Di...
of the American West

The Wordsworth
Dictionary
of the American West

–

Compiled by Winfred Blevins

Wordsworth Reference

First published by Facts on File, New York, 1993.

This edition published 1995 by Wordsworth Editions Ltd,
Cumberland House, Crib Street, Ware, Hertfordshire SG12 9ET.

ISBN 1-85326-356-7

Printed and bound in Denmark by Nørhaven.

The paper in this book is produced from pure wood
pulp, without the use of chlorine or any other substance
harmful to the environment. The energy used in its
production consists almost entirely of hydroelectricity
and heat generated from waste materials, thereby
conserving fossil fuels and contributing little to the
greenhouse effect.

Dictionary
of the American West

A

à la Comanche A description of a rider hanging over the side of his horse; from the style of the Comanches in warfare. [Adams]

Aaronic The lower priesthood of the Church of Jesus Christ of the Latter-Day Saints. For boys 12 to 18 and new converts; these priests assist the bishop and act as teachers and deacons. (*See* Melchizedek)

aboard On horseback.

above my bend Beyond my capabilities; also *above my huckleberry*.

above snakes Above ground; said of a man who's still alive.

abra A narrow valley, a defile between close hills; a break in a mesa; a term of the south-west, especially Texas.

abrazo To say hello or goodbye by embracing someone with both arms and giving a pat on the back, a custom still existing in the south-west today, especially among Hispanics. Borrowed from Spanish, it is pronounced ah-BRAH-soh.

access road Among loggers, a road built into remote areas of commercial timber for access for cutting and hauling. Such roads also give access to fire fighters, hikers, hunters, packers and other recreational users. They are viewed as a benefit by some, as destruction by others.

ace high A poker hand that has an ace but no pair or better combination to bet on. The expression also may simply refer to anything top-notch or first-rate. When Foster-Harris says in *The Look of the Old West*, 'The Spencer . . . was also ace high in the early West, a real frontier gun,' he means it was a humdinger, the cat's miaow.

Aces back to back is an ideal situation, from when a player's first two cards are aces, one face up and one face down. *Ace in the hole* and *ace up your sleeve*, any hidden advantage. These expressions come from stud poker. A gun in a shoulder holster or other hideout might be a figurative ace in the hole.

acequia (1) In the south-west, an irrigation ditch. The main ditch is known

as an *acequia madre*. Borrowed from the Spanish (where it has the same meaning), it is pronounced ah-SEH-kyuh and frequently Americanised to *sakey*. (2) In New Mexico, an *acequia* is the association of land owners that manages a ditch. The shareholders are called *parciantes* and can number from a few to over a hundred; their allotment of water (which varies according to water flow and the location of their land) is called a *sucro* (a share) or a *pión* (a New Mexican variant of *peón*). (*See* mayordomo)

acion In the Mexican-American border country, a stirrup-leather. (*See* stirrup)

Acoma The 'people of the white rock' and their pueblo. Acoma, sitting on a mesa about an hour's drive west of Albuquerque, New Mexico, was visited by Coronado in 1540 and is said to date to the 11th century. The people of Acoma are now known for their pottery. (*See* Pueblo Indians)

acorn calf An undersized calf, often sickly; a runt; a cull.

across lots In the quickest, shortest way; via shortcuts.

actionable fire Any forest fire that requires suppression according to current policy of a national park or national forest.

adamantine candle See star candle.

added money In rodeo, the money provided by the rodeo committee. Together with the entry fees, it makes up the prize money.

adios Goodbye, farewell. Borrowed from the Spanish (where it has the same meaning), it is pronounced ah-DYOS. Literally, it means 'to God' and is a shorthand for *vaya con Dios* (go with God).

adit A passage, roughly horizontal, used to enter and unwater (drain) a mine.

adobe A brick made of earth or clay and straw and dried in the sun; a clay suitable for making adobe bricks; the buildings into which the bricks are made. Borrowed from Spanish it is pronounced uh-DOH-bee, or with a Spanish touch, ah-DOH-bay; often Americans have shortened it to 'dobe.

Usually the bricks are formed in wooden moulds, built into thick walls and plastered over. Adobes are common in the southwest, especially in churches, public buildings and homes that date from the Mexican or Spanish-Colonial periods, many of them handsome and of historic value. Use of adobe brick dates at least to ancient Egypt.

Sometimes, as in the phrase *adobe dollar*, the word connotes an object of little value.

The French in Missouri in the early 18th century used a building material of clay and straw, similar to adobe, called *bousillage*.

adobe-walled Executed; put up against an adobe wall and shot. Watts says that the expression probably arose during the 1870s, when Texas and Mexican cowboys stole cattle back and forth across the border, and some Texans who got caught were 'dobe-walled. (*See* dry-gulch)

afoot Without a horse. In the West, this meant that you had fallen into misfortune or had gone broke or were lame-brained. You couldn't cover enough ground to get to food and water. You couldn't get out of the weather. You were vulnerable to wild critters. Cattle wouldn't respect you. And neither would other men. So to be afoot was to be in sad shape.

agave A succulent south-western plant (*Agave* sp.) with evergreen leaves arranged in a rosette on the ground; commonly called the *century plant*. Each leaf ends in a sharp spine; agaves bloom once and then die. They are used to make alcoholic drinks, soaps and fibres, and by the Indians as food. Borrowed from the Spanish, it is pronounced ah-GAH-vay. (*See* maguey and mescal)

a-going and a-coming Thoroughly, all the way, utterly. A man who beat another man at cards a-goin' and a-comin', or a-comin' and a-goin', has given him a whomping.

agua Water or rain. Borrowed from the Spanish (where it has the same meaning), it is pronounced AH-gwah.

Combinations: agua caliente (hot water); *agua dulce* (literally sweet water – potable water); *agua miel* (the juice of the maguey before pulque, mescal and tequila are made from it); *aguardiente* (liquor).

aguardiente Booze, especially fiery booze. Originally it meant a brandy made in El Paso, but the meaning widened to include almost any kind of spirits. The mountain men loved the aguardiente they got at Taos and Santa Fe in the 1820s, '30s and '40s. Cornelius Smith says that it is primarily a product of the maguey, as pulque, mescal and tequila are, and makes those who imbibe it amorous. (*See* firewater)

Borrowed from Spanish, it is an elision of *agua ardiente* (fiery water) and is pronounced ah-gwar-DYEN-tay. It has been spelled in such creative variations as *awerdenty* and *aquardiente*.

aho! Thank you. An expression in various languages of contemporary Plains Indians (with variations, like *iho!*), it usually offers thanks to the spirits and is said at the end of prayers and in association with rituals and ceremonies, sometimes like amen. At powwows and rendezvous, it may be a rousing affirmation, something like 'Amen, brother!' Among the Dakota, it is usually short for *aho mitakuye oyasin*, a ritual phrase giving thanks to 'all my relations'; it is acknowledgment of the speaker's kinship with all that exists.

AI Artificial insemination; impregnating a cow with a 'straw' of semen; usually done with sperm from a high-quality bull that the rancher could not ordinarily afford. A gomer bull is an infertile bull used to bring the cows into heat so they will be ready to be inseminated.

aim To intend, as in, 'I aim to lick that stupid, stubby-legged, red-eyed son of a she-cat.'

AIM The American Indian Movement, an organisation founded in 1968; one of various organisations formed in the last several decades to increase Red Power. At first an urban movement, it spread to the reservations, especially those of the Sioux and other peoples on the northern plains most dispossessed. AIM activists once took over the Bureau of Indian Affairs office in Washington, DC and, in 1973, AIM members joined some Oglala in what is known to many Indians as the Second Battle of Wounded Knee. A Shoshone man of medicine said, 'It [AIM] takes the role of shock troops because the federal government and American people don't listen, and Indians are second-class citizens in their own country.'

The opinion of its effectiveness in Indian country in the 1970s was divided, but many of the changes sought by the organisation have become policy of the Bureau of Indian Affairs and tribal councils.

air the paunch To throw up after one has drunk too much.

airing the lungs A cowboy term for cussing. Cowboys used to be notorious for their profane and scatological vocabulary, which they barely managed to suppress in front of women. These days most hands blush at the words women use.

air-seasoned Said of timber that has been seasoned in the air rather than in a kiln.

airtights Canned food. The cowboys of the days of the open range did have some canned food, mostly peas, peaches, meat and milk. Tinned food was mass produced after the Civil War and became common in the West in the late 1800s.

ajo A common name for the desert lily (*Hesperocallis undulata*) of the south-west; properly the name of the south-western garlic plant. Borrowed from the Spanish word for 'garlic', it is pronounced AH-hoh.

akicita A Lakota word that translates as 'soldier'. Pronounced ah-GEE-chee-tah. (*See* warrior society)

alameda In the south-west, a road or promenade bordered by trees, especially cotton-woods. Borrowed from Spanish and pronounced al-uh-MEE-da.

Alamo As a common noun, it means the cotton-wood tree. The Franciscan mission in San Antonio that became known as the cradle of Texas liberty was named for this ubiquitous Western tree. Borrowed from the Spanish (where it means 'poplar'), pronounced AL-uh-moh and now used mostly as a south-western proper name.

albardon A packsaddle similar to the aparejo. Borrowed from Spanish, and pronounced ahl-bar-DON.

albino A colour of horse, white with blue eyes. (*See* buckskin)

albondiga A ball of meat or fish. Borrowed from Spanish and pronounced ahl-BOHN-dee-gah, it is common on menus in the south-west.

alcalde The mayor or justice of the peace of a Hispanic community; also called a regidor. The alcalde's territory was known as an *alcaldia*. Borrowed from Spanish (where it means 'mayor') and pronounced ahl-KAHL-day.

alfalfa A leguminous plant (*Medicago sativa*) with purple flowers grown throughout the irrigated West for hay. Both the word and the plant came to the West from Mexico. An *alfalfa cube* is a cake of pressed alfalfa used to feed cows during the winter. Alfaloofee, in Wyoming, is a comical name for alfalfa.

alfilaria The common pin grass (*Erodium cicutarium*) of the plains; also spelled *alfileria* and *alfilerilla* and sometimes Americanised to *fileree* or *filaree*. From Spanish and pronounced al-fil-luh-REE-uh.

alforja A saddlebag for a pack horse; a box of rawhide or canvas (perhaps even wood) carried on a packsaddle. Borrowed from Spanish, it is pronounced ahl-FOHR-hah.

Alice Ann In the south-west, a sorrel horse. According to Cornelius Smith, it's a corruption of *alazan*, which is Spanish for 'sorrel'. American pronunciation of Spanish is generally rough and ready and sometimes sounds like an assault on the music of the original.

alkali (1) Powdery white mineral that salts the ground in so many low places in the West, particularly sinks. It inhabits Western water and whitens the ground where water has risen to the surface and gone back down. It also spoils drinking water and gave many early Westerners the intestinal affliction (*turistas*) known as *being alkalied*. One Western meaning of alkali is a country with alkaline soil. (2) A fellow who's been in the country for a long time. He is said to be alkalied, that is, accustomed to the country. Often he's an old fellow but not necessarily so – any experienced man qualifies. The cattleman in Stewart Edward White's *Arizona Nights* said about the Westerner's attachment to the land, 'An old "alkali" is never happy anywhere else.' Also known as a *grissel heel*, *longhorn* or *sourdough*. (3) As a verb, blinded by booze.

Combinations: alkali desert, alkali dust, alkali flat (a plain ruined by alkali, often an undrained, barren, hostile desert), *alkali grass* (which grows in alkaline soil), *alkali heath* (a plant), *alkali pan* (a shallow depression filled with alkali), *alkali sink* (a spot that doesn't drain), *alkali spot* (an area of gumbo-like alkaline soil), *alkali spring* and *alkali water*.

all hands and the cook Everybody; the entire outfit, all the cowboys and right on down to the cook.

all my relatives A translation of *mitakuye oyasin*, a Dakota phrase frequently repeated during the sweat lodge and other ceremonies, prayers and rituals. According to Lakota shaman Wallace Black Elk, it acknowledges the speaker's 'personal relatedness to everything that exists.'

all-fours *See* seven-up.

Alta California Literally, upper California; what became the state of California in the United States, as opposed to lower (Baja) California, which is part of Mexico.

ama In the south-west, the mistress of a house. Borrowed from Spanish and pronounced AH-mah.

ambulance On the frontier, a light, canvas-topped Army wagon for carrying personnel, wounded or healthy; might mean almost any government wagon for transporting people. Also called a *prairie wagon*, it had no necessary association with hospitals or medical care.

amigo Friend; ubiquitous in the south-west. Borrowed from Spanish and pronounced uh-MEE-goh.

amole A yucca plant, especially the bulb, used to make soap. Borrowed from Spanish, which is borrowed from Nahuatl. Pronounced ah-MOL-ay.

among the willows (1) On the lam, on the run, running from the law. [Adams] (2) When said of a couple, making love.

Anasazi A Navajo term meaning 'the ancient ones'; the Pueblo people who inhabited the Four Corners country of Colorado, New Mexico, Arizona and Utah until seven centuries ago and are the ancestors of the modern Pueblo people. The Anasazi left cliff dwellings, such as those at Kayenta and Mesa Verde, that are today the eloquent voice of their sojourn in the canyon country. They developed pottery, an economy based on agriculture and a highly ceremonial religion. Near the end of the 13th century, they left their large pueblos, perhaps because of drought or pressure from enemies, and started afresh in the Rio Grande Valley and at Zuni and Hopi. (*See also* Hohokam)

Some of the Pueblo people object to the use of the Navajo word Anasazi to denote their ancestors; Navajos and Hopis are traditional enemies.

andale Get going, get a move on. South-western cowboys say this to cows on a trail drive a lot. Borrowed from the Spanish imperative *andar* (to walk), it's pronounced AHN-dah-lay.

angel An innocent at a horse auction, likely to buy unsound horses.

angle iron The metal triangle the cook raised a ruckus on to get all hands to dinner.

Anglo In the south-west, anyone not of Indian or Hispanic blood; a white person, especially a white American; 'black Anglo', though, is not nonsense. New Mexico declares its public pride in being a state of three cultures, Indian, Hispanic and Anglo.

The Indians had and have many words for white man. The Dakotas know them as *wasicun* (the fat-takers). The Crow term for white person is *baaschiile* (person with yellow eyes). Others called them the people with white skin. The Kiowa know the whites as *bedalpago* (hairy mouths), referring to their moustaches (many Indians found facial hair objectionable). *Big knife* and *Long knife* distinguished

Americans from the French, English and pre-Revolutionary settlers. An early Navajo term for white men is 'those who fight with their penises', because they were always woman-hungry. The Mohawk called the Scotch *kentahere*, because their hats reminded the Indians of buffalo droppings. Some Indians knew the German and Dutch as *yah yah algeh* (the ones who say 'ja, ja' all the time). The Iroquois named the white man 'he who makes axes', in their language *asseroni*, which some Indians may want to readopt satirically today.

angoras Chaps made from goat-hide, with the hair on and showing (in fact, showing off); woolies. (*See* chaps)

animal A bull of the domestic variety. It seems that, unlike modern folk, Americans a century ago found any mention of sex in female company indelicate. So, yes, they even substituted *animal* and *cow* for *bull* and stooped to euphemisms like *duke*, *toro* and *bovine*.

Animal Damage Control (ADC) The federal agency in charge of eradicating predators; $30 million are spent annually on destroying predators that threaten (or are perceived as threatening) crops or livestock. Individual ranchers contact the ADC, which then removes (by trapping, aerial shooting or, less commonly, poisoning) the offending animals, usually coyotes. (*See* government trapper)

animal unit Forest Service bureaucratese for a critter that eats a standard amount while grazing on public land. A cow with an unweaned calf equals one cow unit or pair. The Forest Service fellows have also come up with an animal-unit conversion factor, by which a bull is 1.25, an elk 0.7, a weaned calf 0.6 and so on. Different areas of the West support markedly different numbers of animal units. On the plains of South Dakota, rancher and writer Linda Hasselstrom figures 10 to 40 acres of grass, plus hay and cake, are required to feed one cow unit for a year.

anquera A piece of leather at the back of the cantle of a Western saddle, often used for riding double, sometimes mostly for looks. Borrowed from Spanish, it's pronounced an-KAY-ruh.

antelope The common name for what is formally the prong-horn or prong-buck; also known popularly as a goat. The moniker antelope dates at least to Lewis and Clark, who commented on its 'wonderful fleetness'. On the northern plains, this fleet and graceful animal has made a huge comeback in numbers. In the 1920s, less than 100,000 lived in Wyoming, but now the herd is estimated to be 370,000.

Combinations: antelope brush (a Western shrub), *antelope ground squirrel* (a chipmunk), *antelope dance* (a ceremony of the Hopi), *antelope jackrabbit* and *antelope goat* (the Rocky Mountain goat)

anti-godlin In a sideways, crooked or round-about way. Whomper-jawed has about the same meaning.

Apache A tribe of the south-west celebrated for ferocious raiding of its Hispanic, Indian and Anglo neighbours. The name probably stems from the Zuni word *àpachu*, meaning 'enemy'; they call themselves *Diné*, the People (their kinsmen the Navajo use the same term for themselves, and most tribes call themselves the People). The Pueblo Indians called them the Querechos.

The six principal Apache groups (moving roughly south-westward along their traditional lands from south-western Kansas to central Arizona) were the Jicarillas, the Kiowa, the Lipans, the Mescaleros, the Chiricahuas and the largest group, the Western Apaches, also called the Coyotero. Some were purely hunter-gatherers, some raised crops as well, and those on the southern Plains had a buffalo-hunting culture.

The Chiricahua and Western Apaches, who lived in historic times in western New Mexico and east-central Arizona (which was known as Apacheria), became the best known because they fought the Apache Wars until subdued by American armies under Nelson Miles and George Crook. They became known for a remarkable aptitude for surviving and thriving under the extreme conditions of the desert and for resistance to white encroachment.

The Chiricahuas, the last hold-outs under Geronimo, Mangas Colouradas and Cochise, were considerably dispersed and now live at Fort Sill, Oklahoma and on the Mescalero Reservation in New Mexico. The Coyoteros live on the San Carlos and Fort Apache reservations near their historic territory in Arizona. The Mescaleros have their own reservation in New Mexico, as do the Jicarillas. The Kiowa-Apaches, once buffalo hunters, live in western Oklahoma. The Lipans, once the terror of Texas, are said to be culturally extinct.

Apache plume A shrub (*Fallugia paradoxa*) of the south-west, so named because its feathery clusters of seeds reminded someone of an Apache war bonnet; also called *poñil*.

aparejo A Mexican packsaddle that fit the back of a pack mule like an opened, upside-down book. Traditionally, it rested on a jerga (saddle-cloth), which lay on a salea (sheep-skin), and was secured very tightly by a wide grass band so that heavy loads could be borne without chafing. Borrowed from Spanish (where it means 'riding gear'), it is pronounced ah-pah-RAY-ho.

apishamore A saddle blanket of the mountain men and later Westerners, preferably made from soft buffalo-calf skin and often used as the rider's bed at night. From Ojibway, it's pronounced uh-PEESH-uh-mohr.

appaloosa A horse bred by the Nez Percé, distinctively marked on the rump and back with dark spots and known for its excellence as a saddle horse from at least the time of Lewis and Clark. Some lexicographers suggest that the name comes from the Palouse River, where mountain men may first have seen the horse. Variant spellings include *Palouse*, *Pelouse*, *apaloochy* and *appalousy*.

apple (1) An Indian who's red on the outside but white on the inside; the Indian equivalent of what blacks call Oreo, Uncle Tom or Uncle Tomahawk. (2) What you're not supposed to grab when a horse acts up – the saddle horn. South Dakota

writer Linda Hasselstrom jokes that some folks accuse other riders' saddle horns of featuring tooth-marks.

apple-horn A style of saddle with a horn that looks like an apple rather than like a plate, like some early Mexican-influenced saddles; a popular saddle with Texans in the trail-drive period after the Civil War.

appola A word imported by the mountain men from their French-Canadian comrades and meaning 'a method of broiling meat on a stick kebab-style, with fat and lean strips alternated;' also the stick itself. Sometimes spelled *apola*.

apron straps Straps on the skirt of a saddle used to hold slicker, bedroll and other gear.

apron-faced A description of a horse with a white forehead and face. (*See* boomerang stallion)

arancel In the south-west, a tariff or import duty; also spelled *aransel*. Borrowed from Spanish, it's pronounced ah-rahn-SEL.

Arapaho A Plains tribe of the Algonquian family with a buffalo-hunting culture. When first contacted frequently by whites, the Arapaho lived on the plains of eastern Colorado and south-eastern Wyoming. Earlier they had permanent villages and raised crops near the Great Lakes. On the high plains, they allied themselves closely with Cheyennes and were a force in the 1860s wars on the central plains and the fighting in Powder River country in 1865-6. They fought alongside the Dakota (Sioux) and Cheyenne in the climactic Indian wars of 1876-7. Today the southern Arapaho live in Oklahoma and the northern on the Wind River Reservation in Wyoming.

Arbuckle's (1) Arbuckle Brothers coffee, a brand so common in the West that it became a generic term for coffee, just as Levi's has become for jeans, Winchester for rifle and Stetson for hat. It was the word for coffee at Navajo trading posts until World War II. 'During the late 19th and early 20th centuries,' according to historian Francis Fugate, 'the Navajos drank prodigious amounts of coffee, strong and black, boiled with sugar in the pot. They would have nothing but Arbuckle's Ariosa. They would ask the Indian agent for *Hosteen Cohay* – literally translated from the Navajo language, "Mr Coffee".'

The cowboy likes his coffee strong. One Wyoming hand said in the 1980s that the trick to making coffee is that 'it don't take as much water as you think it do'.

Other names for coffee are *black water, belly-wash, black jack, brown gargle, cafecito, Indian Coffee* and *jamoka*.

(2) A hand so green the boss must have sent away and gotten him with the trading stamps that come with Arbuckle's.

Arch A huge span of sandstone created by erosion; a sandstone fin eroded out. Arches are commonly found in the canyon-lands of south-eastern Utah, especially in Arches National Monument and north-eastern Arizona. Delicate Arch, a natural predecessor of the gateway arch in St Louis, is surely one of the grandest sights on this earth.

arena director The director of a rodeo, the person who assures that all goes according to Hoyle as much as it can with unruly stock and more unruly cowboys. He works for the producer or stock contractor, or one of these people may act as the arena director.

Argonaut A California gold rush (1848–9) fortune seeker. The original Argonauts, ancient Greeks, searched for the Golden Fleece with Jason.

Arikara A tribe that lived in earth lodges on the Upper Missouri; an offshoot of the Pawnee. These Indians, commonly known to early Westerners as Rees or Ricarees, had a Caddoan language and lived like their upriver neighbours the Mandans in a half-sedentary (rather than nomadic) style. In the earliest years of fur-trade travel up the Missouri, they posed an obstacle to upriver movement but were stilled by military intervention and disease. They were moved to Fort Clark and then to the Fort Berthold Reservation where they merged culturally with the Mandans and Hidatsa.

Arizona nightingale A burro, known with ironic humour for its song.

Arizona Strip The common name for the huge chunk of Arizona desert bounded by the Grand Canyon on the east and south and the Nevada and Utah state lines on the west and north. It is wild, and then some. A few folks do some herding there. The mythical home of the splendid writer Edward Abbey, Wolf Hole, was there. Before the Strip got littered with too many roads and bridges, it had little law – the nearest authority was on the other side of the Grand Canyon. That's why the Mormon polygamists founded the settlement of Short Creek there, now known as Colorado City.

Arizona tenor A fellow who coughed from tuberculosis – such victims came to the desert for the sake of the dry air.

Arkansas toothpick A humorous name for a wicked kind of knife, dagger-style, with a long, tapering blade, designed for both hand-to-hand fighting and throwing; second in frontier popularity only to the Bowie knife; sometimes called a *frog stabber*.

Arkie A logger's nickname for a worker from Arkansas; also a belittling nickname. It is like Hoosier and Okie in being both an indication of home state and a disparagement. [Adams]

armitas Half chaps, or chinks; a leather apron protecting a rider's legs (as far as his boot tops) against nuisances like brush and the rubbing of the rope. Jo Mora, in *Trail Dust and Saddle Leather*, says they're appealing in hot weather and light brush. They were popular with vaqueros and are still popular with buckaroos but not cowboys of the Texas or northern Plains style. Also known as *armas* or *chigaderos*.

arrastre A primitive mill for pulverising silver and gold ore. Usually a huge stone was dragged round and round on a stone bed by a burro. Also spelled *arrastra* and *rastra*, and also called a drag mill. Borrowed from Spanish (where it means 'mining mill'), it's pronounced uh-RAS-truh.

arriero A south-westernism for muleteer. Borrowed from Spanish and pronounced ah-ree-AYR-oh. Also called a *mulero*.

arroyo A narrow gully with steep dirt walls and a flat floor that is a creek or rivulet when it's wet, but it usually is dry. Arroyos are bad places to camp in – flash floods turn them into melees in no time – and a good place to get a car bogged in the sand. Also called a *wash*, or *dry wash* (*arroyo seco*). Borrowed from Spanish (where it means 'stream') and pronounced uh-ROY-oh. The West has lots of terms for topographical features that are similar but not identical – gully, coulee, ditch, gulch, ravine.

artillery A lightly mocking term for the firearms a man is carrying, especially his handguns.

as they ran To buy or sell cattle as they ran was to take the other man's word for the number, without counting, says Peter Watts.

aspen *Populus tremuloides*, a broad-leaved tree with a straight white trunk, it is common at higher elevations in the West. It reproduces by runners and is dependent on fire for healthy regeneration. When small, it is valuable winter browse for ungulates, and when full grown, it makes a smokeless, ashless fire, important in Indian country. Also called *quakie*, *quaker* and *quaking aspen*. As David Lavender says: 'The tiniest breath of air will twist the light-coloured undersides of the leaves about until the whole tree seems to dance and twinkle.

'The Utes have a legend about these delicious groves. In olden days, they say, the aspens were the proudest of trees. When the Great Spirit visited the earth and all other things shivered with anticipation, the aspens remained stiff and unbending. The Spirit cursed them and ordered that henceforth they should tremble whenever an eye was turned upon them.'

assay In mining, to hold precious metal values, as in, 'That sample assays a hundred bucks a ton.' The noun form is not an Americanism.

Combinations: assay balance (a scale used in assaying), *assay master* (the head assayer [Adams]), *assay office* (the agency that performs assays), *assay stamp* (the mark of the assay office), *assay value* (the calculated value of gold or silver in an ore sample, as determined by assay).

assessment work The effort required by the federal government each year on an unpatented mining claim. If it isn't done, or at least filed, the claimant loses whatever rights he has. In the last few decades, many unpatented claims have really been vacation spots, with a few explosives employed annually to keep up appearances.

Assiniboin Originally a large Plains tribe living in northern Montana and across the border in Canada, the Assiniboin had a buffalo-hunting culture and were particularly known as traders. They were consistently friendly to whites and associated closely with the Americans at Fort Union. Ravaged by smallpox and other diseases, they eventually joined the Atsina and Dakota (Sioux) on the Fort Peck and Fort Belknap reservations in Montana, where they live today.

association saddle A bronc saddle is made to give the rider an advantage in trying to stay on a bronc, but this saddle sanctioned by the Professional Rodeo Cowboys Association 'gives the hoss all the best of it' by removing whatever a rider might anchor himself to. For this reason, it is required for contest riding at rodeos. Also called a *committee saddle* and a *contest saddle*.

Astorian A fur man associated with Astoria; a member of a party sent out by John Jacob Astor's Pacific Fur Company in 1810 (by sea) or 1811 (by land) to found a fur-trading post at the mouth of the Columbia River. Though ambitious as a financial enterprise and an affirmation of American sovereignty, it was short-lived as an American post. The main contributions the Astorians made were the explorations of the unknown West and their discoveries of good beaver country.

atajo A pack-mule caravan in the south-west. British Lieutenant George Frederick Ruxton, travelling in the West in the mid-1840s, described them: 'The atajos, numbering from fifty to two hundred mules, travel a daily distance – jornada – of twelve or fifteen miles, each mule carrying a pack weighing from two to four hundred pounds. To a large atajo eight or ten muleteers are attached, and the dexterity and quickness with which they will saddle and pack an atajo of a hundred mules is surprising. The animals being driven to the spot, the lasso whirls round the head of the muleteer and falls over the head of a particular mule. The tapojos is placed over the eyes, the heavy aparejo adjusted, and the pack secured, in three minutes.'

Borrowed from the Spanish *hatajo* ('small herd'), it's pronounced ah-TAH-hoh; sometimes spelled *hatajo*.

atole Cornmeal; gruel or porridge made from corn; a weak corn soup popular among the poor of the south-west and Mexico. Lt George Frederick Ruxton, that intrepid British traveller of the 1840s, found it 'an insipid compound', but then he found little in New Mexico he liked. The term comes from Nahuatl by way of Mexican Spanish and is pronounced ah-TOH-lay.

Atsina These Indians, commonly known as the Gros Ventre of the Prairie and sometimes confused with the Gros Ventre of the Missouri (the Hidatsa), maintained a buffalo-hunting culture in northern Montana and Canada. An offshoot of the Arapaho, they allied themselves so closely with the Blackfeet that the mountain men sometimes regarded them as the same tribe. Like the Blackfeet, they were hostile to American (though not British) encroachment. In 1873 they joined the Assiniboin on the Fort Belknap Reservation in Montana.

auto camp A place for 'automobilists' to camp, especially in the 1920s in Yellowstone National Park. Cars were permitted into the park in 1916, to the eternal regret of those who love wilderness.

aux aliments du pays The expression of a fur trader or trapper meaning 'to live off the land'; literally, from the food of the land.

avocado Properly the avocado pear, a buttery tropical fruit, especially popular in the south-west in salads and guacamole and with Mexican food. The word comes from Nahuatl (*aguacate*) via the Spanish.

azotea The flat roof of an adobe house. Borrowed from Spanish and pronounced ah-zoh-TAY-uh.

azucar Sugar. Borrowed from Spanish and pronounced ah-soo-car.

B

BBs In logging, an abbreviation for bridge builders.

ba-ah Derogatory name for sheep. For others, *see* woolly.

babiche A thong of skin, especially eel or reindeer skin, often woven into mesh for snowshoes. A French-Canadian term, it is pronounced bah-BEESH.

baby beef A calf under a year old that will be raised for market.

bach To bachelor it; for men to keep house without a women's help. Sometimes spelled *batch*.

back East In the Eastern states; the reverse of out West. With some folks, it had the implication of back in civilisation; with others, it had the implication of back where everything is messed up.

back strap The tenderloin, the strips of meat on either side of the backbone of a game animal, known as fine eating.

back to the blanket Where an Indian goes when he 'reverts' to his old, 'uncivilised' ways. For instance, he might leave off his pants in favour of a breech-cloth, pass up indoor plumbing and fail to show up at his job. Once derogatory, the phrase now describes an Indian returning to his roots and trying to keep his culture alive, generally seen as a praiseworthy activity.

backburn A fire set so that it eats up the fuel of a larger, advancing fire and thus starves the big fire; or a fire set to change the direction of the convective heat created by the big fire; or both. In verb form, to set such a fire. Also called a *backfire*.

backed up to a free air hose To be pregnant, according to *Ten Thousand Goddam Cattle* by Katie Lee, an old Western hand.

back-handed trade A horse trade that was reversed. Usually anything extra thrown in with the horse was not returned with the horse; that is, if you gave cash along with a horse, you lost the cash. Also called a *back-trade*.

backtrack To track backwards, the way someone came; a fellow who does this is a back-tracker. The back track is the back trail.

badman A tough guy; a rowdy, a ruffian, a gunman, a killer; a *bandido*, *cabrón*, holdup man, long rider, outlaw, road agent and all their snaky kin. According to Barrère and Leland's *Dictionary of Slang, Jargon and Cant*, 'This [term] has a special meaning in the West, where it indicates a heartless cruel murderer. Rowdies and bullies in their boasting often describe themselves as "hard badmen from Bitter Creek." '

The badman is ultimately the black hat, the fellow Jack Palance portrayed with such vividness in the film version of *Shane*, and then he is a force for evil, in the mythology of the West to be defeated. But a bit of him is also in Shane himself, the Alan Ladd character, and that is one of the great tensions in the myth: You have to be a little bit bad to be good, to be effective, to get the job done.

bad medicine (1) The less complicated white-man meaning is, a man who is bad medicine is dangerous, an hombre not to be fooled with. (2) The Indian meaning is subtler: A man or woman with bad medicine has spirits set against him or something akin to a hex on him or is out of tune with the spiritual world. The situation bodes ill and needs to be remedied, usually by ritual or a specific healing ceremony. (*See* medicine) And consider what it means when a person's medicine is good.

badger hole A person's cabin, his home.

badlands What the French called *mauvaises terres pour traverser* – bad country to travel through; in Spanish, malpais. It was first applied to a big area of South Dakota that is eroded, barren, gullied and full of strange rock formations; by extension, all such regions all over the West, except that volcanic wastes are more likely to be called malpais. Badlands are likely to be populated by *badlanders*. Sometimes the word appears as *badland*.

baho *See* paho.

baile In the south-west, a Hispanic dance or dance hall; not a particular dance but the entire festivity. Borrowed from Spanish, it's pronounced BY-lay.

bait (1) A trap lure for a wolf or other game animal. 'To make a good bait a buffalo was killed and cut open on the back, and into the meat blood and entrails three vials of strychnine – three-eights of an ounce – were stirred,' explained James Willard Schultz in his classic of life among the Blackfeet, *My Life as an Indian*. Hunters still set baits for bears. (2) In forestry, any offering of food or other necessities to draw animals to an area, whether to improve hunting or for other purposes.

bald-faced Said of a horse or cow with a white blaze on its face. In Wyoming, colloquially know as a *bolly-faced* cow. A bald-faced shirt is a white dress shirt or boiled shirt.

baling wire Wire you fix anything with. Used to tie bales of hay (bale is an Americanism but not a Westernism), it is recycled to fix fences and any sort of machinery, from pick-ups to combines. Its second function is getting under the hooves of horses and cows at the very times they can be tripped. Ranchers everywhere wad baling wire up to keep critters from getting tangled in it. Today, more and more, twine is being used in place of wire.

balky The natural temperament of horses and mules – contrary enough to do anything but what the rider wants; the same as cold-shouldered.

ball (1) What a flint or percussion muzzle-loading rifle or pistol shoots, as opposed to a conical bullet. Not a Westernism but an essential element in the whites' taking of the West. The load for a muzzle-loader is black powder, patch and ball, put down the barrel in that order. (2) Sometimes it meant a shoot-out – the commencement of the ball was the first shot.

balloon What a logger calls his pack or bedroll. Also known as gear or a bindle.

band A herd of critters, whether horses, buffalo, elk or sheep. As a verb it means to group the critters together. A *band wagon* was the wagon of a peddler carrying miscellaneous goods for cowboys.

bandanna In the old days, a cowboy wore his bandanna for the same reason he wore his pants, to be decent and acceptable in society. It might be any colour, though red was the most common, and made of silk or cotton or linen. He folded it into a triangle and tied it around his neck with the knot at the back. It might be used for anything the hand could imagine. Jo Mora listed 'a few' uses in *Trail Dust and Saddle Leather*: as a filter for the dust that moving cattle make, a sling, a water filter, a tourniquet, a towel, a bronc blind, a pigging string, an ear muff and a pad for a hot handle. And as the shoot-'em-up movies have told us endlessly, it made a good mask for a fellow on the prod.

bandbox A conceited dandy given to big words and showing off his knowledge. 'I'd rather have mud on my carpet than that bandbox in any of my chairs,' said Owen Wister's Mrs Starr about the polysyllabic soldier Augustus Albumblatt.

bandido A bandit; often a Mexican bandit. Borrowed from Spanish, it is pronounced ban-DEE-doh.

bandolier A strap over the shoulder that from the 1890s forward held a soldier's extra cartridges; sometimes a ceremonial strap. Also spelled *bandoleer*.

bang juice A chemical that gives a big bang. Among miners, a word for nitroglycerin. Among loggers, a word for dynamite. [Adams] (*See* powder)

bangtail *See* broom-tail.

bank note (1) Currency issued by individual state banks (during the Civil War) and widely distrusted in the West. (2) Metaphorically, anything useful as money – the German physician Frederick Adolphus Wislizenus called beaver skins bank notes.

bannack A kind of bread common among the Métis, and among whites and Indians on the northern plains from the reservation period forward. You mix flour, white ashes and water and cook in a skillet; when you don't have a skillet, you wrap it around a stick, barber-pole style. Also spelled *bannock*.

Bannock A tribe that lived and lives in south-eastern Idaho. The original name,

Ba-nah-qui, mispronounced by trappers as Bannock, means 'water I live by'. An offshoot of the northern Paiute, it has been closely associated with the Shoshones for centuries. During the period of emigration, the Bannocks were known for their predations on the Oregon and California trails. In 1868 they moved to the Fort Hall Reservation in their historic territory in Idaho, but erupted into rebellion once more, led by Chief Buffalo Horn in the Bannock War of 1878. Now they are mostly intermixed with the Shoshone at Fort Hall.

bar (1) A flat line in the design of a brand, such as the B—B, called 'B bar B'. (2) A dialectical pronunciation of bear, as in, 'Diah Smith 'bout got his ear et off by that b'ar.'

bar dog A bartender.

bar mining The washing of gold from river bars (bar diggings), either during low water or by deflecting the water.

barbed mesquite Mesquite grass (*Bouteloua* sp.), a valued winter forage in west Texas.

barber's chair In forestry, a vertical slab, like the back of a chair, left on a stump by not-quite-successful felling.

barboquejo (1) A south-western term for the chin strap for a cowboy hat. Borrowed from Spanish and pronounced bahr-bo-KAY-ho. Peter Watts notes that it should be fragile enough to break before the cowboy's neck does. (2) The chin-strap of a halter. (3) Cornelius Smith says it originally meant a bandage on the chin of a corpse awaiting burial.

barbwire The wire that won the West. This kind of wire, patented (in the form that became dominant) by Joseph F. Glidden, featured strands of wire twisted in various ways to hold barbs that would keep livestock off. It was essential to fencing the Great Plains, which have almost no wood. In fact, it did away with almost all the rail, hedge, board and earth fences; it turned the open range into a lot of private pastures; it made raising purebred stock possible because ranchers could keep the common herd bulls away

from their cows; it made farming possible because livestock could be kept away from crops; it ended the era of the cattle drives and of the great roundups.

Some ranchers liked the old-time ways and hated the damned fences, which they associated with farming, not ranching. They put men after the wire with wire cutters. Range wars threatened, and legislatures had to protect the fences with laws.

In the 1880s, when barbwire sprouted up all over the West, a cowboy's fencing tool became his most important weapon. An old West was unmade and a new one made.

It's fun to fantasise about what the buffalo would have done to it, and how they will trample it if they make the comeback they deserve.

Also spelled *barbed wire* and even *bobwire*, the latter probably a Southerner's soft way of saying it.

bareback riding One of the standard events of a rodeo. The rider must stay on the horse equipped only with bareback rigging (a leather strap with a suitcase-like handle that is cinched around the horse's belly).

barefooted Said of an unshod horse. Indian horses went unshod (except for rawhide shoes, sometimes), but where the white folks went, a blacksmith was sure to follow. A variant is *barefoot*.

bark mark In logging, a sign on a log's bark that indicates ownership. The stamp brand on the end of the log did the same but was hard to see in the water.

barking at a knot A cowman's way of referring to the impossible. In *Western Words*, Ramon Adams says it's like trying to scratch your ear with your elbow.

barracks thirteen According to Cornelius Smith, the guardhouse. When his unlucky number came up, that's where a soldier put in some time.

barranca A ravine, a gully. Borrowed from Spanish, it is usually Americanised to ber-RANK-uh. (*See* arroyo, quebrada and coulee)

barrel cactus A cylindrical cactus (*Ferocactus acanthodes* or *Echinocactus* sp.) that can be as high as 12 feet but usually ranges from two to five feet. Used by travellers as an emergency source of moisture, it is also known as *devil's head*, *Turk's Head*, *hedgehog*, *cotton-top* and *vizniga*.

barrel-jacket punishment A form of discipline that exhibits army humour. According to Teresa Griffin Vielé in *Following the Drum*, at one frontier post 'it consisted of an old flour barrel with a hole cut for his head to pass through, and a pair of holes for his arms. This was a reward for a chronic tendency to "spree", which somewhat interfered with the strict performance of his military duties.'

barrier A rope that bars the way out of the chute for a roper or bulldogger in a rodeo. The barrier is released at the same time the flag is dropped, and the flag starts the time count. To break the barrier is to violate the starting line, which adds a penalty of 10 seconds on to the contestant's time.

barrio Originally a political subsection of a community. It now means an urban ghetto inhabited by Hispanics, and usually afflicted with poverty, unemployment and the attendant problems.

basket maker An Indian of the earliest period of habitation of the south-west, in the first 500 years AD. Their culture preceded with extensive use of pottery there.

Basque barbeque A lamb barbeque; a barbeque where the eaters are Basques, who are often sheepmen. [Adams]

bastos The skirt of a saddle. Borrowed from Spanish (where it means 'saddle-pad') and pronounced BAHS-tohs, it is sometimes spelled *bastas*. Stewart Edward White noted in *Arizona Nights* that a bull would have gored the rider's horse but for his leather bastos.

bat wings See chaps.

batamote The seep-willow tree of the south-west. Borrowed from Spanish, it is pronounced bah-tah-MOHT. Also called *aguatamote*, *guatamote* and *water wally*, which seems charming.

batea A rough wooden bowl used to wash gold. Borrowed from Spanish (where it means 'pan'), it is pronounced bah-TAY-uh. Cornelius Smith says it is still used in out-of-the-way Mexican mining operations.

bayeta (1) A long-wearing wool yarn, used by the Navajo to make bayeta blankets. (2) The cloth made from that yarn. Also appears as *bayjeta* and *vayeta*. Borrowed from Spanish (where it means 'flannel'), it's pronounced bah-YAY-tuh.

bayo In Mexican-Spanish, a dun, brown or sorrel horse with dark mane and tail and a dorsal stripe. It is pronounced BAH-yoh. In *The Mustangs*, J. Frank Dobie lists *bayo azafranado* (saffron), *bayo blanco* (pale dun), *bayo cebruno* (smoky), *bayo coyote* (what Anglos know as a coyote dun), *bayo naranjado* (orange) and *bayo igre* (like a zebra dun). (*See also* buckskin)

Bayou Salado See park.

B-Board A review board of the army in the post-Civil War period that examined the records of officers with questionable ratings and sometimes removed them from the service, according to Cornelius Smith. Since these boards cleaned out poor officers, they were often called *benzine boards*.

bead (1) For Indians all over North America, the most common item of personal decoration. Beads were made (before white contact) of shell, stone, bone, wood, teeth, claws, seeds, bird beaks, clay and other materials and were of many shapes, including tubular. After white contact, glass beads became a hugely popular item in the Indian trade. They came mainly from Venice, which was famous for beads traded all over the world, and from Bohemia and Holland, and were made in many colours, sizes and decorative styles. Some of the distinctive beads during the period of the western Indian trade were the sky-blue chief bead, the cornaline d'Aleppo, the Russian blue, the greasy yellow and the Cheyenne red. They came in such sizes as seed bead (small), pony bead (larger) and multi-coloured beads that might be as large as a joint of a thumb. Such large beads were worn strung on necklaces; seed beads were used for coverage of substantial areas; and pony beads were used for outlines.

Among the Plains Indians, beadwork was done by the women (and berdaches), mostly in geometric patterns until floral beadwork was introduced from the Indians of the Canadian woodlands. Items beaded were clothing and pieces of personal adornment.

Beading is still an important practice among Indians of the West and continues to change according to new ideas, fashions, techniques and materials, like all elements of the cultures. Though the term is not a Westernism, it is essential to an acquaintance with western Indians. (2) A rifle's front sight, which is the source of the expression 'to draw a bead on' someone or something, meaning 'to put your sight on it.'

bean-eater A jocular but derogatory term for a Mexican.

bean-master The cook, the prima donna of the Dutch oven. *See* cookie for his various sobriquets. A beanery is a restaurant, especially a low-class establishment that relies on beans a lot. (*See* grease joint)

bear grass Not a grass but a member of the lily family. In the north-west, it is the common name for *Xerophyllum tenax*, a tall grass-like plant with a conspicuous white flower. In the desert south-west, sotol (*Dasyliron* sp.) and members of the genus *Nolina* (bearing a resemblance to yuccas) are all called bear grass, as in sacahuista, an agave.

bear sign On the range, doughnuts. The cook who made good ones was beloved, which might mean he was cussed only gently.

bear trap (1) A severe horse bit. (2) A style of saddle. (3) In a river, a movable dam.

bear's ass! A common oath of Mormon Country for reasons no one seems to know. Mormons of the early Deseret period, like other frontier people, were prone to scatological talk.

bearberry A low evergreen plant, *Arctostaphylos uva-ursi*, which has a red berry larger than a currant and is a favourite food for moose. It is also called larb or kinni-kinnick, an ingredient in the smoking mixture that goes by the same name.

beard The pointed seed head of some Western grasses that can get stuck in the cattle's soft tissues and cause infections or even blindness.

beat the report For a soldier, to goldbrick, to malinger, to shirk his duty, especially by pretending to be sick.

beaver (1) The semi-aquatic, soft-furred animal that originally lured the French, English, Spanish, Russians, Mexicans and Americans to the western plains, mountains and deserts of the United States, the source of western wealth, the trappers' bonanza and a creature mythical for its industriousness and wiliness.

The beaver had a treasure human beings sought avidly, a soft under-fur (*muffon*) that made perfect felt for hats, which were also known as beavers. Since this fur was valuable, it became the staple of the fur trade and stirred Indians and mountain men to trap the beaver ceaselessly. They also valued the poor fellow for his tail, which was a delicacy when boiled. All this desirability might have been the critter's undoing, some people say, except that in the 1830s beaver hats whimsically went out of fashion, and silk came marching in. The beaver is alive and well and living throughout the modern West.

(2) A word for the felt hat that was made from the under-fur of the critter, both the civilised man's dress hat and the wide-brimmed topper of the out-doorsman. (Thus, when the Scots baronet William Drummond Stewart describes mountain man Bill Williams as wearing a beaver with a hole in it, we need not try to imagine a fifty-pound castor curled on his head) Beaver is still an important source of felt for Western hats. (3) The common term a mountain man used for himself and his compañero (companion). Other terms include child, hoss, coon and nigger. (4) A word for money, because

beaver pelts were a universally accepted medium of exchange. 'Whose beaver you earnin'?' was asking, 'Who's your employer?'

bed ground Where the cattle or sheep lie down for the night to sleep. On trail drives, the hands would then take turns riding in a circle around the cows, singing and whistling to keep them settled down. The bed ground was chosen by the trail boss or the cook, either of whom would ride ahead and find a good spot. Getting the herd to lie down is called *bedding down* or less commonly *fathering the herd*.

To *bed out* is to bivouac, to sleep outside, usually without a tent, as cowboys did on trail drives and roundups. They used a *bed wagon*, which on trail drives hauled along the hands' bedding and war bags and other essential items. It was also known as the *hoodlum wagon*. Small outfits didn't have a bed wagon but carried this stuff in the chuck wagon. The cowboy slept in a bed-roll (also called bedding roll or just roll), usually consisting of a tarpaulin, blankets and a sugan (comforter).

Among cowboys, a critter that's been busted hard enough to make it lie still is called *bedded* [Adams], and to *bed him down* means to kill someone. (*See* bust and dry-gulch).

bedrock (1) The solid rock that alluvial gold rests on. (2) Figuratively, the bottom, the fundamental, the essential. (3) Fine, excellent, first-rate. In *The Virginian*, Owen Wister writes, 'That play is bedrock, ma'am!' (4) To *get down to bedrock* is to go past the small talk and get down to essentials. (5) To bedrock a horse is to ride it down, break its spirit. [Adams]

beef (1) To convert a cow into meat for the pot. Since it was usually someone else's cow in the open-range days, it was said of many a rancher that he never tasted his own beef except when in somebody else's camp. (2) To complain. (3) An ox; a steer, especially one more than four years old.

Combinations: beef book (the account of the ranch's cattle; the tally book), *beef roundup* (the fall roundup in which the cattlemen cut the herd, that is, separated out the animals ready to ship to market, also known as the butt or steer cut), *beef drive* (driving beef to the shipping point), *beef biscuit* (a biscuit of beef and bread made in Texas, or canned beef) and *beef tea* (something completely unappetising – water befouled by cows).

beef issue The distribution of beeves to Indians on a reservation on issue day; also called a *cattle issue*. It was often followed by a mock buffalo hunt, the Indians killing their meat in 'sporting' fashion. The treaty between the federal government and an Indian tribe requiring a beef issue was called a *beef treaty*. Such agreements notoriously were violated. Indian agents so consistently stole rations allotted to Indians by treaty that *agent* became a way of saying *thief*. Indians often rebelled against going to a reservation because it meant virtual starvation. Also called a *cattle issue*.

beef plumb to the hock A description of a person who's big and fat (perhaps two axe handles across the beam).

beefalo Like cattalo, a cross of the buffalo and the beef cow, according to Webster five-eighths beef and three-eighths bison. Various mixtures have been tried. Usually ranchers who crossbreed cows with buffalo are seeking more meat on the frame and so more profit, but the American supermarkets and meat buyers have traditionally resisted the result.

beefsteak To ride a horse in a way that galls its back. [Adams] Light riders don't do this.

beet vacation A distinctive privilege of school children in sugar beet areas, who got out of school for the harvesting.

belduque In the south-west, a big sheath knife; also spelled *berduque* and *verduque*. Borrowed from Spanish, it is pronounced by Anglos bel-DOOK.

bell (1) A belled sheep, used as a marker. Sheep-herders bell about 10 sheep in every 1,000 as a way of keeping track of them. [Adams] (2) Sometimes a jocular term for a rattler's rattles, as in, 'bells on his tail'. A rattler was called a *belled snake*. [Adams]

In the army, *bell sharp* is an expression that describes a trained mule. The experienced mules responded to bell commands and so were said to be bell sharp. The new mules, not yet bell sharp, were called *shave-tails*.

A *belled mare* (or bell) was a mule or horse that led the others in a bunch; sometimes for greater visibility a white mare was chosen.

belly buster A Texas word for the pole used to shut wire gates because of what happens if you let it slip. Also called a *jaw buster*.

belly gun A short-barreled pistol stuck naked into the waistband of your pants instead of holstered.

belly up (1) To go belly up is to die. (2) Most Westerners have been known to belly up to a bar, to bring up a stool and have a drink.

To *belly through the brush* is to be on the dodge, trying to stay ahead of the law [Adams]; a *belly rope* is a roper's loop that ends up on a critter's belly, a comical error. [Adams]

belly wash Weak coffee, or, according to loggers, soda pop.

belly-cheater Also known as *belly-robber*. An army cook.

bellyful of bedsprings A horse that's a good bucker.

bench A flat stretch of land, usually above a river, sometimes below hills, often irrigatable. It is a venerable Westernism, dating to the journals of the Lewis and Clark expedition.

bend To slowly change the direction cattle are moving; especially, to turn a stampede.

bend an elbow To drink booze. When someone is drunk, he's *on a bender* and *paints the town red*. (*See* roostered)

benzinery A low-grade drinking place. Cheap whiskey was sometimes called *benzine*.

berdache An Indian male who dressed and lived entirely as a woman, fulfilling that cultural role within the tribe; sometimes called in Indian languages a 'would-be woman' and sometimes thought of as 'a third sex. Common among the tribes of the Americas, these men-women had social and religious powers: They might be givers of sacred names; first to strike the sun-dance pole; leaders of scalp dances; good luck to war parties; visionaries and predictors of the future; matchmakers; excellent artisans in beadwork, quillwork, hide-tanning and making clothing; creators and singers of songs. Understood as following a vision by most Indians, they were not tolerated by whites. They persist even today, discreetly. Among the Sac and Fox, they were known as the *I-coo-coo-a*; Chippewa, the *Agokwa*; Cheyenne, the *he-man-eh*; Sioux, the *winkte*; Crow, the *ba'te*; Shoshone, the *teni-wiaph*.

between a rock and a hard place Broke or in another sort of tight spot. It also can be called *between hay and grass* – that time of year between winter and spring when the hay has run out and the grass isn't yet up for the stock to feed on.

bible (1) What a waddy (cowboy) calls his cigarette papers. (2) Bible Two was the fugitive list of the Texas Rangers. Rangers read it more often than the real Bible; it was also called the *black book*.

Bible-puncher A preacher. (*See also* black robe)

bicycle To scratch a bucking horse with first one spur and then the other, in a pedalling motion; usually seen in contest rides in rodeos to encourage the horse to bust loose like a tornado.

biddy What a sheep-herder calls an old ewe. [Adams]

bienvenido Welcome. Borrowed from Spanish and pronounced byen-vay-NEE-doh. So common in the south-west today you can hear it on the public-address systems in discount stores announcing the latest shopper's specials.

big In American Indian Pidgin English, big doesn't necessarily mean big physically but means 'special' or 'powerful'. *Big day*, for instance, means Sunday, and *big canoe* a sailing ship. *Big knife* is an American rather than a English white man. (*See* long knife)

Combinations: Mathews gives these other big compounds without defining them, but some of the meanings are clear from usage: *big chief* (important leader), *big dog* (horse), *big hearts*, *big lodge* (fort), *big gun* (cannon), *big medicine* (special spiritual power), *big river*, *big speak*, *big talk* (council talk), *big village*, *big waters* (ocean).

In Anglo usage, big adds emphasis in the following combinations: Among loggers, *big bull* and *big savage* (names for the boss or general superintendent [*see* supreme being]), *big hole* (a logging truck's lowest gear), *big sticks* (the woods).

Among cowboys, *big boss* (the owner of the herd, the owner of the cow outfit; sometimes he's known as the *big augur* or simply *augur*), the *big house* (the main ranch house), *big jaw* (a disease of cattle also known as lump or lumpy jaw), *big jump* (death), *take the big jump* (to die [*see* cash in your chips]); *big loop* (the noose of a rustler), *big windy* (a yarn, a tall tale), *big antelope* (a slow elk, a euphemism for meat from another man's cow).

A *big casino* is an idea or asset you imagine will be a bonanza. [Adams]

Big ditch is an irrigation system's main ditch, in the south-west sometimes known as *madre acequia*.

big Bellies An English version of the name of the Gros Ventre Indians; usually occurs in the plural.

big fifty A .50-calibre Sharps rifle used by professionals for buffalo hunting. It was the buffalo hunter's business tool, 16 pounds unloaded, with three-quarter inch, 120-grain, black-powder cartridges loaded for differing ranges.

big knife An Indian Pidgin English name for white Americans other than the French and English. (*See also* Anglo and long knife)

Big Muddy The Missouri River, traditionally supposed to come from an Indian name, *Pekitanoui*, meaning 'muddy water'.

Big Timber A big grove of cotton-wood trees on the northern bank of the Arkansas River in Colorado, used by the southern Cheyenne as a favoured camping place and a fording place for the river. William Bent built his New Fort there,

downstream from the site of Bent's Old Fort, now a National Historic Site.

bighorn The Rocky Mountain sheep, commonly known as the bighorn sheep. They are distinguished by their huge horns, which curl tightly on the sides of their heads and are bigger around at the base than a large man's biceps. Legendary for their sure-footedness, bighorns live in the high, rocky places, not the forests; there is also an endangered desert variety. They are something of a rare sight: Even the noted hunter and out-doorsman Teddy Roosevelt, when he visited Yellowstone Park as president, stopped shaving and ran lathered to see bighorns at Tower Junction. Lieutenant George Frederick Ruxton, a British traveller in the West during 1840s, reports, 'the hunters assert that, in descending the precipitous sides of the mountains, the sheep frequently leap from the height of twenty or thirty feet, invariably alighting on their horns, and thereby saving their bones from certain dislocation.' This tale demonstrates that Westerners got an early start in stuffing dudes.

bilagaana Navajo term for white man; also spelled *billakona*. Pronounced bee-lah-GAH-nah. Cornelius Smith says it is simply the result of the Navajo attempt to pronounce the word *Americano*. Tony Hillerman, through his mystery novels set in Navajo country, is making this word commonplace.

biler Slang for a snow-mobiler; pronounced BEE-ler. Bilers are sometimes disliked by the other principal winter cavorters in the mountains, cross-country skiers, and vice versa; the skiers complain about the noise and smell of the snow machines, and the bilers complain about being complained about.

bill show A wild West show, like Pawnee Bill's or Buffalo Bill's. A cowboy full of tricks and show was a Bill-show cowboy. [Adams]

billy hell A hell of a lot of hell; what you raise when you're really raising cain.

bindle stiff (1) A Western hobo. (2) In logging, a logger with a bindle (a bedroll, a balloon). Stiff often means 'working man'.

bird cage A 20th-century name for chuck-a-luck, a gambling game that uses a metal cage in the shape of an hourglass.

bird call A wind instrument of southwestern Indians made of two pieces of concave shard bound together with yucca fibres.

birling Log rolling, or log birling; turning a log underfoot as it floats, which loggers known as river drivers did as work and sport. They were called *birlers* and held *birling matches*.

biscuit Another word for the saddle horn, which is also called an *apple*, *dinner plate* and *pig*.

biscuit-shooter A waitress; a cookie pusher. Also one of the many terms for cook, as is *biscuit-roller*. (*See* cookie).

bishop The spiritual leader of the Latter-Day Saint ward. He is a lay minister and receives no compensation, so he often holds a job in the community.

bit (1) Originally an eighth of a Spanish or Spanish-Colonial dollar (thus two bits, four bits, six bits as common ways of expressing monetary value); later a Spanish coin worth twelve-and-a-half cents. A *short bit* was a dime; a *long bit* was twelve-and-a-half cents. A *bit house* was a saloon that charged one bit (or two or another number of bits) for drinks, for cigars and so on. If you asked for change, says William Foster-Harris, they threw you out. (2) The metal bar in a horse's mouth to which the reins are attached. There are many types in the West. The two most common kinds are the snaffle bit and the curb bit. The curb bit has a port (upward curve or extension) and sometimes a roller in the mouthpiece and uses metal extensions to increase the pull of the rein by leverage. The snaffle is jointed in the middle of the mouthpiece and uses no leverage so is less severe. A bar bit has a straight mouthpiece, neither jointed nor curved upward. The bit chain fastens a rein to the ring on the end of the bit (to prevent the horse from biting the rein). Bits are also mounted with silver and otherwise made decorative. Indians used bits of rawhide. (*See* spade bit)

bitch (1) A primitive lamp made by sticking a rag into a cup of grease and lighting it. (*See* happy jack). (2) A sling beneath a wagon for firewood; also called a *cuna* or a *caboose*. (*See* cooney)

bite the dust To be thrown from a horse. Every cowboy gets 'throwed'. Range wisdom has it that 'there ain't no horse that can't be rode, ain't no man that can't be throwed.' When you do get throwed, you're said to have *dirtied your shirt*, *eaten dirt without stooping*, *chased a cloud*, *chewed* (or *eaten* or *tasted*) *gravel*, *eaten grass*, *gone forked end up*, *gone grass hunting*, *gone picking daisies*, *gone up to fork a cloud*, *gotten busted*, *gotten dumped*, *gotten dusted*, *gotten flung away*, *gotten grassed*, *gotten piled*, *gotten spilled*, *gotten spread-eagled*, *kissed the ground*, *landed on your sombrero*, *lost your hat and gotten off to look for it*, *lost your horse*, *met your shadow on the ground*, *picked daisies*, *sunned your moccasins*, *taken a fart-knocker*, *taken a squatter's right* or *taken up a homestead*.

Bit the dust also meant 'to hit the dust with your face from any cause,' such as a blow or a bullet. The climax of a formula Western tale comes when the villain bites the dust. To *bite the ground* is to get killed. [Adams] (*See* cash in your chips) To *bite off more than you can chew* is to take on a job you can't handle; from the notion of biting off a bigger piece of plug tobacco than you can handle in your mouth.

bizcochitos Thick, crisp cookies flavoured with anise. Borrowed from Spanish, it's pronounced bis-co-CHEE-tos.

blab A board fastened to a calf's nose that hangs down and keeps the critter from nursing but permits it to graze; thus is it weaned. Sometimes called a *butter-board weaner* or, in full, a *blab board*.

black blizzard An expression of the Great Plains for a terrible dust storm.

Combinations: dust blizzard, meaning a dust storm, and *ground blizzard*, a storm of snow blowing up from the ground. *Blizzard-choked* is an expression for cattle pushed into a draw or a fence or the like by a blizzard. [Adams]

Black Mike What loggers call stew.

black powder *See* DuPont.

black road In Dakota tradition, a way of living that is full of conflict, danger and difficulty; it runs east and west. The red road, by contrast, is peaceful and fulfilling. (For more information, read *The Good Red Road* by Kenneth Lincoln and Al Logan Slagle)

black robe A priest, especially a Jesuit; a term the Indians of the plains and mountains used in their languages and tried on white folks in the English; a frontierism not peculiar to the West. A black-robe woman is a nun. The most famous of these Jesuit proselytisers was Pierre Jean De Smet, whom the Indians admired.

Other Westernisms for priests and preachers were: *bible-puncher*, *converter*, *cura*, *gospel-sharp*, *sin buster*, *sin twister* and *sky pilot*.

black-balled outfit In the days of the open range, a ranch prohibited from sending a rep (a representative looking for his outfit's strays) to the main roundup. Outfits were blackballed when folks thought they were rustling or helping rustlers.

Blackfeet A tribe of Algonquian origin that became a buffalo-hunting culture that lived in the 19th century in the country around the Missouri and Saskatchewan Rivers. Consisting of the Bloods, the Piegans and the Siksika, the Blackfeet were fiercely proud and aggressive, making war on Indians and whites alike and being especially intolerant of American trappers and traders. The Gros Ventres were closely associated with these tribes, but were detached Arapaho. The Blackfeet tribe was reduced by smallpox in the late 1830s. After the Baker massacre of Piegans in 1870, many Blackfeet went to Canada. Their US reservation is now in north-western Montana. Though the dictionaries say otherwise, the Blackfeet say that their tribal name has no form that looks singular in English – it's correct to say 'one Blackfeet' – and it seems only courteous to adopt the usage they prefer.

black-footed ferret A Western weasel on the verge of extinction. Scientists reintroduced this creature into the wild in 1991.

black-jack (1) The wagering card game *vingt et un*, or 21, imported from France. The goal for the player is to get a total of points (face cards counting 10, aces 11 or one, numbered cards their face value) closer to 21 than the dealer gets; if any player or the dealer goes over 21, he is busted. Principal blackjack terms include *bust*, *drag down*, *hard 17*, *hit me*, *soft 17*, 21 and *vingt-et-un*. (2) A small, flexible, leather club with a weighted head. (The verb form, to blackjack a fellow, is not a Westernism) (3) In logging, coffee (which is also called *black-strap*). (4) In mining, a dark kind of zinc blende.

black-jack steer An undernourished steer from timber country.

black-leg (1) A disease that primarily afflicts yearling calves, causing fever and gaseous swelling. Infectious, it can kill within a day or two. (2) Lieutenant George Frederick Ruxton tells us that scurvy was called blackleg in Missouri in the 1840s.

black-snake A whip of plaited leather used by bullwhackers and other handlers of draft animals.

black-tail More formally, black-tailed deer. Also called a mule deer.

blanc-bec A French-Canadian word for greenhorn, used among the voyageurs. The French literally means 'white-face'.

blanket coat A capote.

Blanket Indian An Indian who holds to the traditional ways of his culture; a 'wild, uncivilised' Indian; now archaic. (*See* back to the blanket)

blatting cart Also *blatting wagon*. Under calf crop, *see* calf wagon.

blaze (1) A shallow cutting away of a tree's bark to mark it, usually to indicate a trail. Trails in the West are still blazed in this way. The verb form means 'to make such a cut.' (2) A white stripe on a horse's face. Such a horse is called a *blaze-face*, or *blazed-faced*.

blazer A bluff, a lie, a trick, a deception. To *run a blazer* is to try to deceive someone. One narrator of Stewart Edward White's *Arizona Nights* runs a blazer with his life at stake. Coming out of his mine shaft, he finds some Chiricahua Apaches waiting for him with bloody thoughts. Luckily, the blasts he has set below start going off. When the third and last one blows, he yells that a fourth is coming. 'It was just a cold, raw blazer,' he admits, 'and if it didn't go through I could see me as an Apache parlour ornament. But it did. Those Chiricahuas give one yell and skipped.'

blazing star A stampede of animals, especially pack animals, not as a herd but bursting in every direction at once. A wonderfully expressive Westernism.

blind Also called a *blinder*. (1) An eye-covering for a horse, used in rodeos to keep the animal still until the rider is in the saddle. (*See* sliding leather blind) (2) A fine levied on a soldier by a court martial; according to Cornelius Smith, a blind cost a soldier his pay but not his freedom. (3) As an adjective, it means 'something concealed, not seen', as in the title of Ralph Beer's good novel of Montana ranching, *The Blind Corral*. A *blind canyon* is a box canyon. A *blind trap* is a disguised corral for catching wild horses or cattle. Brush, branches or camouflaged poles wing the corral, forming a chute, and the hunters of wild horses or wild cattle chase the animals into the trap.

blind staggers A disease affecting the brains of horses, causing them to stagger. One source says it is caused by selenium poisoning. Originally an Americanism, not a Westernism, but now common mostly in the West.

BLM *See* Bureau of Land Management.

bloat The distention of the gut of a cow caused by trapped gas. Bloat is caused by malfunctions of the digestive system or drastic changes in diet and can be relieved by applications of mineral oil, by massage or by inserting a tube down the animal's throat.

blocker loop An over-sized roping loop named for Texas cowman John Blocker, or possibly his brother Ab, and said to descend ultimately from the vaqueros. Sometimes said to be the most versatile of all roping throws, the Blocker, or Johnnie Blocker, may be thrown mounted or on foot and used to catch the head, forefeet or heels. It is thrown from the right shoulder with a leftward twist of the hand so that the loop sails left. It delivers, according to W. F. French, 'a bigger opening at the right place and at the right angle.'

Blond Swede A logger's expression for an elderly man.

Blood Along with the Siksika and Piegan, one of the three principal tribes of the Blackfeet Indians. Also called the Kainai (many chiefs).

blood bay A bay horse (brown or reddish brown with black mane and tail) of especially dark red. (For many horse colours, *see* buckskin)

blossom In mining, a kind of quartz coloured by oxides that promises lead. Also known as *blossom rock*.

blot a brand To make a brand unrecognisable. A *blotched brand* is one that has been blotted.

blow (1) To leave, to clear out of the country. (2) To arrive, to blow in with the tumble-weeds. (3) To take a rest, a breather, as in, 'let's let the horses blow' (or in the noun form, take a blow). (4) To lose a stirrup, which, like pride, often goeth before a fall. In rodeo, blowing a stirrup disqualifies the rider. (5) Among loggers, to head to town to celebrate. [Adams]

blow out his lamp To kill a man. (*See* dry-gulch)

blow the whistle Among contemporary Plains Indians, to participate in the sun dance; also to *use the whistle*. Historically, some warriors were given the right in visions or through membership in a warrior society to blow the whistle while making a war charge.

Today some Indians have the right to blow a whistle at powwows.

blowdown A group of trees felled by a high wind or an area of such trees. A blowdown can be hard for a hiker to get through and worse for a rider. (*See* down timber)

blowout (1) A party, a celebration, a fancy social event. In Santa Fe, General Benjamin Grierson 'attended a number of "blowouts", at which the people were fashionably dressed and the ladies' gowns were described in the local press.' [William H. and Shirley A. Leckie, *Unlikely Heroes: General Benjamin H. Grierson and His Family*] (2) An explosion in a mine. (3) In mining again, a big outcrop with a smaller vein underneath. (4) In dry country, a place where the loose sand has blown away, creating a dip and killing the surrounding grass.

blue meat Flesh from a calf that hasn't been weaned. [Adams]

blue norther or **blue whistler** A particularly wicked north wind.

blue pelt A summer beaver pelt, thin and dry, not worth a cent.

blue ticket A dishonorable discharge from the army and an even blacker mark than the bobtail.

blue-chip Of great value. According to linguist J. L. Dillard, though this term is now mostly applied to stocks and securities, it originated in poker, where the most valuable chips are blue.

blue-sky To chew the dog, to visit, to pass the time of day. It may be an expression mostly of the northern plains.

bluestem A native grass (*Andropogon* sp.) common in the West and valued as forage. Big bluestem (*Andropogon fucatus*) grows up to 12 feet high and is a major grass of the tall-grass prairie; little bluestem (*A. scoparius*) is a bunch grass that is three to five feet tall.

bluff From the mid 1840s and for several decades thereafter, bluff was a common name for poker. A bluff is one of the key ploys of a good poker player, or even a bad one. When you bluff, you raise the bet with a feigned confidence that you hope will convince the other players that you hold better cards than you do; then they may drop out (toss in their hands), leaving the pot to your weak hand. You can run a bluff better if you have the luck to get a couple of good cards dealt face up. Of course, the ploy may not work. Bret Harte, the Western writer, put the eternal question this way: 'But what if he sees that little bluff and calls ye?' Thus the expression to *call your bluff*.

boar's nest What a logger calls a lumber camp and what a cowboy calls a line camp. [Adams] (*See* line rider)

boarding-house man A word for a cook among loggers. [Adams] (*See* hasher)

Bob Ruly The Bois Brûlé (Burnt Wood) Indians, a division of the Teton Sioux, in an amusing pronunciation by ear. In some usages, Bob Ruly refers to the Red River metis. (*See* Dakota)

bobtail (1) A discharge from the army that offered no character reference; not quite so black a mark as the blue ticket. (2) The *bobtail watch* was the first watch of night during a trail drive. (3) Modern cowboys use bobtail to mean short – a bobtail cow is one with a short tail and a bobtail crew is one short of enough cowboys to get the job done properly.

bodega A store that sells wine or liquor. Borrowed from Spanish, it's pronounced boh-DAY-guh.

bodewash *See* bois de vache.

bog hole Boggy ground or quicksand; by extension, anything tricky, hard to figure, likely to snare you in a way you don't want.

bog its head For a bronc to lower its head to jump; thus a good time for the rider to check his balance and try to explain to himself what he's doing on the hurricane deck.

bog rider A cowboy who rides along bogs and marshes to find bogged cows and pulls them out. In the spring in Texas, cows flee to the bogs for relief from the heel flies.

bog them in For a rodeo rider to fail to bicycle, to scratch his horse with his spurs; also called *bog time in*.

boggy-top A Texas expression for open-faced pie, pie without a top crust.

boil over For a horse to blow up, go crazy, start to buck. (*See* buck)

boiled shirt A starched shirt, a shirt with a stiff front. Also known as a *biled shirt*. This was a Westernism for a custom of dress not popular on the frontier. Sometimes called (amusingly) a *fried shirt*. Mark Twain remarked in *Roughing It*, 'The miners [of California] had a particular and malignant animosity toward what they called a "biled shirt", doubtless associating it with snobbishness, or "upper-class" ways of life in general.'

boiler One of a logger's names for the cook. (*See* hasher)

boilermaker and his helper A cowboy's name for a whiskey with a beer chaser. [Adams]

bois d'arc Literally, bow wood; the wood of the Osage orange, used to make bows. It's from French, and the pronunciation is Americanised to BOW-dark. It's also grown as a hedge on the eastern plains.

bois de vache French for cow chips, or buffalo manure (later cow manure), used as a fuel; literally, wood of the cow; Americanised to *bodewash*. Making fires with buffalo chips was a necessity on the plains because trees were few and far between.

bolo tie Strictly a modern ornamentation – Webster shows the word's first usage in 1964. It is a length of cord, often braided or woven, worn as a necktie, especially in the south-west. It is usually clasped with something ornamental, like a fine piece of blossom turquoise, a nice piece of jewellery from Zuni or Hopi or some beadwork or quillwork and is one of the small sartorial indulgences of the conventional Western male. (*See* bead) Occasionally spelled bola.

Bologna bull A bull whose meat will bring a low price and may be used to make baloney (bologna sausage).

bonanza (1) A lucky find of a valuable mineral deposit. (2) The deposit itself.

(3) To be in bonanza is to be producing at a handsome rate. Sometimes a bonanza is, as Maurice Weseen called it, 'a hole in the ground owned by a champion liar.'

bone hunter A person who hunted buffalo bones on the plains, where the buffalo runners (buffalo hunters) and coyotes had left them. Fertiliser plants bought the bones. Surely these fine beasts turned into fertiliser are a symbol of the magnificent brought to naught. Bone hunters were also called *bone pilgrims*.

bone yard A cemetery, boot hill, bone orchard, whether for people or critters.

bone-seasoned In cowboy talk, experienced. [Adams]

boogered Buffaloed; intimidated. Max Evans, in his classic comic novel *The Rounders*, has one cowboy admit of Old Fooler, the meanest critter ever to be bridled, 'This horse had me slightly boogered.' That's classic, leg-pulling Western understatement. *Boogered up* is a cowboy term for crippled.

book count The number of cows the tally book says there are. In the days of the open range, big cow outfits were often bought and sold by absentee owners by book count, which was sometimes a blue-sky tally.

books won't freeze In the cattle country of the northern plains, an expression assuring cattlemen that their investments were safe. Some hard winters froze a lot of cattle there, especially the winter of 1887, and some Eastern and British investors got hurt. But the great herds were often sold by the number of animals on the books (book count), not actual count, and no books froze to death. Adams say the remark originated with Luke Murrin, a saloon keeper who used it to cheer up his Wyoming cattlemen customers.

boom (1) A rush of water used to wash out deposits of gold (also called a *boom flume*); similarly a rush of water in a river. (2) In logging, a barrier of logs or timbers that impounds floating logs in a river; also the logs thus held back. It is also used as a verb meaning 'to form a boom'.

Though not a Westernism, it is an essential term in logging.

Combinations: boom gather (a worker who collects logs in booms), *boom house* (where the boom workers live), *boom man* (a worker who floats logs downstream), *boom master* or *boom tender* (the supervisor of a boom), *boom rat* (a worker who rafts log in a boom), *boom stick* or *boom log* (a log fastened to other logs to make a boom), *boom-stick cutter* (a worker who makes boom sticks).

(3) A rush of business activity, often caused in the West by the coming of a railroad, the discovery of valuable minerals, the arrival of trail herds and the like. Over most of the West, of course, this was often followed by a bust.

Wyoming has a classic boom and bust economy. The fur trappers came in the 1820s and left when the market dropped. The 1840s saw thousands of emigrants in wagons. 1868 brought a gold rush to south Pass. The next century brought oil and gas booms. In the 1970s the exploitation of the overthrust belt set seismic crews and drilling crews to work all over the state. Even in the 1980s the towns of Lander and Evanston suffered depressions when mineral exploitation ceased, and Jeffrey City and Hannah dwindled to nearly nothing.

Boomer A sooner, a fellow who started his land rush before the legal date; also, a man who was a booster for settling lands, especially Indian lands, before it became legal. The expression came into currency in the mid 1880s, just before the whites made several grabs of Indian Territory of the legal-but-not-right variety.

booshway Among American beaver men, a field leader, the fellow who sets procedure and discipline on the trail, and a leader who is one of the backers. It is an Americanisation of the French *bourgeois*. Nowadays, among buck-skinners (mountain-man hobbyists), the booshway is the man who organises camp at rendezvous and sets and enforces rules. Also spelled *bushway*.

booster A shill for a gambler, a decoy, a capper. [Adams]

boot yard A cemetery, especially for those who died with their boots on; also called a *bone yard, bone orchard, grave patch, still yard* and, in this century, *boot hill*.

bootblack cowpuncher An old-time cattleman's expression for an Easterner who got into the cow business for what he hoped would be the profits. [Adams]

boot-jack A device for removal of a cowboy boot. It has a flat part to hold down with one foot and a forked part to stick the heel of the other boot in. Sometimes the forks are designed in the shape of horns or a woman's legs. A boot is difficult to get off with hands alone any time and after a few drinks nigh impossible.

bootleg (1) To sell whiskey illegally. A native Western word, it originally meant to smuggle whiskey to the Indians in violation of law in a flat bottle that fit in the leg of a boot. Later it came to mean selling anything illegally. The fellow who does that is a *bootlegger*. (2) Among miners, an explosive charge that doesn't break the rock. [Adams]

booze For the many words for booze, *see* firewater.

booze blind Very drunk; so drunk he couldn't hit the ground with his hat in three throws; so drunk he could see critters that weren't there; so drunk he thought he could sing. Also known as *gypped, alkalied, roostered, a walking whiskey vat.*

borax lake A lake with lots of borates (compounds of boric acid); a salt or alkali lake.

border shift A tricky manoeuvre to get a loaded gun into your shooting hand. If one hand got short, you threw the loaded gun into the other one.

borracho A border word for drunk or a drunkard. Borrowed from Spanish and pronounced boh-RAH-choh.

borrasca A mine that's poor or worthless; the opposite of *bobabza* or bonanza. Borrowed from Spanish and pronounced bohr-RAH-skuh.

borrow pit In the West, the ditch on each side of a road, where earth was 'borrowed' to form the roadbed. Also called a *barrow pit*, *borrow ditch* and, in Texas, *bar ditch*.

bosal The noseband of a hackamore, usually about finger-thick and braided from rawhide. It does for a hackamore what a bit does for the bridle. From the Spanish *bozal* (meaning 'muzzle'), a spelling that also occurs in American English. A *bosal brand* is a brand burned where the bosal goes, on the nose.

bosque Spanish for forest or woods; pronounced BOHS-kay and used widely in the south-west. Also occurs in an Americanised version, *bosky*. The place of imprisonment of the Navajos at Bosque Redondo in the mid-1860s has been called the first American concentration camp.

boss (1) What you sometimes call a cow – 'Come, boss, here, boss.' (2) The hump on the back of a buffalo's neck. The boss rib is a cut of meat from the boss, and a delicacy. It was eaten roasted by the mountain men and boiled by later whites.

Among loggers, the supervisor of the tree-felling crew is the *boss faller*.

Boss-simple describes a fellow intimidated by his boss.

bossloper An independent fur trader. An Americanisation of the Dutch *bosch-loper*, it is the usual form of the word today and is common among those hobbyists who recreate the mountain-man lifestyle, known as buckskinners. Also spelled *bush-loper*.

Boston A Chinook word for American, as opposed to a Briton. Thus we are told by Sheldon Jackson that certain Indians 'have patriotic ideas, are proud to call themselves "Boston Siwashes",' that is, Indians of the United States. The term arose because the first US ships to touch the north-west coast came from Boston.

bottom Endurance, especially of a horse. A cayuse with bottom can go all day and then some. The same can be said of some men.

bottom-card mechanic In poker, a player skilled in slipping cards off the bottom when they should come off the top. Also called a *bottom dealer*. (*See* card mechanic)

boudin A delicacy made from buffalo intestine, much loved by the Plains Indians and by the mountain men, who learned of it from the Indians. James Willard Schultz, who spent his entire adult life among the Blackfeet, described its preparation in *My life as an Indian*: '[He brought to the lodge] a few feet of a certain entrail which is always streaked or covered with soft, snowy-white fat. This Nät-ah'-ki [his Blackfeet wife] washed thoroughly and then stuffed with finely-chopped tenderloin, and stuffed it in such a manner that the inside of the entrail became the outside, and consequently the rich fat was encased with the meat. Both ends of the case were then securely tied, and the long sausage-like thing placed on the coals to roast, the cook constantly turning and moving it around to prevent it burning. After about twenty minutes on the coals, it was dropped into a pot of boiling water for five or ten minutes more, and was then ready to serve. In my estimation, and in that of all who have tried it, this method of cooking meat is the best of all.'

The word is from the French, meaning blood pudding, and it's pronounced BOO-da (the *a* approximately as in corral and nasal). Modern Louisiana has a dish of the same name.

bounce (1) To turn animals from the direction of their movement. (*See* bend) (2) To startle deer from cover. (3) Rarely, to jump a mineral claim.

bouncer The strapping fellow who collected the late rents in a boarding house.

bounty hunter A man who killed to collect bounties. Bounties were offered on the frontier for animals, Indians and men on the lam. Montanans hunted wolves for bounties; Mexicans hunted Apaches; altogether too many people carried on wars of extermination against other critters for money. Mathews's *Dictionary of Americanisms* shows £100 being offered during colonial times for Indian scalps and 15 and 20 cents in the 19th century for gopher and wolf pelts.

bounty jumper A man who enlisted in the army, collected his bounty for signing up and lit out for other parts. (*See* snowbird)

bourgeois Among French-Canadians, the head of a fur-trading party, and usually a fancy fellow with fine clothes who slept in a tent while his voyageurs slept under the canoes. The second in command in the party was called the little bourgeois. (*See also* booshway)

bovine In *Ten Thousand Goddam Cattle*, Katie Lee says cowboys used this word for a cow that's gentle, not feisty, the opposite of snorty. Range cowboys call cattle owned by farmers 'bovines' as a derogatory term.

bow An arch supporting the cover of a prairie schooner or other plains-crossing wagon.

bow dark *See* bois d'arc.

Bowie knife This famous piece of cutlery was created by Arkansas blacksmith James Black about 1830. A remarkable metal-smith, Black was especially skilled at hardening and tempering steel. James Bowie, a noted knife-fighter, ordered a certain knife from Black. Black made for him instead what became the first Bowie knife. It rose into legend when Bowie died fighting at the Alamo. Lengths of Bowie knives varied on the frontier, 12 or 14 inches being common, and they featured a cutting edge of more than two inches on top as well as the dozen inches on the bottom. Also called a *Kansas neck blister*.

box-and-strip building A traditional, pioneer-style ranch building in Texas, with outer walls of one-by-twelves nailed vertically on a two-by-four frame, the joins covered by one-by-fours, and with a broad front porch.

box canyon A canyon with just one reasonable way in and out; a blind canyon, and so the obstacle of many a hero of pulp fiction, and the come-uppance of many a villain. (*See* blind)

box fit A fit for a pistol in a holster that was ideal – form-fitted enough to allow the wearer a quick draw but snug enough

to prevent the gun from bouncing out when he was riding.

box up the dough Among loggers, to cook.

brace To fix a card game, especially faro. So a *brace box* is a dishonest faro box, *brace faro* a game in which the cards are secretly stacked, a *brace game* a fixed game and a *brace gambler* a cheater.

braceros A Mexican agricultural worker who legally entered the western United States between 1942 and 1963 as a result of the Braceros Treaty. Adapted from the Spanish word *brazos* (meaning one who works with his arms, a manual labourer) and pronounced bra-SAYR-os.

Brahma Cattle imported to the United States from India and popular in the south-west, where they stand up to the elements well. The word is often pronounced BRAY-mur or BRIM-mer. They are sometimes called Brahmins.

brain tablet Among cowboys, a cigarette.

brains What loggers call a representative of the main office.

brake stick A lever that helped the stagecoach driver apply the brakes with considerable force.

branch In a bar, water. A Wyoming bartender said she could nearly get by with knowing how to make only one drink, Canadian Club and water, invariably ordered as C C and branch. In Texas it would probably be bourbon and branch. This usage comes from Southerners' calling a creek a branch, a custom that hitchhiked westward.

brand (1) The brand, along with the earmark, is the sign of ownership of stock. It is burned into the hide with a hot branding iron for permanence. Brands are registered with the state or with a cattlemen's association to prevent duplication, and brand books are issued to show ownership.

Interpreting brands takes some knowledge and experience. They are read from left to right and from the outside in; there are conventions, like translating wings as 'flying', letters turned on their sides as 'lazy', those with little legs as 'walking' and those written in cursive style as 'running'. A brand that isn't clear is called a puzzle brand.

Brands have different names depending on their design. A barbed brand is a cattle brand with a sharp projection; a bench brand is a cattle brand sitting on a horizontal stroke with two legs; a boxed brand is a brand enclosed in a box; a connected brand is one with the figures running together; a county brand was used in the early days of Texas and represented a county; a forked brand is a brand with a V-shape sticking out of any letter or figure; a rafter brand has a roof drawn above it; a rocking brand is above a quarter circle (like a rocking chair's runners); a running brand is drawn in cursive; a tumbling brand is a brand that leans sideways; a swinging brand is a brand hanging from a crescent; a walking brand has little feet.

(2) A cow or herd of cows of a brand. Andy Adams in *The Log of a Cowboy* says, for instance, 'I must have inspection papers before I can move a brand out of the county in which it is bred.' (3) To *start a brand* was to start a cow outfit and by extension to get married and raise a family.

Combinations: brand artist (an artist with a branding iron, sometimes a rustler), *brand blotter, brand blotcher* or *brand burner* (a rustler who mutilated brands so they couldn't be read), *brand book* (a cattle association's record of brands, which established ownership of the brand), *bosal brand* (a brand on a horse's nose where the bosal would go), *fool brand* (a brand too complex of design to read out in a simple way), *fast brand* (a brand deep enough to stay), *jaw brand* (a small brand on the jaw of a horse), *range brand* (to brand calves where they are found instead of at a roundup) *set brand* (a brand made with a stamp iron) and *slow brand* (a brand not registered with the cattlemen's association, a rustler's brand).

(*See* branding, brand inspector, hair brand, road brand)

brand inspector A man hired to check brands on cows to prevent theft. In modern Wyoming, each county has at least one brand inspector, and cattlemen are not permitted to transport cattle out of their home counties without a paper from the brand inspector. Also called a *cattle inspector*.

branding Burning the brand into the hides of newborn calves or other new stock. Branding is done in the spring, when the calves are new and small. In the old style the cowcalf pairs were rounded up and the calves roped, branded (usually on the left hip) and earmarked and the males castrated (cut).

These days branding hasn't changed much. Calves may be trapped by a calf table instead of a rope, and they usually get a vaccination along with their other treatments; but they're still castrated and burned with a hot iron. Some ranchers, however, use liquid nitrogen to 'freeze' a brand.

Stewart Edward White gives a picturesque description of the traditional way of branding in *Arizona Nights*: 'Homer leaned forward and threw [his rope] . . . Immediately, and without waiting to ascertain the result of the manoeuvre, the horse turned and began methodically . . . to walk toward the branding fire. Homer wrapped the rope twice or thrice about the horn . . . Nobody paid any attention to the calf.

'The latter had been caught by the two hind legs. As the rope tightened, he was suddenly upset, and before he could realise that something disagreeable was happening, he was sliding majestically along on his belly. Behind him followed his anxious mother, her head swinging from side to side.

'Near the fire the horse stopped. The two 'bulldoggers' immediately pounced upon the victim. It was promptly flopped over on its right side. One knelt on its head and twisted back its foreleg in a sort of hammer-lock; the other seized one hind foot, pressed his boot heel against the other hind leg close to the body, and sat down behind the animal. Thus the calf was unable to struggle . . . Then one or the other threw off the rope . . .

' "Hot iron!" yelled one of the bulldoggers.

' "Marker!" yelled the other.

'Immediately two men ran forward. The brander pressed the iron smoothly against the flank. A smoke and the smell of scorching hair arose. Perhaps the calf blatted a little as the heat scorched. In a brief moment it was over.'

When the calf had been earmarked and castrated (the latter unmentioned by White), 'The calf sprang up, was appropriated and smelled over by his worried mother, and the two departed into the herd to talk it over.'

What White described was the Texas method, using one mounted roper; in what is called the Mexican or California method, two mounted ropers fell the calf and hold it with their ropes during branding. These ropers are called the *catch hands*.

The *branding chute* is a narrowing chute that ends in a calf table that clamps the steer tight for branding; the *branding corral* is a pen where branding is done; and *branding season* is the time for branding calves, not long after they're born in the spring. The *branding crew* is the men and women who do the branding. On family outfits these days, the branding crew will be made up of hands from several ranches and move from ranch to ranch, generally on consecutive weekends.

The *branding fire* is a fire for heating branding irons. Now a branding heater fuelled by propane is often used in lieu of open fires, and some outfits have electric branding irons.

branding iron The tool used to burn on a brand. The stamp iron was a long-handled iron that branded in one application. Dotting irons, common in Texas in the 1830s, stuck it on one piece at a time, one iron for a half circle, another for a straight bar and so on. The running iron has no stamp at the end but just a little curl, a fish-hook, a circle – any round shape. With this the brand artist sketches in the design free-handed. In some states the running iron is illegal, in part because rustlers like it. A pothook or a cinch ring could also be used as a running iron.

The irons are made of any scrap iron

the blacksmith can work with and average two to three feet long, the longer the better, to keep the handle from getting so hot. Sometimes they have a wooden handle, shaped into a ring at the end. To apply the stamp just right requires a nice touch. The hand must know when the iron is just hot enough. A red-hot one will scorch cruelly, spoil the brand and leave a wound that may get infected. A cold iron will not get through the hair to the hide.

brasada Brush country, especially the impenetrable brush country of Texas and most especially the barbarous brush country of south-west Texas, between the Nueces and Rio Grand rivers, where stubborn steers like to hide and even brush-poppers hate to ride after them. Borrowed from the Spanish *bruzada* (meaning 'brush') and pronounced bruh-SAH-duh. A *brasadero* is a man or critter of the brasada.

A *brasada measure* is the length a man can stretch out his arms and is used to measure a reata.

brave A term of Indian Pidgin English for an Indian warrior; any Indian adult male. Sometimes pejorative and now outdated even more than the use of 'Negro' for blacks. *Brave-maker* means 'booze'.

bravo A nickname for the Rio Grande River, which was also called the Del Norte. From the Mexican name for the Rio Grande, Rio Bravo del Norte.

brea Tar, pitch, especially for use on roofs or as seaming material in the south-west. Borrowed from Spanish and pronounced BRAY-uh.

breachy Descriptive of a cow that has a way of finding her way through fences to where she isn't supposed to be.

bread wallet A person's stomach.

breadroot *See* prairie turnip.

break a horse To train a horse, usually to saddle-riding, sometimes to the bridle or harness. Trained horses in the West are not 'broken' but 'broke' – 'broken' would mean ruined. A horse may be broke to different degrees, from green-broke to cavvy-broke to halter-broke to lady-broke to family-broke (gentled enough for everyone in the family). He may also just have had 'the kinks taken out of him', which means he's been ridden once, is a little bit used to the saddle, doesn't know how to neck-rein, and needs a rider who knows more than he does and is more willful.

The two traditional ways of breaking horses in the West are by hackamore and by bit, which were done respectively where the trainers had learned in the ways of Mexican vaqueros or Texas cowpokes. No doubt each has its virtues, and each certainly has its partisans, partisans who sometimes have their hackles up.

David Lavender, in *One Man's West*, recalls how breaking was done up to the 1930s: 'In earlier days a horse was seldom touched until it was three or four years old. Then a young rider would decide to take the kinks out of it. In a swirl of dust, squeals, and flashing hoofs the colt would be roped, thrown, blindfolded, and saddled. While one man "eared the critter down" – twisted its ears to make it stand still – the rider would mount, reach forward, and slip off the blindfold. Now the horse could see where it jumped, and jump it did, exploding as far and as high as it could go.

'Cowboys who had reached the weary age of thirty regarded this procedure with jaundiced eyes. There you sit, beaten mercilessly between the hard cantle and the hard pommel of the saddle. If you are pitched off the ground is waiting like a club. Or perhaps the horse falls on top of you, snapping a leg or collarbone. Even if you become adept at sticking, your innards simply cannot stand that pounding many times; as the cowboys say, "it makes an old man out of a young one right quick."

'It doesn't do a horse much good either, often leaving the animal sullen, wind-broken, or treacherous. When ranches had more horses than they could use a spoiled colt wasn't so much of a loss. But now that cattlemen have to utilise fully each acre of grass the horseherds have diminished in size. Every animal must be productive, and more care is shown in their breaking. They are eased through their training and cajoled not to buck, instead of the other way around – all of which suits the older hands right to the ground.'

These terms relate to broke horses and their training: *cold-jawed* (hard-mouthed), *dead-mouthed* or *hard-mouthed* (unresponsive to the bit), *head-shy* (leery of the bridle), *halter puller* (in the habit of pulling back on the halter rope), *halter-shy*, *neck-reiner* (broke to respond to the rein against its neck), *one-man horse*, *owl-head* (an untrainable horse), *raw one* (an unbroke horse), *smooth-mouthed* (an old horse), *sour-mouthed* (a horse that fights the bit), *shave-tail* (a broke horse, the opposite of a broomtail), *tender-mouthed* (sensitive to the bit), and *unroostered* (just broken in).

Breaking horses is also called *busting broncs*, *peeling broncs* and *making shave-tails*.

Breaking age is the age when Western horses are broke to ride, usually three to four years old. *Breaking patter* is the soft, comforting talk to a bronc [Adams], and a *breaking pen* is a small corral used to break horses, usually with a snubbing post in the middle. To *break in two* is how a horse feels to the rider when he bucks – head going one way and hind end another.

break your pick Among miners, to get fired or to quit.

break-over In fire-fighting, a term for where a fire crosses over a line or barrier meant to control it. Also called a *slop-over*.

breaks Rough country, terrain interrupted by gullies and the like – thus the breaks of the Missouri River, cut-up country near that river in northern Montana. Also spelled *brakes*.

breast-collar A martingale.

breastplate A large ornament, usually of metal, worn on the chest by Indians or half-breeds or (rarely) Anglos influenced by them.

breech-cloth A strip of cloth worn by a man, usually an Indian or breed or sometimes a mountain man, as a loincloth. It might be short and plain, for work, or long and elaborately quilled or beaded, for show. It was often complemented by leggings. Also called a *breech-clout* or, rarely, *breeching*.

breed *See* half-breed.

breeding range An area used for putting the herd bull with the cows.

bridal chamber Among miners, the far end of the narrow tunnel where the work is being moved forward. [Adams]

bridle-wise Said of a horse trained to neck-rein. (*See* neck)

Brigham (1) In Arizona, gravy or sop. (2) Ephedra, also known as *Brigham tea*, *Mormon tea*, *Brigham weed*, *desert tea* and by other names. Ephedra is a low, wiry bush from which Brigham Young, at least in legend, brewed what was deemed a healthy version of tea. The Words of Wisdom of the Mormons prohibit tea and other drinks with caffeine.

Brighamite An adherent of the Mormon leader Brigham Young; sometimes it was meant in contradistinction to a Josephite, one whose allegiance was to Joseph Smith. (*See* Josephite)

brindle (1) To go. (2) Said of a cow with stripes or spots of different colours; brockled.

bring up the drags (1) To ride at the back of the herd. (*See also* flank, swing and point) (2) Used to describe the way a slow person moves. [Adams]

bristlecone pine A short, often prostrate pine (*Pinus aristata*) that grows on exposed ridge-tops and dry slopes, especially on the mountains in the Great Basin. They are among the oldest living plants in the world; a group near Bishop, California has trees that are over 4,600 years old.

broadaxe brigade A logger's word for a crew of tie hacks, men who cut railroad ties with heavy axes.

broad-horn (1) A flatboat, so called because of the tin horn such boats used. (2) Texas longhorn.

brockled When said of a cow, brindled, bearing spots of various colours.

bronc belt A belt worn by a bronc buster for support of the muscles of the back and stomach. [Adams]

bronc buster A hand who rides the rough string, the unbroke horses. In the old days, he rode them once and called them broke, or at least broke enough to put into some cowboy's string. It was a crazy, man-destroying job, but one a young buck often liked the challenge of. In his wonderful novel *The Rounders*, Max Evans opines that a bronc rider is 'a cowboy with his brains kicked out.' He's also called *bronc breaker*, *bronc scratcher*, *bronc snapper*, *bronc squeezer*, *bull-bat*, *buster*, *contract buster*, *flesh rider*, *gentler*, *hazer*, *horse-breaker*, *jinete*, *mansador*, *peeler* and *rough-string rider*.

A *bronc fighter* is a cowboy who spoils the horse instead of breaking it. [Adams] A *bronc stomper* is what the old-time cowboys called a man who could ride the rough string. [Adams] (*See* break a horse)

bronc saddle A saddle for breaking horses or riding horses with bronco temperaments. It has undercut and back-bulged forks and a heavily dished cantle.

bronc spur A spur whose shank turns in toward the horse, to make scratching the bronc easier.

bronc stall A horse stall small enough to keep a wild horse from kicking or biting.

bronco (1) Strictly, a wild horse, a mustang; then, an unbroke horse. Jo Mora in *Trail Dust and Saddle Leather* gives the traditional view that 'when a horse has been broken he positively ceases to be a bronco'. Less strictly, though, a hard-to-handle horse; sometimes just a synonym for cow pony. Also spelled *broncho* and frequently shortened to *bronc*, it is a borrowing from the Spanish, meaning 'wild, untamed'. (*See* break a horse)

(2) The term is sometimes applied to wild or rebellious people – thus Joseph Porter in *Paper Medicine Man* speaks of 'bronco Apaches', and the *Westerners' Brand Book* tells us that a man who makes mistakes isn't necessarily all bronco.

broomtail A wild mare; sometimes any wild horse; sometimes an unbroke mare or horse. Such a critter is called broomtail as opposed to shave-tail because hands on the northern plains pulled the tails of wild horses when they were broke so that they could tell the broke from the unbroke horses at a distance. Also called a *broomie*. Other terms for wild horses are *bangtail*, *fantail*, *fuzz-tail*, *mesteño* (mustang), *mustang* and *pestle-tail*. Most of these have the implication of a horse with a bushy tail.

brujo In the south-west, a borrowing from Spanish meaning 'sorcerer' or, in the feminine form '*bruja*', a witch. Pronounced BROO-hoh.

brush (1) A little (or not so little) fight, as in, 'We had a brush with the Blackfeet.' (2) The backwoods.

A brush arbor is an improvised south-western shelter with a brush roof to keep the sun off.

brush popper A cowboy who works the brasada, the brush country of Texas (such as the mesquite thickets of the Rio Bravo); also a horse accustomed to working brush.

Breaking brush is hairy work, best left to riders who think they are some hombres. The cattle pick the densest thickets to hide in, and the popper has to move through fast while the brush tears at his skin and clothing. As a result, the brush popper uses nothing on his person or his saddle that snags easily. He has a hard-earned reputation for toughness. He rides a *brush horse* and uses a *brush hook* to slash the brush. A *brush roper* uses a shorter rope and a smaller loop than the cowboy who works the plains and uses less space to swing it. Also called *brasadero*, *brush buster*, *brush hand*, *brush thumper*, *brush whacker* and *limb skinner*.

A *brush roundup* is a cattle drive in the brush, usually the Texas brush country. The cattle are called *brush snakes*, *brush splitters* or *brush steers*. The cattle lie low, so the riders move slowly and try to move them out, often at night. [Adams] A cow that's hiding in the brush is *brushed-up*.

buck Noun usages: (1) A deerskin. (2) A dollar, perhaps deriving from *deerskin*, for

deerskins were money. (3) In extension of the meaning of male animals such as deer and sheep, a male Indian, sometimes with a pejorative implication. (4) Any male human being, as in, 'I was just a young buck then.' (5) In poker, a pocket knife passed around to show who is the dealer (perhaps so called because the knives often had handles of buckhorn) and the source of the expression *pass the buck*.

Verb usages: (1) What a horse (or bull) does to try to unseat its rider – what Texans call *pitching*. Ramon Adams gives a lot of expressions for bucking, many of them wonderfully expressive: *arching his back, blowing the plug, blowing up, bogging his head, boiling over, breaking in two, bucking on a dime, bucking straight away, bucking the saddle, buck-jumping, casueying, catbacking, chinning the moon, circling buck, coming apart, coming undone, coming unglued, craw-fishing, crow-hopping, double shuffling, fall-backing, fence-cornering, fence-worming, folding up, frog walking, goating, hauling hell out of its shuck, hopping for mama, jackknifing, kettling, kicking the lid off, laying a rail fence, moaning, pin-wheeling, pitching fence-cornered, pump handling, pussy-backing, rainbowing, rearing back, sheep-jumping, shooting his back, slatting his sails, straight bucking, sticking his bill in the ground, sun-fishing, swapping ends, swallowing his head, taking you to church, throwing the pack, turning a wildcat, turning through himself, unloading, unwinding, walking beaming, warping his backbone, whing-dinging, wind-milling, wrinkling his spine*.

(2) To carry or tote something heavy, like water. (3) To contend against something, for instance, snow, as in, 'We had to buck deep drifts.'

In saddles, a *bucking roll* is a pad, blanket or even a coat rolled and tied to the fork of a saddle to give a bronc rider something to wedge himself against. It may be manufactured but is often improvised. A *bucking rim* is a projection on a saddle's cantle, and a *bucking rein* is a single rope on the hackamore that helps a rider stay on a bucking horse. [Adams]

The bucking strap is a tight strap around the critter's flank that irritates it, causing harder bucking. It's not the same as a buck strap, a leather loop attached to the fork of a saddle as a hand hold for a rider who's trying to stay on a horse that's bucking. Top riders sneer at such an aid, and it's barred at rodeos.

In rodeo, to *buck straight away* is for a horse to buck in long jumps straight ahead, instead of twisting and turning every which way. Such a horse is easier for some cowboys to stay on, harder for others. *Bucking on a dime* describes a horse that bucks in one place. *Buck the saddle* is what an unbroke horse is likely to do when the empty saddle is first put on its back.

buck ague A hunter's nervous excitement when taking aim at a deer or other game animal. Also called *buck fever*.

buck and rail A style of fence in the parts of the West with rocky ground and plenty of trees. The bucks, made of poles crossed like an X, support the rails.

buck nun A hermit; a cloistered male.

buck out A cowboy term for dying. [Adams] For others, *see* cash in your chips. If you *bucked out in smoke*, you went in a gun-fight.

buck the tiger To play faro. The gambler's faro box and cloth had various pictures of tigers. A faro player was sometimes called a *bucker*, and gambling, particularly playing faro or monte, was sometimes called *bucking*.

buck wood Among loggers, to saw trees. Fallers fell the trees, and buckers saw them into lengths.

buckaroo A cowboy, especially a hand of the desert basins of northern Nevada, northern California, eastern Oregon and western Idaho. According to Jim Bramlett in *Ride for the High Points*, the type of horsemanship seen on these ranges goes back directly to the horse-training techniques perfected by the Californios in the 1700s and 1800s. The Californio style of horse jewellery – silver spurs, bits and conchos – and other Californio-styled horse gear are used by buckaroos today, although this equipment is modified for more strength. These cowboys sometimes wear lace-up boots that sometimes have toe spiders (pieces of leather riveted on to the boots).

The Californio influence has led hands of other styles to use the word buckaroo with a hint of mockery. Said the Pinedale, Wyoming *Roundup* in 1988, 'This is a Nevada/Oregon term for the profession [of being a cowhand] and, around these parts, has a slightly childish ring to it.'

The word may be an Americanisation of the Spanish *vaquero* and has such variants as *buckhara*, *bukkarer*, *buccaroo*, *buckaree* and *buckayro*.

A *buckaroo saddle* is a kind of saddle often preferred by buckaroos, developed from the Californio saddle. It has narrow forks (to keep the legs closer together), bucking rolls and a high cantle and is double-rigged.

buck-board A passenger wagon with a floor of springy boards that provide a certain cushion against the bumps of the road and usually with springs under the seats. It might be drawn by one or two horses and rigged for two or four passengers. Also called a *buck wagon*. The *buck-board driver* is what old-time ranch folks called the mail carrier, who came by buck-board, but seldom came. [Adams]

bucket hunter What a cowboy calls a calf that drinks not from a cow but from a bucket. [Adams]

bucket man A rustler's derisive name for a cowboy. [Adams]

bucket of blood A rough saloon. The name came from a notorious drinking place in Havre, Montana, owned by Shorty Young, and spread to similar dives.

buckshot A shotgun load with large balls, as opposed to bird-shot. It was designed for shooting large game like deer, but since it spread and wrought havoc at close range, it was the choice of stagecoach guards and law officers concerned about defending against groups of men.

buckshot land Soil that's poor, clayey. [Adams]

buckskin From the original meaning, the skin of a buck deer, have come several meanings particular to the frontier or the West: (1) Clothing made from such skin, a complete outfit of which was generally called buckskins. From colonial times, American frontiersmen imitated Indians by wearing buckskin. (2) The colour of buckskin. (3) A popular horse colour is buckskin (golden brown), and the horse was referred to as a buckskin. The old cow pony was of every colour and marking, albino, appaloosa, bay, bayo, bayo coyote, black, blood bay, brown (brown with mane and tail of the same colour), blue, blue roan, buckskin, buttermilk (palomino), calico, California sorrel, chestnut, clay bank, cremello, coyote dun, dapple, dapple grey, fleabitten grey, gateado, grey, grulla, Indian red, iron, iron grey, line-backed, liver chestnut, moro, paint, palomino, piebald, pinto, pinto-overo, sabino, skewbald, sorrel, strawberry roan, tobiano, white, zebraed and zebra dun.

Colour didn't really mean anything – training and temperament were all – but most hands wanted mounts of solid colour. Spotted ponies were supposed to be Indian horses, thus of low breeding.

Buckskin Curtain A recent coinage meaning the obstacles that separate Indian America from the dominant culture, as the Iron Curtain once separated Eastern from Western Europe.

buck-skinner A hobbyist who recreates the lifestyle and physical culture of the mountain man, including going to rendezvous, living in tipis or other period shelter, wearing authentic clothing, shooting muzzle-loaders and so on.

Buenaventura The name of a river that Americans of the early period of Western exploration believed ran west from the Rockies into San Francisco Bay. It turned out to be mythical. Before anyone knew that, the mountain man Jedediah Smith and others spent a lot of time and blood looking for it.

bueno Good. Borrowed from Spanish and pronounced BWAY-noh. Also, during the days of the open range, a cow that was a good find because his brand wasn't in the brand book and you could slip him by a brand inspector. [Adams]

buffalo (1) The Westerner's name for the bison, a magnificent creature standing as tall as a tall man and weighing up to a ton. The term 'buffalo' comes from a misinterpretation by the early Spanish explorers; they called the animal *buffalo*, the name for the wild ox of Africa and India.

Basically a creature of the Great Plains, the buffalo's range extended east to the woodlands of Canada and the United States as well. The Indians hunted the buffalo from the earliest days, at first by driving them over cliffs, later on foot with the bow and arrow, and in historic times on horseback with bow or gun. For them the beast was a source of meat, clothing, shelter, bedding, weapons and other utensils – and it became a focus of Indian religion, the skull and other parts often being used for medicine. Following the buffalo made the Indians nomadic. From the 1840s, white immigrants found the buffalo an excellent supply of meat. (*See* cibolero) From 1870 to 1883, though, professional buffalo hunters (known as buffalo runners) destroyed the great herds for the sake of supplying Eastern markets with hides and bone. Probably over 40 million were killed. Their demise opened the vast grasslands to cattle and cattlemen. Now private and governmental programmes of breeding and preservation have brought the animal back to modest numbers. The Ghost Dancers believed the buffalo will one day come back. We can hope so.

(2) Also used as a verb – buffalo, meaning 'to confuse, cheat or intimidate someone', has been in use since the 1870s. From the same sense comes the mountain man expression *buffalo-witted*, meaning dense and dull.

Combinations: buffalo coat (a winter coat made from a buffalo robe), *buffalo crossing* (a place where buffalo ford a river), *buffalo dance* (a ceremony preparing Plains Indians for a buffalo hunt), *buffalo horse* (a horse used by the Indians for running down buffalo, also known as a *buffalo runner*), *buffalo ground* (where the buffalo roam), *buffalo lick* (where buffalo licked salt), *buffalo pound* (an area where buffalo gathered in the winter), *buffalo range* (the area that had buffalo grass, where the buffalo roamed), *buffalo run* (a trail made by buffalo), *buffalo running* (hunting buffalo on horseback), *buffalo tea* (the fouled water left in buffalo wallows), *buffalo trace* (a trail made by buffalo), *buffalo wallow* (a hollow in the ground where buffalo rolled and scratched themselves, often serving as a catchment basin for rain water), *buffalo whopper* (a hand who chased buffalo off the cattle range), *buffalo wood* (buffalo chips) and *buffalo wolf* (another name for the grey wolf, *Canis occidentaliis*, that preyed on buffalo).

Plants named for buffalo: buffalo burr (*Solanum rostratum* – a short drought resistant annual with sharp spines) and *buffalo berry* (a shrub – *Shepherdia canadensis* – with an edible, but bitter, red berry).

buffalo chip The dried pie of buffalo manure, called by the French bois de vache, literally 'wood of the cow'. It was the universal firewood of the treeless plains. Says Jo Mora in *Trail Dust and Saddle Leather*, 'It made a good hot fire in dry weather, though when too wet it did not burn so readily, all of which scarcely added to the sweet temper or the efficiency of the cook.' It's also called euphemistically *babcock coal*, *prairie chip*, *prairie coal*, *prairie fuel*, *prairie pancake* and *prairie wood*.

buffalo grass A species of grama grass (*Buchloe dactyloides*) common on the arid Great Plains; short and not inviting in appearance, but the principal sustenance of the buffalo. On the northern plains, says David Dary in *Cowboy Culture*, 'because of the dry climate and the high protein content of the slender blades, buffalo grass cured into a dry feed that stayed palatable and nutritious all winter long.' (*See* prairie)

buffalo robe The hide of the buffalo prepared for use with the hair left on. The Indians used the robes as blankets and wraps and as surfaces for painting records of important matters, like battles or visions, or keeping the winter count. The robe of the white buffalo was sacred and was painstakingly prepared and offered to the sun.

Preparation of the robes, done mostly by women, was meticulous. Says David Dary in *Entrepreneurs of the Old West*, 'Most tribes on the northern plains

fastened the edges of a raw or green hide to pole frames, using rawhide thongs, much like an old-fashioned quilting frame made of four stout poles tied together at right angles . . . ' The women scraped the hide 'clean of the last pieces of flesh. They then sprinkled the hide with water and smeared it with buffalo brains and grease. After the hide dried in the sun, the Indian women would rub it [for several days] with a sinew cord until it was soft and pliable.'

Later Anglos used buffalo robes as carriage and sleigh robes and similar warm coverings, and this demand helped nearly exterminate the great beast. According to white Indian James Willard Schultz, a particularly thick, glossy, silky buffalo robe was called a beaver robe.

buffalo runner (1) A buffalo hunter – the term is deceptive in that these professionals did not hunt buffalo by running them on horseback, the traditional sporting method, but in stands, killing large numbers from fixed positions. A buffalo hunter 'never called himself a buffalo hunter – that was the mark of a tenderfoot,' says David Dary in *Entrepreneurs of the Old West*. He was a buffalo *runner*, and Bernard DeVoto in *Across the Wide Missouri* describes the hunt as 'what seems to have been the finest of all sports on the continent, perhaps the finest sport hunters have enjoyed anywhere . . . What gave the hunt an emotion equivalent to ecstasy was the excitement, the speed, the thundering noise, the awe-inspiring bulk of the huge animal in motion, the fury of its death, and the implicit danger of the chase.'

The runners called the animals *buffs* or *bufflers* and were afflicted by *buffalo mange* (lice). They often resorted to drinking *buffalo cider* (the contents of the buffalo's stomach) or *buffalo tea* (the foul water left behind in buffalo wallows). They used a *buffalo gun*, one that could drop a one-ton animal with a single blow, one that delivered a big piece of lead catapulted by enough powder to fly at high velocity. A popular one was the Big Fifty, made by Sharps, a .50-calibre rifle with varying sizes of cartridges. This gun was so powerful that it wiped out tens of millions of buffalo in a dozen or so years, and satisfied the blood-lust and greed of even the buffalo runners.

Buffalo-hunting crews had their own pecking order. At the top was the runner (hunter), who made the shot. Next came the *buffalo skinner*, a fellow with a nice touch and a very sharp knife. They were later followed by *bone hunters*, or pilgrims, who gathered the bones for fertiliser.

(2) A horse used, especially by an Indian, to hunt buffalo.

buffalo soldier An Indian Pidgin English name for a black soldier, probably from the texture of the soldier's hair. In the post-Civil War period, two black regiments of cavalry and two of infantry went to the Indian Wars. Black enlisted men and noncommissioned officers fought under white commissioned officers and rendered yeoman service, especially in the Apache wars. One soldier wrote, 'The officers say the negroes [*sic*] make good soldiers and fight like fiends . . . The Indians call them "buffalo soldiers", because their woolly heads are so much like the matted cushion that is between the horns of the buffalo.'

buford Among rodeo cowboys, a calf or steer that puts up little resistance to being thrown or tied. [Adams]

bug juice Booze. (*See* firewater)

bugged up Dressed up.

bugger To spook; to jump in fright. A cow that got buggered could cause a stampede.

buggy boss A lightly mocking name for an Eastern ranch-owner who inspected his ranch from a buggy because he didn't ride well enough to do it from horseback. The modern equivalent is a *wind-shield farmer*.

bugle A piercing combination of cries, song and grunts made by male elk as part of their fall mating ritual; the noise is intended to let the other bulls know where their territories are.

build a high line Another Westernism for 'to tell a tall tale', this time one native to loggers.

build a loop To shake out the noose of your rope for a throw.

bull (1) The male of the cow, buffalo, elk and moose species. (2) Among loggers, an ox. (3) As a verb, what a cow does when she's in heat – puts her front leg on the hind end of a bull or even another cow.

Among loggers, a *bull block* is a huge pulley block for sky-line logging. A *bull bucker* is the leader of the crew that bucks the fallen trees. *Bull chain* is the big chain that hauls logs uphill. The *bull cook* was, in the old days of logging, the man who fed the oxen and more recently the fellow who takes care of the odd chores in a logging camp. A *bull donkey* is a name for a big donkey engine. The *bull of the woods* is the foreman of a logging camp or the winner of a contest in which loggers fight to see who can stay up on a big log the longest. A *bull-pen* was a bunk-house, and a *bull-pen boy* was the fellow who took care of it. *Bull wheels* are enormous wooden wheels. In the West, bull often simply seems to mean a big version of something.

Among miners, a *bull prick* is not a natural bovine insemination conduit, but a hard-rock miner's drill. Among cowboys, *Bull hides* are heavy chaps, cut from the thick skin of beef bulls. A *bull pen* is a corral for bulls. Another name for a bronc buster is *bullbat*. [Adams] *Bulling steers* or *bullers* are castrated beeves that still have some sexual odour and so draw other steers, which makes them nuisances on the trail. A *bull nurse* is what cowboys call the hand picked to accompany the cattle on their train ride. [Adams] *Bull-puncher* is another name for a cowpuncher.

Bull thrower is an occasional word of a mountain man for his rifle, meaning killer of buffalo bulls.

bull boat A boat made of buffalo hides stretched on a willow frame. It was a favourite of the mountain man because it had little draft and could be jerry-built almost anywhere in beaver country.

In Stewart Edward White's novel *The Long Rifle*, the veteran trapper Joe Crane taught newcomer Andy Burnett how to build one: 'Joe stuck upright in the ground a circle of light willow poles, bent the ends over toward a common centre, and tied them together to form a great inverted basket twelve or fourteen feet long. This he covered with the buffalo skins sewed together. Underneath he built a slow fire. As the skins warmed he assiduously rubbed a mixture of buffalo tallow and resin into the seams, which cooled as hard as the dried hide itself. Then he and Andy, working on opposite sides, carefully pulled up the willows from the earth, turned the thing over, cut off the projecting ends, bound on a rough gunwale of willow.

' "Thar she be!" said Joe. "That's a bull boat." '

You steered it with poles. One made by the mountain man Nathaniel Wyeth was made from three bull skins, eighteen feet long, five-and-a-half feet wide, and was pointed at both ends. The vehicle was indispensable in the fur trade because it could haul a big load of furs down the West's shallow streams.

Bull Durham The celebrated smoke of the cowboy, sold as loose tobacco in a little muslin sack with a famous picture of the bull. Starting at the end of the Civil War, Bull Durham came from Durham's Station, North Carolina. Competing brands were Sitting Bull, Pride of Durham, Duke of Durham, Ridgewood, Navy Tobacco, Navy Plug, Starr Navy and others. In the old West, a man carried the makings and rolled his own. Smoking tailor-mades, also called ready-mades, was looked down on.

bull pen A large empty space in early trading rooms, often with a wood burning stove. The Anglo trader was often alone, so a high wooden counter kept the Indians from direct access to the stock on the shelves. Common practice was for the Indian to bargain for a single item at a time, taking as long as he liked to seal the deal. Traders often provided free tobacco or other treats during the process. Also a term for a mountain hole or park.

bull train A string of prairie schooners drawn by oxen and under a single command. For some reason, Westerners often give oxen, which are castrated, the name 'bulls', whose reason for being is that they aren't. James Willard Schultz described a trader's train on the plains of

Montana in the 1870s: 'Berry's train now consisted of four eight-yoke teams, drawing twelve wagons in all, loaded with fifty thousand pounds of provisions, alcohol, whisky, and trade goods. There were four bull-whackers, a night-herder who drove the "cavayard" – extra bulls and some saddle horses – a cook, three men who were to build the cabins and help with the trade, with Berry and his wife, and I.' Also known as a *bull outfit*, a *bull team*, a *bull wagon* and a *grass train*.

The men who drove the bull teams were called *bullskinners*, *bull pushers*, *bull punchers* or *bullwhackers*. (*See also* mule-skinner) The *bull-wagon boss* (or master) was the chief of a bull train. [Adams]

bull whip A whip of braided rawhide, tapering from a stout wooden stock to a popper at the end, used by bullwhackers and mule-skinners to control their animals. Legends have grown up about the skill of these men with this tool. Not originally a Westernism.

bulldog To wrestle a steer; to throw it by hand. The black cowboy Bill Pickett is said to have been the first man to do it, partly by inflicting his teeth on the steer's nose. Generally, the bulldogger rides alongside the critter's left side, drops on to it, reaches over the neck, grabs its nose or some loose neck skin, grips the left horn with his left hand and with a quick twist brings down man and beast. Bulldogging is a rodeo stunt, since there's little occasion for it in ranch work. Some say it was Bill Pickett's use of his teeth that gave rise to the name *bulldogging*. A *bulldogger* is a rodeo competitor who specialises in bulldogging.

A bulldog is also a short tapadero (stirrup cover), generally of one piece and often lined with sheepskin; it is stitched together under the foot and snugged all the way back to the heel.

Bull riding is a rodeo event. The cowboy indeed rides a bull bareback, an endeavour for neither the faint of heart nor sane of mind. The riders used to hold on to a bull rigging (a surcingle with hand holds built into it) but now use only a loose rope, called a *bull rope*. The rider wraps the bull rope around his hand. The rules permit contestants to hold on with only the wrapped hand, not touching the rope, the bull or himself with the free hand.

Bull tailing was a popular game of early south-western Hispanics. It is like bulldogging in that a bull was thrown down (busted) hard. But the vaqueros did it by grabbing the tail and riding forward and to the side. *Bull-running* was another game of the Californio ranchers, in which riders played bulls with lances and then chased, caught and tailed them.

bullet (1) A gold nugget. (2) A frontier guessing game adopted from the Indians, like thimble-rig, the pea-under-the-shell game. (3) In poker, an ace.

bull-roarer A ceremonial noise-maker of south-western Indians. Made of the sternum of a big animal, or of wood, it is whirled around the head by a cord and makes a whirring or moaning sound. It is associated with wind, thunder and lightning. Also called a *rhombus*, a *whizzer* and a *lightning stick*.

bum calf An orphan calf; a dogie; often has the implication of a runt. Also *bum lamb*, an *orphan lamb*, a *bummer* and a *buttermilk*. To bum a lamb is to remove it from its mother. A *bum steer* is a bad deal or a lie.

bums on the plush The marvellous expression of loggers for the idle rich.

bunch To herd cattle, horses, sheep and so on into a group. The *bunch ground* is where the animals gather during a roundup, and a *bunch quitter* is one that won't stay with the herd.

bunch grass A number of Western grasses that grow in tufts, descriptive of a kind of growth rather than a single species. A *bunch grasser* is a horse that lives on bunch grass or a person who lives in foothills.

bunk (1) A timber on a logger's sledge that supports the logs. (2) In verb form, to put a log on a bunk.

bunkhouse Sleeping and living quarters for cowhands, miners or loggers; sometimes the word carries the implication of being temporary. Historian

David Dary offers these other words for such living quarters: *doghouse, shack, dump, ram pasture, dice-house* and *dive*.

bunkie Bunkmate. The term was first used by soldiers during the Plains Indian wars, where it also meant 'blanket-mate under the open sky', and it may simply have meant 'buddy, pal'. Also spelled *bunkey*.

bunko (1) A swindler. (2) A gambling game played with dice or cards, perhaps derivative of the Spanish *banca*. Also spelled *bunco*. The verb form, to *bunko someone*, and the compounds (*bunko artist, bunko game, bunko joint* and so on) are not Westernisms. The general meaning, any confidence game, came later.

buñuelo A New Mexican term for a sopapilla, a Mexican-style deep-fried fritter.

Bureau of Indian Affairs This bureau of the federal government, commonly called the BIA, was formed in 1824 under the Department of War (and that tells a tale) to administer US policy toward the Indians. In 1849 it was switched to the Department of the Interior, where it has remained. Almost from its inception, the bureau has been notorious for its inefficiency and graft, and it was responsible for much suffering among the Indians and for much resentment. In the 1970s and '80s the BIA almost entirely hired Indians and turned over many of its functions to the tribes, but from the Indian point of view, further improvement is needed. For instance, some call for the establishment of the BIA as a cabinet department.

Bureau of Land Management This Department of the Interior Agency, commonly called the BLM, is the result of the combination of the Federal Grazing Service and the General Land Office in 1946. It manages 270 million acres of public lands in the West (mostly non-forested) and 520 million acres of mineral rights, basically everything left over after forming the Forest Service, Defense Department, Indian tribal lands, and Park Service. Most uses of this land are consumptive and include grazing and mineral exploitation and development; some scenic areas are set aside for recreation use.

Bureau of Reclamation The government department that builds dams and manages waterways in the West, also known as Bu. Rec. Established by the Newlands Act of 1902, it was intended to aid farmers stricken by droughts and to improve on the ineffective job that states and private enterprise were doing. The efforts of the bureau made it possible to farm in areas like the high plains, southern Arizona and most of California; ironically, the large dams also made urban development in the West possible. In theory, some projects are paid for by user fees, but most dams end up being heavily subsidised by the federal government. For a history of water use and the bureau in the West, *see* Marc Reisner's *Cadillac Desert.*

burglar A horse with a hidden defect. A horse trader who isn't on the up and up may have several such horses, say E. R. Jackman and R. A. Long in *The Oregon Desert*, and will avoid guaranteeing the questionable aspect. The burned buyer later brings the horse back for whatever small satisfaction he can get, and the trader sells the same bad horse over and over.

The term horse-trader does not imply generosity, honesty, or openness; it generally suggests a shrewd, tight-lipped, cunning businessman. It is well accepted in much of the United States that what the buyer doesn't discover about the horse is his problem – no refunds. There are hundreds of tricks to cover up specific defects of a horse – usually to hide lameness.

burn cattle A cowman's occasional word for branding; also called *burning rawhide*. To *burn them and boot them* is to brand calves and turn them loose.

burn powder To shoot a gun.

burn the breeze To ride fast; also known as to *burn the prairie*, *burn the earth*, and *burn the wind.*

burrito A food, generally some combination of refried beans, cheese, green chiles and meat wrapped hot in a flour tortilla. As peddled by America's fast-food industry, it has become a hugely popular snack, and in the United States no longer means a small donkey.

burro A donkey. Texas used to have wild herds of them. A borrowing from Spanish, it is pronounced BOO-row, or BOO-r-r-row by those with a nice tongue for Spanish, but often Americanised to BURR-row. Some western deserts still have wild burros, and the Bureau of Land Management sees them as a problem. Also known as *Arizona nightingale*, *desert canary*, *Colorado mockingbird*, *mountain canary*, *Rocky Mountain canary* and *Washoe canary.*

burro milk Cowboy talk for nonsense. [Adams]

burrowing owl A small prairie owl that lives in prairie-dog burrows and is found mostly in the West.

buscadero First a tough, gun-totin' lawman; later any tough gun-toter. Borrowed from the Spanish *buscador* (meaning 'to hunt or search'), it's pronounced boos-kuh-DAY-roh. Also known as a *pistolero*. A *buscadero belt* is a broad belt for two guns, one on either side, and a *buscadero holster* is a holster inserted in a wide cartridge belt, both used chiefly in Hollywood.

bush boy A Navajo country term, used mostly by Anglos, for a Navajo who is very much unassimilated into white culture and modern ways. Typically a bush boy might be a long hair (man with hair uncut, in the traditional style), live on the far western side of the reservation or in the canyons on the south side of the San Juan River, speak no language but Navajo and run his home and get the necessities of life in traditional ways.

busheling Among loggers, paying by piecework for felling and bucking. Loggers also called it *by the inch* or *mile* or *by the bushel.*

bushway *See* booshway.

bushwhack (1) For modern hikers and climbers, to walk (or sometimes crawl or slither) through rough, overgrown country without benefit of trail. It is not anyone's favourite activity but may be a necessity for getting where you want to go. (2) Its older meaning, to ambush, usually had the implication of a cowardly attack. (3) In obsolete usage, to force a keel-boat upstream against a swift current by pulling on bushes and trees along the bank.

business riding Hooking your spurs into the horse's cinch when it bucks; thus the rider 'makes it his "business" to stay on – if possible.' [Adams]

bust (1) To break a horse. (2) To throw a steer or other critter down hard. The right way to do it is to rope it by the head, flick the rope around its far side and bottom, ride off at an angle and so bring it down. Also called *fair-grounding* or *tripping* him. It is sometimes a rodeo event. (3) In blackjack, to go over 21 points and thus lose.

busted flush A flush (poker hand with five cards of the same suit) that's short one card or more. Since it's a worthless hand, the phrase by extension means anything that's gone wrong.

busthead One of many Westernisms for whiskey. (*See* firewater) It has the implication of low quality.

butcher At branding, the fellow who cuts earmarks and puts identifying marks on the wattle or dewlap.

butt log In logging, the section of tree nearest the stump; the biggest log. Also *butt cut*, the length of log just above the stump of a tree.

butte A hill or rocky formation that stands off by itself; if broader and flat-topped, it would be called a mesa.

buttermilk Cowboy talk for a motherless calf. [Adams] Also a bum calf; a dogie.

button (1) A cowboy's affectionate word for a boy. Other cowboy names for children are *doorknob, hen wrangler, pistol, weaner, whistle, yearling* and *younker*. (2) A braided knot of leather or rawhide on tack.

buy chips In poker, to get ready to come into a game; by extension, to put yourself into other situations, such as disputes, without an invitation. [Adams]

buzz saw A spur with a rough rowel with sharp points.

buzzard (1) A turkey vulture; the high-flying scavenger of the West. The Western writer Edward Abbey wrote often that his ambition was to return in his next incarnation as a buzzard. (2) An unflattering epithet for a man, usually an old man.

Combinations: buzzard bait (a worthless horse, fit only to become carrion, or for that matter, a worthless man), *buzzard-head* (cowboy talk for a useless or mean horse), *buzzard wings* (a wide pair of chaps; same as bat wings).

buzzworm A rattlesnake.

C

caballero A horseman; a gentleman.

caballo is a horse, hoss, cayuse, mount, etc.; this version is likely to appear lightly or mockingly. From Spanish and pronounced kah-BAH-yoh or kah-VAH-yoh.

cabaña a small, crudely made cabin; now extended to mean a beach house. Borrowed from Spanish, it's pronounced kah-BAN-yuh.

cabestro (1) A halter made of horsehair rope. (2) A horsehair rope. (3) According to Cornelius Smith, a person who can be led around by the nose.

cabin fever The depression or irritability people get when penned up in a cabin during a long winter. It has been known to lead to quarrels, fights, divorces, insanity and even murder.

caboodle All of it, the whole lot as in, 'the whole kit and caboodle. According to the linguist J. L. Dillard, it's from Indian Pidgin English.

cabree A pronghorn, an antelope. Variants are *cabri, cabery* and *cabril*. From Canadian French, it's pronounced kuh-BREE.

cabron (1) A cuckold (2) A scurrilous outlaw. From the Spanish, it's pronounced kuh-BROHN. Owen Wister said it is, along with *chiva*, one of the two worse insults a Mexican can offer.

cacique Among south-western Indians, a ruler, a chief. Borrowed from Spanish, it's pronounced kuh-SEEK or kuh-SEEK-ay.

cackle-berries What a logger called eggs. (*See also* hen fruit and states)

cactus In reference to a wide variety of desert plants, the word is not a Westernism. But it can also mean the desert country itself. *Combinations: cactus boomer* (longhorns), *cactus candy* (made by boiling the pulp with sugar), *cactus forest, cactus mouse, cactus rat, cactus woodpecker* (the Gila woodpecker) and *cactus wren*.

cager What a miner called the attendant of a cage (shaft elevator). One of his duties was to put the cars on the cages at landings. [Adams]

cahoots To be partners with a fellow was to be in cahoots with him or to be thrown in with him. A verb form existed that appears to have disappeared – to cahoot with. No one seems to know the origin of the term.

cake A supplementary feed made of cotton-seed and other grains compressed into pellets. These days it comes in 50-pound sacks or loose by the pick-up load. The *cake wagon* is the wagon that carries the cake to the cattle for feeding. Called *cotton-seed cake, cotton cake* or, historically, *caddy*.

calabasa (1) A calabash, a gourd, says Cornelius Smith. Borrowed from both French and Spanish. (2) A squash dish made from the calabasa. Stewart Edward White has some starving Anglos offered calabasa by a poor Mexican girl in *Arizona Nights*.

calaboose A jail. Borrowed from the Spanish *calabozo* (which has the same meaning).

calf Calves have a rich bunch of names that allow the cattleman to say just what sort of calves they are: *acorn calf* (a runt), *buford* (a small, weak calf that's easily thrown), *bum calf* or *buttermilk* (an orphan), *churndash calf* (one that runs around a lot), *deacon* (a runt), *dogie* (a motherless, half-starved calf), *free martin* (a sterile heifer born twin to a male), *full ear* (one that isn't earmarked), *green calf* (one with some size but no meat), *hairy Dick* (an unbranded calf), *leppy* (an orphan), *long yearling* (a calf nearer two years old than one), *orejano* (a calf without an earmark), *poddy* (a big bellied, half-starved orphan), *pussy calf* (fat and heavy), *sancho* (a dogie), *short yearling* (a calf that is a year old), *sleeper* (a calf a rustler has earmarked but not branded), *slick* (an unbranded calf), *spike weaner* (a calf being weaned via a circle of spikes on its nose), *weaner* (a calf of weaning age), *wind-belly* (an orphan with a distended belly) and *yearling*.

calf crop The season's newborn calves.

calf fries *See* mountain oysters.

calf puller A winching device used to help pull a calf out of a cow having difficulty giving birth. They range from simple chains to pullers with hydraulic jacks.

calf roping One of the five standard events of any Professional Rodeo Cowboys Association rodeo. The contestant rides after a calf, ropes it, runs to it and ties three of its legs together as fast as he can. A *calf horse* is the horse trained to back away from the roped calf and keep a taut line. This event sprang from a genuine ranching skill, roping and tying calves for branding.

calf table A small chute used to hold calves tight for branding. The calf is pushed into the chute, then the chute is turned into a horizontal position – thus the table. It's sometimes called a *calf cradle*. The *calf roundup* is the spring roundup, for the purpose of branding calves. *Calf fries* are mountain oysters, deep-fried calf testicles.

calf-legs A description of a horse with short legs. To *calf around* is cowboy talk for loafing. A cow that looks like she's about to calve is called *calfy*. Among Texas ranchers, to say 'calf rope' was once an equivalent to saying 'Uncle' – to surrendering, quitting, admitting defeat. The *calf wagon* was a wagon for carrying calves born on trail drives. Before the calf wagon (also called a *blatting cart* or *blatting wagon*) came into use, such calves were sold, given away or killed.

caliche In the south-west, a crust of calcium carbonate on top of the soil, or near the surface; it also refers to hard clay soil. Borrowed from Spanish (where it means 'flakes of lime'), it's pronounced kuh-LEE-chuh or kuh-LEE-chee.

calico (1) A spotted horse or cow. (2) A woman (though not originally a Westernism, it is now common on the range). (3) To go courting (also not originally a Westernism). *Calico fever* is cowboy lovesickness.

calico queen One of the many terms for prostitute. The Westerner is fecund with names of things that interest him, so he has or had many expressions for the woman for sale: *ceiling expert*, *chippy*, *crib girl*, *Cyprian*, *dance-hall girl*, *frail denisen*, *frail sister*, *girl of the line*, *girl of the night*, *horizontal worker*, *hurdy-gurdy girl*, *inmate of a house of ill fame*, *margarita*, *nymph du pave*, *nymph du prairie*, *painted cat*, *soiled dove*, *sport*, *sporting woman* and *woman of evil name and fame*. In the 1870s and '80s, newspaper editors needed to talk about such matters, and propriety led to creativity.

caliente Hot, as in water or salsa. Borrowed from Spanish, it is pronounced kah-lee-EN-tay and is common in the south-west, as in *agua caliente* (hot water).

California To throw a critter down by tripping it.

California, the state, figures in many Western combinations: *California banknote* (a cowhide, when thought of as currency, used in the days of the Californios), *California buckskin* (baling wire [Adams]), *California fever* (laziness, indolence; qualities sometimes attributed to Californios by Anglos), *California greenback* (what California used for currency before statehood), *California moccasins* (sacks wrapped around a cowboy's feet to ward off the cold), *California fan palm* (*Washingtonia filamentosa*, by far the state's most common palm, often found near water in the deserts), *California pants* (striped or checked wool pants popular among cowboys), *California poppy* (*Eschscholtzia* sp.), *California prayer book* (deck of cards), *California twist* (a rope throw) and *California sorrel* (a red-gold palomino).

In tack, combinations include *California saddle* (a single-rigged, centre-fire saddle, that is, a saddle with just one cinch placed in the middle, with a high horn and covered stirrups; also called a *California rig*), *California tree* (the saddle tree for a California saddle), *California skirts* (skirts – the thick, pliable leather of a saddle that sits directly on a horse's back – that are round, as Californians historically liked them [Adams]) and *California drag rowel* (a spur of the Californio type, with big rowels that have sharp points).

California Trail A route emigrants used to cross overland to California, especially the Forty-niners. Though it had variations, the route most often used left the oregon trail at Soda Springs, Idaho, followed the Humboldt River to its sink, struck westward, ascended the Sierra along the Truckee River and crossed the range via Emigrant Gap. Most notorious of all groups to use the trail was the Donner party.

Californio In the 19th century, a person born in California and of Hispanic ancestry.

call (1) A poker player's demand that the other players still in the hand show their cards; in the verb form, to make that demand. The alternatives to calling would be to raise (to increase the stakes) or to fold (to give up). This sense of call can be extended to metaphorical use, to call a person about anything, to challenge him to put up or shut up. (2) A bugle call, the effective measurement of time on an army post. At sunrise comes reveille, at about nine o'clock guard-mount and then, says Martha Summerhayes in *Vanished Arizona*, 'various drill calls, and *recalls*, and sick-call and the beautiful stable-call for the cavalry . . . the thrilling fire-call and the startling assembly, or *call-to-arms*, when every soldier jumps for his rifle and every officer buckles on his sword, and a woman's heart stands still.'

call a brand To give words to the symbols of a brand, which can look arcane to the uninitiated.

call the play In a gun-fight, a suggestion that your adversary start the action by going for his gun. This is probably more common on the sound stage than in dusty streets.

calzoneras Pants popular among Hispanics of the south-west in the 19th century, split on the outside from the knee down and decorated fancily along the split. Borrowed from Spanish and pronounced kahl-sohn-AY-ruhs.

camas (1) A plant (*Camissa esculenta*) with an edible bulb, an important food of Indians of the north-west United States and Canada. The early Oregon settlers ate it so much they got nicknamed camas-eaters. It is sometimes confused with a poisonous plant (*Zigadenus elegans*) – hence the term *death camas*. (2) An area with camas. From Chinook and also spelled *commas* and *kamas*.

Combinations: camas field or *meadow* (flat, plain, prairie ground), *camas pocket gopher* and *camas pouched rat*.

camino real In the south-west, a main highway or principal route. Borrowed from Spanish (where it means 'royal road') it is sometimes used as a proper noun, as in the name of the old road from Mexico City to Sante Fe. Pronounced kah-MEE-noh ray-AHL.

camisa A shirt; a chemise; especially a shirt worn by Indian and Hispanic women of the 19th century in the south-west. Borrowed from Spanish, it is pronounced kuh-MEE-suh.

camote A sweet potato eaten by the Papago Indians. A south-western borrowing from Spanish, pronounced kah-MOH-tuh.

camp inspector A fellow who looks like a logger but is really a drifter, wandering from camp to camp to try the hospitality.

camp robber The Rocky Mountain jay, a plump grey and black fellow that loves to feed on scraps from camps. Watts says 'lone prospectors were said to be super-stitious about them and would offer them no harm.'

camp rustler In sheep-herding, a man who looked after the gear and moved the sheep camp while the herder was with the sheep; also called a *campero*, *camp mover*, *camp jerker* or *camp tender*.

camp wagon The wagon that carried supplies for a trail drive before the chuck wagon came into being, says Peter Watts.

campesino A peasant; as an adjective, rural. Borrowed from Spanish, it's pronounced kahm-puh-SEE-noh.

campo santo A cemetery. Borrowed from Spanish (where it means sacred ground) and pronounced KAHM-poh SAHN-toh.

campoody A hut of the Paiute Indians; a village of these huts; by extension, sometimes an Anglo's cabin.

candy side Among loggers, a well-equipped crew, not a haywire outfit. A *candy wagon* is a crew bus or truck.

canelo A cinnamon-coloured horse; a red roan. (*See* buckskin for horse colours)

canned cow What a cowboy calls canned milk.

canner A useless horse whose final address is Oscar Mayer; an animal fit only to be sent to the canning factory. Other terms for poor (objectionable or defective) horses are *buzzard bait, buzzard head* (a mean horse), *chicken horse* (a canner), *churn-head* (a dumb, stubborn horse), *crock-head* (a dumb horse), *croppy* (an outlaw), *crow-bait, jug-head* or *knot-head* (a dumb horse), *killer* or *man killer, nag, notch in his tail* (a horse that has killed a man), *oily bronc* (a mean horse), *outlaw* (a mean, uncontrollable horse), *plug, salado* (a wind-broke horse), *salty bronc* (a mean horse), *skate, snide, snake-eyed* (a mean horse), *wassup* (an outlaw), *whistler* (a wind-broke horse) and *widow-maker* (an outlaw).

can't keep a secret Said of a horse that's wind-broke.

can't-be-rode horse An outlaw; a horse that's hard to ride. A pungent old Western saying is 'Ain't no horse that can't be rode, ain't no man that can't be throwed.'

can't-hook cattle A cowboy expression for cows without horns. [Adams]

cant dog A peavey, a long wooden lever used by loggers to drive logs.

cant hook A tool similar to a cant dog but smaller and without a spike on the end.

canteen The post exchange on a military base. Into the 1880s this place was known as the sutler's store. Renamed the Post Co-operative store in February 1889, it was popularly known as the canteen. Later that name changed to the PX.

cantina (1) A leather box packed by a mule. (2) In the Pony Express, the pockets of the mochila that actually held the mail. (3) In Texas, a tavern.

cantle The back of the saddle seat, which is raised. Its back is called a *cantle drop*. To *cantle-board* is to ride loosely, so you bump the cantle, or to scratch the horse with your spurs all the way back to the cantle.

canyon A gorge; a steep-sided valley. From the Spanish *cañon*, it was originally a south-western term. To canyon means for a stream to go into a canyon; variant expressions are *canyon up* and *canyon out*.

canyon Country The country of southern Utah and northern Arizona, with adjacent portions of Colorado and New Mexico. All slick-rock canyons, much of it shaped by the mighty gorge of the Colorado River, it is the home of the mule deer, antelope, bighorn sheep, mountain lion, lizard, rattlesnake, and even a few people. It is the strangest, least pretty, most beautiful, most God-forsaken, most God-blessed land the Great Mystery has yet created.

cap rock (1) An erosion-resistant rock that tops mesas and buttes. (2) In mining, barren rock presumed to lie on top of ore.

cap-and-ball gun A weapon fired by percussion cap. These muzzle-loading guns were common in the West in the heyday of the open ranges, even after metal cartridges had been introduced. It cost money to buy a new gun, or to convert your old one, and the cartridges were expensive.

A *cap pouch* was the leather pouch carried on the belts of soldiers of the era of the Indian wars for storing percussion caps. To *snap a cap* was to fire a gun, particularly with a percussion cap. These caps were also known as *cap-locks*.

cap-and-ball layout Cowboy talk for a ranch that's not up to date and hard-working. [Adams]

capitan Chief, head man, captain. A borrowing from Spanish and pronounced with the stress on the last syllable. Also spelled *capitaine*, a borrowing from French.

The boss of a sheep shearing crew is called a capitan. He generally owns the equipment and contracts with the owner. The shearers work for the capitan rather than the rancher.

caponera A herd of geldings. Borrowed from the Spanish *capón* (a castrated animal), it's pronounced cah-poh-NAY-ruh.

caporal Foreman (or assistant foreman), manager or boss on a sheep or cattle ranch, usually with the implication that he's a Mexican. Most common in Texas, borrowed from Spanish and is pronounced ka-puh-RAL, with an *a* like *corral*.

capote The blanket coat of the fur men, made from a blanket that is hooded and closed with a belt or sometimes double-breasted and buttoned. It's pronounced kuh-POHT, but early spellings like *cappo* and *capot* suggest that the *t* may once have been silent.

capper A shill for a gambler. Thus the Abilene, Kansas *Chronicle* in 1871 celebrated the leaving of many 'prostitutes, "pimps", gamblers, and "cappers".'

caracara A south-western, vulture-like hawk. Borrowed from Spanish and pronounced kar-uh-KAR-uh.

carajo! (1) A Mexican's exclamation, ejaculation or eruption of vehement feeling, like the French-Canadian's *sacré bleu*. In Spanish, it means, in Mitford Mathew's euphemism, 'the virile member'. (2) The sort of fellow who would use such language, for instance, a mule skinner or ox driver. (3) The stem of the century plant, visually reminiscent of a 'virile member'. (4) As a verb, to cry out, 'Carajo!' Writes Lewis Garrard in *Wah-To-Yah and the Taos Trail*, he '*sacre*-ed in French, *carajo*-ed in Spanish-Mexican.' Pronounced kah-RAH-hoh and also spelled *caraho*.

caravanserai A fancy name for a hotel, fashionable in the West during the 19th century. Also spelled *caravansary*.

carbine A light, short rifle for use by horsemen. During the Indian-fighting days in the West, US cavalrymen used Sharps, Spencer and Springfield carbines. Not originally a Westernism.

carcage A quiver for arrows. Borrowed from the Spanish word *carcaj* (with the same meaning) and pronounced kar-KAH-huh.

carcajou A French-Canadian word for the wolverine. Pronounced kar-kuh-JOO. In the lore of Canadian fur men and many western Indians, the wolverine was legendary for its astonishing ferocity.

carcel A jail. Borrowed from Spanish and pronounced KAR-suhl.

card mechanic A cheat at cards; a person who manipulates cards to his own advantage. A team of such fellows was called a *card mob*. [Adams] Other such terms include: *bottom dealer*, *bottom-card mechanic*, *broad pitcher* (or *tosser*), *cardsharp*, *gut puller*, *hearse driver*, *heel*, *leg*, *mechanic*, *monte dealer* (or *tosser* or *thrower*), *monte sharp*, *saddle-blanket gambler*, *second dealer*, *square decker*, *tin-horn*.

careless with his branding iron Said of a known or suspected rustler, who finds ways to get his brand on calves that aren't his.

cargador (1) A fellow (usually a Mexican, sometimes an Indian) who packs loads on his back; used by traders in the old days and by the army. Borrowed from Spanish and pronounced kar-guh-DOHR. (2) The freighter who seconds the pack master of a mule train. *Carga*, which was also used in the old south-west, means 'load'. [Adams]

carne (1) In the south-west, meat. Borrowed from Spanish and pronounced KAR-nee or (more properly) KAR-nay. *Carne seca* is literally dried meat; beef jerky. (2) Short for chili con carne.

carnotite Uranium-bearing ore or rock. (*See* yellow-cake) This was the stuff of the money-coloured dreams that caused the uranium boom in canyon country in the 1950s. In more elemental times, the Indians used it to make war paint.

carpieta A Mexican saddle blanket. Borrowed from Spanish and pronounced car-PEE-tuh.

carrera del gallo A vaquero game. Roosters were buried up to their necks in the ground. Riders galloped down on them, leaned out of the saddle and tried to jerk the bird out of the ground by the neck. Usually the birds got decapitated. Anglos called the game chicken pull. The Old South had a similar game, gander-pulling, played with geese tied to a pole or tree. From the Spanish (where it literally means 'run of the roosters' and pronounced kuh-RAY-ruh de GY-oh).

carreta A two-wheeled Mexican ox-cart. It had wheels made of one solid piece or (more often, according to Cornelius Smith) of two pieces joined at the hub and without rims. The hubs were infamous for their squeaking, which could be heard for miles. Borrowed from Spanish and pronounced kuh-RAY-tuh. A *carretela* was a carriage, and a *carretero* was a cart driver.

carrying the balloon Among loggers, hunting for work. The logger called his bedroll a *balloon*.

cart wheel (1) A big coin, usually a silver dollar. (2) A long-pointed rowel.

cartridge box A leather pouch worn on the waist belt or shoulder belt of soldiers of the western Indian-fighting era for carrying the cartridges for their rifles (usually Springfields) or carbines. A *cartridge belt* is a belt worn around the waist that has multiple loops for holding metallic cartridges.

carving scallops on his gun Making notches on the handle of one's pistol to indicate a slaying; more popular in movies than the real world.

casa House, used frequently by Anglos in the south-west. Borrowed from the Spanish and pronounced KAH-suh. *Casa grande*, literally 'big house', in the old days usually was the main ranch-house, where the owner lived. Today 'Mi casa es su casa' ('My house is your house') is the epitome of south-western hospitality.

cascara sagrada The buckthorn (*Rhamnus purishiana*) of the Pacific coast. The Indians used the buckthorn bark as a laxative. Borrowed from Spanish (where it means 'sacred bark'), it's pronounced kahs-KAH-ruh sah-GRAH-duh.

case of slow What was wrong with the loser in a gun battle.

cased wolf A name for the coyote, whose pelt, instead of being split, was peeled from the body and dried on a frame, that is, cased.

cash in his six-shooter What an outlaw was said to do when he used his pistol to withdraw money from a bank. [Adams]

cash in your chips Also *cash in your checks* or just plain *cash in* (1) To quit a game of poker or faro, at which time the player trades his chips for money. (2) Figuratively, to die. Thus *American Humorist* in 1888 asks, 'Do you and each of you solemnly sw'ar that you will . . . cling to each other through life till death calls upon you to cash in your earthly checks?'

Western language has a cornucopia of expressions for dying. You may *ride an old paint with your face to the west*, *hang up your saddle* (or *sack your saddle*), *cross the great divide*, *go to the last roundup* and *go south*. If you die, your friends will *send your saddle home in a feedsack*. Cheyennes *go to the Milky Way*, and Blackfeet *go to the sand-hills*. Anglos also *pass in their chips* (or *checks*), *go belly up*, *take the big jump*, *bite the dust* (or *ground*), *buck out*, *finish their circles*, *land in a shallow grave*, *get a halo gratis*, *get sawdust in their beards*, *go over the jump*, *go over the range*, *go up*, *go up in smoke*, *have no-breakfast-forever*, *ride the long trail*, *shake hands with St Peter*, *turn their toes to the daisies* and so on. Mountain men *come*, *lose their hair*, *go under* or *go beaver*.

castor (1) Castoreum, a substance from a beaver's perineal glands that is the main ingredient of the bait for a beaver trap. It was dried, then mixed with alcohol, cinnamon, nutmeg and cloves, all to attract the wily beaver. The mountain man also called this medicine and carried it in a stoppered horn slung on his shoulder. (2) A plew, or beaver skin. (3) A synonym for beaver.

casueying A Texas term for the bucking (or in Texas, pitching) of a horse. Pronounced kuh-soo-ying. [Adams]

cat wagon A cowboy's name for a wagon carrying prostitutes. (*See* calico queen)

catalogue woman A cowboy's name for a wife a fellow got from a bureau that served such needs; a mail-order bride. [Adams]

catamaran Among loggers, a raft used to raise sunken logs with windlass and grapple.

catch as catch can However you can. The expression comes from a calf-roping contest in which the roper is allowed to throw the rope any old way as long as he snags a calf and holds it.

catch colt A colt that sprang from an unplanned mounting; sometimes used to describe an illegitimate child.

catch dog A dog trained to corner and hold wild cattle. Such animals were used in the early days in south-central Texas when wild cattle were common. J. Frank Dobie says some of these animals were even able to pick mavericks out of branded cattle and to throw them to the ground and keep them down until a man came. The spotted Catahoula leopard dog from Louisiana is one of the more important breeds. Sometimes spelled (and pronounced) *ketch dog*.

Any rope with a noose for catching critters is a *catch rope*. In fancy you might hope to *catch a filly* (human variety). When drunk (alkalied) you may try to *catch the devil*. Often spelled (and pronounced) *ketch rope*.

catgut What a cowboy sometimes calls a rawhide rope.

catlinite *See* pipe-stone.

cattalo A cross of the buffalo and the beef cow; also spelled catalo. (*See* beefalo)

cattle association An organisation for the promotion of the rights of cattlemen. (*See* Stock Growers' Association)

cattle baron A man who had a cattle empire, especially in the days of the open range; also known as *cattle king*, *cattle czar* or *livestock king*.

Various terms for men and women in the cattle business have arisen: *cattle broker*, cattle buyer, cattle detective, *cattle feeder* (owner of a feed lot), cattle inspector, cattleman, *cattle puncher* (cowpuncher), *cattle queen* (a woman cattle baron), *cattle ring* and *cattle thief* (a rustler).

cattle buyer A man (or, recently and rarely, a woman) who makes his living by being a sharp judge of cow flesh, usually for a feed lot owner. He makes his living buying and selling feeder cattle. A packer buyer does the same for a meat packing plant.

cattle country Any big area of land good for grazing cattle, particularly the grasslands of the Great Plains.

cattle detective Usually an employee of a cattlemen's association who is charged with catching rustlers; sometimes a polite term for a hired gun representing big ranching interests against settlers; also called a *livestock detective*. Tom Horn was a cattle detective for the Wyoming Cattlemen's Association, and much feared, when he got arrested in 1901 for killing Willie Nickell. Modern detectives for organisations such as the Texas and south-western Cattle Raisers Association are highly respected professionals.

cattle grubs Heel fly larvae that live under the hides of cattle and horses.

cattle guard Rails in the road (or paint that looks like rails) that keep cattle and horses in a field; sometimes called a *cattle gap*.

According to the Pinedale, Wyoming *Roundup*, a local resident 'told a story at the library [one] night about some friends of hers who thought that cattle guards are actually people. "Well, you have sheep-herders, don't you?" they asked. "You must have cattle guards." '

cattle inspector *See* brand inspector.

cattle issue *See* beef issue.

cattle poor Said of a man who owns lots of cattle when cows are cheap and cash is scarce; the equivalent of land poor.

An old Wyoming joke goes, 'What would you do if you had a million dollars? – Buy a cow outfit and run it until I went broke.' The joke is out of date. A million would buy only a teensy-weensy cow outfit these days.

cattle ring A conspiracy of powerful men and interests to tie up cattle range, available water and so on. Thus the Santa Fe *Western New Mexican* wrote in 1885, 'Revd Sligh's interpreter asserts the existence of a cattle ring in New Mexico whose motto is, "the man with the water hole must go." ' An infamous example was the Santa Fe ring, whose purpose was to promote a land grab by the financial powers behind the Maxwell Land Grant Company – it succeeded.

cattle trail The route of a trail drive. Cow trails were everywhere in the West, but the ones popularly thought of first are the trails north from Texas, where the great drives of the 1860s, '70s and '80s were made. Best-known were the Goodnight-Loving Trail, the Chisholm Trail, the Shawnee (or Sedalia) Trail and the Western Cattle or Dodge City Trail. The Southern Trail led from Texas to California. The Spanish Trail was actually two – one leading from Texas to New Orleans (the Old Beef Trail) and the other to California. The Chisholm and the Western led to the cow towns of Kansas, where the railroad provided cheap transportation to the East for beef, and these gave birth to some of the best Western lore and myth. The Western Cattle Trail later extended north to the grasslands of Wyoming and Montana.

The trail drive is a legendary cowboy activity, celebrated in movies like *Red River* and novels like Larry McMurtry's *Lonesome Dove*. It was a considerable enterprise, headed by a trail boss, with riders for the point, swing, flank and drag positions (perhaps a dozen drivers for a herd of, say, 3,000), strings of horses and wranglers to take care of them and a cook with at least one chuck wagon. The major dangers were stampedes, the crossing of rivers and sometimes people who wanted to steal the trail herd. In some years of the big drives from Texas to the Kansas rail-heads during the 1870s, on trails like the Chisholm and the Western, more than half a million cows went north.

cattleman Not a cowboy but the owner of cattle ranch. It matters not whether it's a rawhide outfit (dinky ranch) or a spread the size of the XIT (a Texas Panhandle ranch once three million acres in size), whether it's a cowcalf operation or a breeding ranch, if he owns it and runs it, he's a cattleman. These days, in the case of the large outfits, the fellows who own them and the fellows who run them are often different people. In that case, a real cattleman would probably see the manager as the cattleman and use the word for the owner only out of politeness. And in the case of certain outlanders, especially those who live on the other side of big oceans, he probably couldn't manage the politeness.

A frequent saying is that a cowboy has a big buckle over his belly; a cattleman has a big belly over his buckle.

catwalk A narrow walkway above a shipping chute, where a cowboy stands to push cattle on to rail cars; a narrow walk on a steamboat.

caution In mining, a posted notice indicating ownership and probably warning that any claim-jumper will be shot on sight.

cavvy The cowboy's version of *cavallard* (the Anglo version of the Spanish *caballada*, 'herd of horses'), used mostly on the northern plains and in the north-west. It refers to the saddle horses kept by a ranch other than the unbroke horses and the ones saddled at the moment. Also known as a remuda. In the open-range days, ranches kept large horse herds, and each cowboy was assigned a string out of them. A *cavvy man* was the wrangler, the *remudero*.

These two words have as many variants as a new heiress has cousins – *cavyard*, *caviard*, *cavalyard*, *cavvie yard*, *cavayado*, *caviya* and *cavvy yard*; in buckaroo country, where Oregon, Idaho, Nevada and California come together, it's usually *cavviada*.

Cavvy-broke is broke enough to be in the cavvy, which meant barely broke.

cayac A young buffalo bull forced away from the herd by the older bulls and not allowed near the cows.

cayuse (1) Horse, especially a wild horse of the north-west; a horse of the Cayuse Indians of Oregon. The term once meant any wild horse and then any horse, but it retained some overtone of condescension: A cayuse was wild, native, nondescript, runty, ill-mannered, and unreliable, not a creature of breeding like the horses brought out from what was then known as the United States (often called by Indians and early Westerners 'American horses'). (2) A cold wind from the east, opposite of a chinook. Spelling variants include *kiuse* and even *skyuse*.

Cayuse An Indian tribe of the Walla Walla country in Oregon, closely associated with the Walla Walla, Nez Percé and Umatilla. When emigration became heavy on the Oregon Trail, the Cayuse traded horses with the emigrants, giving rise to the name cayuse horse. Diseases brought by the Anglos decimated the tribe, and in 1847 they rose against the Whitman mission near Fort Walla Walla. Getting what they thought was revenge for poisonings by Dr Marcus Whitman, they killed him, his wife Narcissa and others there. They were punished militarily in return by the white settlers. Subsequently, most of the Cayuse integrated into neighbouring tribes and now live on the Umatilla Reservation.

cedar brake Rough country covered with cedar, those stunted, shaggy, twisted trees all over the West that are really junipers. Though it's also spelled cedar break, most authorities seem to prefer brake, as in cane-brake. A cow that ranges out in the brakes is called a *cedar braker*.

celerity wagon A mud wagon, or light stagecoach, used by the Butterfield Stagecoach Line, developed particularly for the rough and mountainous sections of roads. The concord coach was heavier. Also called a *celerity coach* or simply a *celerity*.

celestial heathen The Chinese, because an old name for China was the Celestial Empire; not originally a Westernism but common in the West. A Chinese was also likely to be called *John Chinaman*.

cell theory A new theory of range management, also known as 'holistic resource management'. Under this system, cattle are moved from one small division (cell) of a pasture to another every few days, encouraging the cover grasses and discouraging the undesirable weeds. Developed by Allan Savory and sometimes called *intensive grazing*.

centre-fire rig The saddle with a single cinch hung from the centre of the tree (wooden framework). (*See* single-rig)

Centre-fire describes a cartridge with the ignition powder in the centre instead of in the rim.

In forestry, centre-firing is a method of controlling a fire by setting fires in the middle, creating a strong in-draft, and thus drawing the perimeter fire toward the middle.

century plant A species of agave (*Agave desserti*) common in the south-west; some varieties are popularly said to bloom only once or only once in each century.

cerveza Beer. Borrowed from Spanish and pronounced sehr-VAY-suh. It's now commonplace in English, especially in the south-west.

chain To drag a chain between two tractors over sagebrush range-land. This practice is supposed to improve the range for cattle but usually results in erosion, an increase of weed species and destruction of Indian artifacts.

Among loggers, a measurement of length, 66 feet.

chain hobble A length of chain, just a couple of feet, attached to one leg of a horse at one end and left to dangle at the other end. As a method of hobbling, it's hurtful and dangerous. [Adams]

chalchuite A kind of New Mexican turquoise; the green chalchuite is particularly prized. An adaptation from Spanish, it is pronounced CHAL-choo-it.

chalupa In the south-west, a deep-fried tortilla or other bread (usually made of masa) spread with any combination of beans, meat and salsa. Borrowed from Spanish pronounced chuh-LOO-puh.

chamise A shrub (*Adenostoma fasciulatum*) of the semi-arid areas of the south-west; also spelled *chamiso*, *chamizal* and sometimes known as *greasewood*. A borrowing from Spanish, it is pronounced chuh-MEE-soh. The chamise lily is California's redwood lily or chaparral lily (*Lillium rubescens*). The Indians used the bulbs for food.

chaparral (1) At first, chaparral meant scrub oak, then a thicket of scrub oak, then a thicket of mesquite, vines and any sort of shrubbery all tangled together. Now it means brush so thick as to be nearly impenetrable. Longhorns used to love to hide in it and make the brush

poppers work like hell to get them out.
(2) By extension, it means a patch of
chaparral or a plain covered with
chaparral. From the Spanish *chapparo*
(oak), it's pronounced sha-puh-RAL, the *a*
as in *corral*.

*Combinations: chaparral berry, chaparral
bird* or *cock* (the road runner), *chaparral
deer*, *chaparral fox* (a wily person), *chaparral
lily* (chamise lily), *chaparral pea*, *chaparral
berry* (the buffalo berry) and *chaparral tea*.

chaparro The Spanish word for the
evergreen oak of Texas and elsewhere in
the south-west. Pronounced shah-PAHR-
roh or chuh-PAHR-roh.

chapo A stocky, short-coupled horse;
sometimes called a *chupo*. [Adams]

chaps Leggings – leather overalls – the
cowboy wears to protect his legs when
he's thrown from a horse or when the
horse falls on him, pushes him against a
fence or another animal, does its
damnedest to bite him or bolts him
through brush or cactus or chaparral; also
used for warmth or for protection against
rain or snow. One of the cowboy's
essential pieces of equipment.

It's pronounced shaps, with a soft sh-h-
h – Easterners are comically mistaken
when they give it a hard *ch*, as in Chapstick.
It's short for *chaparreras*, which in turn
derives from chaparral, which is one evil
chaps ward off.

It is said that chaps come from the
vaqueros; a brief glance at early paintings
will inform anyone that they also descend
from the mountain man, who copied them
from the Plains Indians. No one rode the
mountains, plains or deserts long without
discovering the need for some hide
covering on the legs.

They can be made from the skin of any
handy beast, the most common being
goat, calf, bull, sheep and deer. They
come in lots of styles. Bat wings (also
called buzzard wings), perhaps the most
popular sort, sport wide wings on the side
and a snap or buckle on in back. Bull
hides are made of the thick hide of a bull.
Shotguns (also called *stovepipe chaps*) wrap
all the way around, like pants, and are
straight and narrow as the barrels of a

side-by-side – these are the usual chaps of
the northern plains. Angoras, the fancy-
looking ones with the curly white hair left
on, are from angora goats; they're also
called woollies. (All chaps with the hair
left on are called *hair pants*)

A *chap guard* juts out from a spur shank
to keep the chaps from hanging up on the
rowel. *Chap strings* hold the chaps together
across the hips. A *chapping* is the beating
of a cowboy with a pair of chaps.

chaqueta A sturdy jacket, made of
leather or cloth, that protects a rider
against the chaparral; most common in
the border country of west Texas. A
south-western adaptation from Spanish
and pronounced chah-KAY-tuh.

charco In the south-west, a pool of
standing water. Borrowed from Spanish
(where it means 'puddle') and pronounced
CHAR-koh.

Charlie Taylor A stand-in for butter
made of syrup or sorghum mixed with fat
and, according to historian Francis Fugate,
'not . . . a compliment to Charlie Taylor,
whoever he may have been.'

charro Among contemporary Hispanics,
the term often refers to the Mexican
riders who compete on the Mexican rodeo
circuit, a separate circuit, quite active in
southern California.

chaw tobacco An expression for
chewing tobacco first recorded on the
Kentucky frontier. Frontier brands were
Star Navy, Navy, Day's Work and Brown
Mule. Contemporary brands include
Beechnut, Lancaster, Levi Garrett,
Swisher Sweet and R. J. Gold in pouches
and Red Man, Skoal, Copenhagen,
Hawkins and Kodiac in the little round
tins that wear circles in the pockets of
shirts and jeans.

cheatgrass Downy brome (*Bromus* sp.),
a grass that was introduced from central
Asia in the late 1800s. It has taken over
much of the sagebrush grasslands,
replacing the native wheat-grasses. Its
sharp seeds lodge in animals' throats. It is
often called simply *cheat*, or occasionally
rescue grass, since it is one of the first
grasses to green up in the spring.

cheechako A tenderfoot. From chinook; also spelled *checaco* and *cheechalko* and pronounced chee-CHAH-koh.

cheek To pull a horse's head around toward you by the cheek strap. A rider does this when mounting to keep the horse from bolting forward or at least to force its motion into the rider to make swinging up easy. Often done when getting on an unfamiliar horse.

Cherokee One of the five civilised tribes, the Cherokee, Creek, Chocktaw, Chickasaw and Seminole. In the 17th century, early in the period of white settlement, the Cherokee lived in the southern Appalachians. Soon reached by white traders, the tribe acquired guns, ploughs, livestock, strong drink, smallpox and other accoutrements of civilisation. They fought on the British side against the French, then warred with the Carolinas, 1759-61, in what was known as the Cherokee War and then fought on the British side during the Revolution.

In the 1820s they became literate (via an 86-syllable phonetic alphabet created by the Cherokee scholar Sequoyah), started a weekly newspaper, adopted a constitution modelled on that of the United States and made large advances in agriculture. The state of Georgia then became determined to have them removed to the West. After various legal battles with the state and federal governments, most of the Cherokee were forcibly removed to what became Indian Territory; the march along what was called the Trail of Tears killed many people. Now the larger part of Cherokees live in Oklahoma, with Talequah as their capital; those who stayed live in the east live in North Carolina.

The *Cherokee outlet* is a bar of land some 57 miles wide in northern Oklahoma, given to the Cherokees in 1828 to provide access from their lands (in what would become Indian Territory) to good buffalo-hunting grounds. It is sometimes confused with the *Cherokee Strip*, a narrow strip (about three miles wide) of the Cherokee outlet in what is now Kansas.

chevrac *See* shabrack.

chew it finer A way of asking the speaker to say something again in simpler terms. [Adams]

chew the dog To visit, talk, pass the time of day.

Cheyenne A nomadic, buffalo-hunting Algonquian tribe of the northern and central plains, well known for its terrible conflicts with US armed forces. The name Cheyenne was the Dakota name for the tribe; it meant 'red talkers' or 'people of a different speech'. They called themselves Tsistsistas, which meant 'the People'. The tribe had a crop-raising culture around the western Great Lakes until the 18th century but moved on to the Great Plains because of pressure from the Dakotas. There they became allied with the Arapahos and Lakotas and roamed in the Powder River country and the area of the North Platte River, following the buffalo and living in a sacred way, guided by their great medicine objects, the four sacred arrows and the buffalo hat.

In the 1830s a tragedy befell them when they lost the sacred arrows to their enemies the Pawnee, and several decades later a horn of the hat was broken, another calamity. They regard these two events as a source of the troubles that followed.

From the mid-1830s, some Cheyennes elected to hunt near Bent's Fort on the Arkansas River in eastern Colorado, so the tribe was divided into northern and southern circles. The Cheyennes were uneasy about white encroachment along the Oregon Trail and toward the Denver gold fields, but the conflagration started only when John Chivington led the Colorado Volunteers in a massacre of Black Kettle's village at Sand Creek in 1864, killing hundreds of Indians. Several years of war followed in the territory between the Arkansas and Yellowstone rivers, with the Cheyennes, Lakotas and Arapahos chasing whites out of the Powder River country. Then George Armstrong Custer perpetrated another massacre along the Washita River in 1868, killing hundreds more, and the southern Cheyennes settled on a reservation in Indian Territory (Oklahoma).

The northern Cheyennes kept fighting and, with the Lakotas and Arapahos, they inflicted a resounding defeat on Custer at Little Big Horn in 1876. After Dull Knife Battle in 1876, they were brought in, starving, and sent to the southern reservation. In 1878 several hundred of them made a defiant break for home, the Powder River country. They eluded and outfought troops for months to get there and eventually were given the reservation they demanded.

Today the southern Cheyennes live at their agency in Oklahoma, and the northern Cheyennes live on the reservation along the Tongue River in Montana.

Cheyenne leg A Wyoming style of chaps, cut away on the under side of the thigh and loose below the knee.

Cheyenne roll A saddle made by Frank Meanea of Cheyenne about 1870, featuring a projecting rim on the cantle. It was popular during the 1870s and 1880s.

chia A south-western desert plant (*Salvia columbine*) of the mint family whose seeds the Indians used to make a drink. Borrowed from Spanish, it's pronounced CHEE-uh.

Chicano A Mexican-American. From the Nahuatl word *Mexica* which the Aztecs used to refer to themselves; hispanicised to *Mexicano*, the later form of the word Xicano or Chicano first appeared in 1848. It has activist political connotations, and many people prefer to refer to themselves as Latinos, Hispanics, Mexicans or Mexican-Americans.

chicharron A crackling, a delicacy to some Hispanics of the south-west. Borrowed from Spanish, it's pronounced chee-chuh-ROHN.

Chickasaw (1) One of the five civilised tribes, with the Cherokee, Seminoles, Creek and Choctaw. The Chickasaws originally lived in Mississippi and Tennessee, an area reached early by traders. The Chickasaws then adopted various elements of the white lifestyle, thus being 'civilised', but in the 1820s they were forced to move West to what became Indian Territory. They allied themselves with the Confederacy in the Civil War. Today they live in eastern Oklahoma. (2) Short for the Chickasaw horse, a calico beast noted for toughness and longevity.

chicken (1) Short for prairie chicken. (2) A boy or young man, especially a soldier or sailor, who is a particular friend of an older man. Homosexual feelings are surely implied, though not all users may have been aware of them. Mathews shows this meaning as Western and dated 1888.

Chicken fixings are high-quality food, not common stuff, and by extension anything fancy or top drawer, whether in food or dress; but a *chicken horse* is a runty horse killed for dog and/or chicken feed, and a *chicken saddle* is a particularly small saddle. [Adams]

Chicken thief, in Texas at least, is a trader's boat, so called because its coming encouraged the light-fingered to steal chickens to sell to the traders.

chico (1) A Hispanic term for greasewood. (2) Also a fond name (although sometimes used derisively) for a little boy; a familiar name for a friend used occasionally in the south-west. Borrowed from Spanish and pronounced CHEE-koh. *Chica* is the feminine version, sometimes an equivalent of 'dear' or 'sweetheart'.

chief's coat In the fur trade, a military-style coat for giving or trading to Indian leaders.

chigaderos Half chaps. (*See* armitas)

Chihuahua (1) A large state in northern Mexico. (2) A tiny Mexican breed of dog. (3) A large rowel on a spur, a type usually worn in the old days by Hispanics. (4) A freighting wagon (called a Chihuahua cart) with two solid wheels and smaller than a carreta. (5) Any town near a frontier military establishment with saloons and other dens of iniquity where soldiers could spend their pay. (6) An exclamation of surprise. Borrowed from Spanish and pronounced chee-WAH-wah.

The Chihuahuan desert lies mostly in Mexico, although there are small portions in southern New Mexico and south-western Texas.

chikaman A north-western expression (from the Nootka) for cash money.

chilchipin A south-western pepper, used to make Tabasco sauce. Borrowed from Spanish, it's pronounced chil-chuh-PEEN.

child The common way a mountain man referred to himself and his companion: 'This child' (or this *beaver*, *hoss*, *coon*, *nigger*), he would say, meaning himself, 'is goin'' to make 'em come,' meaning kill beaver. Or the mountain man might say, 'That child is some,' a way of expressing respect. Thus did the mountain man refer to himself or a companion figuratively. The tireless traveller Lt George Frederick Ruxton wrote in 1849 in excellent trapper talk, 'This child has felt like going West for many a month, being half froze for buffalo meat and mountain doin's.'

chile (1) What greenhorns call a hot pepper – chile the vegetable and not chili the stew. It comes in many varieties, from mild to hot, and is served in forms *verde* or *Colorado*, that is, green or red (vine-ripened). Though for a couple of centuries it was primarily associated with the food of poor Hispanics, in the last decade or so Americans generally have come to recognise the splendid New Mexican cuisine based on the chile. (2) A sauce made from chiles, generally poured over diced meat. It is piquant and delectable. Chile powder is the dried form.

Borrowed by Americans from Spanish and pronounced CHI-lee or CHEE-lay, the word comes ultimately from the Nahuatl word *quachille*.

chileno A ring bit.

chili (1) Strictly, a stew made with meat and red chiles or chile powder. Chili gourmets generally insist that it contain neither beans nor any form of tomatoes; they hold big contests to determine the most delectable. (2) A stew made with chile powder, beans and tomato; it may be *con carne* (with meat) or not. Some variety of this is what you'll get, in either restaurant or grocery store, if you ask for chili outside the south-west. (3) Short for *chili-eater*, a pejorative name for a Mexican.

chili chaser A south-western name for a border patrolman. [Adams]

chimichanga A deep-fried burrito; now a popular menu item in Mexican restaurants.

chimney rock A tall, slender formation of rock, often sandstone, from a couple of dozen to several hundred feet high; it sticks up from the ground like a chimney from a house or like the barrel of a six-shooter pointed to the sky. Hundreds of thousands of emigrants noted 'the' chimney rock on the Oregon Trail, a spire on the north bank of the Platte River a day's travel (by prairie schooner) east of Scottsbluff in Nebraska. It was a sign that the traveller was leaving the prairies and passing into a new kind of country, the real West.

China pump A sort of pump used for extracting tailings and improvised by Western gold miners.

Chinaman's chance A poor chance. During the California gold rush, the Chinese were permitted to work only tailings or played-out claims for gold, so they had a poor chance of striking pay dirt.

Chinatown The section of town, or outside of town, where the Chinese lived in cities of the early West; the only place they were permitted to live. *Chinese laundry* and *Chinese wheel* (a variety of fireworks) also appear to be Westernisms.

chindi A Navajo term for spirit, ghost, evil spirit. The Navajos fear chindis and avoid the dead, belongings of the deceased, burial sites and all else associated with the dead.

chink (1) A chunk of wood used for filling the space between logs in a log cabin. (2) To chink is to fill those spaces with anything – sticks, mud, whatever. (3) A rude name for a Chinese person. (*See also* celestial heathen)

chinkaderos Short chaps; usually shortened to chinks. (*See* armitas)

chinook (1) A blessed phenomenon on the northern plains – a warm, dry wind that sometimes moves in from the West, usually suddenly, raising the air temperature sharply. It will often melt the snow away even in the middle of winter. (2) To chinook is for such a wind to blow. (3) A variety of salmon.

Chinook (1) A group of Indian tribes living along the Columbia River and using salmon for food. (2) A trade language used by Indians of the north-west Coast, based on the Chinook language but simplified.

chip Short for buffalo chip or cow chip, the common fuel of the Great Plains. A *chip sack* was a bag for carrying the chips, and a *chipper* was a rancher so poor he burned cow chips at home.

chip in In poker, to ante up, to put a chip into the pot; by extension, to put money into anything, to join in any enterprise.

chippewa *See* Ojibway.

chiquito Little one; used for children or any little creature. From the Spanish and pronounced chuh-KEE-toh.

Chiricahua (1) A branch of the Apache tribe that lived in western New Mexico. (2) A wild turkey. From the Apache language, it's pronounced chi-ri-KAH-wah.

chirpas According to Cornelius Smith, 'holes worn into rocks by Indians and used as a place] to grind corn.'

chiseler On the northern plains, a prairie dog or Uinta ground squirrel.

chispa A small nugget of gold. Borrowed from Spanish, (where it means spark or flake) it's pronounced CHEES-puh.

chiv A California term for a Southerner; short for chivalry.

chivarras Another word for chaps or leggings, usually made from goatskin. Borrowed from Spanish (where it means 'young goat') and pronounced CHEE-var-uhs.

Choctaw One of the five civilised tribes. The Choctaw lived in western Alabama and Mississippi and adopted many elements of white lifestyle from an early date, especially agriculture and a legal code. In the early 1830s, they were forcibly

removed to what became Indian Territory. Today they remain in the state of Oklahoma. A *Choctaw's mile* is a short distance. *Choc* is what loggers called a beer made by the Choctaw. [Adams]

choke the horn and claw the leather What a rider does when he's desperately trying to stay on a horse that's moving straight, sideways, 'round and 'round or up and down too damn fast. It's supposed to be a mark against pride any time, and in a rodeo, it will disqualify the rider. From my observation, most riders these days have more common sense than pride (or we're just not used to horses that act up any more) and grab leather often enough. One of my favourite woman ranchers, however, denies loudly her husband's allegations that her saddle horn has tooth marks.

  Also called to *choke or grab the apple, reach for the apple, pull* or *hunt leather, grab the nubbin, leather* or *post, shake hands with Grandma, sound the horn, squeeze the biscuit* and *squeeze lizzie.*

chokecherry A shrub (*Prunus melanocarpa*) found in much of the West that bears wild cherries. The Navajo make a purple dye from the bark and roots, and Anglos make jelly from the berries.

chokedamp In mining, gas that suffocates miners. [Adams]

choker In logging, a short steel cable with a loop at one end and a hook at the other, used for looping around logs. A *choker setter* is' the fellow that puts the choker on, and a *choker hole* is a hole that is dug under the log to place the choker. Also a logger's word for cheese.

cholla A south-western cactus (*Optunia* sp.) that grows in weird, twisty shapes and has soft clingy spines that are meaner than your mother-in-law's tongue and never let you forget them. Some of the varieties are *deer bush, jumping cholla, teddy bear, pencil* and *staghorn.* Borrowed from Spanish (where it means 'head'), it's pronounced CHOY-yuh.

chop suey A surprising but genuine Americanism and probably a Westernism. Chop suey (meaning 'odds and ends' or 'hash') is reportedly unknown in China, and Herbert Asbury in *The Gangs of New York* says it was 'invented by an American dishwasher in a San Francisco restaurant.' It is generally a mixture of vegetables, bean sprouts and meat. A *chop suey joint*, naturally, is a Chinese restaurant.

chore boy A fellow in a lumber camp or on a ranch who helps the cook or does other chores, like cleaning the bunkhouse.

chouse To handle cattle roughly and stir them up. David Dary in *Cowboy Culture* quotes old-time Texas rancher Hiram Craig on the subject: 'The roundup boss would let no one ride through the herd and "chouse" or unnecessarily disturb them; these fellows found guilty of such misconduct were called "loco'ed". Oft times it was known for the roundup boss to put him out of the herd and cut his cattle for him.' Also spelled *chowse*.

chow Food; chuck. The word evidently was borrowed from the Chinese in California.

Combinations: chow line, chow time.

Christmas A logger's term for payday. [Adams]

chubasco A severe southerly rain and wind storm that originates in the northern Gulf of California. Borrowed from Spanish and pronounced chu-BAHS-koh.

chuck What the cowboy calls food, grub, chow; also meal-time. It comes from *chuck wagon*. To *chuck it in* is to feed like a trencherman.

Since the old-time Westerner's imagination was fired by the important things in his life, like whiskey and sex, he had lots of words for food. For his over-sized breakfast he might have *hen fruit* (eggs), *hen-fruit stir* with *long sweetenin'* (pancakes with molasses), *chuck wagon chicken* (fried bacon), *sow bosom* (salt pork) and *bear sign* (doughnuts). For dinner (which he ate about noon) he might consume *calf fries* (the testicles of newly castrated calves), *Mexican strawberries* (beans) and *hucky-dummy* (biscuits with raisins). And for supper – *son-of-a-bitch stew* (a stew of sweetbreads, tripe, brains, kidneys and other parts of a freshly-killed calf), *pooch* (tomatoes, bread and sugar) and *boggy top* (pie without crust on the top). All of it, naturally, washed down with *Arbuckle's* (coffee).

Chuck was also known as *chuckaway*.

Combinations: chuck tender (a camp cook or his helper), *chuck eater* (a greenhorn learning to cowboy, but only effective at doing away with the chuck), *chuck away* (the cookie's cry for chow time), *chuck house* (where the food was prepared on a ranch or in a mining camp) and *chuck-line riders* or *grub liners* (unemployed cowboys who would go from ranch to ranch, spend a night or two and get a few free meals).

chuck wagon The mobile cookhouse of the range, used for both trail drives and roundups. Charles Goodnight, first cattleman in the Texas Panhandle, the inventor of good-nighting and pioneer of the Goodnight-Loving Trail, is said to have been the fellow to come up with the chuck wagon. Earlier cowboys carried supplies on pack animals or, on long drives, in carts or wagons. In 1866, according to J. Everts Haley's biography of the rancher, Goodnight had a wagon rebuilt and considerably strengthened and then on the back of the wagon devised the first chuck box, a combination work table and storage box for food staples and utensils for cooking and eating, plus medicines. The box had a lid on a hinge that let out to make a table for cookie to work on. Later chuck wagons carried a little grain for their draft animals, a water barrel, a tool box, a jockey box, big pots and skillets, a shovel, an axe and some dish-pans. By custom the cowboys stored their bedding in the wagon bed.

Underneath the chuck wagon was slung a cooney, which was used to carry cow chips for cookie to use for fuel or wood if he was lucky enough to come on any.

Naturally the chuck wagon became the social centre of the roundup and trail drive, where the fellows ate, got their coffee, smoked their cigarettes, told their lies, sang their songs and had their fun.

Also called a *growler*, a *camp wagon* or simply *the wagon*. In this century the chuck wagon can even be a truck – thus the expression *chuck truck*.

chuck-a-luck A gambling game played preferably with three dice. Not originally a Westernism. The game is of British origin and became immensely popular in the West. Also called *chucker-luck* and *bird cage*.

chuckle-headed Evidently addle-brained (muddle-headed, confused). In *Arizona Nights*, one of Stewart Edward White's narrators says he walked into a trap "chuckle-headed as a prairie dog."

chuckwalla A big south-western lizard, used by the Indians for food. Also called a *chuckwaller*.

chug To spur a horse forward.

chunked In the south-west, impudent.

chupadero The Spanish name for the cattle tick, sometimes used in the south-west. Pronounced choo-puh-DAY-roh.

churn-dash calf A calf whose mother won't stand still and let it nurse.

churn-head A cowboy name for a dumb, stubborn horse [Adams]; crockhead.

churn-twister A cowboy name for a farmer. (*See* granger)

churro A coarse-woolled sheep introduced from Mexico to the Navajo and the Indians of the pueblos. Borrowed from Spanish, it's pronounced CHOO-roh.

chute (1) A passage between fences or rails, sometimes narrowing, through which horses or cattle may be held for chute branding or be driven into a corral, on to calf tables, into rodeo arenas, on to trucks or railroad cars and so on. (2) In logging, a slide for moving timber. (3) In mining, a shaft for moving ore.

In rodeo, a *chute-crazy horse* is one that acts up in the chute. [Adams] This horse is also called a *chute fighter*. His opposite is a horse that gets *chute freeze*, that balks in a chute and won't move at all.

cibola (1) The Spanish word for buffalo, sometimes used in the south-west. (2) The region of the Seven Cities of Cibola, which proved to be the Zuni pueblos and not the source of fabulous riches that the Spanish explorers were looking for. Pronounced SEE-boh-luh.

cibolero A Mexican or New Mexican buffalo hunter. This fellow hunted the bison for its meat, not its hide, and did not participate in the mass slaughter of the herds starting about 1870. Still, in the 1840s ciboleros numbered about 1,600 and, along with the big hunts of the metis at the same time, helped to start the buffalo on its decline.

cienaga A south-western term for a marshy area, often because of a spring or seep on a slope. Borrowed from Spanish, it's pronounced see-EN-uh-guh.

cigarito In the south-west, a small cigar or cigarette. From the Spanish, it's pronounced see-guh-REE-toh.

cimarron (1) The bighorn sheep. (2) A loner, whether critter or man. From the spanish *cimarrón* (which means 'wild and unruly'), it is pronounced see-muh-ROHN or sih-muh-RON.

cinch (1) A girth for a saddle, often made of braided horsehair, canvas, leather or cordage; consisting of the belly band and the latigo, the cinch holds the saddle on the horse's back. In Texas, it is usually called a *girth;* sometimes called a *cincha*. (2) To secure the saddle on the horse's back, to *cinch up*. (3) A card game also known as Double Pedro or High Five; a popular north-western partnership game. It is variation of the game known as all fours or high, low jack.

A *cinch hook* is a hook on a rowel (or a spur) that can be hooked into the cinch to prevent you from being thrown, and a *cinch ring* is the ring at the end of the cinch.

cinch binder A bucking horse that rears up on its hind legs and falls over backward. *See* horse for other terms describing horses.

Cinco de Mayo The celebration of a Mexican victory over the French in 1862, celebrated not only throughout Mexico but in the south-western United States as well.

circle buck Descriptive of a horse's bucking when he does it in a nice circle, usually 30 or 40 feet across. [Adams]

circle riding At a roundup, some cowboys would ride in a circle around a big area, pushing the cattle from the perimeter toward the centre. A hand at this duty is called a *circle rider*, and the horse he rides is a *circle horse*.

citizen band A group of Indians who wanted to give up their tribal identity to become US citizens. Also called a *citizen party*.

claim (1) An assertion of ownership or right of use on public land, especially a mineral claim, patented or unpatented. (2) A piece of land covered by such a claim. In the old days, claims had to be proved up (*see* prove); those not worked for more than a week were considered abandoned. (3) To make such a claim.

clawhammer coat A fancy coat with tails, usually an object of derision in the West.

claybank (1) A yellow-dun colour. (2) A yellow-dun or brownish-grey horse. (*See* buckskin for horse colours)

clean (1) The opposite of bloody. In much of Plains Indians mythology, the red road is straight and clean, the black road (or blue road) crooked and bloody. (2) In mining, to get the mineral that has value out of the gravel and rock in the sluices or the mill is to *clean up*. A *clean-up* is also called a *clearing*.

In logging, *clean-boled* describes timber that is free of branches. [Adams]

Among cowboys, to *clean up* a herd is to cut (separate) all the cows of your brand out of a herd. To *clean his plough* is to give a fellow a beating. A *clean setter* is a rider that doesn't show daylight (let light show between buttocks and saddle). To *clean out a town* is as an 1882 Wichita newspaper describes it: 'The average cowboy is a bad man to handle. Armed to the teeth, well mounted, and full of their favourite beverage, the cowboys will dash through the principal streets of a town yelling like Comanches. This they call "cleaning out a town".'

clear-cut The felling of all the saleable trees in a given area in one cutting; the opposite – selecting only specific trees to fell – is called select cutting. Clear-cutting is a controversial practice in many western forests today.

clear-footed Said of a horse that is sure-footed, one that doesn't stumble, put his feet in prairie-dog holes and the like. (*See* horse for other terms describing horses)

cliff dwelling A house, or usually a group of houses, of the Anasazi, such as those at Mesa Verde in Colorado or Canyon de Chelly in Arizona. They were built all over the south-west in places where steep dirt slope met vertical stone or in cavern-like openings in the stone itself. Such dwellings were easy to defend because they could be approached only up the steep slopes from below. Food was grown on top of the mesa above or on the floor of the canyon, and water was gotten from springs or creeks. Many such dwellings are extravagantly beautiful. Also called, rarely, a *cliff city*.

climax forest The term of a forest ranger or a logger for a plant community that is the culmination of vegetation for a given spot. This community usually endures a relatively long time, and when it burns, decays or is cut, the cycle starts over. A ranger offers this description of how a climax forest of Douglas fir such as might be found in central Idaho comes into being: After a major burn come grasses, herbs and shrubs. Then sunlight-tolerant trees, such as the Ponderosa and other pines. Then, under the canopy of shade provided by the pines, shade-tolerant trees like the Douglas fir. When Doug fir gets big, it wants sun, and so tops out. It will then maintain that state for hundreds of years.

clip a brand To cut away a critter's hair, grown long during the winter, to get a good look at the brand. [Adams]

clip his horns To render someone harmless.

close to the belly In poker, cautious play, without bluffs. Also known as *close to the vest*.

clothesline One of the cowboy's names for the rope used for throwing. [Adams] (*See* rope)

cloud hunter A cowboy's word for a horse that likes to rear. [Adams] (*See* horse for other terms describing horses)

coarse gold Among miners, gold in big grains as opposed to dust.

coaster (1) A longhorn of the Texas coast. (*See* Texas longhorn) (2) A little wagon in a freight outfit, attached to the end; a little wagon for hauling food and gear; a sheep-herder's wagon. Also called a *cooster* or *kooster*.

cobbler A sweet drink made of fruit juice, ice and wine or whiskey. Also called more specifically a *sherry cobbler* or a *whiskey cobbler*.

cocinero A cook; usually a camp cook. When female, a *cocinera*. Also a *coosie, coosy, cosi, cusi, cusie* and so on. Borrowed from Spanish and pronounced koh-see-NAY-roh. (*See* cookie)

cock-a-doodle-doo A cowboy's word for a ranch foreman. [Adams]

cocktail On a trail drive, the last watch of the night; the first was called bobtail. Also called *cocktail guard* or *cocktail relief*. Modern cowboys call a *cocktail crew* one that has lots of help, the opposite of a bobtail crew.

code talker The name for the Navajos in the Marine Corps who made radio transmissions in Navajo to avoid being understood by the Japanese during World War II.

Coeur d'Alene The Skitswish Indians, a Salish tribe that historically lived near Coeur d'Alene Lake in northern Idaho, where their present reservation is. Neither nomadic or warlike, they were generally friendly to whites and receptive to traders. They are also known as *Pointed Hearts* or *Hearts of Awls*. Coeur d'Alene translates to 'awl-heart' from the French and is said by one authority to have been one chief's expression for the size of a trader's heart. Probably he meant the point of the awl.

coffee cooler (1) In the 19th century an Indian who would agree to anything for a cup of coffee; a hang-around-the-fort Indian. (2) Anyone who lazes around instead of facing up to his duty. Perhaps

this sense of the term comes, as Cornelius Smith suggests, from the observation that such fellows give their coffee plenty of time to cool before they down it and head out.

cohab A term of a gentile (non-Mormon) for a Mormon engaged in plural marriage. Same as a polyg, and just as derogatory. A canyon near Utah's Capitol Reef National Monument is named Cohab Canyon. Cohabs continue to be shunned socially and sometimes even persecuted legally today, when most Americans pride themselves on religious tolerance. Owen Allred, leader of the Apostolic United Brethren, a Mormon group that practises plural marriage, comments ironically, 'They say it's all right for a man to live in a commune with a dozen women, unmarried, and make love to all them. But it's not all right for a man to marry more than one woman and support them, and the children.'

cojinillo A south-western expression for a pocket of a saddle or small case attached to a saddle for carrying small objects; a favourite place for a bottle. Borrowed from Spanish (it's the diminutive form of *cojín*, 'saddle pad'), it's pronounced koh-hee-NEE-yo.

colache Boiled pumpkin or squash, a dish of the Californio period. Borrowed from Spanish, it's pronounced koh-LAH-chay.

cold brand A brand that burns just the hair, not the hide, and so will grow over. Also called a *hair brand*. Rustlers apply such brands out of dishonesty, others out of ineptitude. The expression is used both as a noun and a verb.

cold-meat wagon Cowboy term for a hearse.

colear In the south-west, to tail an animal, a method of throwing cows off their feet, literally by their tails, used by the vaqueros from horseback. Borrowed from Spanish, it is pronounced south-western English koh-lee-AR. Also called *el coleo* and *coleada*.

colemanite The most common source of American borax, named after

W. T. Coleman, who led one of the San Francisco vigilance committees.

colonel In the West (as in the South and New England), this is a title of courtesy and respect, without military implications. Or maybe it's really a matter of height and girth: Briton James Robertson wrote in *A Few Months in America*, published in 1855, 'in the South and West nearly all tall men are called generals, stout men judges, and men of middling proportions captains or colonels!'

colonist (1) In the West generally, simply a word for a settler. A *colonist car* was a railroad car intended to transport such settlers. (*See* emigrant) (2) In Texas, an American settler who came to the country before Texas was admitted to the Union. (3) In Kansas, an abolitionist who came to the state in 1854–8 to participate in the struggle over slavery.

colour Prospector talk for a sign of the presence of gold, either in the pan or in dirt. It's colour that makes the miner keep working.

Colorado mockingbird A burro.

Colt A pistol made by Samuel Colt. The Colt revolving six-shooter became the West's most popular pistol. Its common name was *dragoon*. Patented in 1836, it was adopted by the Texas Rangers, carried west by many forty-niners and bought by the government in large quantities during the Civil War, especially the Navy .36 and the Army .44. It was a cap-and-ball weapon until 1873, when Colt introduced a metallic cartridge. In this form, known variously as the *Peacemaker*, the *Single Action Army* and the *Frontier*, it became *the* handgun of the West, dominating competitors like Remington and Smith & Wesson as Winchester dominated the market for rifles, Levi's the market for jeans and Stetson the market for hats. (*See* six-shooter)

Comanche A Shoshonean tribe of Indians known principally for their qualities as horsemen and warriors.

Separating from the Shoshones of historic times on the northern plains, the Comanches lived in the 17th century in what would become eastern Colorado. Then they acquired the horse, followed the buffalo nomadically and began to develop their reputation as superb horsemen and the scourge of all other Indians and whites on the southern plains.

The Comanches drove the Apaches from most of Texas and warred relentlessly on the Spanish colonists there. *Comancheria* is the area of the central and southern Great Plains claimed by the Comanches, 400 miles wide and 600 miles from north to south. In order to trade, though, they excepted the New Mexicans from their raids and welcomed American traders to the country. For more than a century, while Texas was Spanish, then Mexican, then independent, and finally part of the United States, its history was written in white and Comanche blood. Settlers there and in northern Mexico learned to dread the *Comanche moon*, the full moon of August or September when the Comanches most liked to raid, and the *Comanche yell*, their blood-curdling war cry.

In the 1830s and 1840s smallpox and cholera devastated the tribe, and in 1853 it made a treaty with the United States. In the 1870s, due to the destruction of the huge buffalo herds of the southern plains, the Comanches were brought on to reservations in Indian Territory; these reservations in turn were ended early in this century when the US government allocated 160 acres to each Comanche.

From 1879, led by Quanah Parker, the Comanches adopted the peyote religion from the Yaquis of Mexico, and it has evolved into the Native American Church.

Because Comanches were so fierce, their name became synonymous among whites with bestiality and degradation. On the other hand, it was a high compliment to say that a fellow rode like a Comanche. A *comanchero* is a trader (usually Mexican) with the Comanches.

Also spelled *Camanche* and *Cumanche*.

comb To get a horse to buck by spurring it. To *comb someone's hair* is to whack him on the head with a pistol barrel. [Adams]

come To die. To *make 'em come* means to kill 'em. An expression of the mountain man applied equally to beaver, Indians and other critters – 'This child made 'em come.' (*See* cash in your chips)

come off the rimrock Katie Lee says in *Ten Thousand Goddam Cattle* that it means to back away from sensitive conversational territory and get easy and friendly again. (*See* rimrock)

come undone To go crazy; to act wild. A half-broke horse may see something scary and come undone, leaving the careless rider on the ground and undone.

come-along A halter that hurts a horse when it doesn't follow and relaxes when it does. (2) A portable winch used by modern cowboys to get their pick-ups unstuck and to get other heavy moving jobs done.

committee saddle A saddle acceptable for rodeo competition; an association saddle.

common doings Plain, ordinary, no-pretense food; the opposite of chicken fixings (*see* chicken). In *The Far West* in 1838, Edmund Flagg wrote, ' "Well, stranger, what'll ye take, wheat bread and chicken fixens, or corn-bread and common doins?" '

compadre Originally what a Hispanic father and godfather called each other; literally, co-father. In the US south-west, it has come to mean partner, buddy, compañero. *Comadre* is the female equivalent. From the Spanish, it's pronounced kohm-PAH-dray.

compañero Partner, companion, compadre. Borrowed from Spanish, it's pronounced kohm-pah-NYAY-roh. The feminine form, *compañera*, appears not to occur in US.

Comstock Lode The rich silver and gold claim at Virginia City, Nevada, named after one of its partners (who was not the discoverer), Henry T. P. Comstock. Thus compounds like *Comstocker*, *Comstock boom*, *Comstock slang*, *Comstock king*. Not to be confused with *comstockery* or *comstockism*, the sort of rabid censorship of supposed indecencies advocated by Anthony Comstock (1844–1915).

concho Also *concha*. Disk-shaped silver ornaments that typically decorate belts, chaps, leggings, spurs, bridles and so on. Anglos, Hispanics and Indians (especially Navajos) all wear them. They can also be made of brass or leather. Saddle conchos, called *string conchos*, come in sets of eight. From the Spanish word for 'shell' and pronounced KAHN-choh.

Concord The word for stagecoach just as Colt was the word for pistol and Stetson the word for hat. It was named for Concord, New Hampshire, where from 1827 forward Abbott, Downing and Company made what were regarded as the best coaches. The coaches used thorough-braces for shock absorption for the first time. Known for their elegance, these coaches were built mostly by hand of steel, brass and white ash, weighed more than a ton and sold for over $1,250. Up to nine passengers sat in three rows of seats inside, and more sat on the top. Boots in front and back held luggage. Driver and shotgun guard sat on top. The coach might be drawn by four, six or eight horses. Sometimes called a *Pitchin' Betsy* because of its rocking motion.

Combinations: Concord buggy, Concord hack, Concord spring wagon and *Concord stage*.

conducta A south-western term for a caravan, convoy or escorted party, often with the implication of something valuable being transported. Borrowed from Spanish and pronounced kuhn-DOOK-tuh.

Conestoga A big freighting wagon of the early West made in Conestoga Valley, Pennsylvania. It was a behemoth – more than two dozen feet long, nearly a dozen high and weighing the better part of two tons – and was borne on big wheels (even bigger in back than in front) with iron tyres. Ideally, Conestoga wagons were pulled by three pairs of Conestoga horses, big draft beasts, or by oxen or by 10 mules. The Conestoga was sturdy and built to move a lot of freight and so was popular for heavy hauls on the Great Plains. Those big horses typically lugged it 12 to 18 miles a day. It had a boat-shaped body, deeper in the middle than at either end, so the contents would not spill out the end when it was going uphill or downhill, and a hooped canvas covering. Also known as a *Pennsylvania wagon* or *ark*, it was nicknamed prairie schooner because of its ship-like profile, a *Pitt schooner* because it was often manufactured in Pittsburgh and a *scoop wagon* because of its scoop-shaped bed. It came to be the wagon of choice on the Santa Fe Trail. Studebaker made wagons of the same type but slightly lighter for the plains crossing. Later plains freighters came to prefer wagons less bulky.

confidence man   A swindler.

congé   A licence or licensee for fur-trading under the French. Borrowed from French and pronounced kaw-JAY.

consumptive use   In governmentese, use of resources (wood, water or minerals) that reduces the supply. Non-consumptive use, such as boating, hiking, camping and hydro-electric power, does not remove the resource.

contest ride   A rodeo term for a legal ride on a bucking horse.

contest saddle   A saddle approved for rodeo competition; a committee saddle or association saddle.

contract buster   A bronc buster who makes a deal to break a certain number of horses for a certain price.

contrary   Among the Plains Indians, either a man who carried a thunder or contrary bow (and the responsibilities that went with it) or a man or woman who belonged to a contrary society. George Bird Grinnell has described these two sorts of contraries among the Cheyenne Indians: 'The members of the society were people who feared thunder, and from time to time they held a ceremony and made an offering to thunder. During this ceremony they did things backwards, like backing into and out of the lodge, sitting not on their bottoms but their backs, doing the opposite of what was told them, etc. The people enjoyed this silliness, but the ceremony had a serious purpose, to protect the people against thunder.'

The individual contrary also did things backwards and also feared thunder, which had warned him in a dream. But his status as a contrary dominated his life every day. He carried a thunder or contrary bow, a lance that might be touched by no one but him and was used to strike coup. He sat and lay not on hides and beds but on the bare ground. He lived off to one side of the camp and seldom spoke to people. He was a war leader and under some circumstances was forbidden to retreat. Altogether, being a contrary was both an honour and a heavy responsibility. A man bought the lance and the status from another contrary and could not give up his station until another person who had dreamed the thunder dream bought it from him.

converter   A cowboy name for a preacher. [Adams] (*See* black robe for others)

cook mutton   To set fire to a sheep range, an occasional tactic of cattlemen during range wars. [Adams]

cookie   The range cook. In *Western Words*, Ramon Adams wrote this hymn to him: 'If ever there was an uncrowned king, it was the old-time range cook. He had to be good to qualify as a wagon cook because he had to be both versatile and resourceful. He was the most important individual in camp, and even the boss paid him homage. He was conscious of his autocratic powers, and his crankiness is still traditional.

'The present-day range cook follows this tradition. He can absolutely be depended upon to have three hot meals a day, rain or shine, cold or hot, that are good to eat and in sufficient quantity that, no matter how much company drops in, there will be plenty to go round. Through necessity his equipment is limited; yet this does not seem to hinder his speed. On one day he may be trying to cook in the rain with a scant supply of wet wood; on another he may have difficulty keeping the wind from scattering his fire, blowing the heat away from his pots or sand into his food, and yet he works without discouragement. The outfit must be fed on time.

'Though the boys kid him and cuss his crankiness, they certainly will not concede this privilege to an outsider. If he is clean, they will tolerate the poor quality of his bread.

'Almost any cook likes to talk, and while the boys eat, he squats against the rear wheel of the wagon and entertains himself and them by discussing everything from the weather and women to politics and poker. If he is a good cook, the boys do not interrupt him.'

Some authorities say that hands chose the outfits they hired on with by the quality of the cook. If you were already signed on and the cook was bad, says Jo Mora in *Trail Dust and Saddle Leather*, you still had an option. You could kill the son of a bitch. Then you had to cook yourself. Your compañeros might agree to treat your rash act as justifiable homicide, but they would never let you step around the responsibility that came with it. The boys have to eat, don't they?

Though range cooks ran the gamut for type, a few generalisations apply: Most of them were older men, some retired from the hard business of cowboying. Most were Anglos, but you'd also find many a 'Portugee', Negro and 'furriner' among them. And of course they were equally likely to be crackerjack cooks (though never culinary *artistes*) or lead-biscuit klutzes.

The cow-camp cook's name was also spelled *cookee*, but since the historic cook probably neither read nor wrote, he couldn't tell you which was right and didn't give a damn. Some of the nicknames Adams lists for cookie are *bean master, belly cheater, belly robber, biscuit roller, biscuit shooter, cocinero, cook's louse* (a cook's helper), *coosie, dinero, dough-belly* (and *-boxer, puncher, roller* or *wrangler*), *greasy belly, grub spoiler, grubworm, gut robber, hash slinger, kitchen mechanic, old woman* or *old lady, pothooks, pot rustler, rustler, Sallie, sheffi, sop and 'taters* and *sourdough*. The logger uses some of these sobriquets and has a roster of others (*see* hasher). For a lively history of this range archetype, *see* Adam's *Come and Get It: The Story of the Cowboy Cook*.

cooler The jail; the calaboose.

coon Along with beaver, child, hoss, and nigger, one of the mountain man's quiver-full of terms for himself and his compañeros. It's likely an extension of the habit frontiersmen of Kentucky and surrounding regions had of calling themselves and each other 'coon' and 'old coon'.

cooncan A gambling card game of the south-west. It derived from a Spanish game called *con quien?* and was named *rummy* by the English.

cooney In the days of the open range, a cowhide slung under a chuck wagon, primarily as storage for buffalo chips, cow chips and firewood but also for anything else that needed carrying. The front legs of the hide were fastened to the front axle, the back ones to the rear axle and the sides nailed to the wagon sides. For some reason this device has an abundance of names – *bitch, caboose, cradle* and *'possum belly* plus the alternate spellings *coonie* and *cuna*. From the Spanish *cuna* (cradle).

coon-footed A descriptive term for a horse whose rear feet aren't straight. (*See* horse for other descriptive expressions for horses)

coosie The cow-camp cook, short for *cocinero*. (*See* cookie)

cootie cage A logger's word for a bunk.

copa de oro *See* dormidera.

Copenhagen A brand of chewing tobacco that has virtually become a Western synonym for chaw.

cordelle (1) The rope men used to pull boats upstream. (2) The verb form means to heave a boat upstream with a cordelle. A *cordeller* was a fellow who did the heaving. In the early days of travel on the Missouri, before the coming of the steamboat, keelboats were poled and cordelled upriver, and that could be brutal, back-breaking work, grunting along the shore or through the shallows.

cordgrass A native grass (*Spartina pectinata*) of the tallgrass praire that grows six to ten feet tall and prefers wet areas. Its leaves are lined with minute barbs, earning it the nickname *rip-gut*, but it makes good cattle forage and hay.

cordillera A mountain range. From the Spanish, it's pronounced kohr-dee-YAY-ruh.

corduroy (1) Logs (often split logs) laid across soft or wet spots in a road to make them passable for wagons. (2) A road that's been corduroyed. It's also known as a *hickety-crickety* or *hunker-chunker*. Roads in Yellowstone National Park were being corduroyed as late as the turn of the century.

corn freight The freight of a mule train as opposed to a bull train. Oxen (which paradoxically pulled a bull train) lived off the country by eating grass but moved slower. Skinners probably argued about mules versus oxen as modern folk argue about foreign cars and domestic makes, with some feeling.

corona A word for the pad put beneath a saddle or an aparejo; often fancy and usually saddle-shaped. Adapted from the Spanish *corona* (crown) and pronounced koh-ROH-nuh.

corral A pen for livestock (the term is borrowed from Spanish). Most Western corrals are built of posts and planks or poles to withstand the pounding sometimes given by horses and cattle, but they may be constructed of anything, from ropes (and thus the term *rope corral*) to wagons to adobe. They're usually round, so that the critters can't crowd themselves into corners and get hurt. (2) In verb form, it means to get critters penned up. (3) Freighters also corralled wagons at night: They circled their wagons and fastened them tightly to each other with the yokes and chains, as a defense against marauders. (4) By extension, it means to get hold of or control of anything. 'She was slow in corrallin' our idea on account of her bein' no English scholar,' wrote Owen Wister.

corral boss The fellow responsible for a dude ranch's mounts and for matching horse to dude. [Adams] Also known as corral pup.

corral dust A cowboy name for a windy, a yarn, a tall tale. [Adams]

corregidor In the south-west, a magistrate of a Hispanic town. Borrowed from Spanish, it is pronounced koh-REDG-uh-dohr.

corrida A south-western term for a ranch's crew, the men who hunt down the cattle. The *corrida comida* is a large noonday meal of several courses. Borrowed from Spanish, it's pronounced kohr-REE-duh.

corrido A south-western term for a ballad, as in, 'El Corrido de Gregorio Cortez'. Corridos were often written to narrate local legends, love stories or historical events. They are an important part of the oral tradition of the transborder region.

coteau A high mesa; a divide. Borrowed from French and pronounced kuh-TOH.

cotton-wood (1) The tree (*Populus fremontii*) that, with the willow, is the trademark tree of the arid West. A water hog, it grows along the banks of rivers, creeks and, in modern times, irrigation ditches. On the treeless plains, it thus marks water for the thirsty traveller and no doubt for the cow, antelope and elk as well. The bark of the sweet cotton-wood was an important source of feed for the horses of Indians, mountain men and other early Westerners. It provides shade for many a ranch house that would otherwise bake in the sun, and a barrier against wind. It got its name from the downy stuff it broadcasts every spring. (2) To *have the cotton-wood on someone* (rare) is to have the advantage on him.

A *cotton-wood blossom* is a hanged man, especially one hanged from a tree. (*See* string party)

coulee A ravine, with or without a stream. Mostly a term of the northern plains and mountains, it derives from the French *couler*, (to flow) and is pronounced KOO-lee. Also spelled *coolie*, *cooley*, *couley* and *coulie*. (*See* the similar terms arroyo and gully)

count out What a herd is said to do when the tally promised matches the tally delivered. In *Log of a Cowboy*, Andy Adams says, 'just so the herd don't count out shy on the day of delivery'.

counterbrand (1) A new brand put on the other side of a cow or horse, invalidating the original brand, which may be burned over; a *vent brand;* a *sale brand.* (2) In verb form, to make such a brand. Or, if you fouled up the first brand, you might immediately counterbrand the animal yourself. The idea was to do it legally and have it understood that you weren't a brand artist (rustler). (*See also* cross-brander)

country rock In hard-rock mining, the mass of rock alongside a lode or vein or dike. (Not a variety of popular music)

country wife An Indian woman married, according to the custom of the country, to an Anglo fur man. Many traders and trappers had both city families and country families – sometimes a family in each of several different tribes.

county hotel A jocular name of loggers for the county jail.

coup An honour a Plains Indian might gain by a deed of valour. Indian warfare was a dashing sport on horseback with a high purpose. The main object was, acting alone, to do something that showed bravery. The essence of courage was to touch an enemy, alive or dead, with your hand or something held in your hand, like a coup stick. Touching, you would cry out that you'd vanquished a foe so your comrades would take notice and be able to act as witnesses. Honour was also gained by making the second, third and fourth ouches on an enemy, killing an enemy, scalping an enemy, rescuing a comrade, receiving a wound and stealing an enemy's horse, but these were secondary.

After a battle, the warriors would congregate and claim their coups and act as witnesses for other men. A unwitnessed coup was no coup. Back in camp, each man recited in a ceremonial way what he had done, and others testified to it. *Counting coup* entitled a man to wear an eagle feather in his hair, and the feather's position showed the degree of honour. Throughout his life, on appropriate public occasions, a warrior would count coup (recite his war deeds), which were public knowledge. His status in the tribe depended on the number and quality of his coups. An Indian warrior without coups had no standing, couldn't speak up in council, couldn't even give his child a name – he was disenfranchised.

The acquisition of stature via coups explains much of the Plains Indian's longing to fight other Indians even after he had accepted being confined to a reservation. He needed to become a real man.

As for the Anglo custom of killing at a distance, even from behind cover, with guns, without looking your enemy in the eye, the Plains Indians didn't understand it – what was the point?

The term derives from the French *coup* (blow).

coureur de bois A French-Canadian fur trader who operated independently. Borrowed from Canadian French, it is pronounced roughly koo-RUR de BWAH. The big companies proceeded legally on the basis of their congés, but coureurs de bois ignored the regulations, roamed the wilds in small groups and sought the furs. In many ways, sojourning among the red men, they became as much red as white, learning Indian languages, taking Indian wives and having Indian children, adopting Indian customs and becoming men who stood in the circle of the people. They were the first men to penetrate some of the remote regions of North America. And always they brought back the plews (beaver pelts) – and sold them to whoever they pleased. *See* Peter C. Newman's *Caesars of the Wilderness* for an excellent picture of the Canadian fur trade.

courting flute A simple flute used by young men of the Plains and Woodlands Indians to woo young women. It was usually made of cedar or box elder and appropriately carved. The song a young man played might have been composed for him by a berdache, a man-woman skilled in such matters; some of those songs were reputed to be irresistible; on hearing them, their object would come forth and go anywhere with the young man, entranced by him. Also called a *love flute.*

Cousin Jack Among miners, a Cornishman, many of whom were miners in the West. His wife was a Cousin Jenny. Sometimes Cousin Jack meant a Welshman, and his wife was Cousin Anne. Americans sought expertise in underground mining operations from Cornishmen because they had generations of experience in the tin mines of the old country. Welshmen also had valuable experience in smelting techniques. A *Cousin Jack lantern* was a miner's lamp made from a tin can and a candle. [Adams]

covena A Papago bluebell. The Papago and Pima Indians used its root for food.

cover your dog For the roundup boss to get all the cattle in a particular region gathered up. [Adams]

covered wagon A generic word, perhaps more common now than during covered-wagon days, for the wagons Anglos used to haul emigrants and freight across the plains. (*See* Conestoga)

cow (1) The female bovine, but also any bovine, regardless of sex; and a herd of cattle of both sexes and every size is spoken of as 'the cows'. (2) The female of the buffalo, elk and moose species. (3) According to one authority, a purse or kitty. (4) According to Mathews, a log raft with a log cabin on it.

The word gives a start to even more combinations than the ones below: *cow alfalfa* (a weed that grows in Utah), *cow boss* (the man in charge of the roundup or the cattle part of a big outfit), *cow business*, *cow bunny* (a cattleman's sweetheart), *cow call*, *cow camp* (cowboy camp), *cow chip* (dried dung), *cow crowd* (a bunch of cowboys), *cow critter* (any bovine, even bulls), *cow dog* (a canine trained to handle cattle), *cow country*, *cow driver* (a man who trails cows, particularly on a long trail drive), *cow fever* (the fervent desire to go into the cattle business), *cow hunt* (an early Texas roundup of wild cows), *cow game* (the cattle business), *cow geography* (a map of cow country), *cowgirl*, *cowhide*, cow horse, *cow grease* (butter), *cow juice* (milk), *cow outfit* (cattle ranch), *cow pie* (dung), *cow paper* (a promissory note with cows as the security), *cow rigging* (a

cowboy's work clothes), *cow salve* (butter), *cow skinner* (a winter storm so severe ranchers are left with only cow skins), *cow thief*, *cow trail*, *cow waddy* (a cowboy), *cow whistle* (the whistle on a train to keep cows off the tracks), *cow wood* (dried dung) and *cowology* (the science of raising cows). (*See also* cowcalf operation, cow horse and cow town)

cow horse A horse that knows at least something about working cattle, may have some cow sense (that instinctive understanding of cows and how stupid and mean and perverse they are), may even have some skill at cutting or roping, has perhaps only a moderate prejudice against human beings and is only run-of-the-mill dangerous. Generally called by this name with affection and a touch of suspicion. Sometimes they're called cow ponies.

Westerners have scores of terms for saddle horses (not to mention draft horses, pack horses and wild horses). Some of the general ones are *bronco*, *cayuse*, *cowpony*, *cuitan* (an Indian pony), *dilsey* (a saddle mare), *hay baler*, *hay burner*, *jennet* (a small Spanish mare), *mockey* (wild mare), *montura* (saddle mare), *Navvy* (a Navajo pony), *pony*, *pinto*, *rocking-chair horse* (one with an easy gait), *range horse* (one untouched by man except for branding), *ridge runner* (wild stallion), *ridgling* (a stud with testicles not descended), *saddler* (an easy-gaited horse), *stud* (a stallion) and *short horse* (a quarter horse). (*See also* horse, mustang and cutting horse)

cow town The end of the trail; a trail town; the railhead the cowboys finally got to at the end of one of the great trail drives; especially the Kansas destination of any of the principal trails north from Texas. During the days of the great drives, these towns had a few respectable people and facilities and a cornucopia of places that would spoil a Texas cowboy's sobriety, chastity and solvency in about that order. (Naturally, he got ruined with joyous abandon) Cow towns often got to be cow towns because they wanted to be – they wooed the drivers of the great herds – and later turned into decent places to live because their citizens couldn't stand the booze peddlers, gamblers, whores (*See* calico queen), crooks and killers that preyed on the cowboys.

Later, when the days of the great trail drives had passed, cow town simply meant a commercial centre in cow country, like Miles City, Montana or Fort Worth, Texas.

cowboy This most American of terms, at least American in mythology, got its start in medieval Ireland as the word for the literal boys who tended cattle. During the American Revolution it meant, of all things, a Tory. But we know it, properly, as the best-worn of all the handles for the men of the American West of the last century who rode the range and did the hard, down-to-earth jobs required to raise cows. They're still doing them.

The best-known of these fellows rode during the heyday of the cowboy, the 20 or 30 years following the Civil War. He rode, he roped, he branded. He doctored. He nursed. He trailed or, later, fixed fence. (Building and fixing fences were the bane of his existence, partly because he had to do them on foot) On the northern plains, he fed – every winter morning and evening, no exceptions. Depending on his personality, he smelled the air (and the dust and alkali) and felt the motion of his mount and looked about and thanked God for letting him be where he was; if he was of sour disposition, he cussed his horse, cussed the country, cussed his employer and cussed God for sentencing him to . . . everything he resented.

I have known some cowboys, and they're hard to generalise about. The cowboy's main fault, from the modern point of view, is that he is likely to have narrow horizons: He keeps his books in the out-house, and not for his eyes. He likes food from fried chicken to chicken-fried steak and isn't interested in experimentation. Coors Light is his choice over any wine, California or French. In the old days, his musical likes didn't go beyond fiddles and guitars (pronounced GI-tars), these days not beyond country twanging. He's likely to have prejudices, and if you're an Indian or a Mexican or a black, or simply a woman, you may not like some of them.

This fellow works prodigiously, though. He takes care of cows like they were kids, and he doesn't knock off just because the clock says quitting time. He can fix almost anything mechanical. He's decent, and then some. He has a strong sense of justice and will travel many a mile to set things right.

Most important, you can depend on him. In *The Solace of Open Spaces*, Gretel Ehrlich tells of a Wyoming cowboy who cut his foot off by accident. On the way to town for medical help, he stopped his pick-up and got out to close his neighbour's gate after he went through. Otherwise, he said, what would they have thought?

If he's on your side, the cowboy will stick. For most of them, I think, the old expression will do: He's a good man to ride the river with.

The cowboy has gone by more names than you can count, and cowboy wasn't one of them at first. The Texas fellow was first a vaquero (and that didn't suggest he was a Hispanic). Later, after the Civil War, cowboy came into widespread use. In the Great Basin, though, he was more likely to be a *buckaroo*, which also implied somewhat different techniques and gear. He has also gone by *cowpoke* (or just *poke*), *cowprod(der)*, *cowpuncher* (or just *puncher*), *dabster hand*, *gunny sacker* (to sheepmen), *hand* (*cowhand* or *top hand*), *heel squatter*, *leather pounder*, *ranahan* (or *ranny*), *saddle slicker*, *saddle stiff*, *saddle warmer*, *trail hand*, *waddy*, *wrangler* and of course *you son of a bitch*. If he's called a *cowboy of the Pecos*, he's been alkalied in the rough country drained by the Pecos River, which even lizards avoid, and is the toughest kind of rawhide. In this century, a new distinction has become necessary – ranching cowboy means a working hand, as opposed to a rodeo cowboy, a performer.

Cowboy suggests a person who puts action ahead of thought: A speeder is said to be cowboying around, and Ronald Reagan was called the cowboy President. The word is often used as a verb, too, as in, 'I been cowboying over on the Picket-wire,' or in 'cowboy up', to prove yourself as a hand. It is also the basis of combinations like *cowboy hat* (some Westerners prefer *stockman's hat*), *cowboy boot*, *cowboy song*, *cowboy movie* and so on.

A horse that's *cowboy broke* is a horse nobody but a real hand could ride, the opposite of lady-broke.

cowboy boot The cowboy boot is an essential part of the West. I quote Ramon Adams's definition of boot in *Western Words*: 'The cowman's footwear. The cowboy's boots are generally the most expensive part of his rigging, and he wants them high-heeled, thin-soled, and made of good leather. The tops are made of lightweight, high-grade leather, and all the stitching on them is not merely for decoration but serves the purpose of stiffening them and keeping them from wrinkling too much at the ankles where they touch the stirrups . . .

'The boots are handmade to order. The cowman has no use for hand-me-down, shop-made footgear, and no respect for a cowhand who will wear them, holding to the opinion that ordinary shoes are made for furrow-flattened feet and are not intended for stirrup work. The high heels keep the cowman's foot from slipping through the stirrup and hanging, they let him dig in when he is roping on foot and they give him a sure footing in all other work on the ground. Too, the high heel is a tradition, a mark of distinction, the sign that the one wearing it is a riding man, and a riding man has always held himself above the man on foot.

'A cowhand wants the toes of his boots more or less pointed to make it easier to pick up a stirrup on a wheeling horse. He wants a thin sole so that he has the feel of the stirrup. He wants the vamp soft and light and the tops wide and loose to allow the air to circulate and prevent sweating.

'When a man is seen wearing old boots "so frazzled he can't strike a match on 'em without burnin' his feet", he is considered worthless and without pride.'

(2) A rack on a stagecoach that holds mail and baggage. (3) A horseshoe calked at both heel and toe. (4) The scabbard of a saddle gun. (5) Rawhide coverings on hondas or other leather loops to prevent wear. (6) Between two horse traders, whatever extra value (cash or other valuables) a man trades along with the horse to make the deal even.

cowboy change Cartridges used as equivalents of gold and silver coins.

cowboy cocktail Whiskey neat (straight).

cowboy coffee The brew you make on the range, strong enough to float a horseshoe. You use a pot that's been making coffee for months or years without ever being washed – well-seasoned. You keep part of the old grounds and add some new ones and some water (and 'it don't take as much water as you think it do'). You boil it, add cold water to settle the grounds and pour. Also called Indian coffee; for other names for coffee *see* Arbuckles.

cowcalf operation A kind of cow outfit. The owner has cows and at least one bull (or these days, artificial insemination) and therefore calves. He or she sells the calves and keeps the cows for next spring's bunch.

cowhide (1) The skin of a cow. (2) Boots or whips made of cowhide. (3) To flail a man with such a whip. Such beatings were said to be wicked – an early reference says that a lawyer cut a fellow's jacket to ribbons with a cowhide. *Cowskin* is also used in this sense.

cowish An Oregon herb valued by Indians for its edible roots and known to whites since the Lewis and Clark expedition. Also spelled *couse*, *cowas* and *cows*.

cowpen herd A small herd of cows; probably a herd so little it could be gotten into a single corral.

cowpen Spanish Tex-Mex talk; the Spanish Texas hands learned from the Mexican vaqueros.

cowpuncher Another word for a cowboy. Originally, during the days the railroads were making hay by hauling cows on the hoof from the plains to the cities of the Midwest and East, it meant either: (1) A fellow who helped push the cattle on to rail cars by poking them with a long stick or (2) A fellow who used a prod to keep the cows standing during the journey, so they wouldn't get trampled. Maybe it meant both. Maybe *cowpoke* and *cowprod(der)* meant the same, too. David Lavender in *One Man's West* says that movies and magazines first confused cowpunchers with cowboys, and for decades, real cowboys thought the term degrading.

coydog What comes when a coyote and dog get together, male and female. South Dakota rancher and writer Linda Hasselstrom says it's common in her country and that coydogs can be very large. Also called a *coyote dog*.

coyote (1) The prairie wolf, the barking wolf, the prairie lawyer, the song dog, the trickster of Western myth, the irrepressible populater of our plains and mountains. (2) A man who skulks like a coyote. (3) A squatter. (4) An Indian or breed. (5) A Dakotan. (6) A man who guides illegal aliens across the American-Mexican border.

The word has other meanings in verb form. (1) In mining, to run small drifts, dig little holes coyote fashion. (2) To vamoose, to clear out. (3) To drift around, as in, 'I was coyoting around the upper Yellowstone country.' (4) To *out-coyote* a man is to outsmart him at his own game.

Among Indians, the coyote is important in myth, and many-faced. He is a creator but a trickster, mankind's principal helper but a fool; he is victim and villain, saviour and cheat. In some myths, he is like Prometheus, the bringer of fire. In Crow mythology, coyote created the earth and the two-legged, four-legged, winged, rooted and other tribes that inhabit it. In lots of stories, he is sly, devious. In Pueblo myth, he is often the scapegoat, the one who gets tricked or fooled. Always, though, he endures.

Anglos have not liked him so well. While they admire his singing, they don't like his tendency to kill livestock. Though many government specialists insist that *Canis latrans* feeds mainly on small animals like rabbits and mice and attacks domestic critters rarely, most stockmen (especially sheepmen) spit and say quietly, 'Bullshit!' As a result, most states in the West have their government trappers, whose job is to wage ceaseless war on the coyote.

Historian David Lavender, himself raised on a Colorado ranch, argues (along with other authorities) that coyotes save lots of grass for the stockman by getting rid of foraging insects and rodents and so do more good than harm. He admits, 'It is whistling in the wind to say so, however. Most ranchers remain adamant in their determination to exterminate "every one of the danged varmints that walks".'

Yet Anglos do feel a sly love for this creature. Listen to our cowboy songs. Read J. Frank Dobie's *The Voice of the Coyote* or Max Evans's fine little novel *One-Eyed Sky*. Watch the cartoon co-starring the roadrunner and Wile E. Coyote.

And, by God, the coyote is a survivor. Many of the animals who appear to define the old West, like the buffalo and the wolf, exist only marginally these days. The coyote has prospered. We fence the pastures, and he uses the grass along the fences for cover. We build our cities, and he thrives in the foothills. He originally ranged from the Mississippi to the Pacific Coast and from down in Mexico nearly to the Arctic. He's still mostly there and has been expanding his range eastward.

His name, from the Nahuatl *coyotl*, is pronounced ĸɪy-yoht (rather than kiy-yoн-tee) by Westerners and has been spelled creatively – *kiote* most often, also *cayota*, *cuiota* and so on.

Combinations in mining: *coyote gold* (very fine gold dust), *coyote hole* (a digging in a river bank that is neither wet nor dry, but in between), *coyote diggings* (small diggings, especially small drift tunnels, often run down and not productive) and *coyote placer* or *coyote shaft* (a small shaft dug into the hillside).

The early days of settlement in the West, when homesteaders and others lived in dugouts (also known as *coyote houses*) were referred to as *coyote days*. A *coyote well* is a desert water hole, especially if its hard to find. A *coyote dun* is a dun-coloured horse with a dorsal stripe. [Adams]

Plants: coyote tobacco (a name Indians of

Mexico and the south-west gave to tobacco smoked for sacred purposes), *coyote melon* (*Cucurbita palmata*), a south-western gourd said fit to be eaten only by coyotes, and *coyote thistle* (the *Eryngium* of California).

To *coyote around the rim* is to hint, to talk around the edges of a subject. [Adams]

crack shot A first-rate shot, a centre shot; the man who can make such a shot.

crack-a-loo A gambling game. Players pitched coins against the ceiling, and the coin that came to rest nearest a crack in the floor won. Also called *crack-loo*.

cradle (1) In mining, a rocker, like a child's cradle, used to wash gold-bearing earth. (2) In verb form, to do that washing. (3) Another word for cooney, the hide slung under a wagon for carrying cow chips. Also called a *cradle rocker*.

cradleboard The leather, pouch-like home of an Indian infant. Though in pictures the mother is usually carrying her child in the cradleboard high on her back, she was just as likely to hang the board from a lodge-pole or from the pommel of her saddle or to prop it against a tree. The cradleboard had a front of soft, tanned skin, which was usually beaded. Before being enclosed in the cradleboard, the child would be wrapped in a blanket, with some soft material like the inner bark of the cedar stuffed in to absorb his or her soiling.

craps A gambling game with dice that descends from the older game called "hazard". You win if you begin by rolling seven or eleven or by matching a point. If you start with craps (two, three or twelve), you lose. Thus *crap board*, *crap game*, *crap house*, *crap roller*, *crap shooter*, *crap-shooting* and *crap table*. Playing craps is called *shooting craps*.

Principal craps terms are *big natural* (the roll of eleven when it wins), *bones* (dice), *crap out* (to roll a two or twelve), *craps* (the roll of two or twelve), *fade*, *fimps*, *ivories*, *little natural* (the roll of seven when it wins), *no-dice*, *snake-eyes* or *bird eyes* and *viggerish*. The points a player can establish and chants as he rolls the dice are *bird nuts* (double aces); *little Dick*

or *little Joe* or *little Joe from Baltimore* or *Kokomo* (four); *fever dice*, *little Phoebe*, *fee-bee* or just *Phoebe* (five); *two rows of rabbit turds* (double threes); *sixie from Dixie*, *Johnny Hicks*, *Sister Hicks*, *oh so sick* (six); *eighter* (*Ada*) *from Decatur*, *Ada Ross the stable hoss* or *Ada Ross on a fartin' hoss* (eight); *niner from Carolina*, *nina from Carolina* or *Caroline nine* (nine); *big Dick* or *big Joe from Boston* (ten). Seven and eleven cannot be points and are called respectively *little natural* and *big natural*. Two and twelve are craps, and to throw them is to crap out and lose your bet and your turn at the dice.

crawfish To back out, to creep out backwards; especially appropriate when applied to politicians. When said of a horse, it's more violent: It means it's bucking backwards. Hence, of a man or horse, *craw-fisher*.

crawl (1) To creep up on quarry, a usage that surprisingly appears to occur first in the West. (2) To manage to stay on a horse.

crazy as a sheep-herder Plumb crazy. (*See* sent for supplies)

crease To shoot a wild horse in the neck in an effort to stun it so you can capture it. Usually the shot killed the horse, which in the view of early Westerners was no catastrophe. Also, to stun a man with a bullet (to his head, not his neck).

Creek A tribe of Indians that originally lived in what became Georgia and Alabama and properly known as the Muskogee; one of the five civilised tribes. During the 18th century, because of an improved economy (based on methods and trade goods acquired from the white man) and assimilation with other Indian peoples, the Creeks were the dominant tribe in the Old south-west. Staying independent, they leaned toward the British side against the Spanish, who were in Florida, and sided with the British in the American Revolution as well. In time they began to feel pressure on their lands from the governments of the United States and the state of Georgia. Some Creeks fought Andrew Jackson in the Creek War in 1813 and were defeated, and the tribe was forced to cede lands.

In 1834–5 the Creeks were forced to migrate to what would become Indian Territory, with many dying on the way. There they formed a compact with the Cherokee, Choctaw, Chickasaw and Seminole tribes against the buffalo-hunting tribes of the plains, thus creating the Five Civilised Tribes.

Because the Creek split and took both sides in the Civil War, they were again forced to cede land to the United States. In the first years of the 20th century, the Five Tribes made an effort to create a separate state, but in the end Congress merged their lands with Oklahoma and admitted that territory to the union as a state in 1907.

creek diggings In mining, shallow mining for gold beside a creek.

creep feed A pellet feed, usually used for calves. (*See* cake)

cremello An albino horse with white coat, pink skin and china-blue eyes.

Creole A person of mixed European and native blood. In the south-west, a Creole is a person of Spanish and Indian heritage; in Louisiana, French and native or sometimes a native-born black (and sometimes simply a Louisianan who is a descendant of Louisiana colonists); in Alaska, Russian and native.

creosote bush The ubiquitous shrub (*Larrea divaricata*) of much of the south-western desert country, with a yellow blossom, an oily leaf and a bit of a stink. Also called *greasewood* and called by Hispanics *hediondilla*. Some Anglos used to say it relieves rheumatism.

crested wheatgrass An exotic grass (*Agropyron cristatum*) introduced for forage a century ago. It does well in arid areas and is a good forage in the spring, less good later. Generally called simply *crested*. Western wheatgrass (*Agropyron smithii*), largely displaced by cheatgrass, is also called bluestem wheatgrass.

crevice A miner's term for trying to pry gold out of cracks in rock with a knife. [Adams]

crib (1) A saloon, gambling den or whorehouse – usually all three in one high-living, hellacious combination. A *crib girl* was a whore. (2) In mining, the timber lining a shaft.

cribber A word for a horse that sucks air into its stomach while placing its front, top teeth on a bar of wood. This can cause colic, which is often fatal. This nervous habit is contagious in a barn; a cribber is to be avoided. (*See* horse for other terms for horses)

cricket A roller on a horse's bit. With it, the mount can make a kind of music for man and beast. [Adams]

cricksand Quicksand. A wonderful blending of *crick*, the frequent Western pronunciation of *creek*, with the original term *quicksand*; and of course it is crick sand.

crimp A bend in a playing card put there by a cheat; a name for the cheat, who is also called a *crimper* and a *crimp artist*.

crockhead One of the cowboy's many terms for a stupid, stubborn, no-good horse. (*See* horse for other terms for horses)

crop tree In forestry, a tree in a stand chosen to grow to maturity, when it will be harvested as lumber.

crop-eared Descriptive of a critter whose ears have been cropped by nature, as by frostbite. A horse with ears that have been deliberately cropped to show that he's a can't-be-rode critter is called *croppy*.

cross a herd To force a herd of horses or cattle across a stream. You yell, wave your hat, jump up and down and hope.

cross draw A pulling of a pistol from the off-side of the body. It is holstered butt forward for this purpose. Also called a *border draw* since it was popular in the Texas-Mexico border country.

cross-brander (1) A cattle thief, a brand blotter. (2) In the verb form, to cross-brand, it means for a seller to rebrand, or counter-brand, on the shoulder as evidence that he's surrendered his claim.

crossbuck saddle A wooden packsaddle that looks like a small sawhorse. Also called a *sawbuck saddle* and *cross-tree saddle*.

cross-fire (1) For a horse to bump a forefoot against its opposite hind foot when it walks. (2) One of the two branches of the Native American Church, the one with more Christian elements in the ceremonies; the other is the *half-moon* which stresses traditional Indian elements. The *fireplace* is the peyote ceremony of the Church.

cross-hobble To tie one front foot of a horse to the back one on the opposite side to prevent it from kicking.

crotch Among loggers, a small sledge made from the fork of a tree and used to skid logs, hauled by horses. Also known as a *dray*, *go-devil* and *lizard*. [Adams]

Crow A Siouan tribe of Plains Indians with a buffalo-hunting culture. Their name is also rendered in English as *Absaroka*, pronounced ab-SAHR-kuh (not Ab-suh-ROH-kuh, as Charlton Heston said it in the movie *The Mountain Men*), plus dialectical variants like ab-SAHR-kee. It means not 'crow' but 'children of the big-beaked bird', usually considered the mountain raven, which is often mistaken for the crow. Their pronunciation of their own name sounds like ahb-ZAH-loh-gah. Like their neighbours the Lakotas, Cheyennes and Blackfeet, they based their physical culture on the buffalo until the extinction of the great herds and their religion on the buffalo and the sun dance.

The Crow split off from the Hidatsa in prehistoric times and came to live on the southern tributaries of the Yellowstone River, in what now is now eastern Wyoming and south-eastern Montana. Though they made few alliances with neighbouring tribes and were particular enemies of the Blackfeet, Shoshones and Lakotas, they welcomed the mountain men, their first substantial contacts among the whites, and traded willingly. During the period of the Plains Indian Wars (by which time they were divided into the Mountain and River Crow), they furnished the US Army with scouts to fight against their traditional enemies.

In 1868 they accepted confinement to a reservation in their traditional country in south-central Montana, where they live today, beside the Big Horn River and the Custer battlefield.

crow bait A worthless horse.

crow hop Stiff-legged bucking by a horse. It's not a serious effort to get rid of a rider.

crowding pen A small, strong corral where you hold cattle tightly, to do work such as loading into a truck, sorting or branding.

crown In fire-fighting, for a fire to soar into the tops of the trees.

crown dance A religious ceremony of the Apache. Also known as the *Mountain Spirit dance*, it is done to ward off evil spirits or sometimes as a puberty rite for young girls.

cruise To explore forest country for stands of timber worth harvesting. The lumber-men who did this were called *cruisers*, *timber cruisers* or *land-lookers*, and they wore high-laced boots called *cruisers*.

crumb What a soldier or logger (and sometimes a cowboy) called a louse. So a logger called his bedroll a *crumb roll*, and a cowboy called it a *crumb incubator*. Getting rid of your body lice was called *crumbing up*.

Among loggers, the fellow who cleaned the bunkhouse was the *crummie*. [Adams]

crupper A band of leather attached to a saddle or aparejo and passed beneath the horse's tail to keep the saddle from sliding forward. A crupper made in two sections is called a *panel crupper*.

crush pen A narrow branding chute. [Adams]

cuesta A steep, narrow ridge, a hog-back. Borrowed from Spanish (where it means 'slope') and pronounced KWAYS-tuh.

cuff A leather guantlet or wrist guard worn by some cowboys. Some authorities say it was useful to prevent rope burns; some say it wasn't practical but was for show.

cuffy A frontier nickname for a bear. Also *cuff* and *cuffee*.

cuidado! Look out! Or, more accurately for the Western vernacular, Watch your ass! Borrowed from Spanish and pronounced kwee-DAH-doh.

cull (1) In the cattle business, an animal rejected from the herd. Ranchers usually cull cows that no longer yield calves every year. Sometimes called *cut-backs*. (2) In logging, a tree, log or lumber to be rejected. (3) In verb form, to do the cutting out.

cultural resources In governmentese, the remains of sites and implements used by humans in either historic or prehistoric times. Cultural resource management (CRM) is assessing, protecting and preserving the cultural resources on public lands.

cultus Worthless, useless. From Chinook (the trade language) in the same meaning. Also spelled *kultus*. Thus Owen Wister wrote, 'He can't bile water without burnin' it . . . He's jest kultus, he is.' A *cultus potlatch* is a present, a gift (*See* potlatch)

cup (1) A groove in the teeth of a horse that gives away its age. (2) In logging, a notch in a stump or the base of a tree made to hold a chemical. [Adams]

cupid's cramp The ache a cowboy feels when he's in love. Sometimes takes the form *cupid's cramps*.

cura An old south-westernism for a priest. (*See* black robe for similar names)

curandero In the south-west, a healer; a medicine man; sometimes carries the implication of quackery. Borrowed from Spanish and pronounced koo-rahn-DAY-roh.

curb bit One of the favourite bits of Western riders, one with an upward curve (called a port) in the middle; a popular curb bit was called a *grazing bit*. The *curb strap* runs from the bit underneath the horse's chin. (*See also* spade bit)

cured grass Grass that has matured where it grew, uncut. In the West an important source of nutrition for cows in the winter.

curl him up One expression of Westerners for killing someone. (*See* dry-gulch)

Curly Bill spin *See* road agent.

curly wolf A mean fellow; a tough guy; maybe a bit of a bastard. Peter Watts says it's a rough-and-tumble compliment.

curry him out To rake a horse with your spurs. To *curry the kinks out* is an expression for breaking a horse. [Adams]

cuss word A profane word. The convention of not using these words in front of women, naturally, is a fountainhead of Western verbal creativity. Though cuss (in both the noun and verb forms) appears not to be a Westernism, the first use of cuss word I've seen is in Mark Twain's *Roughing It* (1872).

Custer hat A version of the Kossuth hat with both sides pinned up. But what General George Armstrong Custer often wore was the planter's hat, a leftover of the pre-Civil War South.

custom-mades A cowboy's term for his boots when they're not store-bought but made to order. *See* cowboy boot. The old insistence on custom-mades seems to be waning.

cut A word with a parfleche-full of Western meanings. *Verb:* (1) To cut a herd is to divide it into groups. (2) To separate a particular cow or a group of cattle from a larger group. This manoeuvre is best done on a cutting horse. It is a tricky matter, and these days the skill may be exhibited at a *cutting competition*. Here is David Lavender describing the work in *One Man's West* (1943): 'Four or five men cut at a time, their wise ponies slipping back and forth through the close-packed animals. A flick of the reins, a touch with the spurs, and the horse knows which steer is to go. Slowly, so as not to excite the rest of the bunch, he crowds the yearling to the edge of the herd. Suddenly the steer senses all is not well. It tries to dodge, but with a swift leap the horse blocks it off. The steer whirls. Spinning on a dime, the horse heads it again. The rider jerks off his hat, slaps it in the brute's face. Back and forth they lunge. Men working between the main bunch and the "cut" [the segregated animals] dash up and take over.'

Cutting-horse riders say the horse does the work: Without guidance, it sees how to force the cow the way it wants the critter to go and does the dodging and darting. It is worth noting, though, that unless the rider anticipates the horse's moves and leans with it, he ends up in the dust himself.

Cowboys at a big roundup would make both a *calf cut*, grouping the cowcalf pairs in one bunch, and a *steer cut* (or beef cut), separating out the steers that are to go to market, for each ranch.

Cutting double-barreled is to use two cowboys to cut a herd at once; a *cut herd* is a bunch of cows separated from the main herd; and a *cutting gate* is a swinging gate that forces cattle into one pen or another.

(3) To castrate a steer, so he'll put on weight instead of burning off pounds chasing heifers, changing his attitude 'from ass to grass', as Westerners say. It's usually done at branding with a sharp knife.

(4) To *cut down* is to level a pistol at a man, as in, 'I cut down on him with both hands.' (5) To *make the final cut*, jocularly, is to get thumbs up at the Last Judgment.

Noun: (1) A group of cows separated from the main herd, whether for branding, trailing, shipping or whatever. (2) In mining, an open drift.

Many cow-country expressions use cut: *cut a trail* or *cut for sign* (to come on a trail and identify it by signs), *cut a rusty* (cowboy talk meaning to do your best), *cut her loose* (what the rodeo cowboy says when he's ready for the gate to be opened), *cut him some slack* (to give him a break), *cut straw and molasses* (a cowboy's description of food he doesn't like), *cut plug* (a piece of tobacco cut from a plug of tobacco), *cut the bed* (what a cowboy called sharing his bed) [Adams], *cut the beef* (to separate the market-ready animals), *cut the deck deeper* (to explain more fully, to come again), *cut the dust* (to take a drink, preferably alcoholic) and *cut over* (said of land that has been logged).

cut your wolf loose To go on a bender, to do something outrageous, to raise some hell while stimulated by strong drink. (*See* roostered for similar expressions) Ramon Adams's example is riding a horse into a saloon. He tells of a bartender who received a complaint from an Eastern customer about the horses in the saloon. The bartender answered that the Easterner had a lot of nerve coming in on foot.

cutbank An overhanging bank on a stream, on the outside of a bend where the water has undercut the bank. Also spelled *cut-bank* and *cut bank*.

cut-throat (1) The object of the Rocky Mountain fly fisherman's affections, the native brook trout, distinguished by a pair of orange slashes on its throat. (2) A Shoshone name for a Lakota (Teton Sioux) Indian, because the sign language for the Sioux is a slash of the hand across the throat. The two tribes were long-term enemies.

cutting horse A horse skilled at cutting cows out of a herd. They're also called *carvers* and *carving horses*, *choppers* and *chopping horses*, *sorting horses*, *whittlers* and *cut horses*. The rider points the horse toward the cow and calf to be cut out and lets the animal take over. Stewart Edward White describes the precision work of a cutting horse called Little G: 'The cow and her calf turned in toward the centre of the herd. A touch of the reins guided the pony. At once he comprehended. From that time on he needed no further directions. Cautiously, patiently, with great skill, he forced the cow through the press toward the edge of the herd . . . When the cow turned back, Little G somehow happened always in her way. Before she knew it she was at the outer edge of the herd. There she found herself . . . facing the open plain. I felt Little G's muscles tighten beneath me. The moment for action had come. Before the cow had a chance to dodge among her companions the pony was upon her like a thunderbolt. She broke in alarm, trying desperately to avoid the rush. There ensued an exciting contest of dodgings, turnings, and doublings. Wherever she turned Little G was before her. Some of his evolutions were marvellous. All I had to do was to sit my saddle, and apply just that final touch of judgment denied even the wisest of the lower animals . . . At last the cow, convinced of the uselessness of further effort to return, broke away on a long lumbering run to the open plain. There she was held by men forming the new herd, called a cut herd.'

A cutting horse is a source of pride to its rider and to the whole outfit. Nowadays the tradition is kept alive in the *cutting competition*, a contest for cutting horses and their riders. It's judged by how efficiently the rider can cut out a cow critter from a herd in three minutes.

D

D ring A metal ring on a saddle, used to attach the cinch or a martingale. It may be flat on one side (like a D) or completely round.

dab To toss, as in, 'Just dab your rope on.'

Dakota A large, powerful tribe commonly known as the Sioux that became celebrated because of their fierce resistance to white encroachment on the northern plains. Dakota leaders like Crazy Horse, Red Cloud and Sitting Bull and events like the Little Bighorn battle and the Wounded Knee massacre have become legendary in the Anglo and native cultures.

Dakota is a word in their Siouan language meaning 'alliance of friends'. It has two other dialectical forms, Nakota and Lakota; the latter may now be the word they most commonly use to refer to themselves. Historically, they also called themselves the 'seven council fires'. The word Sioux is a French version of their Ojibway foes, meaning 'adder' or 'enemy'. Historically they lived near the Western Great Lakes but, because of pressure from the Ojibway, gradually migrated further and further on to the plains, as far West as modern Wyoming.

The Dakota divided themselves into seven tribes: Mdewakanton, Sisseton, Wahpekute and Wahpeton (these four known to whites as the Santee); Yankton and Yanktonai (these two known to whites as the Yankton); and Teton. The Santee were Minnesota farmers, the Yankton a semi-agricultural culture in the eastern Dakotas and the Teton (much the largest group) a nomadic, buffalo-hunting culture in the Dakotas and Wyoming. The Teton Sioux, themselves comprised of seven tribes – the Blackfoot (not to be confused with the Blackfeet), Brulé, Hunkpapa, Miniconjou, Oglala, Sans Arc and Two Kettle – were the principal Dakota combatants of the Indian Wars of the 1860s and '70s.

Their religion was centred around the vision quest, the sun dance and other ceremonies seeking blessings from the spiritual power they saw in nature, and emphasised an individual gaining of rightness with that divine spirit.

The Teton Lakota fought against the US government, especially about the Bozeman Trail and use of the Black Hills, during the middle and late 1860s. After an 1868 treaty many accepted reservation life; others continued to fight. They inflicted defeats on troops led by George Crook and then George Custer in the spring and summer of 1876, but during the following winter they suffered severely from lack of food. Many surrendered the following summer; others stayed in Canada until 1881. The government ended the ghost dance fervour in 1890 with a slaughter of unarmed men, women and children at Wounded Knee Creek.

Since that time the Dakota have lived principally on reservations in South Dakota, with other reservations in North Dakota and Nebraska. They have suffered under government policies that suppressed their culture, their religion, even their language. In their terms, the sacred hoop was broken.

In the last two decades a new consciousness of Indian rights has helped them to reassert their customs and values. In 1973 some occupied the village at Wounded Knee for two months against FBI opposition and brought international attention to their circumstances. Now the Dakota are fighting to regain the Black Hills.

Combinations: Dakota sandstone, a common rock formation in the Black Hills and on the eastern slope of the Rockies; *Dakota Territory* (formed in 1861 with Yankton as its capital and continuing until the admission of North Dakota and South Dakota to the union in 1889) and *Dakota turnip* (the prairie turnip).

Dalles The name of a tribe of Chinookan Indians living on the east side of the Columbia River near the Dalles, Oregon near the falls. It's pronounced *dalz* (the *a* as in *corral*). Dalle was a word of the voyageurs for rapids in a river, and they also named eastern rapids the Dalles. A variant of this word is *dells*.

dally When roping, to wrap the rope, or take a turn or turns with the rope, around the saddle horn, then use the saddle horn as a kind of snubbing post to bring the cow short when it hits the end of the rope. Since the critter is trying to get away, this turn must be taken quickly and with care not to get the fingers or especially the thumb caught between rope and horn. A cow going hard away from a planted roping horse generates considerable force, and careless placement of fingers has cost many a cowboy a digit.

The technique was invented by the vaqueros of New Spain. After years of tying the rope to the cinch or the tail of the horse, they developed this use of the saddle horn. The word is an Anglo version of the vaquero term for it, *dar la vuelta* (to take a twist or turn around something), or in the form of a command as it would have been used in a pinch, *dale vuelta*. The cowboy simply shortened it to dally. Sometimes he tried to keep the Spanish *vuelta* and said *dally* (or *dolly*) *welter* or *dally welta*.

Some cowboys, especially Texas cowboys, instead of dallying tie the rope to the saddle horn, and are known as tie-hard-and-fast men. They generally work with a shorter catch rope, 30 to 40 feet, as opposed to the 40- to 80-foot reata of the dally man. And the tie-hard-and-fast men generally stick to shorter throws.

You can cause some excitement by stirring hands of each technique to argue about which is better. Dallying has the advantage of not subjecting horse, saddle, rope and cow to a severe jerk when the critter hits the end of the rope, because the rope slips on the horn. But it's harder on fingers, and Texas saddles are double-rigged (equipped with two cinches) to take the jolt. Another disadvantage of tying hard and fast is that you can't let go of what you've roped. There are stories of cowboys' having the saddle ripped straight off the horse by a big bull. In *Trail Dust and Saddle Leather*, old hand Jo Mora opined: 'I'm not saying one system is better than the other . . . It just depends on what the job is that's got to be done. The hard and fast for rough and ready speed; the dally for the artist. In flat, open country the former is tops; but take it in the rough hills with lots of trees and patches of chaparral, the long reata and the dally system, in the hands of an expert, are unbeatable.'

The end of the rope you dally, the one opposite the noose, is called the *home end*.

This verb has some uses by extension: A fellow who advises you to *dally your tongue* is telling you to shut up.

A *dally man* is a cowboy who uses dallies instead of tying hard and fast. They joke that if a hand is missing a thumb, you know he's a dally man.

dance Among Indians, a term for a religious ritual. It is not simply a dance (a series of rhythmic, patterned movements) nor is it primarily a social event, like an Anglo dance. Such rituals, the sun dance of the Indians of the plains or the snake dance of the Hopi, for instance, are likely to be religious observances that last a week or more. Though these observances generally involve a measured, stately form of dancing to drums, singing and other music-making, this part is merely the most accessible part of the ceremony to the rest of the tribe and to the public. The ceremonies involve much more (prayer, sacrifice, meditation, ritual and so on) and are imbued with high religious purpose. Such dances include the antelope dance, crown dance, green corn dance, dog dance, snake dance, and sun dance. (*See also* sing, the Navajo name for similar ceremonies)

Indians also dance for substantially social purposes (though never entirely without religious connotations) and even hold dance competitions these days. Some dancers (both Indian and Anglo) travel from powwow to powwow, the Indians competing for substantial prizes.

dangler A pear-shaped metal ornament hanging from a spur. Also called a *jingle-bob*.

Daniel Boone A derisive term of a cattleman of the open-range days for a long-haired Anglo who dressed the part of a scout or badman. [Adams]

dashboards A cowboy's mocking name for someone else's big feet. Historically, cowboys have taken pride in their small feet.

datura In the south-west, *Datura meteloides*, a poisonous weed of the nightshade family, commonly called *jimson weed*. It is a hallucinogen and is used ceremonially; some tribes of California Indians had a cult that centred around it.

daunsy A cowboy word for downcast, depressed.

day herd (1) The herd left after the cowcalf pairs have been cut out for branding. (2) As a verb, it means to watch the cattle by day.

day hole Among miners, a level of a mine that connects with the surface. [Adams]

day money The prize money paid for one day's go-round at a rodeo. Many rodeos have a go-round of each event on Friday and again on Saturday, with day money paid each time, and then a final go-round of the competitors with the best averages for the big prize on Sunday. A *day-money horse* is one that bucks well enough to get a rider a decent score but not well enough either to help him win or to land him in the dust.

day wrangler The hand (remudero) who minded the horse herd (remuda) during the day. At night, the night-hawk did it. (*See also* wrangler)

day's drop Among sheep-herders, the number of sheep born (dropped) in one day. [Adams]

day-lighting Letting daylight show between your bottom and the saddle. It's poor riding technique.

de nada A south-western expression meaning 'It's nothing', often used in response to thanks for a favour or kindness. Borrowed from Spanish and pronounced day NAH-duh.

deacon seat The characteristic piece of furniture of a logging camp, a bench-like seat made of a log split in half.

dead man (1) On the range, a support for a fence post, usually a heavy object like a rock or a piece of wood, to help anchor the fence. (2) In logging, a spar or log sunk into the ground and used as an anchor for lines.

dead man's hand   In poker, a hand with a pair of aces and a pair of eights. By tradition Wild Bill Hickok was holding this hand when he was shot dead by Jack McCall; the linguist J. L. Dillard thinks the tradition dubious. Some sources also say the hand has two jacks, not aces, and two eights.

dead-mouthed   Descriptive of a horse that's insensitive to the bit. Also *hard-mouthed*.

deadfall   (1) A low-class den of drink and gambling. (2) In forestry, a dead tree that has fallen down; an area covered with such trees.

deadline   A line some man or critter is not supposed to cross, sometimes on penalty of bodily harm. Cattlemen set down deadlines for sheep. In Kansas during the days of the big trail drives, the deadline prohibited Texas cattle from coming into the eastern part of the state because they were thought to bear Texas fever. The sheriff's deadline in Texas for a while was the Nueces River – no lawman was supposed to cross it. In mining, deadlines warned workers away from dangerous workings.

deadwood   An advantage – to have the deadwood on someone might be to have the drop on him.

deal from the bottom of the deck   In poker, to deal a player the bottom card instead of the one he is due, the top one. By extension, to cheat or take unjustified advantage in any situation.

deal me in   In poker, a request to be included as a player in a hand. By extension, to ask or agree to be part of anything. *Deal me out* means the opposite.

Dearborn   A light carriage, usually covered and curtained, named for General Henry Dearborn. Common in the east and used on the Santa Fe and Oregon Trails.

death   For words on death and dying, *see* cash in your chips.

death camas   The variety of the lily family (*Zigadenus elegans*) poisonous to stock. It's also called *poison camas*.

death song   Among Plains Indians a warrior's song given to him by a spirit helper to prepare the singer appropriately for death. It is what a warrior wishes to intone as the last words of his life, a call for strength to do whatever is necessary and to accept what comes. It is not a traditional or communal song but is unique to the singer.

decoy brand   A brand put out of easy sight; used to trick rustlers. [Adams]

de-horn   (1) Among cowmen, to take the horns off cows or (more often) calves. In the old days, the horns were sawed off. Now the operation is usually done at branding, when the horns are just nubs, with a tool called a scoop. The wound is then treated for coagulation and against infection and flies. Cattle with horns are a nuisance to each other and to the people who work with them. (2) To act up when inspired by whiskey. Also, as a noun, the whiskey itself and the man who gets mean on it. (3) Among loggers, to saw off the end of a log with the owner's mark and give it a new mark.

Del Norte   A name for the Rio Grande until the mid-19th century. From the Mexican name for the river, Rio Grande del Norte, it's pronounced del NOHR-tay. The Rio Grande was also called the *Bravo*.

Delaware   The Algonquian Indians who lived in New Jersey and adjacent areas before white contact and called themselves Lenni-Lenape (real men). Displaced early in the colonial period without much resistance, they moved gradually to what is now Ohio. In the latter half of the 18th century there, they joined the Shawnee in raids against American frontier settlements. Defeated, they dispersed widely. Some went to a reservation in Kansas, and some joined the whites in Rocky Mountain beaver-trapping. They became in Bernard DeVoto's words, 'the only Indians the mountain men ever thought of as companions in their trade' (*Across the Wide Missouri*). Many eventually became citizens of the Cherokee Nation in Oklahoma and still live there.

democrat pasture   A grazing area that was mostly unfenced but was bounded by rimrock or other natural barriers.

den A frontier verb meaning to track a bear to its den. Animals (and sometimes people) were said to *den up*, to hibernate, to stay in their dens for the winter.

depance A storehouse. From the French *dépense* and pronounced day-PAHNS.

depouille A thick layer of fat on the back of the buffalo, valued by Indians and mountain men as food. Also called *depuis* and *depuyer*. From the French *dépouillé*, it's pronounced day-POO-yuh.

derringer The common percussion hideout pistol of the antebellum frontier, named after its inventor, Henry Deringer (with one *r*). Small, single-shot and often of large calibre, it was effective at short range. Remington made a particularly popular model. Occasionally the word was even used as a verb – 'he got derringered.'

Deseret (1) The name of the utopia founded in the desert by the Mormons, the state of Deseret. Deseret, as mapped by Brigham Young and his advisors, included what is now Utah, most of Nevada and Arizona, and parts of California, Idaho, Oregon, New Mexico and Wyoming. The Territory of Utah, the official Deseret established by Congress, was smaller but was larger than the modern state. (2) A word coined in the *Book of Mormon* meaning 'honeybee'. The Utah state symbol, the beehive, comes from the word. To Mormons, the honeybee symbolises the spirit of cooperative industriousness. (3) A Mormon name for Salt Lake City.

The *Deseret alphabet* was a set of characters invented by Mormon George D. Watt in hope of helping the Saints establish a new written language.

desert canary A jocular name for a burro.

desert rat A human denizen of the desert, especially a prospector who wanders the desert.

desert varnish A black glaze or patina on desert rock, formed from manganese and iron oxide, often appearing where water streaks the rock.

devil's backbone A name given to various spiny ridges (hogbacks) all over the West.

devil's corkscrew A name of local cowmen for Daimonelix, a large, spiral fossil of the Badlands, South Dakota.

devil's kitchen The name given to a variety of hot and unpleasant rocky areas in canyon country.

devil's slide A name describing gullies that are bordered by parallel fins of sedimentary rock.

dewlap To cut this loose skin on a calf, done for the same reason you brand it or crop its ears, to make a mark of ownership. The cut skin is left to hang in a distinctive way.

diamondback A rattlesnake (*Crotalus atrox*) with diamond-shaped markings on its back. Common in the south-west and known for its deadliness, this is the second largest rattler, sometimes reaching seven feet in length. (*See* side-winder)

dice house What a cowboy sometimes called the bunkhouse. He also called it a *dive*, *doghouse*, *ram pasture* and *shack*.

dicho A south-western term for a saying, proverb or epigram. Borrowed from Spanish, it's pronounced DEE-choh.

die on their backs What sheep sometimes do when they turn turtle. The critters have a hard time getting right side up again, especially when they're heavy with wool, and the sheep-herders must put them back on their feet.

die-up The deaths of substantial numbers of cattle from cold, disease, starvation and so on. In Texas, die-ups brought on what was called the *skinning season*, a period of cutting the skins off dead cattle and selling them. Some of the most famous die-ups occurred in the winter of 1886 on the northern plains. Some ranchers were said to be able to walk across their entire ranches on the carcasses of their cattle.

differential grasshopper A big, particularly destructive grasshopper (*Melanoplus differentialis*), found from the plains to the Pacific Coast.

difuntos The dead, corpses. Borrowed from the Spanish, it's pronounced dee-fun-TOS.

digger (1) An Anglo name for an Indian of the south-west, Great Basin or Pacific Coast who lived on roots and other vegetables he gathered. Usually Diggers wore few clothes and lived in primitive brush dwellings. Most of these Indians were Shoshones or Paiutes. Though the name may first have been a translation of the name of a Paiute tribe of south-western Utah, it quickly became an epithet of Anglo contempt. They were also called *Shuckers* or *Root-eaters*. A *digger ounce* is a lead weight that came to more than an ounce, sometimes much more. It got its name because it was often used to cheat Digger Indians when weighing the gold they brought in. [Adams] (2) When not capitalised, a cowboy's name for his spurs. (3) A stove-up (crippled) horse. [Adams]

diggings An area of placer mining. People spoke, for instance, of the diggings at Virginia City, Montana or at Last Chance Gulch.

dilly road A miner's name for the mine railroad.

dilsey A mare used as a saddle horse. In the older West, mares were not commonly ridden. [Adams]

dime novel A short piece of adventure fiction published in the latter half of the 19th century, usually set in the West or on the frontier and written with stereotypical characters and formulaic plots.

Erastus Beadle brought out the first series of dime novels starting in 1860, and some were hugely successful with the mass audience. Typical dime-novel characters were Deadwood Dick and Hurricane Nell. Buffalo Bill and Calamity Jane were actual Westerners used as characters in these adventure stories. Perhaps the best-known dime novelist was Edward Z. C. Judson, who wrote under the pen name Ned Buntline.

The term came to be used as descriptive of an improbable heroic fantasy – *dime-novel hero*, *dime-novel Indian*, *dime-novel rescue*. It also yielded the forms *dime novelist*, *dime-novelism*, *dime-novelish* and even *dime-novelly*.

There were also half-dime novels, which sold for a nickel.

Not a Westernism but an Eastern term for a psuedo-Western product.

dinah One of the names of miners and loggers for dynamite. They also call it *dine*. (For other Westernisms for dynamite, *see* powder)

dinero A south-western term for money, often used flippantly. Borrowed from Spanish, it's pronounced dee-NAY-roh.

dingus A thingamajig; something you can't think of the name of. This borrowing from Dutch seems first to have appeared in the West in the 1870s.

dink What rodeo cowboys call a person or a horse for the steer-wrestling or roping events that isn't well trained, doesn't give a good performance.

dinner plate What American cowboys called the horn of the old Spanish saddle, which was as big as a plate.

dip (1) On the range, an insecticide for ridding stock of ticks and lice. You swim the livestock through a deep vat (the *dipping vat*) containing the insecticide. (2) A cowboy word for pudding; a sauce of sugar and flour.

dirt The substance a forty-niner hoped would make his fortune. He spoke of *rich dirt, poor dirt, pay dirt* and so on. This use of the word then spread to other Western diggings.

dirt-washing A name for placer mining.

dirty your shirt To get thrown from your horse. (For other such expressions, *see* bite the dust)

discovery The location of a valuable mineral on a claim. Discovery is required under mining law for valid title. The first locator of a mineral is entitled to what is called the discovery claim. The General Mining Act of 1872 established the right of discovery. By getting the rewards of their discovery, ordinary people were sometimes able to accumulate fortunes.

On a placer (streamside) claim, other claims are numbered up or down from the discovery claim. On a lode claim, the opening the first locator makes is called the *discovery shaft* or *tunnel*.

dish The seat of a saddle, which is referred to as either deep-dished or shallow-dished, depending on the depth of the seat below the fork and cantle.

dish-wheeled Descriptive of a man or beast that's knock-kneed. [Adams]

ditch company In the latter half of the 19th century, a company that sold water to miners for their sluices and brought it to them via ditches. Later, and presently, a company that brings water to ranchers for irrigation via ditches.

A *ditch rider* is the man who patrols the irrigation system, checking the condition of the ditches and perhaps turning the water into laterals. The fellow in charge of the fair distribution of the water is sometimes called the *ditch boss*.

ditty A cowboy's word for a gadget or contrivance new to him; like a dingus.

dive A name for the ranch bunkhouse. (For other such names, *see* dice house)

divide The point of division between watersheds, where water flows one way or the other.

A divide is usually formed by ridges in hills or mountains. It may be conspicuous or imperceptible. Those who travelled the Oregon Trail couldn't tell where they passed from Atlantic to Pacific waters on so major a divide as South Pass, which is on the continental divide.

Divides were crucial to explorers and other early travellers: In an unmarked land, watercourses and divides were guideposts. Later, divides helped ranchers define their ranges. And from the time of the mountain man to today, 'Go over the divide', meaning 'cross from one watershed to another', has been a staple of Western direction-giving.

Sometimes a divide was called a *dividing ground*.

To *cross the great divide* (sometimes just to cross the divide) means 'to die'. (*See* cash in your chips)

Dixie Now the south-west corner of Utah, around St George, a country with magnificent rimrock scenery and, since it's warm, a fruit-growing centre. The early saints also attempted to establish a cotton and silk industry there. Originally Dixie was larger, extending into Mormon Arizona.

doctor A logger's name for a camp cook. (For other logging names for cooks, *see* hasher)

Doctor C C What a logger called the doctor who came to his camp. The initials stood for *compound cathartic*. (*See* sawbones for other names for doctors)

dodge out To cut (separate) calves out of a herd. [Adams]

dodger Among loggers, a worker who takes the dogs (steel-grabbing spikes) out of logs.

dofunny Doodad, trinket, such as an open-range cowboy might carry in his war bag (sack for personal belongings). [Adams]

dog (1) Short for prairie dog. (2) A logger's term for a spike that was pointed at one end, bent in the middle and with an eye at the other end, used to grab logs. In full, *log dog*. In this sense it's also used as a verb – to *dog a log*, to grab or hold it. (3) Short for bulldog, to wrestle a steer to the ground.

dog-fall To throw a steer down with its feet underneath it, instead of getting it all the way off its feet.

dog hole A saloon.

dog loop A small noose used for roping calves. [Adams]

dog pole A travois pole pulled by dogs for Indians.

dog robber A striker, an orderly, a soldier acting as attendant or servant to an officer. Strikers are gone from the modern US army. Strikers ate in the officers' mess. Cornelius Smith says the term came into being because they were jokingly said to be cheating the dogs of the officers' left-overs.

dog soldier A member of an important warrior society of the Cheyenne or other plains tribes. These warriors were charged with keeping order when the entire tribe was hunting, moving camp or the like, and with protecting the rear in tribal flights from enemies. They were known for their group discipline and fierceness. Because of the belligerence of some Cheyenne dog soldiers, whites in the latter half of the 19th century misunderstood the term to mean rebellious, outcast or especially savage warriors.

The people selected to enforce the camp rules at modern buckskinners' rendezvous are also called dog soldiers.

dog travois A travois pulled by dogs.

dog warp A rope with a hook used to break up log jams (and as a verb, to *dog warp* a log jam).

doghouse (1) An extra-wide stirrup of bent wood, mostly of the early period on the range. Ramon Adams says they had enough wood in them to make a doghouse. (2) One of the cowboy's words for a bunkhouse. (*See* dice house for other names) (3) The room on a oil rig or a seismic crew where all the controls are kept.

dogie An orphan calf, usually runty, usually unbranded; a bum calf; sometimes simply any calf. On trail drives, dogies weren't strong enough to keep up well and so were a nuisance.

The dogie has entered Western mythology as an occasion of sentiment and pathos. One of the most famous cowboy songs, 'Git Along, Little Dogies', is addressed to him:

Oh, you'll be soup for Uncle Sam's Injuns;
It's, 'beef, heap beef,' I hear them say.
Git along, git along little dogies,
You're going to be beef steers by and by.
Whoopee, ti yi yo, git along little dogies,
It's your misfortune and none of my own.
Whoopee, ti yi yo, git along little dogies,
For you know Wyomin' will be your new home!

Since the word was variously spelled in the early days (*doughie, dogy, doge, dogey*), lots of folk, both ordinary and academic, have speculated widely about its origin. Some note that starved calves have swollen bellies and so were sometimes called *dough-guts*, which could have become dogie. Linguist J. L. Dillard says dogie may have come from the Creole *dogi-man*, meaning 'short man', or from *doga*, a term Owen Wister heard in the West and recorded as meaning any 'trifling stock'.

By extension came *dogie lamb*. Later the word came to be applied to anything unlikely to survive, often meant in a jocular way, as in, 'this dogie enterprise'. It also became a verb, *dogied* (orphaned). And a *dogie man* was a farmer or rancher who took in dogies to raise.

dogtown grass A variety of prairie grass (*Aristida*) also known as *needle grass* and *red threeawn*. It has sharp bristles that work into wool, and even skin, and so is dangerous to sheep.

dogwood A cowboy word for sagebrush.

doings Food, as in *buffalo doin's* or *chicken doin's*. In this sense, it is an equivalent of *fixings*. Also, any particular activity, from a Taos dance to a rendezvous to a good Indian fight, any of which may be grand doin's.

doll baby A small, whittled-out, wooden peg used to spin mecates (horse hair lead ropes or reins).

dolly (1) A variant of dally, a wrap, or turn, or two of the rope taken around the saddle horn to make an anchor to bring whatever critter you've roped to a sudden stop. (2) In logging, a wheeled platform used to move logs.

dome Any landscape feature that looks like an overturned bowl; as a technical geological term, a symmetrical upfold in which the rock layers dip downward in all directions. Teapot Dome, near Casper, Wyoming, was the downfall of the Harding administration, when federal oil reserves there were secretly leased in the early 1920s.

don This Spanish title, once commonly inserted before Christian names in the south-west as an indication of respect, became a common noun in English meaning 'Mexican'. Thus early California history may be called 'the days of the dons' and Mexico 'the land of the dons'. Though borrowed from the Spanish, it's usually pronounced like the American first name *Don*.

donkey A portable engine used in cable logging.

doodlebug A divining rod, a device used to locate (or pretend to locate) valuable deposits of oil, water or ore. Hence *doodlebug artist*, *doodle-bugger* and *doodle-buggery*.

door knob A small boy, a kid. (*See* button for other such names)

dope (1) To treat or doctor almost anything, animate or inanimate. Cowmen doped calves, and sheepmen doped sheep. Drivers doped (greased) stagecoach wheels. Early-day skiers even doped the bottoms of their skis. (2) As a noun, the word meant any preparation that you administered – medicine, opium, sawdust in dynamite or pitch for the bottoms of shoes.

dormidera The California poppy. It was also called the *copa de oro* (*cup of gold*). This name, from Spanish and pronounced dohr-mee-DAYR-uh, means 'sleeper' and comes from the fact that this poppy unfolds only in sunlight.

dotting iron A primitive branding iron. The cowhand burned on the entire brand in one effort with a stamp iron, but he had to make several applications with a dotting iron. It had half circles of two different sizes and a bar. By combining these, you could make a lot of brands. (*See* brand and running iron)

double eagle A twenty-dollar gold piece. It gave way to the term *double sawbuck*, a twenty-dollar bill.

double out (1) To hitch more teams to a wagon to pull it out of the muck. (2) To put grass on to mud to make a way to pull a mired wagon out. [Adams]

double rig A saddle cinched twice, front and back, the way tie-hard-and-fast men like it because of the stability it gives the saddle. It's also called *double-barreled*, *double-fire* and *double-cinched*. (*See* single rig)

double roll A stunt with two pistols.

double shuffle An abrupt change in the rhythm of a horse that's bucking.

double-wintered An old expression for cows kept on northern grass for two winters to get them prime.

dough boxer A name of both cowboys and loggers for a camp cook. They also called the cook a *dough-belly*, *dough puncher*, a *dough roller* and a *dough wrangler*. (For many cowboy names for cooks, *see* cookie)

doughboy An American infantry-man. The origin of this term is unknown, but some suggestions have to do with the American West. Libby Custer said the spherical buttons on Civil War infantry uniforms were called doughboys because they were shaped like the doughboys (doughnuts) of sailors. In time the name passed naturally to the soldiers themselves, she says. Mitford Mathews speculates that Hispanics in the south-west applied 'dobe (adobe) to US soldiers for unknown reasons, and it converted to doughboy. Cornelius Smith conjectures that infantrymen of the plains were called doughboys because they were dough-faced, comparatively paler than the cavalrymen who spent long hours riding in the sun. Smith also tells a charming story about American soldiers storming the Bishop's Palace in Monterrey during the Mexican War. They seized flour and rice and, since they were starved for a hot meal, made biscuits. The results were half-done and doughy, so they jokingly called each other doughboys.

Dougherty wagon A passenger wagon, called an ambulance in army parlance. No one seems to know who Dougherty was or how he gave his name to this conveyance. Also spelled *Doherty* and also called a *Dougherty ambulance*.

doughgod To the cowboy, a biscuit; to the logger, bread.

Douglas fir *Pseudotsuga douglasii*, also known as the red fir, Oregon pine, Douglas pine and Douglas spruce. Named after the Scottish botanist David Douglas, it is the great lumberman's tree of the Rocky Mountains, the north-west and Alaska. Now Douglas fir is so common as lumber for houses in the West that carpenters sometimes refer to framing up a house as *firring up*.

Other important Western firs are: Red fir, Subalpine fir, Pacific silver fir and white fir.

down in your boots A cowboy expression for afraid or cowardly. [Adams]

down timber Trees that are no longer standing. In some places in the West, down timber can extend for many square miles and make travel impossible. The terms *down log* and *down tree* are applied to individual trees either blown or cut down.

down to your last chip Broke, busted, cleaned out, financially embarrassed. Also known as *down to the blanket*.

downer A cow that for some reason is too weak to stand, whether because of a hard winter or a hard ride in a cattle car. You have to tail up such critters (grab them by the tail and force them up). An animal on the floor of a cattle car is also called a *down steer*.

drag (1) The back end of a trail herd, which is also called the tail. The drag position (called *at drag* or *eating* or *swallowing drag dust*) is no fun for the hands assigned to ride it – they have to make the sick and the stragglers keep up, chase the breakaways and suffer the dust. They're likely to use cow calls and noise-makers for the job. Since it's unpleasant, green hands usually get assigned to ride drag. The other positions for riders with a trail herd are flank (on the side almost halfway forward), swing (on the side most of the way forward) and point (at the front). The cowboys at drag are called *drag riders* or *drag drivers*. (2) A cow that's dragging, falling behind. (3) The trail and spoor left by a snake. (4) A log or other weight roped to a horse's leg as a hobble. This kind of hobbling is called logging.

draw (1) A gully, a ravine. (2) A form of poker (or bluff, a 19th-century name for poker) that permits the player to discard some cards and be dealt others. In full, *draw poker* (or *draw bluff*). (3) In poker, the deal that follows the discard. (4) The

motion of pulling a pistol, as in, 'He beat me to the draw.' Typical Western draws were the cross draw, hip draw and shoulder draw. (5) As a verb, to pull out a pistol. (6) Also as a verb, in poker or other card games, to take new cards after discarding.

Combinations: draw a bead on someone (to aim a weapon at someone, the front sight of a gun often being a bead), *draw dead* (for a rodeo contestant to draw a bad horse or steer, a critter he can't win any money with because the horse won't buck or the steer won't run) [Adams] and *draw to an inside straight* (in poker, to draw a card hoping to get the single number within a sequence to make five in a row; figuratively the phrase has come to mean showing bad judgment by taking a long chance).

dray A log sledge, a sledge used to reduce the friction in skidding logs because one end was on the sledge. It forms the verbs *dray-haul*, to convey logs in that manner, and *dray in*, to haul logs from the forest to the landing or skidway.

dreadnought Unafraid. Washington Irving used this word to indicate the fearlessness of some Kentucky frontiersmen in *Astoria*.

dream book What some cowboys once called a pack of cigarette papers. [Adams]

dreamer cult A religious group of Columbia River tribes from about 1850. Followers of the Indian prophet Smohalla, they resisted white ways, opposing moves to the reservation, agriculture and white religion. Yet they incorporated portions of Mormon and Catholic dogma, using trances and revelations; Smohalla claimed to have risen from the dead. This movement had some impact on Nez Percé Chief Joseph's decision to resist white encroachment. Also called *Smohalla Indians*.

drench sheep To worm sheep by squirting medicine down their throats.

dressed up like a sore toe Dressed up in a fancy way. [Adams] It appears to imply that the decked-out fellow feels embarrassingly conspicuous.

drift (1) Of cattle, to wander as a herd in some direction, usually in front of a cold wind or a snow storm. When they drifted in the days before fenced grazing lands, they sometimes got far off their range or came against a drift fence and stood and froze to death. Cattle also drifted to better grass or water. In this sense the word was also used as a noun – 'the season's drift'. (2) For cowboys to move cattle (his own outfit's or a neighbour's) slowly and gently, as though they were meandering that way of their own will. (3) For a man to wander, go slowly, almost aimlessly – 'I 'spect I'll drift down there sooner or later.' (4) Among miners, a horizontal tunnel, usually following a vein off a main shaft. By contrast, a crosscut intersects a vein.

Combinations: drift cattle (cattle that have drifted), *drift fence* (a fence to prevent cattle from drifting far – a barrier, not an enclosure) and *drift smoke* (fire smoke drifted from where it started and now without its billow).

On the drift, though, when said of a mine shaft, means crooked.

drive (1) For cowboys, to herd cattle from one place to another. It may be a trail drive, a roundup or a drive of cattle to different range, depending on context.

On a trail drive, cowboys often drove cows a long way, even from Texas to Kansas or on to Wyoming and Montana. At a roundup (or gather or cowhunt), they drove them out of the far reaches of their range to a central spot where they could be branded (in the spring) or could be cut (separated) for shipment to market (in the fall).

Now cattle are driven mostly to move them from one range to another, as from summer range to winter pasture or from deeded land to national forest and the like.

(2) To drive logs is to float them downstream from the forest to the sawmill or the shipping point. Log drives were dangerous – they led to log jams – and required expert handling by *log drivers* (birlers). Now this transportation is entirely by logging truck. To *drive the river* also meant to drive logs down the river. Water high enough to drive logs was called *driving pitch*. (3) In stagecoaching, a drive was the distance coach and driver usually travelled before being changed, about 60 miles. [Adams] (4) A drive was also a V-shaped trap to chase animals into. (5) The group action of chasing animals (such as rabbits or others regarded as pests) from an area and killing them.

The word is commonly both noun and verb – the cattle drive, and to drive cattle; the log drive, and to drive logs. (*See* trail)

driving pike A tool of a log driver, with a wooden shaft, a sharp point and a hook. (*See* drive)

droop-eyed Descriptive of a calf with cut eyelid muscles. Cattle thieves cut them to keep the calf from seeing its mother and following her.

drop (1) The advantage in a shooting situation. To *get the drop on someone* means 'to get your gun pointed at him before he can do the same to you.' Now it has been extended to mean any kind of advantage. Mathews implies that the phrase may come from military positioning: artillery on elevated ground literally has the drop on lower targets. (2) The top, front part of a pair of drop-front trousers.

drop band A herd of ewes about to lamb (drop or give birth to their lambs). They're tended by a *drop-band herder*.

drop gap A place in a barbwire fence where a rider can let himself through.

drop stirrup A strap that hangs below the stirrup to give a short rider (once usually a woman) a leg up.

drop your rope on a heifer Figuratively, to marry.

drouthy Descriptive of calves suffering from drought, of arid country or of grass needing rain. It's usually pronounced to rhyme with mouthy, but sometimes Easterners or others eager to be proper correct the spelling to *droughty* and the pronunciation to match. The term also applied to unhappy visitors to Kansas, when that state was dry – short of booze, not water.

drugstore cowboy A fellow who's got the name but not the game; a person who acts and dresses like a cowboy but may not have the skills of a hand. A contemporary of a skim-milk or mail-order cowboy; also called a *phildoodle*.

drum (1) To solicit (*drum up*) orders, to make sales. The fellow who travelled soliciting trade in the West after the Civil War was called a *drummer*, and as a greenhorn he was the object of a lot of fun. (2) Among contemporary Indians, a drum is not only a rhythm instrument but a group of singers in traditional Indian style, a band of musicians that makes music for powwows; short for *drum group*. In 1990, for instance, Red Bull was a popular drum on the powwow circuit. (3) For a grouse to make a reverberating noise with its wings.

dry A thirst for booze, as in, 'Hosses, this child's got to wet his dry.' New Englanders had long used this word as an adjective in this sense, according to linguist J. L. Dillard, but the mountain man exhibited a little creativity by making it into a noun.

dry cow A cow that didn't bear a calf this year and so isn't giving milk. According to South Dakota writer and rancher Linda Hasselstrom, these cows gain weight fast and are inclined to be troublesome. Because they don't support another critter, they have too much energy left over. A cow that's dry one year may live to see another season. If she's dry again, she'll surely be a cull, one of the cows taken to the sale ring. Also known as an *open heifer* or *dry stuff* (a lactating cow is called *wet stuff*).

The term is also applied to ewes, and a group of such ewes is called a *dry band*.

dry diggings A placer-mining operation that was away from water. When water wasn't available to wash the dirt, miners dry-washed with cloths, with a dry-washing machine (a device for sifting dirt for gold with air currents), or used a crude pulveriser called an arrastre.

dry drive A cattle drive across a piece of country that has no water. A *dry camp* is a camp made without water. The terms are also used as verbs, to dry-drive, to dry-camp.

dry farming Farming without irrigation. The dry farmer uses water stored in the soil. By ploughing deeply, breaking up the soil, using dust mulches and growing appropriate crops, he is sometimes able to farm successfully west of the 100th meridian, the traditional line of demarcation of the West.

A *dry-lander* is a person who farms west of the 100th meridian, using either irrigation or dry farming.

dry fire To practise shooting with a gun that isn't loaded.

dry painting *See* sand painting.

dry storm A rain storm that brings negligible rain to the ground. Commonplace on the high plains and deserts, you can see rain falling from the clouds and coming to nothing halfway down. A dry storm can also be a sandstorm.

dry up Among contemporary Plains Indians, to make the sacrificial fasting of a sun dance, which includes going without water.

dry wash In the south-west, a wash; an *arroyo*, especially an *arroyo seco*; a dry, flat-bottomed gully with steep walls created by occasional run-offs. These washes can flood suddenly and violently.

dry-gulch To ambush someone, especially by hiding near a road in a gully or gulch and shooting him in the back as he rode by. It was regarded as the method of a coward. Other Western expressions for killing people are *adobe wall him*, *bed him down*, *bushwhack him*, *curl him up*, *down him*, *kick him into a funeral procession*, *make wolf meat of him*, *Pecos him*, *put a window in his skull*, *salivate him*, *sarve him up brown*, *save him*, *strap him on his horse with his toes down* and *wipe him out*.

dubber An Indian instrument for scraping fat and flesh off a buffalo skin; also called a hide scraper. The handle was usually made of bone or elk antler, and the business end (shaped like an adze) was iron (or flint or obsidian). The word has a verb form – to dub (to scrape a buffalo hide).

dude A person from the East who vacations on a ranch. Probably the word still carries some of the original implication of a greenhorn, a person who doesn't know his way around a ranch, a horse or a cow. It sometimes suggests a person decked out in city clothes or in a fancy way. (One authority traces it back to the British use of the word a century ago, when it meant fop) Now, though, dude is generally offered as a term of genial welcome, and the owners of guest ranches don't really mind if you call them *dude ranches*. (Dude ranches are also known among cowboys as wild willow West)

In most of the West 50 or 100 years ago, dudes came to a ranch for the entire summer and spent some serious time learning to ride and even participating in the cowpunching. This life is wonderfully depicted in Strothers Burt's book set in Jackson Hole, *Diary of a Dude Wrangler*. Today, most dudes come for a week or two for a pack trip, a float trip or some trail rides and pack it in. Some dude ranches are even becoming (heaven help us!) spas and diet centres. And dudes come not only from the East but from all over the world.

The word dude has lots of offspring – not only *dude ranch* and *dude rancher* but *dude puncher* and *dude wrangler* (cowhands who take care of dudes instead of cows and horses, respectively). A female dude is either a *dudess* or a *dudine*. A dude you're taking pity on is a *dudie*. Dudes exude a quality known as *dudeness, dudism* or *dudery*; besides, they're *dudish*. They live in *dudedom*, which is not only any spot on the map outside the West but a place in their minds. Unfortunately, dudes are occasionally susceptible to the blandishments of *dudolos* (the word plays on *gigolo*). A *dude horse* is so gentle it will permit dudes to sit on it and will even let their children play around its legs. *Dude chaps* (or any other of gear or clothing) means a fancy-looking item that would embarrass any self-respecting hand.

You can find out a lot about dudes by seeing the fine movie *City Slickers* (1991).

dueño A south-western term for a proprietor of a store, ranch or other enterprise. Borrowed from Spanish, it's pronounced DWAYN-yoh. The feminine form, *dueña*, meaning 'chaperone', is rare in the West.

duff The bed of half-decayed matter found on the floor of forests and made of leaves, cones, needles and bark. When dry it burns easily.

dugout (1) An Anglo dwelling dug out of the side of a hill or, like a basement, into flat ground. Those built into hillsides were usually finished with a log-framed door and a log roof, the roof topped with sod. The ones in flat ground often had sod walls above the ground. Most people who lived or visited in them seem to have agreed that dugouts were unpleasant places, earning the name half-human. They were frequently used by Mormons, especially in central Utah, and by keepers of stage stations who feared Indian attack. (2) Among cowmen, a shallow hole with sloping sides dug down to water level so cattle can water. (3) A canoe made by hollowing out a big log. Not originally a Westernism.

dugway Now a road scraped out of a steep hillside. During the heyday of the great trail drives, though, it meant a cut (called a cutting) in the bank of a river to let cattle and wagons get to the stream and out of it on the other side. (Western rivers often have vertical, or undercut, banks) But among Mormons, in the days of their emigrations, it meant a 'rut dug deeply in the slope.' According to David Lavender in *One Man's West*, 'the inside wheels of the wagons fitted into this slot so snugly that the vehicle could not fall out – maybe.' The ultimate dugway descends 1,800 vertical feet from the hole in the rock to the Colorado River; it served as the main route for Mormon settlers to reach south-eastern Utah.

dulce (1) In the south-west, a sweet, a dessert, especially a candied fruit or similar confection. *Pan dulce* is a sweet bread or roll. (2) south-western Anglos have extended the word to mean sweetheart. From the Spanish word meaning 'sweet', it's pronounced DOOL-say, or no doubt often Americanised DOOL-see or DULL-see. The Americanisation *dulcie* also occurs.

dun A horse of yellow-brown colour with black mane, tail and socks and often with a dorsal stripe. (*See* buckskin for horse colours)

DuPont A brand name that became the common word among the mountain men for black powder, as Stetson and Winchester became common for hat and rifle. The manufacturer, E. I. Du Pont de Nemours and Company, was founded in 1802. The predecessor of modern smoke-less gunpowder, black powder was made from saltpetre, charcoal and sulphur, then caked and rolled into grains – fine for pistols, more coarse for rifles. All guns were fired with black powder until the 1890s. The shooter measured the powder into his weapon for each shot (though the measuring was often imprecise, especially when done on a galloping horse). 'Here's damp powder and no way to dry it' was an expression of the mountain men for a bad fix. Wet powder, of course, wouldn't ignite. Hobbyists are still shooting black powder today for fun and even hunting with it – the shooting has a spirit that's said to be addictive. (*See* powder horn)

Durham (1) A breed of cows also called *shorthorns* in the West. They were imported to interbreed with Texas longhorns and other cattle on the northern plains in the 1870s and 1880s, until Herefords became more commonly used for that purpose. (2) Short for Bull Durham, a smoking tobacco that came in small cloth bags, used a Durham bull as a trademark and was ubiquitous in the West after the Civil War.

dust As a noun, short for gold dust. As a verb, (1) To get gone, to leave in a hurry. In this meaning, it appears as to *dust along*, to *get up and dust*, to *dust for* and to *dust out*. (2) To move around quickly or in a spry way. (3) To cover a cow with powdered insecticide. (4) To fan a horse with your hat. [Adams]

Combinations: dust bag (a sack for gold dust), *dust blizzard*, *dust cutter* (a glass of whiskey after a dusty ride), *dust mulch* (a layer of dust used in dry farming to prevent evaporation) and *dust pneumonia* (a lung ailment of people and livestock,

usually in dust bowls, that comes from breathing air full of dust). (*See* dust bowl and dust devil)

Colloquial phrases: dust the trail (to travel), *have dust* (to get into a fight), *eat dust* (to get out-raced by someone) and *be out for the dust* (to have money as a motive).

dust bowl A piece of country often afflicted with drought and dust storms, bringing grief to farmers. When capitalised, it refers to a region of the south central plains in Texas, Oklahoma, Kansas, Colorado and New Mexico, where drought and dust storms ruined a lot of farmers in the 1930s.

dust devil A little whirlwind of dust or sand, such as can be seen anywhere on the plains and in the deserts. Also called *wind devil*, *dancing devil*, *Idaho brain storm*, *remolino* (Spanish meaning 're-grinder') and *sand auger*.

duster (1) A light overcoat, especially one made of linen, used to keep dust off. Now (but not originally) associated mostly with the West. (2) A dust storm or sand storm. (3) A dry hole, a hole drilled for oil that is unproductive.

Dutch oven A heavy, three-legged, cast-iron pan with a lid that cookie was always using over open fires, especially to make sourdough biscuits. The pan sat directly on coals and coals were heaped on top of it to cook the food from all directions. Dutch ovens were used by pioneers and cowboys alike because of their versatility, being useful as an oven, a stew pot and a frying pan. Named *Dutch* for either the Pennsylvania Dutch or the Dutch peddlers, it is still used today, particularly by packers and outfitters.

Dutchman In the West this term was not limited to the Pennsylvania Dutch (German and Swiss immigrants to Pennsylvania). It meant any European or, depending on the speaker, any European who didn't speak English and wasn't a Frenchman, Italian or Spaniard. Such a fellow was often addressed as *Dutch* or *Dutchy*.

dyno A miner's word for the fellow who handles the explosives. [Adams]

E

eagle bill A tapadero (leather toe fender worn on the stirrups). Probably so called because it looks like the beak of an eagle.

eagle feather The feathers and other parts of the golden eagles, and to some extent the bald eagle, were prized by most western Indians for their medicine, the qualities of spirit associated with the birds, especially swiftness, courage, prowess in hunting and war.

Single eagle feathers, tied to headdresses, shields and coup sticks, were symbols of coups. Ceremonial eagle-wing fans were (and are) made from 37 feathers of the immature golden eagle (preferably the larger feathers of the female). These fans are used in dancing, in healing (to gather and disperse smoke) and in various other religious ceremonies, including the sweat lodge and peyote meetings. Entire eagles were skinned and used as medicine bundles. Heads and talons were mounted on ceremonial staffs and dance sticks. Talons were used in necklaces or shields. Headdresses were made from the skin and head. Large numbers of feathers were used together in war bonnets, bustles and shields, to suggest the motion of the bird in flight; the fluffs on these were the eagle's downy breast feathers. Any part of an eagle awarded by a medicine man might become part of a medicine bundle. One-note whistles were made from the upper wing bone and used in war and in the sun dance. Feathers of the grey (immature bald) eagle were also valued, especially for war bonnets, and gave protection against the wearer's being wounded.

Some Indians raised eagles (often tethered) and plucked the feathers. Plains Indians usually caught their eagles by baiting them to camouflaged pits and grabbing their legs as they fed. This eagle-catching was done only by older men given the power by established practitioners. The catchers prepared by making medicine and did not eat or drink in the pits. They then traded the feathers to other members of the tribe. Found feathers were not used unless caught before they hit the ground. If a feather is dropped at a powwow, the whole powwow stops for a feather-pick-up ceremony. Feathers from live eagles are particularly prized for their power.

Some tribes (including the Choctaw and Cherokee) held eagle or eagle-tail dances.

Many traditions associated with eagles are still alive or making a comeback. Eagles and their feathers are protected by federal regulation, but native Americans can use them ceremonially.

ear The point of the upper flag of a tipi. The ears are held up by long poles and adjusted to control the venting of the smoke.

To *keep your ear to the ground* is to keep an eye out; it came from the plainsman's practice of listening at the ground for far-off sounds.

ear down To twist or bite the ears of a horse to get him to stand still; said especially of broncos, where one cowboy ears down the horse while another saddles it for a first ride. Horses that are often eared down and thus wary of having their ears touched are called *ear-soured*.

ear head A headstall with a loop for one of the horse's ears but without nose band, browband or throat latch; used only on well-broke horses.

earmark A cut in the ear of a cow that is made at branding and, like the brand, indicates ownership. Also called an *ear crop*. Used as both noun and verb.

Earmarks, not originally Western, became much elaborated in the West. Typical earmarks were the barb, bit (a nick in a cow's ear used as an earmark), comet split (looks like a comet), crop (cut straight off), double over-bit, double under-bit, ear tag, fanned split, full split, grub (entire ear removed), hack, jingle bob, key split (cut like a cotter key), over split, over sharp, over hack, over slope, over-bite, saw-set, saw-tooth, seven under-bit, seven over-bit, sharp, slope, slash, split (split in a horse's ear), steeple-fork, swallow-fork, under-bite, under sharp, under split, under slope, under hack, ear tag and tattoo.

These days earmarks have been replaced by ear tags.

Americans often use the term metaphorically – as in, 'he's earmarked for stardom' – without being aware of the original meaning.

Earth Firster An adherent (the organisation does not have members) of the environmental activist group Earth First! Inspired by Edward Abbey's novel *The Monkey Wrench Gang*, Earth First! is known for its strong and controversial positions and for the kind of direct action known as ecotage.

easy keeper A horse that thrives on any feed.

easy on the trigger Short-tempered; ready to explode.

eating irons Cowboy talk for silverware. [Adams]

eighty-niner A person who participated in the Oklahoma land rush of 1889 – 50,000 to 60,000 white people are said to have flooded into the newly opened lands on the day of April 22 alone.

ejido In the south-western border country, the village common. Borrowed from Spanish, it's pronounced ay-HEE-doh.

El Dorado Wherever in the West the adventurer imagines he will find his fortune, usually in gold; especially a place where gold has been discovered and especially California after the strike at Sutter's Mill. By implication the fortune is a will 'o the wisp.

The Spanish term means literally 'the gilded man'. Originally it was applied to a 16th-century chieftain of Colombia, who, according to legend, had his body oiled and then sprinkled with gold dust. Sometimes the English place name is now spelled as one word, *Eldorado* or shortened to *Dorado*. And sometimes it's pronounced el doh-RAY-doh instead of doh-RAH-doh.

elder In the Mormon Church, an office of the Melchizedek priesthood. Only men may be elders. Male missionaries are called elders; female missionaries are called sisters. The general authorities of the Church are commonly addressed as Elder (Smith, Jones, etc).

embarcadero A wharf or port; frequent in California place names. Borrowed from Spanish, it's pronounced em-bar-kuh-DAY-roh.

emigrant An American who left the East or South to settle on the frontier, especially the frontier that was not part of the United States in the first half of the 19th century and particularly one who went to Texas before its statehood, one seeking a new life in Oregon Territory, a Mormon who went to deseret (Utah Territory) or a California gold-rusher. Sometimes spelled immigrant.

Combinations: emigrant agent (a person employed by a railway or land company to promote emigration to the West), *emigrant aid society* or *company* (an organisation devoted to bringing anti-slavery settlers to the West, especially to Kansas), *emigrant cattle* (cattle not native to the country and by implication perhaps not hardy), *emigrant car* (a railway car set aside for transporting emigrants, usually at special rates), *emigrant gravy* (butter), *emigrant rate* (a special rate established by railroads wanting to populate the West to support their own operations – for instance, in 1869, $40 instead of the regular $75 from Omaha to California), *emigrant road* or *route* (a trail established by use for the passage of emigrants in wagon trains, especially the Oregon Trail), *emigrant train* (either a group of emigrants, wagons and livestock making its way West or a railroad train carrying emigrants) and *emigrant wagon* (a prairie schooner, a wagon carrying emigrants and their belongings West).

empresario A coloniser of Texas during its days under Mexican sovereignty. The government of Mexico gave these empresarios large grants of land in return for bringing in settlers. An individual settler was granted 4,428 acres (a *sitio*), which he could purchase from the Mexican government for a nominal fee. Borrowed from Spanish (where it means 'manager' or 'contractor'), it's pronounced em-pruh-SAHR-yoh.

empty saddle On a ranch, a sign of trouble. If the horse came home empty-saddled, where was the rider?

enchilada A tortilla with meat, beans and chiles (or some combination of these) rolled inside; tortillas stacked and covered with meat and chile sauce. Borrowed from Spanish, it's pronounced en-chee-LAH-duh.

The *whole enchilada* is contemporary slang meaning the whole thing, and the *big enchilada* is the *head honcho*, the boss.

encina In the south-west, especially California, the live (evergreen) oak, in contrast to the deciduous oak, which in American Spanish is called a *roble*. Common in place names, it also occurs in the form *encino*. Borrowed from Spanish, it is pronounced en-SEE-nuh.

An *encinal* is a grove of these oaks.

end town A town sprung up at the temporary end of the tracks of a rail line, especially the Union Pacific line west of Omaha. (*See* hell on wheels)

endowment A course in understanding the Mormon religion, undertaken by the devout. They are recommended by their bishop and stake officials and participate in a service of instruction where they pledge to keep the commandments of virtue, charity and tolerance and serve their fellow man according to the teachings of Christ. To complete it is to *receive your endowments*, given in a ceremony in a Latter-Day Saint temple. Before the temples were built this ceremony took place in an *endowment house*.

enemy One of the miner's names for the shift boss. [Adams] Also called a *gaffer* or a *shifter*.

engagé A French-Canadian trapper or canoe-man (often of mixed blood) who paddled wilderness streams to conduct the fur trade. The engagé was a trapper hired for wages, in contrast to a free trapper, who was on his own. (*See also* voyageur)

Ephraim A mountain man nickname for the grizzly bear, especially in the form old Ephraim.

Ermatinger money Currency issued in Oregon Territory in the 1840s and 1850s by the Hudson's Bay Company; named after Francis Ermatinger, one of the company's traders.

escopeta In the south-west, a muzzle-loading musket or a shotgun of a type old-fashioned even in the 19th century. Borrowed from Spanish, it's pronounced es-koh-PAY-tuh.

esposa In the south-west, an occasional word for wife (but *esposo*, husband, is rarely used). Borrowed from Spanish, it's pronounced es-POH-suh.

estancia In the south-west, a ranch, especially a big ranch. Borrowed from Spanish, it's pronounced es-TAHN-shuh.

estanco In the south-west, a government trading post or store. Borrowed from Spanish, it's pronounced es-TAN-koh.

estufa In the south-west, a big, circular, underground, ceremonial room of the Pueblo Indians, with a sacred fire. Only men lived there. Also called a *kiva*. Borrowed from Spanish (where it means 'heated room'), it's pronounced es-TOO-fuh.

euchred Outwitted. From the card game euchre, which, though not originally Western, was commonly played in the West.

excuse me, ma'am Cowboy talk for a bump in the road.

exoduster Originally a Negro who joined in the black migration to Kansas and other points west in the late 1870s; later a dust bowl refugee.

eyeball In early Texas, to cut off the upper eyelids of cows to keep them from going into the brush where their eyes would easily get scratched. *Eye openers* were little sticks used to prop the eyes open, for the same reason. But an *eyeballer* was a meddler.

F

face-licking A good time, with people extra friendly, as at a reunion.

factory (1) A combination Indian agency and fur-trading house of the type established and operated by the US government on the frontier from 1796 to 1822 with licensed agents appointed by Congress. Common trade goods were firearms, lead and powder, axes, traps, blankets, cloth, sewing materials, clothing, jewellery, kitchen utensils, food (such as salt, sugar and coffee), tobacco, pipes and wampum. The system was not intended to make a profit but to help pay for the operation of the posts and the maintenance of armed forces on the frontier and to make the Indians dependent on the white man, and thus more agreeable to white settlement. The main Canadian posts were also called factories.

The Indian agent, or the principal officer of a fur-trading company, at a trading post was called the *factor*. The head of a big post like the Hudson's Bay Company's Fort Vancouver was called the *chief factor*.

(2) After the Civil War, a Texas business specialising in hides, tallow and salted beef.

fag In cowboy talk, to get out fast.

fall-back A backward fall by a bucking horse. Trying to stand on its hind legs, it goes over backward. Also called a *rear-back*. [Adams]

fallen hide The hide of a cow that dies naturally. The custom of the Texas range was that this hide belonged to the finder.

faller A logger who fells trees. Loggers often say he falls them. He's also called a *feller* and a *sawyer*. Fallers worked in pairs.

false front A building with a front sticking above and to the sides of the principal structure; also, the façade itself. Sometimes in early Western settlements, the false front hid a tent.

fan (1) To shoot a revolver by holding it in one hand and with the other palm knocking back the hammer and letting it spring forward while holding back on the trigger. A method of shooting often used in movies and in practice but seldom by experienced men in a serious scrape. Also known as *flip-cocking*. (2) To wave your hat while riding a bucking horse.

fandango A Hispanic dance in triple time. Used by mountain men and later most Americans to mean any Hispanic dance or, by extension, any get-together of a crowd, even for a fight. It also had a verb form – to fandango someone, to throw a celebration for him.

fantail A wild horse, whose tail is ungroomed; the opposite of a shave-tail. (*See also* broomtail)

faro A gambling game played with cards and popular in the West of the 19th century. The name is said to come from the French word for 'pharaoh'.

In faro, the players bet on the order in which the cards will be turned over by the dealer. The cards were kept in a dealing box with wires like an abacus on top to keep track of the play. (Since this box usually had a tiger painted on it, to play faro was called to *buck the tiger*) The players could bet on any card either to win or lose (a bet to lose was coppered, that is, marked with a Chinese coin or similar marker). The dealer turned the cards over in turns of two from top to bottom, from the first (soda) card to the last (hock) – thus the expression from soda to hock. Both soda and hock were dead cards.

Principal faro terms are *behind the six* (the money drawer, usually behind the six in the layout), *blaze, brace, cage, call the turn* or *call it both ways, case, case-keeper, case card, copper the heel* or *the odds* or *the deal* or *the pile, cross colours, cutter, faro bank, from soda to hock, layout, one side against the other, paroli* (an Italian term meaning 'a bet of your original stake plus everything you've won'), *play the bank, play the evens, short faro, single out, sleeper, snap* (an improvised game of faro), *Spanish monte* (*a form of faro*), *strippers, sure-thing bet, tell box* or *sand tell box* or *snake tell box* and *twist the tiger*.

feather duster An occasional Anglo word (no doubt mocking) for an Indian. (*See* siwash)

feathered out Cowboy talk for dressed up. [Adams] Same as *decked out in full war paint*.

feed bag (1) A morral (nose bag), a sack with oats or other feed that fits over a horse's head. (2) A restaurant (by extension from the first meaning). Restaurants were also called *beaneries*, *grub houses* and *swallow-and-get-out troughs*.

feed off your range To be nosey, to inquire inappropriately into another person's affairs. [Adams]

fence-cornering Bucking in a zig-zag pattern, as certain fences run. Also called *fence-worming*. (For similar words, *see* buck)

fence-crawler A horse or cow that has a way of getting through a pasture or corral fence. Also called a *fence-breaker*.

fence-cutter A man who cut fences during the Western wars over fencing the open range. Usually big cow outfits fenced public land and the small farmers cut the fences, but sometimes it was the other way around. Fence-cutting often was the start of big trouble.

fence-lifter A goose drowner; a gully washer; a heavy rain.

fencing tool The modern cowboy's ever-needed tool, a combination cutter, hammer and pliers the size of a big pair of pliers. Also called *fencing pliers*.

A *fence stretcher* is a tool that stretches the barb wire tight before the cowboy staples it.

fender On a saddle, a leather shield between the rider's leg and the horse. Also called a *rosadero*.

fever line *See* quarantine line.

fiador A light rope used with a hackamore, usually of hair but sometimes of rawhide or cotton. It ties to the bosal (nose band) and acts as a throat-latch, holding the hackamore in place. A common corruption of this term is *theodore*.

fiddle An occasional word for a horse's head.

fierro In the south-west in the 19th century, a buying brand, the brand the new owner of livestock applied. When he sold animals, he put on a venta, a sale brand. Literally, a fierro is a branding iron. Borrowed from Spanish, it's pronounced fee-EH-roh. (*See* brand)

fiesta In the south-west, a celebration, a festivity with a Hispanic accent. Borrowed from Spanish, and pronounced fee-ES-tuh.

fifty-four forty The latitude many Americans of the 1840s insisted on as the permanent boundary between US and British possessions between the Rocky Mountains and Puget Sound. Their rallying cry was 'fifty-four forty or fight!'

fight the bit For a horse to toss his head when reined; for a person to act impatient, unruly. [Adams]

fighting wages Cowboy pay when there were rustlers to be rousted or range wars to be fought. Except when fighting wages were paid, cowboy earnings were low.

fill a blanket To roll a cigarette. To *fill your hand* is to draw your gun.

filly A young female not only of the equine but the human species.

fire In Indian Pidgin English, a group of related Indians, from a family to a nation. Thus the Dakota were the people of seven council fires.

Combinations: fire boat or *fire canoe* (a steamboat) and *fire box* (a stagecoach escorted by soldiers).

fire break A strip of earth several yards wide cleared to keep fire from spreading. Sometimes called a fire guard or fire land.

Combinations: fire boss, the boss on a large fire suppression effort; *fire finder*, a device used by spotters to locate forest fires; *fire line*, a strip of ground bared of trees and vegetation (similar in appearance to a hiking trail), made to prevent the fire from spreading; *fire sector*, a section of fire control line under the command of a sector boss; *fire tower*, a forest watch tower used to spot fires. An *escaped fire* is a *prescribed fire* that is burning out of specified conditions, a prescribed fire is a prescribed burn, and a *wild fire* is an out-of-control forest fire.

Among miners, the fire boss is an official who inspects the mine for gas each morning. He posts his findings on a blackboard called the *fire-board*.

fire escape Among cowboys, a preacher. (*See also* black robe)

fire out a brand To change it to show a new owner. [Adams]

fire steel A piece of steel bent by a blacksmith into a D-shape to fit around the fingers for striking against flint to create sparks to start a fire; thus the expression *flint and steel*. When the steel struck the flint, sparks fell on to charcloth, a prepared linen, and began to glow. Blowing and the adding of tinder soon gave forth a flame and thence a fire. Not originally a Westernism.

fireman Keeper of the fire, or *fire tender*; the person who tends the fire that heats the rocks outside a sweat lodge.

firewater A Pidgin Indian English term for booze. (*See* the introduction for a discussion of Indian Pidgin English) In the Indian trade, it was often pure alcohol cut with the water of the closest creek and seasoned with tobacco, red chiles and whatever pleased the imagination of the trader, according to rumour even snake heads. The term came from a custom developed by Indians trading with the Canadian fur men. The alcohol was customarily diluted, often with water from the nearest creek. The Indians, knowing that, would spit the first mouthful of booze on the fire. If it flamed, they'd trade for it; if it put some of the fire out, they wouldn't.

Booze (along with death and other central preoccupations) appears to have set the Westerner's imagination aflame. Other names for it include *aguardiente*, *base burner*, *boilermaker and his helper*, *brave maker*, *Brigham Young cocktail*, *bug juice*, *bumblebee whiskey*, *cactus juice*, *choc*, *coffin varnish*, *conversation fluid*, *corn*, *cowboy cocktail*, *de-horn*, *drunk water*, *dust cutter*, *dynamite*, *forty rod*, *fool's water* (a term of Indian Pidgin English), *gut warmer*, *honeydew*, *Indian whiskey*, *irrigation*, *jag*, *jig juice*, *joy-water*, *Kansas sheep dip*, *lamp oil*, *leopard sweat*, *lightning*, *lightning flash*, *mescal*, *mountain dew*, *neck oil*, *nose paint*, *Pass brandy*, *Pass whiskey*, *pine top*, *pop skull*, *prairie dew*, *red disturbance*, *red-eye* (and *hundred-yard red-eye*), *red ink*, *rookus juice*, *salteur liquor*, *scamper juice*, *scorpion Bible*, *sheep-herder's delight*, *shinny*, *snake-head whiskey*, *snake poison*, *stagger soup*, *station drink*, *strong water*, *strychnine*, *sudden death*, *tangle-foot*, *Taos lightning*, *tarantula juice*, *tiswin*, *tongue oil*, *tonsil paint*, *tonsil varnish*, *tornado juice*, *trade whiskey*, *valley tan*, *white mule* and *wild mare's milk*. (For booze's effects, *See* roostered)

first rattle out of the box Cowboy talk for quick.

fish What a cowboy called the yellow slicker he always kept (and still keeps) tied behind his saddle, so named because the trademark was a fish. Aside from keeping the water off, it served to cover his bedroll (sometimes called a *slicker roll*), to wrap gear in for a river crossing, to cover a pack and even to wave at stampeding cattle.

five beans in the wheel Cowboy talk for five cartridges in the cylinder of the six-shooter, with the hammer on the empty chamber. Cowboys usually carried their hand guns this way for safety.

Five Civilised Tribes An Anglo term for the Cherokee, Chickasaw, Choctaw, Creek and Seminoles, because these tribes, in the view of the whites, took up 'civilised' ways readily. The confederacy was established formally in 1843, with an inter-tribal code of law. Despite their being 'civilised', these tribes were removed from the south-eastern states to Indian Territory by carrot and stick, mostly stick. They confederated partly to form a united front against the 'wild' tribes of the Plains.

Since the tribes had black slaves, many of them sided with the Confederacy during the Civil War, and in retribution the federal government reduced their lands. Later, as a result of the work of the Dawes Commission, talks at the Sequoyah Convention and laws passed by Congress, the members of the Five Civilised Tribes became citizens of the United States and their lands part of the new state of Oklahoma, admitted to the union in 1907.

fix for high-riding To get ready to vamoose (go) quick, or to do something that will necessitate vamoosing quick. Other expressions with similar meaning are *flag your kite* and *jump a lot of dust*.

fixings Among fur men, possibles (essential personal gear). Also, food to prepare for dinner, material needed to make something, camp gear, the makings for a cigarette and any equipment or supplies you wanted it to mean, sometimes with the implication of something extra or fancy.

flag (1) To flag antelope was and is to decoy them close by waving a red bandanna or similar object in the air. Insatiably curious, antelope often come to a flag. (2) Among sheep-herders, to set out white flags or lanterns to keep coyotes away. [Adams]

Among loggers, *flag's up* was the call to eat. They called dinner *flaggings*. In rodeo, the *flagman* is the man who signals the start or end of the timing for a competitor.

Flandreau Indian One of a group of Santee Dakota who separated from the tribe, became Christian and lived at Flandreau, Dakota Territory. Dr Charles Eastman, the Dakota physician, was a Flandreau Indian.

flank A riding position alongside a trail herd on a drive – it's on each side most of the way to the rear. A man in this position is called a *flank rider*. The other positions (from front to back) are point, swing and drag.

At branding, *flankers* are men who work in pairs to throw and hold calves. When the roper has heeled and dragged the calf, one flanker grabs the calf's tail, the other the rope, and they jerk in opposite directions at the same moment. Down goes the calf. Then they hold the calf's legs and keep it down while others brand, earmark, vaccinate and (if a bull calf) castrate it. This sort of flanking can also be done by a single man: he reaches across the calf, grabs the loose skin under the brisket and jerks the beast off its feet. It's commonly called *wrestling calves*.

flank rigging In rodeo bronc riding, the back cinch (also called the *scratcher cinch*), which adds incentive to the horse's bucking. [Adams]

flapboard A board at the back of a chuck wagon that was let down on hinges to make a table.

flare In the oil patch, burning off oil from a well to let the workers know something is happening.

flash rider Cowboy talk for a bronc buster (or *peeler*, *fighter*, *squeezer* or *twister*); a fellow who makes shave-tails.

flasharity Cowboy talk for fancy riding clothes, those that are too fofarrow or fumadiddle – fancy.

flatboat The first principal vehicle of westward migration down the Ohio River. The 30- or 40-foot long boat was built cheaply, with heavy timbers and a kind of house on the deck. When you reached your destination, you probably took it apart and built your house from it, because it wouldn't go upstream. That's why it was succeeded by the keel-boat, which would go both upstream and downstream and was the instrument of expansion on the Mississippi and Missouri rivers. Also called a *broadhorn*.

flathead Among loggers, a lawyer. Spirited dislike for lawyers is old in the West – *son of a bitch stew* and *district attorney stew* are synonymous.

Flathead Indians A Salish Indian tribe who have been living in western Montana since the early 1800s. Their culture was like that of the buffalo-hunting tribes to the east. Though some north-western Indians did, the Flatheads did not flatten their heads; the name has several possible origins, including the sign language expression for them (two hands on the side of the head) and the fact that the heads of the slaves among them were flattened. They were also called the *Cat Indians*. The Flatheads were notably friendly to whites during the period of westward expansion and responded enthusiastically to the Catholic missionaries who came among them. Today they live in their home country on the Flathead Reservation in northern Montana.

flea trap Cowboy talk for a bedroll. Later a sleeping bag was a flea bag.

flea-bitten A cowboy's description of a white horse with freckles.

fleece (1) A mountain-man term for the flesh along the hump, ribs and spine of the buffalo. (*See also* dépouille) (2) The inner lining of a saddle, usually made of fleece or a similar product.

float gold (1) Gold in the form of flakes and dust washed down from the hills; the gold obtained by placer mining. Also called *floated gold* or simply *float*. (2) Gold that floated away – escaped – in the mining process.

float stick A stick the beaver trapper attaches to his trap. If the beaver swims away with the trap, the stick shows where it is. This stick is the source of one of the best-known expressions of the mountain man, 'he don't know which way the stick floats.'

floater A person banished from a tribe for a serious offense, such as killing another member of the tribe. Some Plains Indians still float people by action of the tribal council; the law they use to do it may be called a *floater clause*.

floating outfit A group of cowboys, usually half a dozen men and a cook, riding the winter range to brand calves missed at the roundup and to keep cows from drifting. Their chuck wagon was called a *floating wagon*.

flour gold Gold in very fine particles, ground fine as flour. Also called *flour dust*.

fluff duffs Hotel food, fancy food; the food women cooked back at the ranch to show the hands they weren't at the chuck wagon. Cowboys also called it *soft food*, *chicken fixings* and *throat-tickling grub*.

flume A wooden channel that brought water to a placer operation.

fly A sheet used to keep water off, especially at the back of a chuck wagon to protect the cook.

fofarrow Among the mountain men, trinkets, gaudy clothing and similar show-offy stuff. Thus Lt George Frederick Ruxton has one of his trappers complain, 'First I had a Blackfoot – the darnedest slut as ever cried for fofarrow . . . There warn't enough scarlet cloth nor beads, nor vermillion in Sublette's packs for [her].'

The word also took an adjective form – thus a woman might be described as *too fofarrow*. Adapted from the Spanish fanfarón (meaning 'braggart'), with perhaps some influence from the French *frou frou*, and spelled variously.

fog To move along fast, make dust, get along pronto, especially on horseback.

follow the tongue What a freighter did with his wagons. At night he would spot the north Star and point the tongue of the lead wagon to it for the right direction for the morning's travel.

fonda In the south-west, a restaurant or an inn. Borrowed from Spanish and pronounced FON-duh.

fool hen A common name (originally from the mountain men) for the sage grouse. The bird sits so still (for whatever reason) men can get close enough to hit it with a stick, stone or whip.

fool's gold Iron pyrite, which looks like gold. By extension any sucker's notion of riches.

foot-and-walker line A term for a stage line that made its passengers get out and walk – or push – across hard places in the road or up steep hills.

Forest Service The agency of the Department of Agriculture that administers public lands. The Forest Reserve Act of 1891 protected significant forested reserves on public land, not to prevent their being used but to provide for their conservation and wise use for the greatest number of people in the long run. Under the Department of Agriculture, the US Forest Service manages this land to promote multiple use – timber, water, grazing, wildlife, mineral development, wilderness, recreation and other uses.

forge For a shoed horse to hit its back hoofs against its front ones when running. It's a bad habit and makes a sound like the ring of hammer on anvil. To do this is also called *to anvil*.

fork (1) A tributary of a river. Thus the Lewis Fork, the original name of the Snake River, and Henry's Fork, its main tributary. Some Westerners have so forgotten the meaning of this word that state highway signs sometimes give streams redundant names like Henry's Fork River. (2) The front of a saddle tree, below the horn. (3) In verb form, to mount up. Sometimes it's a command – fork your horse, get mounted and ride. To fork a horse is also known as to *hairpin a horse*.

forked end up Where a rider may end up if he's thrown – on his head. Thus a man who speaks of being still forked end down means he's OK.

forked tongue To speak with forked tongue (a term of Indian Pidgin English) is to lie.

fort up To barricade yourself; to take a position defensible against attack, especially Indian attack. Emigrants forted up by driving their wagons into a circle. Mountain men sometimes killed their horses and forted up behind the bodies.

forty years' gathering What a cowboy calls his personal gear – sometimes it's a 30 years' gathering. A logger calls his a 50 years' gathering.

Forty-niner (1) A California goldrusher in 1849. A Fifty-niner is a Colorado front range gold rusher; a Sixty-niner is a Montana gold rusher; and a Seventy-niner is a Leadville, Colorado gold rusher. (*See* eighty-niner) (2) A person who advocated the 49th parallel as the final boundary between US and British territory in the north-west.

forty-rod Booze. (*See* firewater)

Four Corners The place where Utah, Colorado, New Mexico and Arizona all meet. The surrounding area is called *Four Corners country*.

four directions The Indian Pidgin English term for the four main directions of the compass; also called the *four winds*.

The four directions are integral to the religions of many Indians – pipes are ritually offered to the sky, the earth and the four directions. The directions appear often in Plains Indian art in *four-directions wheels*, circles of quillwork or beadwork. They also have colours and themes associated with them: west is often black, home of the thunder beings, and of middle age; north is white, home of the white giant, and of old age; east is red, home of the eagle, the sun, the dawn, the new day and birth; south is yellow, where you are coming from, spring. The colours associated with sky and earth are often blue and green. The contemporary shaman Wallace Black Elk says, 'The "power of the Four Winds" is the power over space.'

four-flusher A trickster, a bluffer. It comes from poker and the daring experience of bluffing that you have a flush when you have only four cards of the suit.

fox *See* sauk.

fraggle In Texas, to rob.

fraidy hole Where you go to get away from a tornado; a storm cellar or cave.

freak What a cowboy calls a man who is reluctant to work or is a complainer.

freddy Contemporary slang for an employee of the US Forest Service; it has a derogatory connotation when used by earth firsters.

free grass The public range; open range; the paradise for cattlemen that was the original Great Plains. The intrusion of private ownership and fences forced some of the most fundamental changes of the 19th century West. It also led to range wars. The big cattle companies needed their free grass and did their damnedest to keep farmers and small ranchers out. If a fellow owned the land right around the water source, he could control the range for many square miles around. An advocate of cowmen running critters on the public grass was called a *free-ranger*.

Combinations: free lunch, the custom (apparently started in California in the early 1850s) of taverns' providing free food at noon to those buying drinks; *free trader*, an independent fur trader (rather than a trapper), not outfitted by one of the large fur companies. (*See* free trapper)

free trapper A beaver man who went it alone instead of working for one of the fur companies. He was usually a fellow, French-Canadian or American, who had begun in the trade as an employee, acquired his skills and struck out on his own. Some still had to get outfitted by the big companies and so were obliged to sell their plews (beaver skins) to their creditors; others were completely free. Their opposite number was the engagé (hireling).

Free trappers sometimes worked in small groups of coequals but often travelled with the large company brigades, where their savvy made them welcome. They were the zenith of one line of development of the North American frontiersman, celebrated by writers such as Washington Irving. Many also became nearly as Indian as white, with native wives, children, languages and customs and suffered notably with the flooding of whites into the West.

freeze-out A winner-take-all variety of poker. Each player stayed until broke, the last man getting everything.

freight train A caravan of prairie schooners or other wagons, often 10 to 20, enough to provide defense against whatever Indian opposition might be expected. The crew was a captain and several lieutenants (or in the Hispanic world a *caporal* and several *capitans*), a wrangler, a night-hawk, the drivers (muleskinners for a mule train, bullwhackers for a bull train) and swampers, who were men-of-all duties.

Trains moved mornings and evenings and nooned through the worst heat of the day. A bull train, one drawn by oxen, would average 12 miles a day on a fair trail, a train drawn by mules half that much again. Oxen were slower but surer and could carry more freight because they thrived on grass alone. Mules were faster but delivered less load and needed corn.

Also called a *freight outfit*. (*See also* jackass mail)

freight your crop To get liquored up and kick up your heels; to go on a bender. (*See* roostered)

fremontia Another name for greasewood, named after the Western explorer John C. Frémont. A variety of cotton-wood tree, holly-grape, herb, pine tree and pine squirrel are also named after him.

Frenchman Usually in the West, not a Gaul but a French-Canadian of mixed blood. The term was common among the mountain men and probably did not reflect the scorn for other cultures characteristic of many later Westerners.

The French-Canadians (sometimes called Franco-Canadians) preceded the Americans in the Western beaver trade, explored much of the country, learned the native peoples and developed many of the ways. They brought many words to the mountain man's vocabulary, including *appola, bois d'arc, boudins, carcajou, coulee, engagé, hivernant, mangeur de lard, parfleche, plus* and *voyageur*.

freno Either the whole bridle or just the bit. Borrowed from Spanish, and pronounced FRAY-noh.

fresno A buck scraper; a scoop used to move earth to build a dam. Drawn by horses, it looked like a wheelbarrow without a wheel. It took its name from the Fresno Agricultural Works in Fresno, California.

fried chicken Cowboy talk for bacon that's breaded and fried. [Adams]

friendly An Indian who wasn't a hostile. Sometimes it meant an Indian like the Lakota leader Red Cloud or the Shoshone chief Washakie, men who decided with independence and integrity on a road of peace and even accommodation with the white man. Sometimes it meant an Indian who was fighting on the white side temporarily to get back at hereditary enemies. Often it meant a hang-around-the-fort Indian, who was unfaithful to his own traditions, not walking his good red road.

frijol A bean. When pinto beans are boiled and then mashed and fried with lard, they are *refried beans* (frijoles), a favourite of the Hispanics and known to Anglos primarily through Mexican restaurants. In Texas, they are sometimes called redundantly frijole beans. Borrowed from Spanish, it is pronounced free-HOHL (plural free-нон-les) and spelled in English variously. For the names cowboys called beans, *see* whistle-berry.

frog-eye pudding Cowboy talk for tapioca pudding.

frog walk A form of mild bucking in short hops, not likely to throw a rider. (*See* buck)

from who laid the chunk Descriptive of something terrifically well done. Ramon Adams cites the example 'He burned the breeze from who laid the chunk,' meaning 'He rode very fast.'

front-door puncher Cowboy talk for a cowpuncher who spends all his time in town. [Adams]

frontiersman A man knowledgeable in the outdoor ways of the Western wilds (surprisingly, apparently not of the East or the Middle Border).
Combinations: Frontier Colt (a model of Colt revolver popular in the Far West after 1873), *frontier day(s)* (a celebration of the ways of the old West, usually annual; one of the best known is held in Cheyenne, Wyoming each July) and *frontierism* (an expression or custom of the frontier, often by implication crude or barbarous).

froze To yearn for something, to have a powerful itch for it. Thus hungry mountain men spoke of being froze for meat. It rarely or never occurs in the form *freeze*.

fry bread A deep-fried puffy bread usually associated with Indians. Originating in the south-western tribes, it has become pan-tribal. Also called *fried bread*.

frying size A cowboy's description of a kid or a small man.

full house A very good poker hand consisting of three cards of one kind and two of another. By extension, any good situation.

full sixteen hands high Descriptive of a cowman of integrity and ability. [Adams] The phrase comes from the conventional way of measuring the height of a horse, the number of hand-spans from the ground to the withers – sixteen would be sizeable.

full war paint Cowboy talk for dressed up, as to go to church; *feathered-out*. [Adams]

full-stamped saddle A saddle whose leather is stamped with designs. Aside from looking fancy, this stamping gives a rider's legs something to get friction against. Its opposite is called a *slick saddle*.

fumadiddle Descriptive of something fancy, frilly, unnecessarily extravagant, something faradiddle, something fofarrow.

fur trade The commerce in the skins of animals, which was a key impetus in the exploration and colonisation of North America. The main object of the hunt was always beaver, which was used to make felt, which in turn was made into hats. At various times other animals' skins were important in the trade, especially buffalo, deer and sea otter.

The search for beaver began in the early 17th century by the French in what later became Canada, and led directly to the exploration of that country all the way to the Pacific and Arctic oceans. In the United States it was a motivating force for westward exploration, and the mountain men roamed over most of the Far West before emigration or settlement were dreamed of. Russian ships plied the trade in otter skins along the north-west Pacific Coast starting in the middle of the 18th century.

In both Canada and the United States the quest for furs dominated relations with the Indians, and set patterns for later Indian-Anglo relations. Principal fur-trading companies were the Hudson's Bay Company, the Northwest Company and John Jacob Astor's American Fur Company.

When the silk hat became popular in the 1830s, the price of beaver fell sharply. Then buffalo became the centre of the trade, leading in the 1880s to the near-obliteration of that animal.

Many Western terms spring from the fur trade. (*See* beaver, engagé, free trapper, hivernant, partisan, plew and voyageur)

fusil A muzzle-loading musket of the type the Hudson's Bay Company and Northwest Fur Company traded to the Indians; a trade musket. Also called a *fuzee* and a *fuke*. It generally was not a weapon of high quality. The term is borrowed from French and is pronounced foo-SEE.

fuste In the south-west, a Mexican saddle or a saddle tree with cloth thrown over it. Borrowed from Spanish, and pronounced FUHS-tee.

fuzztail A wild horse; a mustang; an unbroke range horse with a bushy tail. (If it was broke, it would be a shave-tail) Also called a *fuzzy*, and to *run fuzzies* was to catch wild horses.

G

GTT *See* gone to Texas.

gabacho An epithet for Anglos used by Hispanics, usually disparagingly. Adapted from Spanish (where it originally meant 'French-like' or 'foreigner') it's pronounced gah-BAH-cho.

gaberel The tin horn used as a dinner bell in a logging camp. [Adams]

gachupin A south-western term for a Spaniard. From Spanish, it's pronounced gah-choo-PEEN. It may derive from a Nahuatl word that refers to the 'prickers' (spurs) worn by horsemen. Though J. Frank Dobie says it means 'an upper-class Hispanic', another source calls it derogatory.

gaff (1) To spur a horse. (2) Among loggers, the metal point on a pike pole.

gaffer (1) Among miners, a shift boss. (2) Among loggers, the general superintendent. (*See* supreme being for more logging terms for bosses)

gage d'amour A hide pouch that hung around the neck of a voyageur or mountain man and held his pipe. According to the 1840s British adventurer Lt George Frederick Ruxton, it was usually 'a triumph of squaw workmanship, in shape of a heart, garnished with beads and porcupine quills.' Originally, it was simply any token of love given a fur man by an Indian woman, but came to mean the most common of such items, the hide pouch.

gain Among miners, an amount of gold or silver mined.

galena The main ore for lead. This word was usually used in the West to mean the lead in bullets. Thus when the mountain man spoke of needing DuPont and galena, he meant powder and lead (and he probably formed his own balls from a bar of lead). When the frontiersman spoke of a *galena pill* (or *blue pill*), he meant a bullet: 'One Galena pill is no dose for me – come on with a whole lead mine.'

gall bitters A drink popular among mountain men. The recipe of plainsman Rufus Sage: one pint water with one-quarter gill buffalo gall. Sage describes it as 'a wholesome and exhilarating drink' and a sure cure for dyspepsia. Also known as *prairie bitters*.

gal-leg A spur with a shank shaped like a woman's leg, at least in the eye of a cowboy who hasn't been to town in a while.

galleta A south-western grass (genus *Hilaria*) popular as graze for livestock. Borrowed from Spanish, it's pronounced gah-YAY-tuh.

galling Cowboy talk for courting.

galoot A fellow, especially one who's a bit of a character.

gambusino A gold prospector, a small-time miner, even a fellow who pilfers gold. Borrowed from Spanish and pronounced gam-buh-SEE-noh. Also spelled *gambucino*.

game of the arrow A game George Catlin found the Mandan Indians playing in the 1830s. The object was to get the most arrows in the air at once. The term is an English translation of an Indian (probably Mandan) phrase. The game is still played among the Crow in a somewhat different form.

ganadero A south-western term for a cattleman. It is borrowed from Spanish and pronounced gah-nuh-DAY-roh.

Ganado red A bright red colour produced by an analine dye. Named for Ganado, Arizona, it was the first non-vegetable dye used by the Navajo.

gancho A shepherd's crook or a hook made of metal. Borrowed from Spanish and pronounced GAHN-choh.

gant up To get gaunt, thin, skeletal-looking. Said especially of livestock. Such critters were said to be *ganted* or *ganted down*.

gaper In card games, a tiny mirror the dealer holds, to sneak a look at the cards.

garbage can What a logger called a Bunyan camp, a camp with miserable living accommodations.

garment A white undergarment worn by Mormons that symbolises purity and modesty. It is worn by members who have received an endowment.

gate horse A rider posted at a corral gate to count cows, to keep them in or out or for any other reason.

gateado A dun-coloured horse striped like a cat, much like a zebra dun. Borrowed from Spanish, it's pronounced gahtay-AH-doh. (*See* buckskin for other horse colours)

gather As a noun, the cattle that have been rounded up.

gauntlet A cowboy's glove, generally sewn of buckskin, fringed and embroidered with handsome designs, especially (in Texas) with a star. Gauntlets were also sometimes decorated with beadwork.

geed up Crippled, banged up, out of action.

gente de razon In the Hispanic south-west, a term meaning people of quality, educated people, members of the upper class. Literally, it means 'people of reason', and it distinguished the so-called higher class from the poor, the Indians and others thought beast-like. Sometimes used in the short form alone, gente. Borrowed from Spanish, it's pronounced HEN-tay day rah-SOHN.

Gentile Among Mormons, any non-Mormon. It consistently means 'not one of us'. Shakers used it to mean non-Shakers. Jews use it to mean non-Jews.

gentle To break a horse, especially to train it gradually and with its cooperation, not quickly and roughly, as cow ponies were often broke. Horse trainers are sometimes called *gentlers*. Other horses are also called gentlers when they are necked (tied by the neck) to wilder horses in an effort to teach the wilder ones some manners.

Genuine Jimmy What a logger called a camp doctor, perhaps a corruption of Quinine Jimmy. [Adams] (*See* sawbones for other names for doctors)

geoduck The giant clam found on the entire Pacific Coast, eaten first by Indians and now by all. It gives the forms *geoducker* and *geoducking*. It is said to be a Nisqually Indian word and is pronounced GWEE-duhk.

get her made For a logger to accumulate enough of a stake to move on. [Adams]

get there with both feet To succeed in a big way. Thus a gambling fellow 'got there with both feet at the starting, and was eight hundred ahead once, but he played it off at monte.'

getaway money The cash a rodeo cowboy has at the end of one rodeo. He hopes it's enough to buy gas, sandwiches and beer until another rodeo in another town the next weekend.

getter A coyote trap that's now illegal. The coyote pulls on a scented wick and cyanide is injected into its mouth; often other animals are poisoned by it.

ghost bead A bead of cedar sold by Navajos today.

ghost cord A string tied by a bronc buster around a horse's lower jaw and tongue and used to punish him for bucking. Not regarded by Westerners as good horse-training technique.

ghost dance A practice and ceremony of the Indians of the Great Plains and Great Basin. Although it is now mostly associated with the Paiute prophet Wovoka (Jack Wilson) and the cataclysmic events among the Lakotas in 1890, it existed among Shoshonean peoples from a much earlier date in a form called *naraya*. Tradition says it was given to the people by coyote to keep away sickness and harmful events. New impetus was given to the ghost dance by the visions of the Paiute Wovoka during an eclipse of the sun in the late 1880s. In his vision, Wovoka was given songs and a dance that would make white people disappear and bring Indians back to their former high estate.

This religion spread quickly to the Plains Indians. The Lakota adopted it in 1890 and added a new revelation, a ghost shirt thought to protect the wearer from danger, even from bullets. The ghost dance excitement on the Sioux reservations alarmed many white people and led indirectly to the massacre at Wounded Knee in December 1890. The ghost dance ceremony was held as recently as 1974 and 1975 on the Rosebud and Fort Hall reservations, respectively.

Additional forms are *ghost dancer* and *ghost dancing*.

ghost town A town that is abandoned, or nearly abandoned. Evidently, it's strictly a 20th-century term. It is generally a mining town, widowed when the ore (or rumour of ore) played out. The terms *ghost cabin*, *ghost camp* and *ghost city* also occur.

ghost walks What a logger called payday.

gig (1) To spur a horse. (2) To swindle.

gila monster The only poisonous lizard (*Heloderma suspectum*) in the United States. This dweller of the south-western deserts stands a hand span high and a foot and a half or more long. He is nocturnal and shy and is coloured pink, beige and black. He takes his name from the Gila River in Arizona and New Mexico, whose valley he haunts. Gila is pronounced HEE-luh.

gilsonite An asphalt found in Utah and brought into common use by S. H. Gilson of Salt Lake City in the late 19th century.

gimlet To ride a horse so badly that you make its back sore.

gin To disturb cows, to make them move around unnecessarily, which chases the fat off them. Cattlemen will grumble at foolish hands who gin cows around. Similar to chouse.

giraffe A car used in a mine to hoist ore up inclines, 'absurdly called so,' says Charles H. Shinn's *The Story of the Mine*, 'because the hind wheels are very large and the front ones low, so as to keep the car level.'

girl of the line One of the many Western words for a prostitute. These women were called girls (or ladies) of the line because they did their business in tents lined up in cow towns, mining camps, railroad camps and the like. (For other names for prostitutes, *see* calico queen)

girth The Texas word for the cinch of a saddle. Pronounced *girt*.

giveaway. A custom among many Indian tribes of giving gifts freely to all as part of a ceremony (for instance, a naming ceremony). Shoshones have giveaways at funerals; among Pueblo peoples giveaways are goods thrown from the roof-tops into the plaza where the dancers are performing the ceremony. (*See* potlatch)

glance In mining, an ore with a metallic luster. Miners speak of silver glance, lead glance and so on.

go under To die. First an expression of the mountain men. Says the linguist J. L. Dillard in *American Talk*, 'The sign language . . . expresses die by moving one hand from above the other to below it. The mountain man's *go under* is clearly a verbalisation of this sign.'

Go over the range also means to die. *Go wolfing* is a term of early Western traders meaning to leave a body on the plains for the wolves. (For other Western expressions for dying, *see* cash in your chips)

go-devil (1) A logging sledge. (2) A wire from bank to stream, along which a bucket was pulled, hauling water. [Adams]

gomer bull *See* AI.

go-round A round in a rodeo, one sequence in which all competitors get an opportunity to compete in one event, such as saddle bronc. The winner of each go-round gets some day money (prize money for winning that day's event). Often rodeos hold one go-round in each event each day and on the last day match the top hands in the go-rounds.

goat (1) Antelope, a pronghorn. This usage is common both historically and today. (2) Sometimes a bighorn sheep. (3) For a horse to buck half-heartedly.

goddam (1) An Indian term for a white man (and for once really an Indian term, not a translator's word), naturally based on the white's frequent expression. (2) An Indian's term for a freighting wagon, an unceasing object of Anglo cursing.

gold The word gold yielded lots of Western combinations:

Tools used in gold-mining: *gold borer* (an auger), *gold canoe* (a cradle), *gold* (or *gold-mining*) *dredge*, *gold monkey* or *goldometer* (a locating rod), *gold pan* (a pan), *gold rocker* (a cradle), *gold separator*, *gold sluice* (a sluice), *gold washer* (a cradle) and *gold weight*.

Other mining terms, some of obvious meaning: *gold blossom* (gold-bearing rock detached from the vein), *gold camp*, *gold digger* (a placer miner), *gold digging*, *gold dirt* (pay dirt), *gold excitement*, *gold fever* (or *gold colic*) (the acute desire to find gold), *gold hunter* (*gold hunt* and *gold-hunting*), *gold mania*, *gold nugget*, *gold panning* (*see* pan), *gold rush* (and *gold rusher*), *gold seeker* and *gold strike*.

Miscellaneous combinations: *gold brick* (before it became a swindle and a way of avoiding work, it was a real brick of gold, a form in which gold was transported), *gold coast* (on the Pacific shore, a coastal area of northern California and southern Oregon), *gold fish* (a soldier's term for canned salmon served commonly in army messes in the south-west), *gold mountain* (the name Chinese immigrants gave to California) and the *gold spike* (a railroad spike driven at Promontory Point, Utah on May 10, 1869, to symbolise completion of the first transcontinental railroad).

gold dust Gold in fine particles, as commonly found in placer mining (panning and the like). Dust became an important medium of exchange in the second half of the 19th century, when Westerners were sharply suspicious of paper money (Confederate paper having proved worthless). This term was not originally an Americanism.

Gold dust gave rise to two combinations: *gold dust scales* (used for weighing the dust accurately) and *gold dust exchange* (where you traded dust for money).

Golden Bible The *Book of Mormon*, which Mormons believe was given to Joseph Smith inscribed on golden plates.

golden eagle *See* eagle feather.

gome A Papago Indian game somewhat like soccer, and the name of the ball used in the game, according to Cornelius Smith in *A south-western Vocabulary*. The ball was wooden and baseball-sized; it was not kicked but thrown with the tops of the feet.

gone beaver Originally a mountain-man term meaning trapped, dead – what a beaver was when it got trapped. Later it also referred to a man who got sick or fell in love or otherwise got lost or done for. Similar expressions are *gone coon, gone gander, gone goose, gone gosling, gone nigger* and *gone sucker*. Of these, coon and nigger were mountain-man usages.

gone over the range Cowboy talk for death. *Gone up* was an occasional term for killed. One source reports it as Denver slang, short for *gone up a tree*, that is, hanged. (For other terms for dying, *see* cash in your chips; for other terms for getting hanged, *see* string party)

gone south An expression of Indian Pidgin English for those who have died and are travelling the Milky or Spirit Way.

gone to Texas This sign hung on the doors of Yankee and Southern folks who decided they could do better with a fresh start. It was particularly a way of kissing lawmen and creditors goodbye. At first the expression was literal, later metaphoric. Often abbreviated GTT.

good enough for government work What a carpenter or other labourer says of a job that's good enough but not good.

good Indian Sometimes this meant a 'decent redskin', one friendly to whites; sometimes it meant simply a good fellow; most often, in the old West, it meant a dead Indian. Little Phil (General Phillip Sheridan) said when the Penateka-Comanche chief Toswai referred to himself as a good Indian, 'The only good Indians I ever saw were dead,' which over time became 'the only good Indian is a dead Indian.'

good scald Cowboy talk for a good job. Scald comes from dipping the pig in boiling water (to remove the hair) when slaughtering hogs.

good stick A successful mounting or successful breeding session. [Adams]

goodnighting An operation on the scrotums of bulls to help them on trail drives. Cattleman Charles Goodnight noticed bulls' testicles getting banged around on long drives; sometimes the testicles would swell, and the animal would have to be cut (castrated); sometimes it died. So Goodnight started cutting off the scrotum and sewing the testicles up tight against the body. This procedure worked well, did not even impair the bulls' breeding ability and was soon adopted widely, although it's seldom used today since it can sometimes cause sterility.

goosey Describes a horse or a man that's jumpy, nervous, unpredictable. As a verb, to put the spurs to a horse.

Combinations: goose moon (an occasional Indian Pidgin English term for the month when the Canada geese come back from the south, heralding spring), *gooseneck* (a hairpin curve in a river so severe that the stream bends back on itself, as in the goosenecks of the San Juan River near Mexican Hat, Utah; also a spur with a shank shaped like a goose's neck and head [Adams] and *gooseology* (the philosophy of people who were 'sound on the goose'[in favour of slavery] during the struggles about slavery in Kansas; why the goose was pro-slavery is unexplained).

gopher A burrowing rodent of the genera *Geomys, Thomomys* or *Citellus*, ubiquitous on the prairies (there are so many in Minnesota that it's known as the Gopher State); not the same as a prairie dog. The burrows gophers make were and are dangerous to horses and so to riders. By extension, a gopher may be a man who digs, either a miner or a logger who makes holes under logs for the choker. In verb form, to make exploratory diggings for gold on a small scale. The result is a *gopher drift, gopher hole* or *coyote hole*. A gopher hole also means a dugout (half-underground house) of the sort early settlers lived in.

gorper Contemporary slang for a certain kind of back-packer or other back-country goer, usually urban or with urban attitudes and with a romantic view of the wilderness and back-to-nature values. The teasing term comes from gorp, a trail food of mixed nuts and fruits popular among such folk. They're also called *hanky-heads* or *granolas*.

gospel sharp A preacher. The term is based (wonderfully) on the similarity to cardsharp. Also *gospel shark*. (*See* black robe for other names for preachers)

gossan In mining, an out-cropping of a lode, usually a rich one.

gotch ear A droopy ear on a cow, caused by ticks that weaken the cartilage. Also spelled and pronounced *gotched ear*.

gouch hook The pothook cookie uses to handle heavy lids. [Adams]

gouge In mining, a layer of soft matter alongside a vein, affording the miner easier access. But a *gouger*, in boating, was the bow oar of a flatboat.

government job What a logger called personal work done on company time. [Adams]

government trapper A hunter who works for the federal government, usually for Animal Damage Control in the Department of Agriculture. His duty is to reduce predators, mostly coyotes.

gracias Thank you. Spanish, of course, and now common, especially in the south-west; pronounced GRAH-see-uhs.

grain To scrape a beaver (or other) hide clean of flesh fat, or hair. The mountain men accomplished this task with a graining block, which the 1840s adventurer Lt George Frederick Ruxton described as 'a log of wood with the bark stripped and perfectly smooth, which is planted obliquely in the ground.' After graining, the hides were stretched and dried, often on hoops made of willow branches.

grama From Spanish and short for *grama grass*, any of the species *Bouteloua* common in the West. These grasses are noted for their nutritive value. Explorers and overland pioneers were often surprised to find that grama seems as nutritious when dry and brown in the winter as when green in the spring and summer. Also spelled *gramma*; not the same as gama grass, which grows from eastern Texas eastward.

grande Big, grand, great. This Spanish word, pronounced GRAHN-day, is ubiquitous in south-western place names (for example, Rio Grande).

This word also appears frequently in the West in its English cognate, grand, as in the Grand Canyon (of the Colorado, the Yellowstone, the Snake or the Arkansas rivers). One of the two principal bands of the Pawnee Indians, the Chaui, was known to Anglos as the Grand Pawnee.

grandfather A term of the Lakota and many other Indians for the deity, often seen as embodied in the sun. Says the contemporary Lakota shaman Wallace Black Elk, Grandfather is 'the male aspect of the Creator personified by wisdom, the sky, light, etc., [the Lakota called him] Tunkashila.' Thus Nicholas Black Elk begins his well-known prayer in *Black Elk Speaks*: 'Hey-a-a-hey! Grandfather, Great Spirit, once more behold me on earth and lean to hear my feeble voice.' Also, among many Indians, a term of respect for any older man. Sometimes, in Indian Pidgin English, Grandfather meant the president of the United States. The healing stone of the Lakota is called the *grandfather stone*.

Grandmother is also a term of the Lakota and other Indians for the deity. Wallace Black Elk calls Grandmother 'the female aspect of the Creator personified by knowledge, the Earth, birth, etc.' Also, among many Indians, a term of respect for any older woman. Sometimes, in Indian Pidgin English, Grandmother meant Victoria, Queen of England.

granger What the cattleman called a farmer. The National Grange, the origin of the word, was founded in 1867 and was strongest in the upper Mississippi valley. The word *granger* was more common on the northern prairies and plains than in the south-west, where nester was more usual. In the days of the open range, farmers were often unwelcome intruders.

Granger formed several combinations of obvious meaning: *granger agitation*, *granger laws*, *granger legislature*, *granger movement*, *granger party* and the like. *Grangerism* meant the philosophy of the farmers' movement.

grapevine Short for grapevine telegraph, the mysterious way news appeared to get around on the frontier. The Indian equivalent is moccasin telegraph.

grass The word inspires a couple of fine colloquial expressions: *As long as grass grows and water flows* was a phrase that occurred often in treaties made with Indians, meaning 'forever'; forever came pretty quick. To *get grassed* means to get thrown off a horse. [Adams] (*See* dirty your shirt for similar expressions) *Grass-bellied* means bloated, big-bellied; and in *Lin McLean* Owen Wister used *grass-bellied with spot cash* to mean flush with money.

grass dance Historically a dance of Indian warriors using grass as a symbolic substitute for scalps. (It was also called the *grass lodge dance*) Now the grass dance is primarily a social dance at powwows.

grass fat A cow fattened on grass alone, without supplements; such a cow is called a *grasser*. (Once, having to eat beef from such a critter was regarded as a sign of poverty. Now it's fashionable for its leanness)

grass freight Goods freighted across the plains in wagons pulled by oxen, not mules. It was so called because oxen (bull teams) would feed on grass along the way. Mules had to have corn hauled along. Goods hauled by mules (called *corn freight*) got there faster but cost more. Ox teams were also called *grass teams*.

grass question The issue of grazing rights, an inflammatory issue in the days (approximately the 1880s) of the closing of the open range.

grass roots The soil just under the surface of the ground, where some optimistic miners predicted grass-roots bonanzas.

grass rope Originally a rope made from bear grass, later a rope made from sisal, manila hemp or any fibre except cotton.

Like the use of the double-rigged versus single-rigged saddle, dallying versus tying hard and fast, the grass rope versus the rawhide reata provides never-ending contention among cowboys. It also used to be a sign of where a hand got his cowboying education. Good Texas hands, Stewart Edward White reminds us in *Arizona Nights*, were 'addicted to the grass-rope, the double cinch, and the ox-bow stirrup.' Buckaroos and Californios went for the reata and single-rig. (*See also* lariat)

grass staggers The illness a horse or cow got from eating locoweed.

grasshopper (1) In Western steamboating, to pole a boat over a sand bar or shoal area with spars. Also called *walking a boat* (over a sandbar). (2) Short for *grasshopper plough*, which was adapted for breaking up the tough sod of the plains.

gravel in his gizzard Descriptive of a brave man. [Adams]

graveyard shift In trail-driving, the watch on the herd from midnight to two o'clock in the morning. Also known as the *graveyard stretch*.

Graveyard stew was a range term for milk toast.

gravy run In rodeo, a fortunate draw of critter, such as a horse that's a good bucker, making it easier to win. [Adams]

grazing permit Permission from a federal agency (primarily the US Forest Service or the Bureau of Land Management, but sometimes the National Park Service, US Fish and Wildlife, and even the Department of Defense) for a stockman to graze cows, sheep or horses on government lands. Such permits usually last for 10 years and are dependent on certain provisions, such as limiting the number of animals and the amount of time in a given area, maintaining fences and developing water sources. Most ranches in the West have grazing permits since they have insufficient land to grow hay and graze cattle in the summer. Permits, also known as *grazing allotments*, are theoretically available to anyone, but in practice existing allotments are continued, and the permits are 'sold' with a ranch, although the permit is always the property of the US government. Grazing on public land is a bone of contention between the environmental and agriculture communities; a rallying cry for environmentalists is 'Cattle free by '93'. (*See* animal unit)

grease joint A cowboy term for a restaurant, which he also calls a *beanery*, *feedbag*, *grub house*, *nose bag* or *eat-and-get-out trough*.

To *grease the skids* was what loggers did to make the logs move more easily down the skid road (the path or road from the forest to the loading point). Now, by figurative extension, what anyone may do to facilitate another fellow's fall.

greaser Now a derogatory Anglo name for any Mexican.

The term dates at least to 1836 in Texas. In historic usage, it appears to have meant not just any Hispanic but a male of the lower classes. Yet there are also references to 'greaser girls'.

Some uses may indicate that the term wasn't always demeaning. Two army wives, Teresa Vielé and Libby Custer, appear to use it relatively innocently. Vielé wrote of Texas in the 1850s in *Following the Drum:* 'One Mexican girl, as she milked her goats, talked and smiled most coquettishly, the while showing her beautiful eyes and teeth to great advantage to a "greaser", who evidently appreciated her charms! His slouched sombrero and enormous black moustache, with traces in his dress of the picturesque garb of Spain, produced an exceedingly artistic effect.'

The etymology of greaser is uncertain. One folk version: The Red River carts had wooden wheels on wooden axles, and they squealed like the devil. A Mexican would walk alongside and constantly grease the axle, thus he was a greaser, a job suited only for a flunky. On the other hand, Lt George Frederick Ruxton, who travelled in Mexico and New Mexico in the 1840s, traces the term to the Mexican-Spanish *pelado*, meaning 'peasant' or 'ill-bred person'.

Greaser also came to mean 'the Mexican-Spanish language'. The cowboy was also likely to call Hispanics *bean-eaters, chilis, chili-eaters, Mexicanos, never-sweats, oilers, pelados, pepper guts, shucks, spicks, sun-grinners* and (when the Mexicans are cowboys) *vaqueros*. Most of these names have been spoken in the past in a spirit of denigration, a spirit that needs to die.

Greaser madhouse was what cowboys termed Mexican brands, which were elaborate, and were also known as maps of Mexico. New Mexico was occasionally called, derisively, *Greaserdom*.

greasewood A name for various resinous shrubs (especially of the goosefoot family, *Sarcobatus vermiculatus*) abundant in the arid parts of the West. Also called *toroso*. (*See* creosote bush)

greasy sack outfit A small cow outfit (cattle ranch). The name got started because little outfits had their cowhands carry their food to roundup in sacks tied behind the cantle. Outings by such riders became known as *greasy sack rides*.

Great Basin The interior West, the central part of the continent between the Rockies and Sierra Nevada; more strictly, those areas of eastern California, Nevada, south-eastern Oregon and western Utah that do not drain to the sea – the rivers end in sinks (dry lakes) and marshes.

The Great Basin Desert is one of the four desert types in the United States. It's characterised by cold winters, high elevations and rainfall of four to ten inches. Sagebrush, shadscale, rabbit brush and winter fat are the dominant plants; there are no cactus except the smaller species of prickly pears. Home of the sage grouse and the pronghorn antelope, it is far from the classic desert.

The Great Basin had Indian cultures distinct from those in the surrounding regions. The Indians were primarily what the whites called Diggers, Shoshones and Paiutes who maintained a pre-horse culture and subsisted primarily on roots and other vegetables that they gathered.

great divide The boundary of life and death. To *cross the great divide* is to die. Divide here is a metaphoric extension of the word for a ridge that separates two watersheds. (For other Western expressions for dying, *see* cash in your chips)

Great Plains The steppes of the American West, the region between the prairies and the Rocky Mountains from the provinces of Canada to Texas. Generally considered to start at about the 100th meridian, they are defined principally by aridity: If there's enough moisture for farming, it isn't the Great Plains. Anglos at first didn't appreciate this area, calling it the Great American Desert, the name given by Major Stephen H. Long after his 1820 exploring expedition to the Rocky Mountains; for decades afterwards, Americans thought of the plains as a barren wasteland, untillable and useless. Promotion by the states, territories and railroads eventually changed this idea. Despite setbacks because of periodic droughts, irrigation and dry farming have turned the Great American Desert into a huge producer of beef and wheat. Ian Frazier celebrated the plains in *Great Plains* (1989).

Less strictly, the term sometimes includes the prairies as far east as the Mississippi River Valley.

great spirit American Indian Pidgin English for the chief deity, also called *great spirit father* and the *great mystery*, with or without capitals. In this language, great meant 'grand' or 'important', as in *great white father* for the president of the United States, *great water* for the ocean and *great medicine* for a big mystery or impressive machine.

Since *great spirit* was a term of Indians speaking a sort of English to white men or of translators rendering Indian languages to white men, it is not to be trusted as reflecting anything genuinely Indian in philosophy or religion. From Indian attempts to convey something of their religion to unsympathetic ears came this great spirit, a creation who also goes by the name *Manitou*.

Great spirit necessarily implied a simple monotheism only to Christians eager to hear that and nothing more. George Bird Grinnell, for instance, in his seminal study *The Cheyenne Indians*, writes: 'The Cheyennes say there is a principal god who lives up above – Heammawihio – and that there is also a god living under the ground – *Ahk tun o' wihio*. Both are beneficent and they possess like powers. Four powerful spirits dwell at the four points of the compass. In smoking, the first smokes are offered to these six

powers.' Though other Indian religions often identify a creator, they also commonly identify two principal deities.

green corn dance An important annual ceremony of the Creek and Cherokee Indians and other tribes originating in the south. It lasted up to eight days and was a time of renewal of the spirit and making new possessions such as clothes. Also called the *green corn ceremony, feast* or *festival*.

Green River knife The knife of the beaver men, according to Lt George Frederick Ruxton in *Life in the Far West* (1848) and much popular history since. Some people have thought the knife was named after that beaver haven of the mountain men, the Green River, one of the great streams of the West, or that it was manufactured at Green River, Wyoming (half a century before that town existed).

Recent research indicates that the knife of the heyday of the Rocky Mountain beaver trade, 1820–40, was a knife made by John Wilson and that the Green River knife, manufactured at the Green River works of John Russell on the Green River in Massachusetts, came to the mountains in the 1840s. Other manufacturers stamped their blades Green River to exploit the popularity of the Russell knife, which was of high quality. The initials GR on a British trade knife of the 1820s actually stood for Georgius Rex, king of England.

Up to the Green River became an expression of the 1840s meaning 'to the hilt' (in the sense of all the way), because that's where Green River was stamped on the blade. And to *go up Green River* was to die.

green up What the grass does in the spring. Also used as a noun, as in *come greenup*, meaning 'come spring'.

green-broke Descriptive of a horse that's only had the kinks taken out of it, that is, has been ridden only once or twice and so is apt to be hard to control. (*See* break a horse)

greener A fellow who doesn't know his way around the West yet; a *green hand*, a *greenhorn*, a *juniper*, a *gunsel*, a *pilgrim*, a *tenderfoot*, what was known during the time of the mountain men as a *mangeur de lard* (pork-eater), the opposite of an *alkali* or *sourdough*. The word also appeared in the form *greeny*.

Greeners have been the source of a lot of fun among Westerners. To *string a greener* means to play a trick on one, such as putting a snake in his bedroll.

Grindelia A range shrub named after the Russian botanist David Hieronymus Grindel. One plant of the *Grindelia* genus, curly-cup gumweed, is used in the treatment of swelling caused by poison oak or poison ivy.

gringo A derogatory word of southwestern Hispanics for an Anglo, a stranger, someone who doesn't speak Spanish; the reverse angle of greaser. Various folk etymologies for the word have been offered – short for 'greens go home' during the Mexican War (Americans had green uniforms) and a shortening of 'Green Grow the Lilacs' (a favourite American song during the same war). A form of the word originated in Spain in the late 18th century. In Malaga, the word *greigo* (Greek) referred to people speaking Spanish with a foreign accent; the word may have been transformed into *gringo*. The etymology remains uncertain.

grizzly bear The great American bear, huge, quick, immensely strong, dangerous, and damned hard to kill. Teddy Roosevelt argued that this magnificent creature, and not the bald eagle, should have been the national emblem of America.

Its scientific name is *Ursus arctos horribilis* (and even the name strikes fear); some of its common names are *Old Ephraim*, *Old Caleb*, *silver-tip*, *white bear*, *yellow bear* and just plain *griz*. The species used to inhabit North America from Alaska to Mexico. The version that still roams Wyoming, Montana and Idaho can run as much as 1,000 pounds; the Canadian and Alaskan grizzly, sometimes called a *brown bear*, goes half again that big. Its fur is often tipped with silver (grizzled), and its back is humped. The critter feeds largely on vegetation and carrion and also kills for meat.

Indians of the plains and mountains respected the bear hugely – those with the courage to fight and kill a bear wore its claws in a necklace. To the first whites into the country, the mountain men, the bear quickly became legend. One of the great tales of the West is how trapper Hugh Glass fought a grizzly in 1823, was left for dead by his companions in South Dakota, crawled a couple of hundred miles eastward to the nearest fort, walked west to the Rocky Mountains to take revenge on the men who abandoned him but in the end forgave them. John G. Neihardt and Frederick Manfred have written splendid books, respectively *The Song of Hugh Glass* and *Lord Grizzly*, from the Hugh Glass tale.

Nineteenth-century adventurer Lt George Frederick Ruxton expressed in *Ruxton of the Rockies* the admiration of whites and Indians for the bear: 'The grizzly bear is the fiercest of the *ferae naturae* of the mountains. His great strength and wonderful tenacity of life render an encounter with him anything but desirable, and therefore it is a rule with the Indians and white hunters never to attack him unless backed by a strong party. Although, like every other wild animal, he usually flees from man, yet at certain seasons, when maddened by love or hunger, he not infrequently charges at first sight of a foe, when, unless killed dead, a hug at close quarters is anything but a pleasant embrace, his strong hooked claws stripping the flesh from bones as easily as a cook peels an onion.

Those of us who go into the backcountry in or near Yellowstone and Glacier National parks are still plenty wary of grizzlies. Sightings are frequent. And nearly every summer someone who's insufficiently careful is injured or killed by a griz. Unfortunately, the National Park Service has had difficulty finding a way to let the bears live free and still keep people safe.

Grizzlies are also chaps made of a griz skin with the hair left on. Grizzly was once a Western lager. In mining, a grizzly was a screen in a sluice that caught the larger rocks. The grizzly bear was a dance craze about 1910, preceding the turkey trot. And the *grizzly bear cactus* is a prickly pear, *Opuntia erinacea*.

groaning cart What a cowboy sometimes called a heavily loaded chuck wagon. [Adams]

grocery A sometime name during the 19th-century for a tavern.

Gros Ventre of the Prairie *See* Atsina.

ground apple What a logger called rocks in the section he was cutting.

ground fire In forestry, a fire that burns the combustible material on and in the soil layer along with small vegetation. A fire in the tops of the trees is called a crown fire.

ground hog (1) A logger's name for a tie hack who camped away from the main camp. (2) What miners called a truck that pushed cars up a grade.

ground money Among rodeo cowboys, money split equally among all competitors in an event because no one qualified and thus no one won.

ground-hitched Descriptive of a horse standing as though hitched with the reins on the ground. Many Western horses are trained to stand this way, and many a rider has had to walk home because he thought his horse was so trained.

grown stuff Fully grown cattle (as opposed to calves and yearlings).

grub An earmark that consisted of cutting off the whole ear of the critter. Grub, as in food, is not a Westernism but slang dating from the mid-17th century Britain.

Combinations: grub cache (stored food), in forestry, *grub felling* (felling by cutting the roots, which also is called *grubbing out* or *stubbing out*), *grub house* (restaurant), *grubliner*, *grub rider* or *grubline rider* (an out-of-work cowboy riding from ranch to ranch looking for free meals; also called a *chuckline rider*), *grub loco* (for a critter to nose at loco weed and try to eat it; critters who grubbed loco were called *grubbers*),

grub pile (among cowboys, stored food, a meal and the call to dinner), *grub slinger*, *grub spoiler* or *grubworm* (cook; *see* cookie), *grub wages* (pay just enough to eat on) and *grub wagon* (chuck wagon, a wagon carrying food and cooking utensils for cowboys).

grubstake The supplies needed by a prospector to go on a search for valuable mineral. The supplier took the risk of perhaps losing his money, and he shared in any discovery. He was known as a *grubstaker*, and so was the prospector he staked. The deed of putting up the supplies was called *grubstaking*.

grullo A horse the slate-blue colour of the sandhill crane. This crane, which inhabits Western marshes, is called in Spanish a *grulla*, and the word for the horse is also spelled *grulla* (and *gruya* and *gruyo*). The horse has a dark mane, tail and socks and often has zebra stripes or a dorsal stripe. When the colour is greyish, the horse is also called a mouse dun. It has a reputation for hardiness. Pronounced GROO-yoh or GROO-yuh. (*See* buckskin for other horse colours)

grunt What a logger called pork.

G-string A 19th-century name for a breech-cloth.

guacamole Mashed avocado. This south-western term has now spread throughout the United States. Borrowed from Spanish, it's pronounced gwah-kah-MOH-lee or gwah-kah-MOH-lay.

guaco *Cleome serrulata*, the Rocky Mountain bee plant. Its juice is used by Pueblo peoples to make a black pigment for decorating pottery. Borrowed from Spanish, it's pronounced GWAH-koh.

guage A south-western term for a gourd used for drinking, mentioned by both Josiah Gregg and Lt George Frederick Ruxton in the 1840s. Borrowed from Mexican Spanish (which got it from Nahuatl), it's pronounced GWAH-heh.

guapa Descriptive in the south-west of a woman who is both beautiful and sexy. Borrowed from Spanish, it's pronounced GWAH-puh; the masculine equivalent, which appears occasionally, is *guapo*.

guayacan A shrub or small tree of west Texas, *Porlieria angustifolia* or *Guiacum angustifolium*, used to heal various illnesses. Borrowed from Spanish, it's pronounced gwah-yuh-KAHN.

guayave A bread made by some Pueblo Indians from corn. It looks like a hornet's nest. Borrowed from Spanish, the word is pronounced gwa-YAH-vuh.

guayule A south-western shrub, *Parthenium argentatum*, that yields rubber. Recently scientists have experimented with using guayule, which grows wild over much of the south-west, as a potential commercial source of rubber. The word came to Mexican Spanish from Nahuatl and is pronounced wy-oo-lee. Another plant of the south-west producing an inferior rubber is *pingue*.

guerrillero A south-western term for a guerrilla, probably from the Mexican War for Independence, and by implication a raider or even a bush-whacker. Borrowed from Spanish, it's pronounced gayr-ree-YAY-roh.

guest ranch A euphemism for a dude ranch, now used everywhere.

guia A written permit allowing merchandise into Mexico; once used to admit American goods into that country on the Santa Fe Trail. Borrowed from Spanish, it's pronounced GEE-uh, with a hard *g*.

guisado A south-western term for a meat and vegetable stew, a south-western version of *pot au feu*. Borrowed from Spanish, it's pronounced gee-SAH-doh.

gulch A ravine; a deep, steep-sided gully, with or without a stream at the bottom. The term was especially applied to areas of gold diggings, as in Alder Gulch (Virginia City, Montana) and Last Chance Gulch (Helena, Montana).

Mining combinations: gulch claim, gulch diggings, gulch gold, gulch mine (or *miner* or *mining*), *gulch washings*.

To *be gulched* was to be trapped in a gulch, as sheep might be. To *gulch* was to mine in a gulch. If you hauled wood down the gulch, you said you *gulched it down*.

gullet The hole on a saddle just below the horn, often used when carrying the saddle by hand.

gully-washer A very heavy rain, one powerful enough to clean out the gullies or dig new gullies. Also known as a *fence-lifter* or a *goose-drowner*.

gum plant A range shrub of the species *Grindelia*. Used to treat bronchial afflictions and poison ivy.

gum rocker In a sluicing operation, a split, hollowed log below the sluice box and splint basket that received the gravel. (*See* placer)

gumbo A soil (primarily of the northern plains) that gets gummy and sticky when wet. According to Sinclair Lewis in *Free Air*, it is 'mud mixed with tar, fly-paper, fish glue, and well-chewed, chocolate-covered caramels. When cattle get into gumbo, the farmers send for the stump-dynamite and try blasting.'

gummer A horse with the teeth worn down to the gums.

gun In the West, a pistol, not a rifle.

Combinations: Gun battle and *gunplay*, as far as the evidence shows, are strictly modern terms for a *gun-fight* (which first appeared in the very late 1800s and means 'a shooting affray'). (*Gun-fighter* appeared about the same time, *gun-fighting* a generation later) Evidence does not appear to confirm a distinction sometimes made between *gun-fighter* and *gun-man*, that the first is a good fellow, the second a badman; the first use of *gun-man* is in 1903 – in a New York newspaper. *Gun hand*, meaning the hand you shoot a pistol with, is about the same date. *Gun toter* (a man who carries a gun) and *gun-toting* come from the 1920s. An authentically old term is *gunsman*, which was used on the frontier of the Revolutionary period but was probably not restricted to the use of pistols. Cowboys sometimes called a gunman a *gunny* or a *gun shark*. *Gun-slinger* is another word for gun-fighter.

The *gun-man's sidewalk* is said to have been the middle of the street, for visibility. [Adams] *Gun-shy* was cowboy talk for cowardly. *Guns on the table* is descriptive of something fair, above board. [Adams] *Gun wadding* was cowboy talk for white bread. *Gun cap* is another name for a percussion cap.

The verb forms to *gun*, *gun after* and *gun for* are not especially Western.

Other Western names for a gun-fighter are *buscadero*, *leather slapper*, *pistolero*, *pronto bug*, *quick-draw artist*, *shootist*, *short-trigger man* and *tie-down man*.

gunning stick In logging, a pair of sticks attached to a tree to control the direction of its fall.

gunny-sacker What sheepmen sometimes called cowboys who attacked sheep herds with gunny-sacks over their heads.

gunsel A greener, greenhorn, pilgrim, tenderfoot; a newcomer, a fellow who doesn't know what's what in the West yet. Ramon Adams says that the word was invented at a California rodeo in 1938 by John Bowman to poke fun at a dude.

gusano The worm in the bottle of mescal, which reportedly concentrates the alcohol in its body. It's very macho to eat it after draining the bottle.

gut hammer A logger's term for the triangle the cook dings to call dinner.

gut twister A horse that bucks well. [Adams]

gyp Alkaline water, brackish water not fit for drinking. A well of such water is called a *gyp well*. Getting sick from drinking it is called *getting gypped* (but *gypped* also means drunk). Bad water is called *gyppy*.

gypo A small logging contractor; in full, *gypo outfit* or *gypo contractor*. The term was uncomplimentary originally. Also spelled *gyppo*.

H

hacienda In the south-west, a big ranch, especially one owned by a Hispanic; the main house on the ranch. Its owner is called a *hacendado*.

Hacienda now often refers to secluded Spanish-style houses that may even be in town, the implication being that the home was there before civilisation intruded. Borrowed from Spanish, it's pronounced ah-see-EN-duh or hah-see-EN-duh.

hackamore A halter with reins (mecate) and a noseband (bosal) instead of a bit, used for breaking horses and riding. It is a cowboy adaptation of the Spanish *jaquima* ('headstall'), which, is pronounced in a similar way.

The vaqueros (especially in Spanish California) developed the old method of breaking horses with a hackamore, a method sometimes still used. It takes lots of time but is said to yield sweet-mouthed mounts. They used the hackamore alone for some months, then got the horse used to a bit without reins and eventually graduated to a spade bit. A colt thus trained is called a *hackamore colt*.

hair A euphemism for scalp, especially among the mountain men. Taking scalps was called *lifting* or *raising hair*. 'Hang on to your hair' was a favoured mountain man farewell. If the Blackfeet went out hunting hair, they were seeking scalps, that is, at war. Sometimes *hair-lifter* was a joking name for an Indian.

hair brand A brand applied lightly (or through a wet blanket) so that it burns only the hair and not the hide. Rustlers put on hair brands so they could re-brand the animal after the hair grew back. Trail brands were sometimes hair brands. When grown back, such brands are said to be *haired over*.

hair in the butter Cowboy talk for a delicate spot.

hair off the dog Descriptive of a person who's experienced.

hair of the bear A mountain man expression for bulldog courage, and a high compliment.

hair pipe An Indian pipe whose stem was decorated with hair. Originally, it was made from conch shells, and prized. Later it became a trade item manufactured from compressed cow bone. In the late 19th and early 20th centuries this pipe was a symbol of wealth and prestige among Plains Indians.

hair rope A light rope made from hair taken from the tails of horses, too light for throwing but often used as a mecate.

half-breed A person with parents of different races, usually a white father and Indian mother. Though many Indians accepted half-breeds generously, some did not. Whites usually treated them as Indians and often said half-breeds combined the worst elements of both races. The term originated on the eastern, not western, frontier. Also called a half-and-half. (*See also* metis and Red River metis)

Combinations: *half-breed bit* (a bridle bit with a small curb and an uncovered roller), *half-breed legging* (a legging covering only the calf, popular among mountain men and often decorated with beads) and *half-breed scrip* (a certificate given to a half-breed in return for his land, entitling him to other lands).

hame-headed What a cowboy sometimes calls a stupid horse, which he also calls a *jug-head* and an *owl-head*. (*See* canner for similar names)

hand Another term for a cowboy; short for *cowhand*. By modern extension, a worker at anything. It is usually complimentary. As the Pinedale, Wyoming *Roundup* noted in 1988, 'If some[one] calls you a real hand, you know you are doing a good job no matter what it is you are doing.' Historically, *top hand* got to be a recognised rank. In Texas in the 1890s, says David Dary in *Cowboy Culture*, 'first-class' hands got $35 a month, 'top hands' $40 to $45. (*See also* buckaroo, cowboy, ranahan, vaquero and waddy)

hand game A hugely popular gambling game of many Indian tribes (and not only western tribes) played in teams. The Scots baronet William Drummond Stewart described it in his novel *Edward Warren*: '[Players were] seated in a circle . . . A small piece of carved bone, often taken from the body of a fox, was held by the gambler, who joining his closed fists together one above the other, could thus pass it into either, he then separated them and threw his arms wide apart, singing and jerking his body up and down, and again bringing his hands together, and changing or pretending to change the bone, the gamblers choosing only when the hands were held wide apart. If the guess is right, the guesser pulls away his pile with that of the bone holder, previously arranged beside it. If inclined, a new bet is made.'

Also called the *stick dice game*, *stick poker* and *Indian poker*.

handcart company A name given to groups of Mormons who emigrated to Utah in the 1850s and 60s, toting their belongings in hand-pulled carts. They sometimes suffered terrible hardships and became legendary in Mormon history. Some non-Mormons also crossed the Great Plains with handcarts, for instance, some gold-rushers to Denver in 1859. The word also takes the form *handcarter*.

hang To catch trout with the bare hand. The technique was to ease one hand under the fish, gently stroke toward the gills, grab it in the gill region and throw it on to the bank.

hang-around-the-fort Indian An Indian who spent most of his time around a trading post; by implication, he or she had abandoned some of his traditional ways and might have descended to drunkenness, prostitution, begging or the like.

happy hunting ground An Anglo phrase for the presumed Indian version of heaven; often jocular. By extension, the Christian heaven. Also by extension, any ideal situation, such as a treasure trove of rare books for a bibliophile.

happy jack Cowboy talk for a lamp made of a tin can and a candle. (Compare *bitch*)

hard chink Hard money, minted coins, the most common money of the West, where paper currency was distrusted. [Adams]

hard goods Among the Navajos, a term taken to mean coins, jewellery and other durable objects of accepted value.

hard-mouthed Descriptive of a horse with a mouth unresponsive to the bit.

hard-rock stiff A miner who works the big rock formations underground. Also called a *hard-rock man* or simply a *rocker*.

hard-wintered Run down, in poor circumstances, as though after a hard winter.

Harvey House Any of a chain of restaurants built by Fred Harvey to serve meals to customers on the rail lines. They are remembered in the literature for good food and good-looking waitresses. Harvey, a former railway mail clerk, opened his first eatery at Topeka, Kansas on the Atchison, Topeka and Santa Fe line in 1875. Later his son Ford expanded the line to include hotels and railway dining-car service.

hasher One of a logger's names for a cook, whom he also calls a *boiler*, *dough boxer*, *dough puncher*, *dough roller*, *dough wrangler*, *grease ball*, *grease burner*, *gut burglar*, *gut robber*, *hash burner*, *hash slinger* (which also means a waitress in a hashery), *kitchen mechanic*, *lizard scorcher*, *mess boiler*, *mess moll* (if a woman), *mulligan mixer*, *pot walloper*, *sizzler*, *star chief*, *stew builder* and *stomach robber*.

Hassayampa From this Arizona river came a legend and a character. The gold rush on the river gave rise to the myth that whoever drank its waters, especially when drunk, would become a liar. Thus old-time Arizonans, when bragging or yarning, were called Hassayampers.

hasta la vista So long; see you later. In the south-west, a common Hispanic-flavoured substitute for goodbye. *Hasta luego* has the same meaning. Borrowed from Spanish, it's pronounced AHS-tuh lah VEES-tuh or HAHS-tuh lah-VEES-tuh.

hat Indian An Anglo term for an Indian who favoured what was thought of as progress. His stance was suggested by his wearing an uncreased government issue hat (a reservation hat). A *blanket Indian* favoured the traditional ways.

hatchet pipe Among the Indians, an implement that was both smoking pipe and tomahawk. Also called a *pipe tomahawk*, it was made by the English for the Indian trade. It was used both as a weapon and for smoking. When you sank the blade into the ground, you were left with the pipe, the symbol of peace – thus the phrase *bury the hatchet* as a synonym for making peace.

hatchetman A Chinese gangster, especially in San Francisco's Chinatown; also called a *high-binder*.

hatrack A name for a cow that's tick-ridden and a bag of bones or for a wide-horned cow, as in, 'look for that speckled cow with the hatrack.'

haul in your horns To back off, back down. *Haul in your neck* is another way of saying it.

haul out To get going (the opposite of haul up).

Havasupai A Yuman-speaking Indian tribe whose name means the blue or green water people. An agricultural people who also hunt and gather, they live primarily along the Colorado River, especially in the Grand Canyon. Living in isolation, they now make much of their living from tourism.

Hawken A muzzle-loading percussion rifle made by St Louis gunsmiths Jacob or Samuel Hawken from the 1820s until the Civil War. Though most Hawkens probably got to the mountains relatively late in the heyday of the fur trade (1820–40), they are celebrated in the literature as *the* mountain man rifle. The Hawken brothers adapted these rifles (known as plains or mountain rifles) from the long rifle for horseback travel in the West – they were heavy, sturdy, either full stock or half stock, often percussion rather than flintlock, with an octagonal barrel.

Some other makers of plains rifles carried by the mountain men were Dickert, Gill, Henry, Leman, Mills and Tryon. (*See also* fusil)

hay burner A horse, which is also called a *hay baler*; also a stove rigged to burn hay.

hay hand A man hired for haying season. Also called a *hay slayer*, *hay waddy*, *alfalfa desperado* and other teasing terms.

hay shaker Cowboy talk for a farmer.

haywire Messed-up, crazy; from the cow-country practice of twisting up loose wire before throwing it on the ground. A *haywire outfit* is a poorly run ranch or a logging outfit with poor equipment, which must by implication be kept together with haywire.

haze To chase cows, for instance out of a corral; to ride alongside a bronc and keep it from running into obstructions while the bronc buster is trying to break it. In rodeo, to ride alongside a steer and keep it going straight so the bulldogger has a chance at it. The rider who does the last two jobs is called a *hazer*. To *haze the talk* is to lead the subject in a certain direction.

HBC *See* Hudson's Bay Company.

head for the setting sun What a wanted man did when the law got close.

head gate In ranching, the main gate on an irrigation ditch.

head taster A ranch manager.

head-and-tail string A string of pack animals tailed up (their halter ropes tied to the tail of the animal in front).

header The team roper whose job is to throw a head catch (the other is the heeler).

Combinations: head and heel (a team roping event in rodeo, the steer being roped by the head and heels against time) and *head catch* (a rope throw on to an animal's head or neck rather than its feet).

headright In the Republic of Texas (1830s and 40s), a land grant to every man over 21. Similar in purpose to the Homestead and other land acts, but it required only surveying, not residency on the land (*see* homestead). It also means the right of Indians to their tribal lands and oil or mineral royalties.

heap A lot, very much, in Indian Pidgin English. Thus *heap hungry*, *heap scared*, *heap mad*. And a *walk-a-heap* might be an infantryman.

hear the owl hoot To kick up your heels with the help of whiskey; to have lots of colourful experiences. [Adams] (*See* roostered)

heart-and-hand woman A wife gotten from a matrimonial agency, especially from the publication put out by one such agency, *The Heart and Hand*. [Adams]

heat your axles In cowboy talk, to run fast. [Adams]

heathen Chinese A mocking term for a Chinese person that appears to have come from a line in Bret Harte's poem 'Plain Language from Truthful James'.

heel (1) To rope cows by the hind feet (which isn't done to horses); also called to *hind foot*. (2) To *heel yourself* or to *be heeled* is to get a gun, to be armed. Owen Wister reports that Doc Holliday warned Ike Clanton, 'Heel yourself and stay that way.'

A *heeler* is a roper who catches the steer by its hind feet. In rodeo, he works as a part of a team with a header against time. In a *heeling catch*, the loop is thrown so that the critter runs into the rope, and it is then jerked tight. It was and is commonly used on ranches to catch calves for branding and, according to David Dary in *Cowboy Culture*, was even used by California vaqueros to rope grizzly bears. Other principal roping catches are the pitch, slip, backhand slip, fore-footing, hoolihan and Blocker. (*See* blocker loop)

A *heeler* is also an Australian shepherd, a dog that works cows by nipping at their heels. *Heel squatter* is a name for a cowboy, who can get comfortable squatting on his heels. A *heel band* is the part of a spur that goes around the heel of a boot.

A *heel fly* is a tiny fly that lays its eggs just above cows' hooves on the back side and drives them crazy. *Heel flies* is sometimes a name for Texas rangers, who made themselves a nuisance with persistence. *Heel-fly time* is spring.

heifer brand A handkerchief on a man's arm at a dance, signifying that he's prepared to take the role of a woman and accept male dancing partners. [Adams]

hell around To raise hell, to pursue a wild lifestyle.

hell on wheels (1) A big, temporary town that kept moving westward with the construction of the Union Pacific Railroad, carried on freight cars to the end of the track. These towns consisted of one huge tent and lots of smaller tents and shacks, together with housing places for drinking, gambling, dancing and whoring, and sleeping as many as three thousand residents. Also called *end towns*, *end-of-line towns*, *hurrah places* and *towns with the hair on*. (2) A name for a horse that's hard to keep from bucking.

hell's half acre (1) A low dive. Also called a hell. (2) A rough piece of country. Many places in the West have carried this as a place name, including (temporarily) Yellowstone National Park's Middle Geyser Basin and the lavaflow wilds of Craters of the Moon National Monument in Idaho.

People could be described as *hell bent for breakfast* (quick, lickety-split); *hell for leather* (same as hell-bent for breakfast); *hell in his neck* (stubborn) [Adams]; *hell West*, or *hell West and crooked* (cockeyed); and *hell with the hide off* (strictly trouble).

hemp Cowboy talk for a rope; in verb form, to hang (someone).

Hemp fever was a morbidly jocular term for a hanging; *hemp party* meant the same. A *hemp committee* was a group of vigilantes or a lynch mob, depending on your point of view, and a *hemp necktie* was the rope they did the deed with. (*See* string party)

hen fruit A logger's name for eggs (as States fruit meant eggs from the United States). *Hen-fruit stir*, among cowboys, meant pancakes (which were also called splatter dabs). The *hen wrangler* was the chore boy.

hen-skin A feather-stuffed comforter.

Henry A first practical repeating, breech-loading rifle, .44-calibre, developed by Benjamin Tyler Henry in 1860 and made by the New Haven Arms Company. The Henry was the forerunner of the Winchester, for New Haven Arms reorganised as the Winchester Repeating Arms Company.

Hercules powder A miner's explosive charge, primarily nitrate of soda.

herd *Combinations: herd boss, herd guard, herd law, herd ground* (a herd's range, or where it was bedded down). *On herd* meant on duty watching the cows; to *keep cows under herd* meant to keep them in a group; to *ride herd on cattle* meant to watch them and keep them under control; to *be the whole herd* was to be a person of importance.

A *herder* was either a sheep-herder or a foreman of a Chinese railroad gang.

herd-broke Descriptive of a bunch of cows used to moving as a herd and so not requiring such hard riding.

here's how A frontier toast meaning 'to your health'. Derived from the Indian Pidgin English salutation 'How!'

Hereford The most common breed of Western range cattle today, red with white faces. Originally Herefords were imported from Herefordshire, England in the 1880s to improve the Texas longhorns.

Also a cowman's jocular name for the white shirt he wears when dressed up in a suit.

hi-yi A cowboy's interjection used to urge cows to move along.

hiaqua Among Indians of the Pacific north-west, shells and strings of shells used as money. Adapted from Chinook jargon, it's pronounced hi-AHK-wuh, with a short *i* like the one in *city*.

hickory A strong, durable cloth (thus *hickory shirt, hickory trousers*).

hidalgo In the south-west, a Hispanic landowner, usually an aristocrat. Borrowed from Spanish, it's generally pronounced by Americans with an *h*, hee-DAHL-goh.

Hidatsa A tribe with an agricultural economy that lived along the Missouri River in the Dakotas. Also known as the Minataree, the Gros Ventre of the Missouri and the River Crows, they had a culture similar to their neighbours the Mandans and spoke a Siouan language. (The Indians known to whites as the Crows were a group that broke off from the Hidatsa.) Reduced by disease and warfare with the Dakotas, the Hidatsa joined with the Mandans and Arikaras to form the Fort Berthold Reservation, where descendants of the three tribes live today.

hide drogher In 19th century California, a vessel that plied the coast transporting cow hides; a man who worked on such a vessel.

hide hunter (1) In the 1870s and 1880s, a professional buffalo hunter. Also known as a *buffalo runner*. These men killed the animals for their hides alone. (2) More broadly, any person who hunted animals for their hides.

A *hide buyer* was a person who bought buffalo or cow hides. A *hide camp* was a camp of buffalo hunters.

hide rick A stack of buffalo hides waiting to be sold. In the old pictures, these stacks are often the size of a house.

hide rustler A man who killed another's cow for its hide; also called a *hide thief*. The skin of a dead cow in early American Texas belonged to the finder. A *hide with a stovepipe hole* was a cowhide with the brand cut out, as a canvas tent may have a hole cut out for a stovepipe.

hide-and-tallow factory A pen where cattle were slaughtered for their hides and fat alone.

hideout A shoulder or hip pocket holster. A hideout gun was a small, concealed pistol.

high *Western combinations: high lonesome* (a big drunk), *high lope* (a fast lope on a horse, a gallop), *high roller* or *high poler* (a bucking horse that jumps high), *high-headed* (descriptive of a horse that holds its head too high, blocking the cowboy's view), *high-tail it* (to make tracks fast, to move fast, from the way scared cows run with their tails up), *high-line rider* (an outlaw, a man obliged to keep to the high country) and *high-grass constable* (a country lawman. [Adams])

high-centred Stuck on the centre of a two track in your car or truck. The differential hangs in the dirt and lifts the rear wheels off the ground.

high grade Descriptive of rich ore. A *high-grader* is both a fellow who works rich ore and a fellow who steals it, which is called *high-grading*.

high heel Among cowboys, to walk.

high plains The part of the Great Plains that mediates between the plains and the mountains. It is characteristically higher, more broken, steeper; marked by rimrock, buttes, mesas and other steep formations; drier even than the plains and even less suited to farming; treeless and subject to high winds; characterised by alkaline soil. The western half of Nebraska is plains, for instance, and the eastern half of Wyoming high plains. This country is best suited to growing antelope, which in Wyoming are doing splendidly.

high-ball outfit Among loggers, a top, hard-working outfit.

highfalutin Fancy, pretentious.

hillbilly cowboy A hand on an outfit that works far from civilisation. [Adams]

hip shot A shot with a gun from the hip, so not aimed but only pointed; used strictly at close range.

hippodrome stand *See* Roman riding.

his leg is tied up Descriptive of someone at a disadvantage. The expression comes from the custom of tying up the legs of broncs to shoe them. [Adams]

hishi Strands of disc-shaped beads, usually made from shell or turquoise. In modern times the best hishi comes from Santo Domingo Pueblo. Other types of beads and turquoise nuggets are often strung on hishi. From the Navajo, and pronounced HEE-shee.

hit the trail To get going. Anyone ever notice how many words and expressions the West has for 'Let's get the hell out of here'?

hit the breeze also means to get going, probably with more suggestion of hurry; *hit the flats* and *hit the sod* meant the same.

hitches In the West, knots are called hitches. The *diamond* (or *Kit Carson* or *pack hitch*) is favoured by packers for its dependability. When 'throwed' right (you throw a hitch – you don't tie it), it makes a diamond shape on top of the load. Other hitches are the *basket hitch* (used for a load likely to slip), *half-diamond*, *pole hitch*, *prospector's* (or *crosstree* or *sheepherder's*) *hitch*, *one man hitch*, *S hitch*, *sling hitch*, *squaw hitch* and *W hitch*.

hitching rack A pole to hitch your horse to; also called a *hitch rack*, a *hitch* (or *hitching*) *rail*, *hitching bar*, *hitching pole* and *hitching post*. Not necessarily Western but most common in the West.

hive off To leave, hit the trail. [Adams]

hivernant A French-Canadian term for an experienced beaver trapper or trader; literally, a 'winterer', a man who has spent winters in the wilderness. In the late 18th century, the hivernants of the Northwest Company in Montreal formed an exclusive club, the Beaver Club. Also occurs in the form *hivernanno*. (*See also* coureur de bois and voyageur)

hobble your lip Advice to shut up.

hobbled stirrups Stirrups tied beneath the horse. They make it easier for the rider to keep his seat during bucking but are regarded by skilled riders as not only unnecessary but dangerous. In the early part of this century, women rodeo riders competed in the saddle bronc competition with hobbled stirrups.

Western types of hobbles, some of them nice improvisations, are the chain hobble, clogs, cross-hobble, crow (or Scotch) hobble, double hobble, running W and sideline.

hobble-tongued Descriptive of a stutterer. [Adams]

hoddentin The sacred meal of the Apaches; the pollen of the tule (bulrush).

hoe dig The dance the cowboy sometimes called a *hoe-down*. He also used the verb, to *hoe it down*. (Easterners *hoed it off*.) Joseph McCoy, a mover and a shaker in Abilene, Kansas during its cowtown years, described this colourful phenomenon: 'A more odd, not to say comical sight, is not often seen than the dancing cowboy. With the front of his sombrero lifted at an angle of fully forty-five degrees, his huge spurs jingling at every step or motion; his revolvers flapping up and down like a retreating sheep's tail, his eyes lit up with excitement, liquor and lust, he plunges in and "hoes it down" at a terrible rate, in the most approved yet awkward country style; often swings "his partner" clear off of the floor for an entire circle, then "balances all" with an occasional demoniacal yell, near akin to the war whoop of the savage Indian.'

hoe man A cowman's derisive term for a farmer. (For more such terms, *see* nester)

hog ranch An establishment pretending to be a ranch but actually supplying whiskey and whores to soldiers. In the late 1870s, the Hayes administration prohibited liquor sales at Western military posts. The soldiers responded by going to the nearest hog ranch for satisfaction.

hog wallow A depression in a prairie, of a type frequently found in Texas; the grass found in such depressions (and now elsewhere) is called *hog-wallow mesquite*.

hogback A steep, narrow ridge that arcs back to earth; sometimes also a horse that's the opposite of a swayback. [Adams]

hogleg A revolver, originally a Bisley single-action Colt, later any big pistol.

hog-tie To tie a cow so that it's helpless, as for branding. The two hind legs and one front one are pulled together and tied with half-hitches. A special soft rope about three feet long is used – it's called a *pigging string*, *hogging string* or *hogging rope*. Sometimes this job was called *hogging down*.

hogan The one-room dwelling of the Navajo. Traditionally, it is octagonal, made of horizontal cedar logs calked with mud and with the entrance facing east. The roof is a dome with a smoke hole. These small houses are still common on the reservation.

When someone dies in a hogan, a hole is made in a wall to let the *chindi* (spirit) of death out, and Navajos will not enter that dwelling again; if one is forced to enter, he will purify himself ceremonially later.

hohokam The Pima Indian word meaning 'the extinct people', those who left the pueblo ruins along the Gila River and may be the ancestors of the modern Pima and Papago. In Mormon belief, these people were the Lamanites.

hoja In the south-west, a corn shuck used as cigarette paper. Borrowed from Spanish (where it means 'leaf'), it's pronounced OH-hah.

holdup (1) An armed robbery, especially of a train or stagecoach. (2) A robber, also called a holdup man. (3) A rider who stationed himself at a junction to keep a trail herd headed in the right direction. [Adams]

hole Open meadows surrounded by mountains, like Jackson Hole, Wyoming, Brown's Hole, on the Utah-Colorado-Wyoming border; and Pierre's Hole, Idaho, a mountain park. Some of the most beautiful places in the West are holes, yet the term is falling toward disuse.

hole card An unrevealed weapon or advantage. The term comes from stud poker, where the first card, or two cards, are dealt face down, and said to be 'in the hole'.

hole up To take refuge in a shelter or hiding place.

Hole-in-the-Rock A remarkable piece of wagon road cut by Mormon pioneers down the cliffs on the west side of the Colorado River near the mouth of the Escalante River in what is still some of the wildest country in the United States. The pioneers cut the road in 1880 so they could colonise the San Juan River area in south-eastern Utah.

Hole-in-the-Wall A notorious hideout for outlaws in Wyoming's Powder River country. It was used by the Wild Bunch, led by George LeRoy Parker, better known as Butch Cassidy.

holiday Among loggers, an unwooded area in the timber. [Adams]

holler calf-rope To throw in the towel; to cry uncle; to say, 'I've had enough, I quit.'

hombre Especially in the south-west, man. Sometimes it implies a rough fellow, a tough; but sometimes it refers to a real man, a stand-up guy (*see* Elmore Leonard's fine novel *Hombre*). Borrowed from Spanish, it's pronounced AHM-bray or OHM-bray.

Combinations: hombre bueno (an arbitrator), *hombre del campo* (a skilled outdoorsman) and *hombre viejo* (literally 'old man', the *Cereus schotti*, the old man cactus of New Mexico and Arizona).

homestead The principal sense of homestead, as a tract of public land given rather than sold to settlers, follows the Homestead Act of 1862. It was the result of a land reform movement to prevent speculators from buying up land in hopes of making a high profit and creating 'speculator's deserts' that actual settlers couldn't use, except at daunting prices. It provided that citizens might claim up to 160 acres (or at some times and in some places up to 640 acres) in exchange for living on the land and making certain improvements. By combining the Timber Culture Act of 1873 (another 160, 40 of which needed to be planted in trees), pre-emption (the right to live on and then file for 160 acres at $1.25 an acre) and the Desert Lands Act of 1877 (640 acres could be obtained for a small fee and the proof of irrigation), 1,120 acres could be obtained. Homesteading thus became a major factor in the settling of the West. The rate of failure was high, however, for much of the land was difficult to farm, too small to irrigate or ranch and too large to farm conventionally. Not long after the Homestead Act came the term *homesteader* (which usually carried the implication farmer) and usage of *homestead* as a verb.

Combinations: Homestead Exemption Law (in most states, a law exempting homesteads from attachment or sale for debt), *homestead act* (or *bill* or *law*), *homestead claim*, *homestead entry*, *homestead grant*, *homestead right* and *homestead settlement* (or *settler*).

homestake A stake that's enough to get a person home, usually back to the States.

homesucker A derisive cowboy term for a homesteader.

honda An eyelet at the end of a cowboy's lariat or rope for making a noose. In a lariat, the honda was usually braided in. On a rope it was simply a slipknot. It could also be made of horn or metal. Borrowed from Spanish *hondón* (eyelet), it's pronounced HON-doo or HON-duh and also spelled *hondo* and *hondou*.

honest Injun Anglo slang meaning, 'Is that so?' or 'Really?'

honest pitcher Cowboy talk for a horse that starts bucking right when mounted, instead of waiting for a bad time. [Adams]

honey mesquite A common mesquite of the south-west, *Prosopis juliflora*, also known as *algarroba*.

honky-tonk A dance hall, saloon or other place of low amusements. Thus towns at the ends of cattle trails were called honky-tonk towns.

hooden A cabin for cowboys to sleep in.

hoodlum wagon The bed wagon on a trail drive, often called simply a hoodlum. It carried bedding and other supplies not in the chuck wagon. Its driver, usually the fellow who watched the horses at night, was called the *hood*.

hoodoo (1) One of various fantastical rock formations in the Yellowstone River region. Hoodoo is an Americanisation of *voodoo* and implies a place of weird doings. Yellowstone National Park has a Hoodoo Basin and the Hoodoo Mountains. (2) Another name for a rustler. (3) In south-western Colorado, a hoodoo was a small hut or a cave converted into a hut. (4) A hoodoo stick was a divining rod for ore instead of water.

hooey The last half-hitch in the process of hog-tying (tying three legs of a calf together).

hoof it To walk, usually not a preference among cowboys.

hoofed locust Cowboy talk for sheep, because of their supposed destructiveness to the range.

hooligan wagon On a trail drive, a wagon carrying fuel and water.

hoolihan (1) A quiet, no-fuss rope throw for catching horses in a crowded corral – one quick whirl, a flat noose and a head catch. A hoolihan loop is also called a *herd loop*. (2) A method of bulldogging. When the rider leaps on to the steer, instead of twisting its head, he uses the force of his weight to knock it down. This technique is prohibited at rodeos. (3) Hoolihaning is raising hell, painting the town red.

The origin of the term is unknown. Sometimes spelled *hooley-ann*.

hoop-and-stick game A game played by Indians all over the continent, of such importance that the Cheyennes name a month after it. It's played in many ways. The Cheyennes roll hoops with rawhide mesh in the centre and try to make little lances stick in the mesh. When they succeed, they capture the hoop and throw it at their opponents.

hoopla An interjection of a stage driver to his horses. Perhaps the sense of an excited outcry came from this usage.

hoorow Among Texas cowboys, to tease.

hoosegow A jail. Adapted from the Spanish word *juzgado* (courthouse).

hoosier Among loggers, a beginning logger. The term started when a lot of inexperienced Indianans were recruited as lumbermen in the Pacific north-west.

Hoosier belt is cowboy talk for farm country. [Adams] To hoosier up was to conspire against someone or malign him. [Adams]

hooter A hoot owl or an outhouse.

hoot-owl hollow Cowboy talk for some very remote dwelling place. [Adams]

Hopi A pueblo people of the high mesas in north-eastern Arizona. They speak a Uto-Aztecan language and were traditionally farmers and hunter-gatherers. They have occupied some of their present villages for seven centuries and more, and one of these, Walpi or Oraibi, may be the oldest settlement in the United States to be inhabited continuously. Their name means 'the peaceful people'. Other peoples, including whites, have called them Moquis.

The Hopi have a rich religious and ceremonial life centred around dances held at traditional seasons, including the *famous snake dance*. Their *kachinas*, carved to teach the children the names and characteristics of the various spirits, are widely collected as art objects. The Hopi are also known for their weaving, pottery, baskets and silversmithing. (*See* pueblo)

They are now engaged in a struggle with their Navajo neighbours for control of lands. Though the two tribes have a historic enmity, Navajos have lived on land allotted to the Hopi for a century. A recent US government effort to get each tribe on to its own lands has caused controversy and may result in the forced removal of several thousands of Navajos from Hopi lands.

horn On a stock saddle, a leather-covered protuberance meant for help with roping (and not for the rider to hang on to). A cowboy dallies his rope around the horn when he's roped a calf, or he ties the near end of his throwing rope there. Some Mexican horns were big and flat (some Americans mockingly called them dinner plates). American cowboys and saddle-makers reshaped the Mexican horn to suit their own inclinations. (*See* dally)

To *horn people out* was to drive them off; to *horn a prospect* was to sell dubious mining stocks; an over-aggressive person was said to be *horning the brush* [Adams]; and to *have your horns sawed off* was to have the starch taken out of you.

Combinations: horn string (used to tie a coiled rope to the saddle horn), *horned toad* (one of several lizards, especially of the south-west) and a *horn-tossing mood* (an angry mood).

horn spoon A tool made from a cow horn and used to assay crushed rock; often called simply a horn. The process was called *horning a prospect* or *assaying with a spoon*.

horno The outdoor, earthen oven of the Hispanic south-west. Borrowed from Spanish, it's pronounced OHR-noh.

hornswoggle The wriggling motions of a cow to get rid of a rope; in later usage, to deceive.

horse In cow country, traditionally not any equine but a grown male horse. Females are designated *mare* or *filly*; a *colt* is a young male. Mares were generally unwelcome on the range as saddle horses in the early days because they might be in heat.

Descriptive terms for horses include *barn sour* (one in a hurry to get back to the barn), *camp staller* (one resistant to starting out), *cinch binder* (a bucking horse that rears up on its hind legs and falls over backward), *clear-footed* (agile of foot), *cloud hunter* (a horse that rears and paws), *cloud watcher* (a horse that holds its head too high), *cold collar* (a balky horse), *cold-blooded* (not pure-bred), *cold-jawed* (a horse with a hard or insensitive mouth), *cold-shouldered* (one that is newly harnessed and balky), *coon-footed* (one whose rear feet aren't straight), *cribber* (a horse in the habit of sucking on wood), *crow bait* (a worthless horse), *dead-mouthed* or *hard-mouthed* (insensitive to the bit), *halter puller* (a horse in the habit of pulling back on the halter rope), *halter-shy*, *man-killer* (a vicious horse), *outlaw*, *pie biter* (one that snoops in the chuck wagon), *puller* (one that pulls eagerly on the bit), *ripper* (a big horse with plenty of endurance), *second saddle* (a bronc buster's name for a horse that has been ridden twice), *shadow jumper* (a skittish horse), *skate* (a lousy horse), *snorter* (an excitable horse), *snorty* (a high-spirited horse), *sugar eater* (a pampered horse), *switch tail* (a nervous horse), *watermelon under the saddle* (one that arches its back a lot), *widow maker* (an outlaw horse) and *wring-tail* (a nervous horse).

Other terms for physical characteristics of horses: *calf-legs* (a short-legged horse), *chapo* (short-coupled horse), *close-coupled* (short-bodied), *cowhocked* (with legs nearly touching at the hocks), *coon-footed* (long and low-pasterned), *ewe-necked* (with a bowed neck), *fiddle-foot* (with dancing or nervous feet), *fiddle-headed* (with an ugly head), *light in the timber* (light-boned in the lower legs), *gotch-ear* (with a drooping ear), *moon-eye* (glassy white eye), *mule-footed* (round-hoofed), *mule-hipped* (with hips sloping too much), *nigger-heeled* (the opposite of pigeon-toed in front), *parrot-mouth* (with buck teeth), *pudding foot* (big-footed, clumsy), *rat-tailed horse* (with a thin tail), *snipe-gutted* (with a slender barrel), *tender* (saddle-sore or sore-footed), and *whey-belly* (big-gutted).

Terms for horses that do jobs are *brush horse* (good in the brush), *buffalo runner*, *calf horse* (a roper), *circle horse* (one used to ride circle), *dink* (a horse poor for roping or bulldogging), *gut twister* (a good bucking horse), *night horse* (one good for night use), *peg pony* or *pegger* (a horse with unusual ability to change directions), *rimrocker* (one sure-footed in rough rimrock), *roper* or *rope horse*, *snub horse* (a horse used to snub buckers at a rodeo), *Sunday horse* (one for show), *swimming horse* (a horse to cross rivers on), *whittler* (a good cutter), *winter horse* (one kept at the main ranch for winter riding) and *wrangle horse* (a horse for bringing up the cavvy).

(*See also* cutting horse, mustang and shave-tail. For horse colours, *see* buckskin. For terms for unfit horses, *see* canner. For names for saddle horses, *see* cow horse)

Combinations: horse apple (a horse turd; sometimes it means the fruit of the bois d'arc, which horses eat), *horse-breaker*, (a professional horse trainer [*see* break a horse]), *horse-hocky* (horse manure), *horsehair rope* (a braided rope, preferably from mane hair), *horse heaven* (a place in Cayuse country where horses formerly roamed), to *be horsing* (when said of a mare, to be in the breeding period), *horse jewellery* (metal ornaments on tack), *horse man* (a horse breeder), *horse opera* (a Western movie, and by implication grade B), *horse ranch* (a horse-breeding outfit), *horse restaurant* (in California, a livery stable), *horse sense* (good, practical sense such as a cowpony has), *horse smoke* (among the Osages, a ceremonial pipe-smoking that promises the gift of a horse), *horse-thief's special* (rice pudding), *horse fighter* (a bronc buster), *horse Indian* (a Plains Indian with a nomadic culture), *horseback outfit* (a mounted crew), *horseback work* (a cowboy's work) and *horse pestler* or *horse rustler* (a wrangler).

hospital cattle Cows weak from the winter.

hosteen A Navajo title of respect for a man, usually an older man; also used as a common noun to indicate a Navajo man, as in, 'Is that hosteen tall?'

The journalist and historian Francis Fugate points out that the Navajos of the trading-post days called Arbuckle's coffee *Hosteen Cohay*, which translates literally to Mr Coffee.

hostile An unfriendly Indian, as opposed to an Indian on one's own side or a reservation Indian. An Indian perceived as on the warpath, inimical to white interests. The term is sometimes used today, in reference to a person who wants little to do with Anglos.

Since military units in the West often had Indians as guides or comrades in arms, they spoke of the enemy as hostiles. In official eyes, sometimes any Indian who was off the reservation.

hot iron! The brander's holler when his branding iron gets too cool – the iron must be hot or you get a hair brand (one that burns the hair but not the hide).

hot rock A biscuit. *Sinker* and *sourdough bullet* were other names for biscuits. The terms show the inclination of the minds of Westerners to work in homely and colourful metaphors.

hot shot An electrical charge that makes a horse buck; used in rodeo. [Adams]

hot stuff Branding irons right out of the fire. [Adams]

hot-foot To burn a calf's hoof to keep it from following its mother, a nasty trick played by some rustlers.

hot-spotting Among firefighters, stopping the spread of a fire where it's moving fast or in an especially dangerous way. This is usually of high priority.

hound ears and whirlups A range dessert, sourdough balls with a sugar-and-spice sauce. [Adams]

hounds Rowdies of the gold-rush days in San Francisco.

hovel A logging-horse stable.

how! A salutation from Indian Pidgin English, usually accompanied by a raised, open right hand to show the absence of a weapon. The original Lakota greeting was 'How, Kola?' meaning roughly, 'How are you, friend?'

hoz Sickle. Borrowed from Spanish, it's pronounced hoz.

hua! A command of a Santa Fe Trail trader to his draft animals meaning 'Get going!' From the Spanish exclamation *Gua!* which is pronounced similarly. [Adams]

huarache In the south-west, an open-toed sandal of Mexicans and Indians. Borrowed from Spanish, it's pronounced wah-RAH-chay. Also spelled *huaracho*.

hucky-dummy Cowboy talk for biscuits with raisins. [Adams]

Hudson's Bay Company A mammoth British trading enterprise often known by its initials, HBC. Since HBC was first in the West and liked to assert its seniority and pre-eminence, some Americans called it 'Here Before Christ'. The American trappers did not like it, as they did not like John Bull generally.

hueco tanks Water holes in rock whose rainwater sometimes provided salvation for travellers, especially in Texas. In Spanish, the noun *hueco* (pronounced WAY-koh) means 'hole'.

huero In the south-west, a man with light or red hair and a fair complexion. Borrowed from Spanish, it's pronounced WAR-roh.

hug rawhide To keep your seat stuck to the saddle during tough times. [Adams]

huisache *Acacia farnesiana*, a shrub of the Mexican-American border country known for its yellow flowers and sweet smell. Borrowed from Spanish, it's pronounced wee-SAH-chay.

hull Cowboy slang for saddle.

human fruit A dead body hanging by a rope from a tree. [Adams] Such a body was also said to have been hung up to dry. (*See* string party)

Humboldt house A kind of dugout built by Nevada miners into the side of a mountain. (The Humboldt is a principal Nevada river.) A Humboldt, among loggers, was a wedge-shaped undercut. [Adams]

hump rib A prolongation of the vertebrae that support the hump of the buffalo and the meat on it. The mountain men prized this meat.

hump yourself Get a move on. Also *hump your tail*. A *humper* is a thing that goes fast. To *hump up*, for a horse, is to arch its back high, hoofs together.

hundred and elevens The marks of raking spurs on a horse's side.

hundred and sixty A quarter section of land, the amount claimable under the Homestead Act of 1862. Often used as a noun, as in, 'the West hundred and sixty'.

hung up Descriptive of a rider who has fallen out of his saddle, has a boot caught in a stirrup and is in trouble.

hunt In the fur trade, the year's take of pelts. A *hunting boat* was a boat used by fur men.

If you're caught where you shouldn't be, you say you're *hunting a horse* or *hunting strays*.

A sheep-herder who's gone a little loco is said to be *hunting water* and should be sent for supplies.

hunt dirt To fall off a horse. Also *hunt grass*. (For similar terms, *see* bite the dust.) To *hunt leather* is to hold on to the saddle horn.

hunter spider A name for a tarantula.

hurdy-gurdy (1) A dance hall or similar establishment with prostitutes, sometimes called a *hurdy* for short. Thus *hurdy-gurdy girls*, *hurdy-gurdy house*, *hurdy-gurdy saloon*, etc. The name perhaps came from the musical instrument of the same name, which was similar to a barrel organ. (2) Among miners, a water wheel such as might be used to run a stamp mill.

hurricane deck The saddle of a bucking horse; a nicely descriptive term.

hydraulicking Among miners, using water under high pressure to wash down gold-bearing earth. The pressure was directed by *hydraulic giants*, or *chiefs*, with nozzles. Thus *hydraulic diggings*, *hydraulic mining* (and *miner*), *hydraulic hose*, *hydraulic nozzle*, *hydraulic washing*, etc.

hymn Cowboy talk for a song he sings to the cows. As shown in Guy Logsdon's book *The Whorehouse Bells Are Ringing and Other Songs Cowboys Sing*, the words were often decidedly unacceptable in church.

I

ictas In Chinook, merchandise, trade goods.

immigrant *See* emigrant.

in a bind Among loggers, to be stuck in a hard place. It comes from the notion of having your saw bound by the weight of a log.

incense cedar The white cedar or post cedar, *Libocedrus decurrens*, of the Pacific Coast.

incomplete act of worship A euphemism for an act of coitus interruptus and, according to Shirley Leckie, the editor of the correspondence of army wife Alice Kirk Grierson, 'the most common form of birth control in the nineteenth century'.

Indian The term Indian, because of Columbus's famous mistake in thinking he was contacting the people of India, is of uncertain acceptance these days. In political circles, speakers show their sophistication by saying 'Native American'. In 1979 a legislative assistant to a US congressman told the author that it was impossible to say 'Indian' in the capitol.

Indians themselves are less impatient of the older term. They do joke about it. Some say they're glad Columbus wasn't looking for Turkey; others are glad he wasn't seeking the Virgin Islands. One well-known member of the Gros Ventre tribe likes to say he's an Indin [*sic*] on the reservation, an Injun in the nearby town, an Indian all over the state and a Native American in Washington, DC. Though some Indians (perhaps those who are college-educated) prefer the usage Native American, many others (perhaps traditional Indians) do not; most accept either term. Even more would like to be identified more specifically as Cherokees, Shoshones, Hopis and so on. The *Lakota Times*, a leading Indian newspaper, says it is returning from Native American to Indian.

Historically, Indian was sometimes short for something associated with Indians, such as Indian corn or an Indian language – 'She was speaking Indian.' It also meant temper, anger, as in, 'He had his Indian up.'

Many Western terms have been formed from the word Indian (and contemporary speakers may want to be alert to the denigration in some of them):

Animals: *Indian cattle* (one name for longhorns), *Indian devil* (the wolverine) and *Indian pony* (a mustang, usually disparaged by Anglos).

Plants: *Indian breadroot* (prairie turnip), *Indian currant* (*Lonicera symphoricarpos*, or St Peter's Wort), *Indian grass* (*Sorghastrum nutans*, a four- to eight-foot grass of the tallgrass prairie), *Indian medicine* (any of a number of plants used for healing), *Indian paint* (*Lithospermum canescens* or *Sanguinaria canadensis*, also called puccoon root, red root and blood root, used by Indians to render a red body paint), *Indian paintbrush* (*Casileja linariaefolia; see* paintbrush), *Indian pine* (*Pinus taeda;* the lob-lolly), *Indian potato* (one of several plants with edible roots) and *Indian tobacco* (also called *Indian weed*) (any one of a number of native tobacco plants, including mullein). Many more plants begin with the word Indian.

Food: *Indian bread* (the fatty meat along the spine of the buffalo, much favoured by Indians and mountain men; evidently an equivalent of fleece; in colonial times, this meant bread made from meal made from Indian corn), *Indian coffee* (coffee made by whites by a second boiling of the grounds, thought to be good enough for Indians but looked down on by Anglos) and *Indian taco* (a beef salad on fry bread, now a popular food in restaurants on and near reservations.

Government: *Indian annuity* (an annual payment due from the federal government for cessions of lands, minerals, or rights to a group of Indians, often not paid or much reduced by middle men), *Indian Bureau* (Bureau of Indian Affairs), *Indian service* (a person's service either in the Bureau of Indian Affairs, presumably to help the Indians, or in the US Army against the Indians), *Indian police* (from 1878, a force of Indians organised on reservations to keep order among Indians, prevent traffic in liquor and control the distribution of annuities, usually under the direction of a white Indian agent), *Indian right* (an Indian's, or group of Indians', entitlement to land), *Indian superintendent* (from 1824, the commissioner of the Bureau of Indian Affairs; previously any official in charge of Indian trade), *Indian ring* (a group of politicians, contractors and the like organised to rob Indians of the annuities sent them by the federal government) and *Indian scout* (either a scout for the US military who was Indian or an Anglo scout used against Indians).

People: Agency Indian (an Indian who lived on a reservation that had an agency, not a 'wild' Indian), *church Indian* (a Christian Indian), *good Indian* (in the bad old joke, a dead Indian). *Indian countryman* (a white who chose to live among Indians; also called a *white Indian*), *Indian doctor* (a healer, sometimes Anglo, practising traditional Indian medicine, usually including the sweat lodge), *Indian lover* (a derogatory term applied to anybody who argued in favour of, supported, helped or sympathised with Indians), *praying Indian* (an Indian who had switched to Christian prayers), *treaty Indian* (a member of a tribe 'pacified' by a treaty with the United States), *whiskey Indian* (an Indian inclined to drunkenness) and *white Indian* (either an Indian of a tribe noted for light skin, such as the Zuni, or an Anglo living as an Indian).

Places: Indian country or *ground, land* or *territory* (a land area in Indian control, which was a changeable matter; the military still uses this [as recently as the Persian Gulf War] to mean any land under the control of the enemy); capitalised, *Indian Territory* (a region assigned to Indian nations for their own use in what is now the state of Oklahoma) and *Indian frontier* or *border, boundary* or *line* (the rough demarcation between white settlement and Indian country).

Miscellaneous: Indian broke (descriptive of a horse trained to be mounted from the Indian side – the right side, which was customarily used by Indians), *Indian deading* (an old winter Indian camp where steamboatmen found downed and limbed cotton-woods for fuel), *Indian file* (single file, as Indians are presumed to move

through woods), *Indian goods* (trade goods – *see* fur trade), *Indian list* (cowboy talk for a blacklist), *Indian mortar* (a natural depression in rock, used for grinding), *Indian poker* (Indian version of the popular card game, usually played by women), *Indian post office* (a mound of rocks where Indians left messages), *Indian razor* (a pair of tweezers or a shell used as tweezers by Indians to pluck facial hair), *Indian shoe* (a horseshoe of rawhide dried on to the hoof), *Indian trace* or *road* (a trail worn by regular use by Indians), *Indian trade, Indian trail* (usually the trail made by a village of Indians, complete with scrapings left by lodge-pole travois, not just the hoof prints of a war party) and *Iron Indian* (the figurehead on a steamboat).

Phrases: Indian up (to sneak up), *play* or *do the sober Indian* (to stay sober while others drink), *play Indian* (to show no emotion in your face or for children to pretend to be Indians) and *seeing Indians* (a disease now unidentifiable but also known as *blue-devils, man-with-the poker* or *red-monkeys*).

(*See also* Bureau of Indian Affairs, dance, Indian agent, Indian chief, Indian trader, Indian whiskey, reservation, sun dance, tipi, trade blanket, Welsh Indian, wickiup and the names of principal tribes)

Indian agent Since 1824, a functionary of the Bureau of Indian Affairs, usually a person in charge of the administration of a reservation. Though some such agents were good people, in the 19th century many were notorious for stealing the provisions sent to the Indians by the federal government. The office of the agent was called the *Indian agency*. Now such agents, called superintendents, are Indians.

Indian chief A leader of a band or tribe of Indians. This term often represents a misunderstanding of leadership among Indians. There were leaders generally and leaders for war (or hunting, travelling and so on) in particular; whites often mistook war leaders as over-all leaders. In any case, leadership among Indians usually was more flexible than among whites, with individuals and families having more autonomy.

Indian trader An Anglo or Hispanic who traded (or still trades) with Indians, either from a trading post or by going to their camps or villages. In the north, these traders were almost invariably fur traders, but in the south-west, they traded for other goods.

Often traders came to know the Indians intimately and sympathetically, even marrying into a tribe. In *Entrepreneurs of the Old West*, David Dary writes that Navajo trader John Lorenzo Hubbell 'became something of a teacher, helping the Indians understand the ways of the white man. He was also a trusted friend, translating and writing letters for the Indians, settling family quarrels, explaining government policy, and even helping them when they became ill.'

Indian whiskey Alcohol for trade to Indians, weakened by water and strengthened with spices. Acknowledging its origin with early fur traders, trail hand Teddy Blue gives one recipe in *We Pointed Them North*: 'Take one barrel of Missouri River water and 2 galls. of alcohol. Then you add 2 ozs. of strychnine to make them crazy – because strychnine is the greatest stimulant in the world – and 3 plugs of tobacco to make them sick – because an Indian wouldn't figure it was whiskey unless it made him sick – 5 bars of soap to give it a bead, and half of a pound of red pepper and then you put in some sagebrush and boil it until it's brown. Strain this into a barrel and you've got your Indian whiskey, that one bottle calls for a buffalo robe, and when an Indian got drunk it was two robes.

See also firewater.

Indio In the south-west, the Spanish word for Indian, becoming more and more common. Pronounced IN-dee-oh.

individual What a cowboy of the old days called the horse he owned personally, as opposed to those in the string provided by the ranch.

inner circle Among cowboys riding circle (riding a wide loop to gather cows for roundup), a short circle, usually assigned to a hand with a horse of uncertain quality. [Adams]

instream flow The prescribed level of water flow released from a dam. It's the subject of much quarrelling between fishermen and wildlife advocates versus ranchers and other water users, who often have needs hard to reconcile.

intendente In the south-west, a high-ranking government official. Borrowed from Spanish, it's pronounced in-ten-DEN-tee or in-ten-DEN-tay.

invitation stick Among some Plains Indians, a small piece of wood carved and marked. When placed by a lodge, it could declare a desire to court a woman, or invite people to a feast or ceremony.

Irish baby buggy What miners and loggers called a wheelbarrow.

iron Iron was short for a *branding iron* or slang for a revolver or a horseshoe. *Iron burner* was a logger's term for a blacksmith. An *iron man* (or *iron tender*) is a hand who heats branding irons in a fire and produces a hot one at a brander's need. To *iron out a horse* (or *iron the bumps out*) is to take the kinks out of it. To *iron the calf crop* is to brand it. [Adams] But to be *ironed by a blacksmith* was to have your legs shackled. [Adams]

iron horse A railroad. An Anglo term in half-jocular imitation of Indian Pidgin English.

irrigation (1) Slang for alcoholic refreshment. (*See* firewater) (2) Irrigation of crop lands is a particularly Western practice in the United States and has yielded the combinations *irrigation bill* (law), *irrigation district* (a group of ranchers on one irrigation system), *irrigation ditch*, *irrigation pump*, *irrigation rancher*, and so on.

issue day *See* beef issue.

it is all wheat A Utah expression meaning, 'It's on the square, it's OK.'

ivories Cowboy talk for poker chips [Adams] or a gambler's term for dice.

iztle In the south-west, a kind of obsidian used by Indians for arrow points and the like. Borrowed from Spanish, which got it from Nahuatl, it's pronounced IST-lee.

J

jacal In the south-west, a mud hut, a shack of the Indians or Mexicans. It was generally made of upright poles covered with mud but might be anything from an Apache brush shelter to a rude adobe house. A temporary shelter was a *jacalito*. Borrowed from Spanish, it is pronounced hah-KAHL. American spellings (and pronunciations suggesting spellings) ranged from *hackel* to *hayrick*.

jack rabbit A hare with long ears and long legs. There are several varieties in the West, including those called black-tailed, white-tailed and white-sided. *Jack* is sometimes short for jack rabbit.

A *jackalope* is a taxidermist's creation, a jack rabbit with antlers.

jackass mail Mail hauled by teams of mules (sometimes called *jack trains*), especially on the stage lines of John Butterfield or James Birch. Mules were sometimes thought tougher than horses for the work of pulling stage coaches. It also meant slow, inefficient mail lines, which were apparently operated by jackasses – thus *jackass express*.

jacket To cover a bum (motherless) lamb with the skin of a dead lamb. Going by smell, the mother of the dead lamb will then nurse the bum lamb.

jackleg An incompetent fellow, a shyster, as in, 'a jackleg lawyer'.

jackpot (1) Originally, in poker, a pot, especially one in a hand when jacks or better are required to open. Later, money won on a single go at a slot machine. (2) In rodeo, an event with no added money, with the winners getting only the entry fees. (3) Among cowboys, a confounding or messed-up situation, and among loggers, a confusing pile of logs.

jam the breeze In cowboy talk, to go full steam ahead. [Adams]

jamoka Coffee. (For coffee words, *see* Arbuckle's)

jaquima The Spanish word meaning 'a horse's headstall' that got corrupted to hackamore. Sometimes this turns up among cowboys as *jakoma*. Pronounced HAH-kee-muh.

jarabe A Hispanic dance of the south-west. Borrowed from Spanish, it's pronounced hah-RAH-bay.

javalina The peccary (*Tayassu tacaju*) of the south-west. A pig-like animal, it lacks the tail and tusks of the Old World pigs. In Spanish, *jabalina* is the feminine form and *jabalí* the masculine, but in American English *javalina* is used for both genders. (The Spanish *b* sounds much like a *v* to American ears) Pronounced hah-vah-LEE-nuh or ha-vuh-LEE-nuh, with the first *a* as in *corral*. Also spelled *havalina*.

jaw cracker As late as the 1930s, the travelling dentist. David Lavender described him in *One Man's West:* 'He went from town to town, dragging his shop in a trailer behind his automobile. Whenever he appeared, all the possessors of toothaches, recurrent headaches, neuralgia, rheumatism, lumbago, or morning stiffness flocked to see him. He jerked out their teeth . . . and sent them home to let their wounded gums shrink into shape. On his return trip he measured his now-hungry clients for plates, made the dentures in his home office, and shipped them out COD.

jawbone (1) Talk, especially mere talk. It also takes a verb form – to jawbone. (2) To buy something on jawbone was to get it on credit. Some cowmen have lived on jawbone.

jayhawker (1) A man who fought in the war in Kansas during the mid- and late 1850s over slavery. (2) A Kansas guerrilla during the Civil War, on the Union side. These jayhawkers fought secesh (Confederate) sympathisers, especially Missourians. (3) A man who harassed the Texas cattlemen after the Civil War, claiming that the herds they brought north were infested with Texas fever. Texas trail driver Jim Daughterty wrote, 'The Jayhawkers were said to be soldiers mustered out of the Yankee army. They were nothing more than a bunch of cattle rustlers and were not interested about fever ticks coming into their country but used this just as a pretence to kill the men with the herds and steal the cattle or stampede the herds.' (4) Any lawless person.

Jehu A sobriquet for a driver of a stagecoach.

jerga A twilled wool made by Mexicans and used for carpets, saddle blankets and clothing. It was checked black and white. From the Spanish word *jerga* (coarse cloth), it was pronounced KSAYR-guh and also spelled *xerga* or *gerga*.

jerkline A single line used as a rein by a mule-skinner or other driver of teams. The line was attached to the bit of the lead animal only. One pull signalled a move to the left, two pulls right. Sometimes it was called a *jerkrein*.

Combinations: jerkline express (horse or mule team), *jerkline outfit* or *string* (a team of mules or horses so driven), *jerkline driver, jerkline freighter* and the idiom *to have a hold on the jerkline* (to have a situation under control).

jerky Meat preserved by drying. The Plains Indians jerked meat (primarily buffalo, but any red meat) by cutting it into strips and drying it on a rack of twigs head-high above a low fire for several days. The Californios added the trick of dipping it in brine first. Many similar methods have been employed. The crux of the process is not smoking but drying.

Jerky is the basis of pemmican, the other principal Western form of preserved meat. Since jerky will last for months without spoiling, it was commonly carried by Indians on journeys, by mountain men and by other Western travellers. Though what's sold in stores as jerky today isn't jerky, the real McCoy is still made in Western homes.

It's also called *jerk* and, by Hispanics, *tasajo*. To *jerk meat* means 'to make jerky'. The word is an Americanised version of the Spanish term for jerked meat, *charqui*.

In Montana in the latter 19th century, jerky also meant a wagon without springs.

jesse A scolding, a thrashing, a person's come-uppance. A fellow in a fight was sometimes encouraged, 'Give him jesse!'

jewellery In cowboy talk, guns, especially hand guns.

jigger To run a horse until it's overheated.

jiggle The usual, relaxed gait of a cow horse; to ride at that pace.

jimson weed The common name for datura (*Datura meteloides*), which is hallucinogenic.

jinete A skilled rider; a bronc buster; a cavalryman. Borrowed from Spanish (where it means 'horseman'), it's pronounced hee-NAY-tay.

jingle To round up the horse herd, which is kept in a *jingle pasture* (fenced and near the cowboys' quarters) for quick access in the morning. Sometimes the wrangler is called the *jingler*.

jingle bob (1) An earmark known for its ugliness. The ear was cut from tip to base, and the bottom half flapped loosely. It was the earmark of the herds of John Chisum, one of the protagonists of the Lincoln County War, and his crew was known as the jingle bob outfit. (2) The jingling danglers on a cowboy's spurs.

jingle your spurs! Get a move on!

job To joke, to poke fun, to play a practical joke.

Job's comforter Cowboy talk for a boil.

jockey box A box carried on a wagon for miscellaneous small articles. On a chuck wagon, it held horseshoeing equipment, hobbles and maybe extra ropes.

jocla An earring, usually a rope of turquoise *hishi* (disc-shaped beads) that dangles from the ear. The word is an Anglo corruption of *jahklo*, a Navajo word meaning ear rope. Pronounced jo-KLAH.

John Chinaman Cowboy talk for rice; a Chinese person. Formed as *John Donkey* and *John Q. Public* were. *John Henry* (a signature), *John Law* (any law officer) and *Johnny Navajo* are similar Western formations. According to Cornelius Smith, so was *John Daisy* (an army word for a mule adapted from the similar-sounding Navajo word *tsanez*).

Johnnie Blocker *See* blocker loop.

Johnson bar A stinger; the hand-held bar of a fresno (buck scraper), known for stinging like hell when it kicks.

jojoba A south-western plant, *Simmondsia chinensis*, also called *coffee-berry*. Valued by Indians as food, the seeds are now prized for the oil they yield that is very similar to the oil of the sperm whale.

Jones' place A line camp; a privy; a saloon. [Adams]

jornada A day's journey; more often, a waterless stretch of country that can be crossed in a single day, or at least a single drive, and usually hard on men, horses and cows. Some jornadas made a hell of a day. The Jornada del Muerto (Dead Man's Journey) on the Rio Grande in New Mexico (between San Cristbol and Rincon) was about 80 miles long. The Jornada del Diablo (Devil's Journey) was a piece of rough, dry land in Papago country.

Josephite A Mormon follower of Joseph Smith III (founder of the Reorganised LDS Church) rather than Brigham Young. After the death of Joseph Smith, the Mormon Church chose Brigham Young as its head, and he led them to the Great Salt Lake. The Josephites split off and formed the Reorganised Church of Jesus Christ of the Latter-Day Saints. Centred in Independence, Missouri, it is generally abbreviated RLDS Church to differentiate it from the LDS Church.

Joshua tree A strange tree (*Yucca brevifolia*) with twisting branches. Found in the southern California desert and sometimes called the *yucca palm*, it is ubiquitous near Joshua Tree National Monument.

joss house A temple. From the Chinese Pidgin word *joss* (god). *Joss-sticks* are incense.

Judge Lynch Lynch law personified. In California, a *Judge of the Plains* was a county official who decided issues of livestock ownership.

jug handle A slit in the loose hide under a cow's throat and a sign of ownership like an earmark or a brand. It forms a loop resembling a jug handle.

jug-head A dumb horse, one that doesn't understand what its rider wants. A mule or a man may also be called a jug-head. (For other words for dense horses, *see* canner)

juice A cowboy's verb meaning to milk a cow.

jump To come upon a man or animal suddenly, catching it unawares, as in, 'to jump a deer out of brush'.

Idioms: (1) To *jump a* (mining) *claim* means to take it illegally, by force or skulduggery. One who does so is a *claim-jumper*, and *claim jumping* is sometimes referred to euphemistically as relocating a claim. (2) To *jump the cut* means for the dealer to cut the cards for his own advantage. (3) To *jump over the broomstick* is to get married. (4) To *jump up a lot of dust* means to come or go (on a horse) in a hurry.

juniper Americans everywhere use this word to mean various conifers; in the West, its berries are used occasionally for seasonings. The distinctly Western meaning of juniper is a 'greener' or 'pilgrim'. Thus the narrator in Owen Wister's 'A Pilgrim at Gila' rattles up to a water stop in a stage and says, 'I jumped out to see the man Mr Mowry warned me was not an inexperienced juniper.'

justins Cowboy boots. The name comes from a fine boot-maker, Joseph Justin, whose firm started on the Red River and is now in Fort Worth, Texas. Some people say Justin is to boots what Stetson is to hats and Levis is to jeans.

K

kachina In Hopi religion, a spirit, a demi-god; a masked dancer or a doll representing these spirits. Youths of both sexes are initiated into kachina societies, become dancers and participate in the principal Hopi ceremonies.

The kachinas, said to winter in San Francisco peaks south-west of the Hopi Reservation near Flagstaff, Arizona, appear at various times of the year and in many shapes.

Kachina dolls, made of wood, feathers and so on and brightly painted, were originally made for Hopi children but now are often made for Anglo collectors. Some Hopi carvers have made names for themselves as kachina artists.

Spelled variously (especially *katcina*), it comes from the Tewa language and is pronounced kuh-CHEE-nuh.

kangaroo rat A rodent of the Western deserts. He survives without drinking any water, relying on the water that is a by product of food metabolism and by water-conserving behaviour (limiting activity to night, temporary periods of hibernation, concentrated urine, etc).

Kansa Indians; Kaw Indians A tribe similar to the Osage.

Kansas *Western Combinations: Kansas banana* (the pawpaw), *Kansas brick* (a square of prairie sod used to build a soddy, also called a *Nebraska brick*), *Kansas sheep dip* (both a treatment for scab in sheep and, later, one of the many cowboy terms for whiskey – for others, *see* firewater), *Kansas stable* (a stable built of forked posts and poles and covered with sod and brush), *Kansas zephyr* (a devil of a wind) and *Kansas City fish* (salt pork; sow-belly).

keelboat During the quarter century up to 1820, the keelboat was the primary mode of transportation for people and supplies from Pittsburgh west. Named for its heavy timber keel (and it was also called simply a *keel*), 50 to 80 feet long, pointed at both ends and light of draft, the keelboat was distinguished from the broad-horn or flatboat in that it could go upstream. The keelboat moved slowly by a combination of sailing, poling, bush-whacking (pulling on bushes and trees) and towing by a rope that might be 1,000 feet long (cordelling). It could haul up to 300 barrels of freight. A trip to, say, St Louis, was easy down the Ohio River and hellish going up the Mississippi.

The keelboat required a tough, strong bunch of men to crew it, usually six to ten per boat, plus a captain who acted as steersman. One such fellow, Mike Fink, became legendary as the half-horse, half-alligator king of the boatmen.

keep the double doors swinging To kick up your heals with the help of whiskey. The double doors are the saloon doors. (*See* roostered)

Kelleys Spurs and bits of high reputation once made by the firm P. M. Kelley and Sons in El Paso, Texas.

keno (1) A lottery-like gambling game, first known as lotto and first popular along the Mississippi River and now in Nevada. The globe that held the numbered balls was called a *keno goose*. (2) A cowboy exclamation meaning everything's OK.

Kentucky breakfast Stewart Edward White explains this one eloquently in *Arizona Nights:* 'He staked me to a Kentucky breakfast. What's a Kentucky breakfast? Why, a Kentucky breakfast is a three-pound steak, a bottle of whisky, and a setter dog. What's the dog for? Why, to eat the steak of course.' Another source describes a Kentucky breakfast as three cocktails and a chaw of tobacco.

kettle For a horse to buck or pitch.

ketoh The leather bracelets mounted with silver once worn by Navajo men. They derived from the wrist guards once used to protect the bare arm of an archer from the twang of the bowstring. Navajos added heavy silver elements, often sand-cast silver, or rows of buttons to the basic leather band. Also spelled *getoh*.

kick the frost out To loosen up a horse; to get the kinks out. To *kick the lid off* is for a horse to start bucking like the devil. (For other similar expressions, *see* buck)

kick up your heels To indulge in vigorous play or celebration, often when drinking. The linguist J. L. Dillard says this is a Westernism. (*See* roostered)

kicked into a funeral procession Descriptive of a person done in by a kicking horse. (*See* cash in your chips)

kidney pack To tie your gear behind the saddle, on the horse's kidneys. Also called a *banana bag*.

kidney plaster A mocking cowboy name for an Eastern (hornless) saddle; also called a *kidney pad*. (*See* postage stamp)

killed pottery Among various Indians, especially in the south-west, ceremonial pottery that has been broken, usually in conjunction with burial practices, or the ritual cleansing or ritual leaving of a house.

killpecker guard A cowboy name for the night watch on a cow herd.

kinky When said of cows or women, whimsical, unpredictable.

kinnikinnick Among many Indians, smoking tobacco. It is a mixture of tobacco and other ingredients, especially dried sumac leaves and the inner bark of the willow or dogwood. Different tribes made different mixtures, sometimes with red osier and bearberry.

Since kinnikinnick was part of many religious gestures, from private prayers to public ceremonies, tobacco was an immensely important item in the Indian trade. Kinnikinnick was and is used for smoking or as a gift to the earth.

A Cree word adopted by the Indians, the mountain men and subsequently other Westerners, it is spelled variously and pronounced KIN-i-kuh-NIK. (*See also* medicine pipe)

Kiowa A Uto-Aztecan tribe of Indians associated principally with the southern plains.

In the 16th century the Kiowa lived around the Three Forks of the Missouri River in Montana. They gradually moved through eastern Wyoming and Colorado to the Arkansas River. There they became horse Indians with a buffalo-hunting culture much like the cultures of the northern plains and with a religion featuring the sun dance. They allied themselves closely with the Comanches and fought with other Indians to the north and the whites to the south, primarily in Texas where, in 1864, they fought at the battle of Adobe Walls.

Following decimation by disease and defeat in the Red River War (1874–75), the Kiowa accepted reservation life peacefully. They were briefly involved in the ghost dance in 1890, and like their Comanche friends, many adopted peyotism and the Native American Church. The reservation period ended with allotment of private land to individual Kiowas.

kip pile A buffalo hunter's term for a pile of buffalo calf skins.

kit fox A small fox of the Great Plains, *Vulpes velox*, important in Indian mythology.

kitchen flap The flank strap on a saddle. [Adams]

kitchen string The horses that haul the chuck wagon, which was occasionally called the *kitchen wagon*. Packers called the mule that carries the kitchen gear the *kitchen mule*. [Adams]

kiuatan Chinook for an Indian pony. Pronounced KYOO-uh-tan.

kiva An underground ceremonial chamber of Pueblo Indians. For men only, kivas are circular, are entered by a ladder and are used for social, political and religious gatherings. Also called an *estufa*.

klootchman In the Pacific north-west, an Indian woman. From Chinook jargon, it also appears in the short form *klootch*.

knee To cut a tendon in the lower leg of a wild cow or mustang. After this surgery, the critter no longer can run but can be driven slowly and can bear young.

knight of the ribbons A driver of a stagecoach. [Adams] The ribbons are the reins.

knob-head A mule.

knot-head A brainless cowboy or a brainless horse; a jug-head.

know how to die standing up To be brave. [Adams]

know which way the stick floats To know which end is up, know your ass from a hole in the ground, know poor bull from fat cow – to know what's what. The stick here is the beaver trapper's float stick, which attaches to the trap. Some specialists think an experienced man would know that the stick floats downstream in the creek; others think he could read information from the exact way the stick was floating.

koshare Among Pueblo Indians, a clown at ceremonies.

Kossuth hat One of the two hats worn by the US soldiers in the post-Civil War period. Named for the Hungarian patriot Louis Kossuth, it was high-crowned, made of felt and embroidered with insignia indicating the corps. Also called a *Jeff Davis hat*.

kowtow To show deference in the Chinese manner, by touching the head to the ground. It has come to mean any obsequious behaviour.

kyack A pannier (carrying sack for a packsaddle).

L

lace your tree up To saddle your horse. [Adams] A fanciful expression from the notion of tying your saddle tree on.

ladies of the line *See* girl of the line.

ladino A south-western word for a cow or other brute that's cunning and ready to hurt you, especially a longhorn of the Texas brush country. In Spanish, it first meant a person who was learned and educated in Latin, then meant a cunning person. *Ladina* means the lead mare in a herd of wild horses. It's pronounced luh-DEE-noh.

ladrone A south-western term for a thief. Borrowed from Spanish, it's pronounced luh-DROHN.

lady-broke A description of a horse so well-trained that even a lady can ride it. The other end of the spectrum is cavvy-broke. (*See* break a horse)

laguna A pond, lagoon or lake. Laguna Madre separates Padre Island from the mainland of Texas on the Gulf of Mexico. This word has become common in proper names of towns and real-estate developments in the south-west, where if they have water, they brag about it. The word is from Spanish, literally meaning 'lagoon', and is pronounced luh-goo-nuh. (*See* pueblo)

Laguna A pueblo and a tribe of Keresan people located about 45 miles west of Albuquerque near a pond, where a Spanish mission was established in 1699.

lair rope Among packers, the rope you tie the pack cover on with. [Adams] Called *lair* for short. To do that tying was called to *lair up*.

Lakota What the Indians known to Anglos as the Teton Sioux call themselves. One of three dialectical versions of the word – the others are Dakota and Nakota – it may now be replacing Dakota as the most accepted form among these Indians. The Teton Sioux were the branch of the Dakota most prominent in the Indian Wars, when they were led by (among others) Crazy Horse, Red Cloud and Sitting Bull.

lallygag To dawdle, to lie around. The word first appeared in print in Idaho and Iowa in the late 1860s. Also spelled *lollygag*.

Lamanite Among Mormons, American Indians, whom they speak of as their Lamanite brothers. According to the *Book of Mormon*, they are descendants of the prophet Lehi, who with his wife, sons and daughters, and their families migrated to the New World in 600 BC. Sons Laman and Lemuel were sullen, disobedient and rebellious, and because of this they and their descendants were marked with a dark skin. Pronounced LAY-muhn-yt. (*See also* nephite)

lamber On a sheep ranch, a man who takes care of ewes and the new lambs during lambing season – spring, when the ewes give birth. Cowboys call sheepherders lamb lickers, an unflattering name derived from the way ewes lick their lambs. [Adams]

lame pen A pasture for a ranch's crippled animals. Also called a *sick* or *hospital pen*.

lampers Inflammation of the mouth of a horse.

land The first cut in a hayfield – you mow out a land near a fence and then back-cut, explains South Dakota writer and rancher Linda Hasselstrom. Some ranchers cut their lands far enough from the fences to leave cover for birds and other wildlife.

land grab The seizing of big tracts of public land, usually not honestly; one of the great Western crimes. The perpetrator is called a *land grabber* or *land pirate*. If he only steals one or two claims, he's called a *land jumper*. If he hooks and crooks something the size of a New England state, he's called a *capitalist*. For instance, the Maxwell Land Grant Company grabbed 1.5 million acres more than it was entitled to in New Mexico. A land grab was also called a *land gobble;* a group intent on so defrauding the public was a *grant ring*.

land grant An issuance of public land to a school or a railroad by the federal government.

Twenty-four colleges and universities in western states have been supported by the Land Grant Act of 1862, also known as the Morrill Act. These are called land-grant colleges or universities.

The government also granted lands to railroads as incentives for development and settlement, thus making the remaining government lands appreciate in value. From 1862 forward, these grants inspired a great rush of railroad-building in the West, thus the term *land-grant railroad*. At first, the new railroads received 10 sections of public land per mile, later as much as 40 sections. This policy resulted in huge land holdings by the railroads and considerable public resentment.

Land in the West always meant land available for settlement, land up for grabs. Many terms rose up around it. Some *combinations: land agent* (an official in charge of a government land office or a private land broker), *land boomer* (a promoter of the value of certain lands), *land booster* (a speculator in land), *land certificate* (an entitlement to a tract of land, often given by the government to soldiers), *land claim* (a legal claim to a tract of land, sometimes based on a Spanish or Mexican grant), *land commissioner* (the head of the General Land Office in Washington), *land leaguer* (a member of a group of Kansas settlers on former Osage land who fought railroad claims to their land), *land opening* (an occasion of making public land available to be bought and settled), *land rush* (a hurry by the public to settle former public lands), *land scalper* (a man who staked a claim on good farmland on the plains in hopes of selling it to a settler), *land scrip* (same as land certificate) and *land state* (a state with land available for homesteading). *See* homestead, empresario and school section.

land in a shallow grave To die or be killed, then buried unceremoniously, usually in the middle of nowhere, as on an emigrant crossing or a trail drive.

laning For a rider to mistakenly approach a cow on the opposite side of the cow from another cowboy, creating a lane between the two riders. The correct procedure is to have the two cowboys on the same side of the cow.

lap and tap What rodeo cowboys call a simultaneous start for the roper and the calf or steer, with no head start for the critter. [Adams]

lap robe A buffalo robe, hair on, used for warmth on carriage rides and the like. Though it could be of wool or other cloth or fur, in the 19th-century West it was usually buffalo.

lapboard A way to poison coyotes, wolves and other predators. A board was drilled and larded with strychnine. When the critters lapped it up, they died. A relic of a West hostile to wildlife that is not entirely past.

lariat Though this word first meant a picket rope, it came to mean the cowboy's catch rope, whether made of rawhide, horsehair or fibre (hemp, maguey, even linen or cotton). The word is an Anglo adaption of the Spanish *la reata*, meaning 'rope' (*See reata*). Hands also call the rope a *lasso* (or one of the variants of that word), a *lass rope* or a *string*. All have a honda, which is like the loop that makes a slip knot work, at the end. The fibre ones are generally 30 to 40 feet long; the ones braided from rawhide have the advantage of stretching when a critter hits the end, lessening the jolt to rider and mount.

According to old hand Jo Mora in *Trail Dust and Saddle Leather*, the linen and cotton varieties are for show ropers more than stock work. Reata (a term favoured in California) refers to rawhide variety; making and handling reatas requires considerable craft. A rawhide lariat is also called a *skin string* to distinguish it from one of hair or fibre.

Originally lariats were always rawhide. Says Mora, 'The laws of supply and demand and the matter of economy was what first gave the grass rope its popularity. Modern trends for more speed and less time for leisure, a laziness and more often an inability to braid their own gear, and the grass rope came into the picture to stay. A waddie could stump into the trading post or general merchandise emporium and buy him 30 or 40 feet of whale line from a big coil at a small cost and whenever he wanted it . . . I've used both rawhide and grass, and I've seen them used for many years, and to classify them broadly, I would say that the grass rope was the efficient tool of the rough and ready, "let's go" operator: and the reata that of the finished artist, a sensitive, elastic, vibrant gear.'

The word lariat is sometimes used as verb meaning 'to catch with a rope' or 'to stake a horse out'.

It is usually pronounced LAYR-ree-uht but occasionally layr-ree-ET.

lariat pin A stake for picketing horses. Also called a *picket pin*, *stake pin* or *hitch pin*.

larigo The saddle's cinch ring; what the cinch is tied to. Also called a *larigo ring*.

lark bunting The state bird of Colorado, *Calamospiza melanocarys*. Also called the *prairie bobolink*.

larkspur A blue-flowered plant (*Delphinium nelsoni*) of the buttercup family with sharply different associations for Anglo and Indian. Cattlemen call it poison because it can kill cows by stopping the heart and the breathing. The roots are especially dangerous, and the leaves when wet are thought virulent. To Navajos, though, larkspur is a sacred plant and is used in ceremonies.

larrup To beat, to whip. Larruping as an adjective means 'great, big, extra-big' or the like.

lasher The fellow who used the whip on the *jerkline* team. As assistant to the driver, he also applied the brake.

lass rope Another word for a catch rope. (*See* lasso)

lasso One name for the cowboy's catch rope, used primarily on the West Coast. It dates from the vaqueros of New Spain and, like a lariat, is mainly for roping cows and horses. Originally, like the first lariats, it was of braided rawhide. Also called a *lass rope*. Lasso also occurs as a verb, meaning 'to rope' something. From Spanish or Portuguese, depending on which authority you believe, it is generally pronounced LAS-soh (the *a* as in *corral*) but sometimes las-soo.

last roundup One of the Westerner's many expressions for death. It even appears as a past participle – *last round-uped*. (*See* cash in your chips)

last year's bronc A horse in his second year of working cows.

lateral In an irrigation system, the ditch leading out of the main ditch.

latigo The wide leather strap that goes through the cinch ring and secures a stock saddle on a horse.

Latter-Day Saint A Mormon; a member of the Church of Jesus Christ of the Latter-Day Saints. This Church calls itself 'latter-day' because it regards itself as a re-establishment of the Church of Jesus Christ on earth, which in its view was lost after the deaths of Christ's apostles.

The Church was founded in 1830 by Joseph Smith in New York. Smith attempted to establish a spiritual centre for the Church in Missouri, then in Illinois. Under Brigham Young, the Church did establish itself in what is now Utah.

The word also appears in adjective form, as in the phrase Latter-Day Saint newspaper, and occasionally in the form Latter-Day Saintship. Mormons often refer to themselves by the abbreviation LDS.

lay (1) Among miners, a lease given by the owner of a claim to a person who proposes to work the claim for a percentage on shares rather than for wages. This lessee is called a *layman* or a *leaser*. (2) Another word for a cow outfit. [Adams] Also called a *layout*. A ranch run with badmen for hands is called a tough lay. (3) A cowboy's bed. [Adams]

A *layout* can be a person's clothing and other personal gear or a group of people, as in, 'I never liked him nor anybody in his layout.' A *lay-up* or *lay-over* was a halt in a trail drive or wagon journey.

Expressions using lay: *lay a rail fence* (for a bucking horse to pitch in a zig-zag direction, also called *fence-cornering*), *lay the dust* (to kick up your heels when inspired by whiskey or to settle the dust a little in a rainstorm), *lay the trip* (for a roper to bust a steer [Adams]) and to *lay them down* (a poker term meaning 'to quit; to die').

lazy board A plank on the left side of a Conestoga wagon where the driver rode, instead of having a seat inside.

lead In mining, a vein or lode; by extension, any good discovery, including someone to talk to.

lead chucker One of the names a cowboy called his six-shooter. [Adams] He also called it a *lead pusher*, and when he got shot he *got leaded*, *got lead poisoning* or *leaned against a bullet going past*. To *swap lead* or *swing lead* is to have a gun fight.

lead steer On a trail drive, the steer that gets out front and stays there. Cowmen saw stamina and even character in lead steers and gave them names and even affection. Some herds were led by a lead ox, which would be available for the task repeatedly, since steers were slaughtered on a yearly basis.

A *lead ox* was also an ox used for necking. That meant he would be tied neck to neck with a sulling longhorn in the Texas brush country and would bring the brute by force to the main gathering place of the cow hunt or roundup.

The *lead mule*, in a pair of draft mules, was the left one or in a team larger than a pair, the one at the head left. The *lead wagon*, in a freighting outfit, was the wagon the horses were hitched to, drawing several wagons.

The *lead drive men* are the widest circle riders at roundup. [Adams] These riders make the widest loop because they know the ins and outs of the country.

lead the pelican For a soldier to be under arrest. This is a funny expression of the Seventh Cavalry, according to Libby Custer. The outfit had caught a pelican and was bringing it along at the rear of a column. Says Mrs Custer, 'as an officer or soldier is condemned to this ignominious position also, when deprived of his place with his company, it became the custom to describe arrest as "leading the pelican".'

league In the south-west, this term may describe either linear distance or an area –

either miles or acres. The distance meant is probably about two and a half miles, the area about 4,400 acres. An adaptation from Spanish, it was often used to denote the size of Spanish and Mexican land grants.

leaky mouth Descriptive of someone who talks too much.

leather-root A plant (*Psoralea macrostachya*) valued by the Pomos and other California Indians for the toughness of its fibre.

leather-stocking A name for a frontiersman who wore hide leggings, which is how James Fenimore Cooper's Natty Bumppo got his nickname. The term originated on the Eastern frontier (the first reference is from Cooper) and was carried west.

leave him in the soup To leave someone in hot water, to run off in a fix. An expression first recorded in a Dakota Territory newspaper.

leaving Cheyenne A sentimental cowboy expression for going away. It comes from the old cowboy song 'Goodbye, Old Paint, I'm leaving Cheyenne':

My foot's in the stirrup,
My pony won't stand;
Goodbye, old paint,
I'm a-leavin' Cheyenne.

This song was traditionally the last tune at cowboy dances.

Larry McMurtry put the sentiment perfectly in his novel of the same title: 'The Cheyenne of this book is that part of the cowboy's day circle which is earliest and best: his blood's country and his heart's pasture-land.'

lechuguilla A name for several agaves of the south-west, indicator plants of the Chihuahuan desert. From Spanish, it's pronounced le-choo-GEE-yuh. A pocket gopher that feeds on it is called the *lechuguilla pocket gopher*.

ledge In mining, the lode, the lead, the ore deposit. The *ledge rock* is the true bedrock.

left side The correct side for getting on a horse; also called the near side. The other side is the *off side* or *Indian side*, which is the wrong side (among Anglos) to get on a horse. To Anglos, *Indian* often seemed to mean wrong.

leg bail Flight from the law while on bail. To take leg bail was to *skip*, to *take a powder*. Likewise, to *show leg* was to run away.

leg knife A knife worn by a long hunter or mountain man in a thong or strap that circled his legging like a garter. He also wore a belt knife and a patch knife.

legging (1) Giving a cowboy a whipping with a pair of leggings or chaps. (2) An irksome way of separating sheep of different brands that have gotten mixed. You grab each one by the leg and pull it out.

leggings The leg coverings of an Indian, long hunter, mountain man or cowboy or other mounted Westerner. They cover the legs but not the groin region, where a breech-cloth sufficed among Indians and among some whites; usually whites wear trousers under leggings. They are usually made of deerskin, which is lighter and easier to sew than elk, moose and buffalo and more durable than antelope.

Among cowboys, they're generally called *shotgun chaps*, but leggings were native sons of the movable frontier long before cowmen ever got to Texas and heard of *chaparral* or *chaparejos*, the words that are the source of *chaps*. The Kentucky long hunters of the 1770s adopted them from Indians or previous American frontiersmen and bequeathed them to the mountain men. Later they were a common style of chaps on the northern plains.

An abbreviated form is the *knee legging* (or *breed legging*), which ties on to the leg of an Indian woman or the pant leg of a white man and hangs to the top of the moccasin or boot. It was often made of blanket. East of the Mississippi, leggings worn by Indians were sometimes called *Indian boots*.

The word is sometimes spelled *leggin* without an apostrophe.

legitimate smoke In fire-fighting, smoke from any acceptable fire, as in permitted burning or machinery – useful to know when a spotter calls in a sighting of smoke.

lemon sugar An instant form of lemonade at south-western military bases in the 1870s and 1880s, according to Cornelius Smith, and so a precursor of modern convenience foods. It came in cans containing powdered sugar and a vial of lemon extract.

lemonade sumac One of several sumacs (*Rhus tribolata* or *R. integrifolia*, *Schmaltzia tribolata* or *S. emoryi*) whose fruits are used to make a drink. They range over the entire West and are sometimes used as ornamental shrubs. Also called *lemita* and *lemonade berry*.

lent One of the cowboy's words for a green hand. In adjective form, he was *lenty*. (*See also* Arbuckle's)

leopard sweat Mormon home-made whiskey, also known as *Valley Tan*. (*See* firewater)

lepero A low, scurrilous Mexican. Borrowed from the Spanish, it's pronounced LAY-puh-roh.

leppy An orphaned calf. Also called a *dogie* and a *bum calf*.

level In mining, a drift, a horizontal passage.

lever bit A severe form of the curb bit, known to be able to inflict pain.

Levis The most famous brand of blue jeans in the West, to jeans what Stetson is to hats, Winchester to rifles, Colt to pistols. Levi Strauss, a tailor, originally made this bib-less overall in California in 1850, using canvas and riveting the seams and pockets with copper to make them withstand the hard uses Westerners give them.

lick Short for *salt lick*.

lift hair An expression of the mountain men meaning 'to take scalps' and by implication 'to kill people', though not all scalped were necessarily killed.

light To get down off your horse. A cordial but succinct expression of Western hospitality to a rider was sometimes, 'Light and set.'

light a shuck To leave quickly. Since corn was the universal food and was carried in its shuck, there were shucks around the camp fires. Leaving one fire to go to another, a fellow found himself abruptly in blackness and his eyes not adjusted. So he lit a shuck, which would burn only briefly, and took off.

light burn In forest management, limited burning to reduce available fuels, which might otherwise make fires difficult to suppress and likely to cause great damage. A good deal of the controversy about Yellowstone National Park's management of its forest prior to the fires of 1988 centres on its decision to do no light burning.

light in the timber Said of a horse light-boned in the cannon bones (lower legs). (*See* horse)

light rider A rider who sits in the saddle lightly and so does not need to redo the cinch often and doesn't chafe the horse's back with the saddle.

lightning Low-grade whiskey. Though the earliest citation to lightning in Mathews's *A Dictionary of Americanisms* is 1858 in San Francisco, various authorities refer to *Taos lightning*, meaning the rough brew distilled in Taos, a couple of decades earlier. It occurs not only in that expression but in *Jersey lightning, white lightning, flash lightning* and *lightning whiskey*. In British usage, it meant gin. (For many Western expressions for booze, *see* firewater)

lightning frame A frame like a folding lattice that represents lightning in some art of the Navajo.

like a steer, I can try A wry expression indicating the futility of effort. Steers are impotent because they're cut (castrated).

like getting money from home Easy and pleasant. Though this phrase sounds collegiate, notes linguist J. L. Dillard, it is Western – Owen Wister recorded it in 1893. British aristocrats sojourning in the West often depended on remittances from home, and so were known as *remittance men*.

Lincoln shingle Hard bread issued as rations by the army during the period of the Indian Wars, according to Peter Watts. The bread was about three inches square and evidently very hard – other nicknames were sheet-iron cracker and teeth-duller. Watts says it was also called a *Lincoln pie* and a *McClellan pie*. The use of Lincoln's and McClellan's names (George B. McClellan was a Union general in the Civil War) indicates that the bread was probably a leftover from the Civil War. Some soldiers must have thought it was a literal leftover.

line (1) The boundary of a range, marked or unmarked. Sometimes it divided cattle outfits, sometimes cattle from sheep. In some uses, it meant the boundary between Anglo country and Indian, thought of as the extreme limit of civilisation. (*See also* line rider, sheep deadline and sheriff's deadline) (2) A cowboy name for a rope. (3) A logger's name for a cable. (4) An expression for the line seismic crews follow.

As a verb, it means to fetter a horse by tying its forefoot to its hind foot, instead of hobbling the forefeet together in the usual way. Also called *side-hobbling* and *side-lining*.

line breeding Breeding cows to make sure of descent from a particular family, particularly on the female side.

line rider A cowboy who rode the line and lived in a *line camp*. In the days before fences, big cow outfits used such riders to keep their own cows mostly on their side of the line (on their own range) and other outfits' cows on the other side. They also pulled cows out of bogs, doctored them, nursed them and kept predators away. With the coming of fences, they became known as fence riders, and their job was keeping the fences in good repair.

Now a line rider, also called a *line cowboy*, is simply a man who lives in a line camp in a remote part of the ranch and does cowboying. Though cow outfits are not as gargantuan as they sometimes were in the early days, they're often split up into pieces, some of which may be far from the main house.

The *line shack*, *line cabin* or *line house* is a small cabin where a cowboy lives when he's riding the line. The *line boss* is the rider in charge of a group of cowboys.

line your flue In cowboy talk, to eat.

lineback A horse or cow with a stripe down its back. On Texas longhorns, this stripe is called a lobo stripe.

link strap In the US cavalry during the period of the Indian Wars, a thong hooked to a horse's ring bit and the throat-latch buckle. When a trooper dismounted to fight he linked the strap to the ring bit of another horse; one man could hold eight horses, freeing his comrades to fight.

literary A gathering devoted to literary culture, as in, 'We went to literary last night.' Such meetings were held on the central plains from the turn of the 20th century forward, almost always on winter evenings. People read literature aloud, recited poems, debated, read their own works and the like. Like the Chautauquas elsewhere, such gatherings provided some intellectual stimulation and a little social life.

little giant In placer mining, a metal pipe that carries water and has a nozzle (called a *giant*) at the end. As the water pressure goes up, the nozzle gets smaller, controlling the flow.

Little Mary What the cowboys on a trail drive called the fellow who drove the blatting cart, the vehicle for the newborn calves that couldn't keep up. [Adams]

little old This combination of adjective, observed Owen Wister, was 'applied to anything, e.g., a little old pony; hard to say what it means'. Two qualities it does not indicate are small and aged. Usually it's just a fond diminutive.

Little Phil A Western soldier's nickname for General Philip Henry Sheridan (famous Civil War general), a commander of the Division of the Missouri known for his lack of sympathy for the Plains Indians his armies fought.

little red wagon Among miners, a portable toilet.

live dictionary What some cowboys called a schoolmarm or any other woman with lots of words. In Elmer Kelton's splendid novel *The Good Old Boys*, the protagonist, Hewey, a good old cowboy, meets a live dictionary, falls for her and in the end has to decide whether to settle down with her or keep on rolling.

live oak The common name of a variety of oaks that grow in California and the desert south-west. Acorns and foliage are an important wildlife food source, and the hard wood was used by California pioneers to make splitting mauls and carriage parts.

living firebreak In forestry, a strip of ground where flame-resistant vegetation is growing. This is particularly popular in California.

lizard-tailed outlaw Katie Lee, author of *Ten Thousand Goddam Cattle*, says this is a bad guy who is 'mean and scrawny and quick to get away'.

llano A south-western expression for a steppe, a dry, treeless plain. A fabled one is the Llano Estacado (or staked plain) of New Mexico and Texas, inhabited by Indians called *llaneros*. Borrowed from Spanish, it's pronounced YAH-noh.

Lo A generic name for Indians that has now fallen into disuse. Usually it was used like a proper noun – 'Cowardly Lo prefers to attack none but very small parties' – but sometimes as a common noun – 'the Lo's are passing . . . rapidly from the face of the earth'. Its source is Alexander Pope's *An Essay on Man*:

Lo, the poor Indian! Whose untutor'd mind

Sees God in clouds, or hears him in the wind;

That first phrase became a mocking watchword among Americans, who for more than a century after it was written (1733) suffered from what they regarded as the maraudings of the Indians. (For Anglo terms for Indians, *see* siwash)

load Among cowboys, a verb meaning to tell tall tales. Also, a cowboy used to describe a fellow with long hair as having a *load of hay on his skull*. [Adams] Some cowboys still might.

loaded for bear To be fully armed, prepared for trouble, with a full head of steam up, spoiling for a fight. It can be a metaphoric preparedness: an angry wife waiting for a late husband is often described as loaded for bear. The phrase comes from the choice of loads a hunter has with his rifle, the option of more or less powder or lead. A heavy load would be chosen for a creature as big as a bear.

loading chute A fenced ramp for getting livestock on to trains in the days of the great trail drives, usually from pens called *loading corrals*. Now loading chutes are primarily for getting critters on to trucks.

loading jack In logging, a rig for loading logs and trucks. It is now a rig with a loading block for picking up logs from the ground but was once a framework for hoisting logs out of the water. The logger who is doing the work is a *loader*.

lobby In a logging camp, where the workers wash up and wait for mealtime. [Adams]

lobo The grey wolf or timber wolf. The term was borrowed from Spanish and also appeared in an anglicised form, *loafer*. He was also called a *loafer wolf*, a *lover wolf* and a *lobo wolf*.

The wolf is an animal that symbolises the conquest of the West. In the 1800s, wolves were an important part of the ecosystem, keeping populations of hoofed creatures in check. With white settlement, the wolf was viewed as a threat to both livestock and civilisation and was ruthlessly exterminated. Government officials trapped, poisoned and shot wolves. Wolves remain in the lower 48 states, in only northern Minnesota, Montana and, perhaps, Wyoming. Considerable controversy surrounds the reintroduction of the wolf to Yellowstone Park; ranchers, hunters and politicians don't want the wolf, but wildlife biologists and environmentalists do. The wolf may take care of reintroduction on its own.

lobo stripe The stripe down the back of a lineback, especially a Texas longhorn. It may be white, yellow or brown.

locate (1) To file a mining claim. Usually the phrase is 'to locate a claim'.

The person who does the locating is called a *locator*. (2) To file a claim to land, especially land with springs and streams, under the homestead law. (3) To put cows on to a new range.

The act of filing a mineral claim was called *location*. The area of the claim, which is traditionally marked with *location stakes*, was also called a location. Staking a claim was also called *pegging it*.

lock horns To fight. As applied to human beings, it often means to come into confrontation, to argue, to engage in a struggle of wills. From the behaviour of buffalo bulls, elk bulls and other male beasts – they fight with their horns to achieve dominance and the right to mate with the cows.

locked spurs Spurs with the rowels tied so they won't move. Then, if the rider puts them into the cinch (called screwing them down), the spurs will hold him fast; if the rowels rolled, the spurs wouldn't hold him. In rodeo, it's illegal to lock your spurs.

loco As an adjective (the most common use), it means crazy and can be applied to man or beast. As a noun, it can mean the locoweed, the poisoning that comes on livestock that eat locoweed or a preparation made from locoweed that affects human beings. The poisoning is sometimes called *locoism*. Loco also occurs as a verb – to *get locoed* (to get crazy) or to *let something loco you* (make you crazy). The word is borrowed from Spanish, where it means 'crazy', and is pronounced LOH-koh.

locoweed Any of a number of plants widespread in the mountain West, especially of the genera *Astragalus* and *Oxytropis*, that make livestock act crazy when they eat them. It can be fatal to cattle.

lode claim In mining, a legal claim to gold or other mineral in a lode or vein. A *placer claim* entitles the miner to wash gold from sand or gravel.

lodge A tipi of the Plains Indians; also the family that lived in the tipi. Sometimes the word refers to permanent dwelling places of agricultural Indians, such as the earth lodges of the Arikara. Since the word *lodge* was often a way of saying family, Westerners used it to express the number of families of Indians, as in a village of 20 lodges.

A *lodge skirt* is the lower part of the covering of a lodge or tipi, which was often raised in the summer to bring in cooling breezes.

lodgepole (1) A variety of pine, *Pinus murrayana*, with a straight trunk that makes a good pole for a tipi (lodge). This pine has cones that open in the heat of a forest fire; it played an important role in the Yellowstone fires of 1988. (2) A pole, usually cut from the trunk of a lodgepole pine, used by Plains Indians (and some Anglos) to hold up a tipi. The Dakota-style tipi, according to Reginald and Gladys Laubin's *The Indian Tipi*, requires 17 poles – trimmed and peeled and anywhere from 20 to 30 or more feet long – for lodges of family-dwelling size. The poles were also used to transport each family's material goods – they made travois when travelling. And the travois left what was called a *lodgepole trail*, a track dug into the earth by the dragging butts of the poles. (3) To lodgepole is to drub or thrash, from when an early trapper used a lodgepole to beat an Indian wife. Later the meaning extended to all beatings.

log To take the timber from an area and cut it into logs. Such an area is called *logged off* when it is completely cleared of trees, *logged over* when it is partially cleared.

log sledge A wooden platform on runners that supports one end of logs as they are skidded, reducing friction. Also called a *log sledge*, *bob*, *crotch*, *drag sledge*, *dray*, *go-devil*, *joe-log*, *lizard*, *log boat*, *mud-boat*, *scoot*, *sloop*, *stone boat*, *travoy* and *wood boat*.

Combinations: *logging berth* (a logging camp), *logging berry* (a prune), *log birling* or *riding* (rolling a log underfoot as it floats, done as work, as sport and even in competition), *logging chance* (a patch of forest suitable for logging), *log drive* or *log run* (the movement of logs down-river), *log interest* (the companies with a commercial interest or stake in logging), *log road* (not only a road for logging but one made of logs, that is, a corduroy road), *logging show* (a logging enterprise) and *logging side* (transporting logs from the woods to where they're to be loaded).

Combinations pertaining to logging equipment: log measurer (a tool for gauging the usable board feet in logs), *log rule* or *scale* (a table of the number of board feet in logs of different diameters and lengths), *log shoot* or *chute* (a chute made of split logs for skidding logs downhill), *log stamp* (a device for marking the number of board feet on logs), *log way* or *jack* (a chute or slide for logs), *logging wheels* (a pair of wheels usually about 10 feet in diameter used to transport logs, which are slung beneath the axle) and *log wrench* (a cant hook or peavey).

logger The name for labouring men in logging in the West – they do not call themselves lumberjacks. Other names for loggers generally, not designating workers with specialised tasks: *Arkie, bindle stiff, brush ape, brush cat, brush rat, bush rat, gabezo, jack, log cutter, logman, long logger, lumberer, lumberjack, lumber rustler, lumber stiff, Paul, Paul Bunyan's boy, savage, shanty boy, shanty man, slave, tame ape, timber beast, timber-jack, timber savage, timber wolf, wood head* and *wood hick.*

Some more specialised loggers are: *log cuffer* (a worker who birls [rolls] logs), *log driver* (a worker who floats logs down-river), *log jockey* (a worker in booms), *long logger* (a West Coast logger who works with log lengths of 40 feet), *log maker* (a worker who cuts trees into log lengths) and *log watch* (an expert river driver).

Logger's smallpox is the calk-shaped scars on a logger's body. They came from getting kicked by loggers' boots, which had calks (metal studs) on the soles.

Novelist and historian Bill Gulick says a logger is a man who shaves with a double-bitted axe, cuts his hair with a chainsaw and stirs his coffee with his thumb.

loggering In rodeo, to come out of the chute grabbing the saddle horn, an embarrassing lapse. [Adams]

logging Hobbling a horse by tying a light log to its leg. Such a weight is also known as a drag.

logging chain A levered chain grab hook used in loading logs. Also any heavy chain used in logging, which may be more strictly a *log chain.*

loma A south-western term for a rise or low hill. Borrowed from Spanish and pronounced LOH-muh, it is often used in place names, for instance, Loma Linda.

lone ranger Cowboy lingo for an unmarried man. Compare *buck nun*, which means hermit, and *lone wolf*, which means a man who goes it alone. Lone wolf occurs in verb form – he's *lone-wolfing* it.

Lone Star Pertaining to Texas. The flag and seal of the Texas republic used a single star. Thus *Lone Star banner, Lone Star flag, Lone Star rattler, Lone Star State* and *Lone Star Stater.* But some caution is required: The state flags of Louisiana and South Carolina are also Lone Star flags; so is the Cuban flag. Sometimes 'lone star' is printed in lower case; sometimes the phrase 'single star' substitutes for it.

long chance A chance against long odds. Mathews records as its earliest citation Stewart Edward White's *Arizona Nights*: 'He's plumb scared at the prospect of suffering anything, and would rather die right off than take long chances.' Drawing to an inside straight is a long chance. So was homesteading on the Great Plains. A great many people went broke doing each.

long hair An old-timer, a long-time resident of the West, an old alkali, a longhorn. In the early West, men wore their hair long, perhaps because of the lack of barbers. In *Arizona Nights*, just after the turn of the last century, Stewart Edward White described one such fellow: 'The old man was one of the typical "long hairs". He had come to the Gailuro Mountains in '69, and since '69 had remained in the Gailuro Mountains, spite man or devil.'

Near the Navajo reservation today, a long hair means a traditional male Navajo, usually but not always elderly. The uncut hair itself shows an inclination to follow tradition.

long hunter A frontiersman and fur man of the Appalachian region in the second half of the 18th century, such as Simon Kenton or Daniel Boone. A precursor of the mountain man.

long knife Indian Pidgin English for white man. First applied to a fighting force of Virginians, it is said to have come from the swords carried by white soldiers. How much it was used in the West is unclear. It's in the Anglo literature but may have been supplied by the white writers for whatever native word was actually used. Another Indian Pidgin expression for whites is *long beard* (for other names Indians had for whites, *see* Anglo).

long rifle The first truly American firearm. Also called the *Kentucky rifle*. A flint-locker, it was adapted by Pennsylvania gunsmiths from the European rifle to the conditions of the frontier – made lighter, more slender and of lighter calibre. It went over the mountains with frontiersmen to Kentucky and then went west to the Rocky Mountains with the mountain men. Late in the heyday of the western beaver trade, in the 1830s, it began to be replaced by the plains rifle, which had a shorter stock and was heavier. Also called a *long tom*.

long sweetening Molasses, the most common sweetener in the West in the early days – sugar was scarce. It was also called *black-strap*, *larrup*, *lick*, *long lick* and *long-tailed sugar*. Sugar was called *short sweetening*.

long time Califorin' In the early 20th century, what Chinese immigrants would tell immigration officials to establish they had lived in California and were legal citizens.

long tom In placer mining, an inclined trough for washing ores that bear gold. It is sometimes capitalised.

long rider An outlaw.

long rope A rustler.

long trail A Western expression for death. (For various expressions for dying, *see* cash in your chips)

long yearling A cow that's nearer two years old than one. Likewise, another year older is called a long two.

long-ear A cow without an earmark, by implication an unbranded cow.

longhorn cattle *See* Texas longhorns.

look at a mule's tail In cowboy talk, to plough. [Adams] Traditionally, cowboys despised work that couldn't be done on horseback.

looking up a limb What a hanged man is said to be doing. He's also said to be *looking through cotton-wood leaves*. [Adams] (*See* string party)

lookout (1) A rider who goes out ahead of a herd of cattle to find graze. (2) At a gambling table, a house man who watches the play, particularly to guard against cheating. (3) A fire-spotter.

looloo An eccentric hand in poker that under local rules is a top hand. When three clubs and two diamonds was a looloo in Butte, Montana, one celebrated afternoon, it even beat the four aces held by a stranger to town.

loop What a cowboy calls the noose of his lasso. Sometimes he spins the loop before throwing it, but often he just uses a quick flip. But if people say a fellow swings a *wide loop*, they mean he's a rustler.

loose-herd To herd cattle so that they're neither widely scattered nor tightly bunched, giving them room to graze. The opposite is *close-herd*.

lop-horn Descriptive of a cow with a horn that points down.

lope A smooth, relaxed gait for a horse, faster than a trot and slower than a gallop; a canter. It is used not only as a noun but a verb, as in, 'We loped our horses across the meadow.'

lose your hair To get scalped; to die. The expression was recorded by Lt George Frederick Ruxton in the 1840s. (For various expressions for dying, *see* cash in your chips)

lose your hat To get bucked off. A hand spotted on the ground near his horse is likely to say he lost his hat and dismounted to get it. His explanation may cause some joshing. [Adams] To *lose your horse* meant the same.

louse cage What a logger calls both his hat and the bunkhouse. [Adams]

low-neck clothes A cowboy's Sunday-go-to-meeting clothes. [Adams]

lubber grasshopper The common name for three different kinds of grasshoppers, primarily desert dwellers, that are major pests in the Great Plains region. One of them, *Brachystola magna*, a big clumsy creature, is also known as the 'Clumsy Locust'. New World grasshoppers are often called locusts because of their resemblance to the biblical locusts, with their voracious appetites and swarming in dense clouds.

lucifer A match, colourfully named. Matches were invented in 1827 by the English druggist John Walker and were quickly available in the United States. They came in wooden blocks, and you broke a single one off a block. The word is not a Westernism, but British.

lumber To log a tract of timber. The worker who does this work is sometimes a *lumberer*, *lumberjack*, *lumberman*, *lumber rustler* or *lumber stiff*. In the West, the equivalent words that stem from log are more common – log and logger.

luminarias Among New Mexican Hispanics, a candle, these days in a sand-filled paper bag, particularly associated with festivals. Also called *farolitos*.

lump oil Cowboy talk for kerosene or coal oil.

lump-jaw (1) Actinomycosis, an infection of cattle and sheep that causes tumours around the jaw. Also called *lumpy jaw*, *lumped jaw*, *big jaw* and *wooden tongue*. (2) Swelling or infection of a horse's mouth.

lunger A person who came to the West in hopes that the dry air would benefit his health.

lynch To punish an alleged criminal without due process of law. Though lynching usually means hanging in the West, early in the period of Western settlement it often meant beating or tarring and feathering. Associated with vigilance committees (made up of vigilantes), lynching did not, in fact, originate in the West but was named after a lynch-law policy started by Captain William Lynch of Pittsylvania County, Virginia during the Revolutionary War. *Lynch law* was the practice of punishing without a proper trial, a *lynch mob* was a gang hot to do some lynching and a *lynching bee* was a hanging. For a while, even the modifier *lynchy* had some currency, as in, 'The mob had a lynchy look.'

M

machada In the south-west, a flock of billy goats. Borrowed from Spanish, it's pronounced muh-CHAH-duh. A single male goat is a *cabron* in Spanish.

machero In the south-west of the 19th century, a lighter for cigarettes and cigars. Adapted from the Spanish *mechero* (which has the same meaning), it's pronounced muh-CHAY-roh.

machete A heavy knife used for chopping. Borrowed from Spanish, it's usually Americanised to muh-SE-tee.

macho Now usually an adjective with the derogatory meaning 'ultra-masculine', it originally meant a number of things connoting masculinity, from a male mule to a male mescaline plant to the hook of a hook and eye. Borrowed from Spanish (where it has those original meanings), it's pronounced MAH-choh. It gives rise to the noun *machismo*, meaning 'a code of masculine courage and virility'.

mackinaw (1) A heavy blanket originally traded to Indians of the Great Lakes region. The name may derive from the strait of Mackinac, between Lake Michigan and Lake Huron, or the trading post situated there. (2) A scow-shaped boat used by fur traders around the Great Lakes and on the Missouri River, 40 or more feet long and 10 feet wide, controlled by a steersman and four oarsmen, with a very shallow draft, strictly for downstream travel. (3) A plaid coat made from a blanket and popular among woodsmen. (4) Variously a hat, shirt or gun with the same name.

made wolf meat Descriptive of a person who was killed and his body left on the prairie. [Adams]

magpie Cowboy talk for a Holstein cow. [Adams]

maguey A common name of the agave. Borrowed from Spanish, it's pronounced MAH-gay or mah-GAY, and occasionally spelled McGay.

The fibres of the maguey were used by Indians for weaving and by whites to make a slender rope more useful for roping tricks than for hard cow work. The maguey also yields liquors known as mescal and pulque.

mahala In 19th century California, an occasional word (from the Mariposan Indian) for squaw, Indian woman.

mail-order cowboy A tenderfoot decked out too fancily in what he hopes is cowboy clothing. This fellow used to be more elaborately described as a *mail-order catalogue on foot*. [Adams]

make Several Western expressions use *make*: to *make a hand* (to become competent at cowboying), *make a port* (among old-time freighters, to find a camping place [Adams]), *make hair bridles* (to spend time in jail, where cowboys passed the time by doing just that), *make medicine* (to hold a conference or do some conjuring), *make shave-tails* (to break horses *see* shave-tail]), *make the town smoky* (to shoot it up), *make tracks* or *make dust* (to hurry), *make a nine in your tail* (to clear out, vamoose, get gone; from the shape a scared cow's tail makes when she takes off [Adams]) and *make a hat* (among loggers, to take up a collection).

make meat To make jerky (to cut meat into thin slices and dry it for preservation). An expression of the mountain men. Sometimes simply 'to hunt animals for food'.

makings Paper and tobacco for making a cigarette. The first citations for this term are Western. Old-time cowboys seldom smoked 'tailor-made' (manu-factured) cigarettes, and to refuse a man the makings was considered an insult.

mal de vache The diarrhoea common to early travellers on the Great Plains, thought to be caused by alkali water or by the change to an all-meat diet. Borrowed from French and pronounced MAHL duh VAHSH.

maleta In the south-west, a rawhide saddlebag. Borrowed from Spanish, it's pronounced muh-LAH-tuh.

malpais Lava-bed country; badlands. The original French means 'bad country, bad to travel through'. Pronounced MAL-pie (the *a* as in corral). Sometimes occurs in the form *mallapy* or the like.

mamelle A rounded hill. Borrowed from Canadian French, where it means 'a woman's breast'. Also occurs in the form *mammilla*.

man at the pot! A cow-camp cry. If you went to the pot for coffee, the cry obligated you to fill everyone else's cup. [Adams]

man for breakfast A murder; a body in the streets at dawn. Said to have been commonplace in the early days of Los Angeles and in Denver.

manada In the south-west, a band of breeding mares with a stallion; any herd of horses or cows. Borrowed from Spanish, it's pronounced muh-NAH-duh.

manadero The stud or herding stallion that claimed a band of wild mares. From the Spanish and pronounced mah-nuh-DAY-roh.

mañana In the south-west, tomorrow, sometime later, whenever – the indefinite future, considered in a leisurely way. Borrowed from Spanish (where it means 'tomorrow'), it's pronounced mahn-YAH-nuh. Mexico is sometimes called *mañana land*.

Mandan A Siouan tribe of the Missouri River Valley, living near the Heart River in North Dakota at the time of white contact. The Mandan economy was based on both hunting and agriculture; they lived in earth lodges and were skilled makers of pottery. Their society was based closely on clans and on ceremonial religious practices.

When the Mandans were reduced in number by smallpox in the middle of the 18th century and were under pressure from the westwarding Dakota, they settled near the Knife River with the Hidatsa, who also had a semi-sedentary way of life. There they were visited and studied by various whites (including Lewis and Clark, Catlin and Prince Maximilian), some of whom thought them the long-sought Welsh Indians. In 1837 the Mandan were again ravaged by smallpox – their tribe was reduced from 1,600 to 125 – and eventually were forced to merge with the Hidatsa and Arikara on the Fort Berthold Reservation in North Dakota.

Mandan Corn is an upper Missouri River corn with white, blue and yellow kernels.

manga In the south-west, a poncho, a cloak. Borrowed from Spanish, it's pronounced MAHNG-guh.

mangeur de lard Among fur men, a beginner, a greenhorn. Originally a French-Canadian term of the voyageurs, it means, literally, 'pork-eater' and occasionally appears in that form. It comes from the custom of the French-Canadians' feeding canoe-men pork in their corn mush on the river routes between Montreal and Lake Superior. The canoe-men of the further interior were skilled at living *aux aliments du pays* (off the land).

Manifest Destiny The doctrine held by many Americans, especially in the 19th century, of the inevitable domination of North America by white people or by the United States. It swept the country during the 1840s, at the time of the US expansion in the south-west through the Mexican War and in the north-west through treaty with Great Britain.

manila The most popular of the hemp cowboy ropes, three-strand and tough.

mano In the south-west, a stone used to grind grain by hand on a metate (bed stone). Borrowed from Spanish (where it means 'hand'), it's pronounced MAH-noh.

mansador In the south-west, a Hispanic horse-breaker, especially of the old style of training horses with hackamores, once the preferred way in California. Borrowed from Spanish, it's pronounced man-suh-DOHR.

manso A Christianised Indian; also called a *mansito*. Borrowed from Spanish, it's pronounced MAHN-soh.

manta In the south-west, a pack cover of coarse cotton cloth; also the cloth itself or a big shawl made from it. Borrowed from Spanish (where it has similar meanings), it's pronounced MAHN-tuh. A *mantilla* is a woman's shawl.

manteca In the south-west, lard. Borrowed from Spanish, it's pronounced man-TAY-kuh.

manzanita A bush of the genus *Arctostaphylos* that covers hillsides in dry parts of the south-west, sometimes growing more than head high. In Spanish, it literally means 'little apple', a reference to its fruit. Pronounced man-zuh-NEE-tuh. Also called *mountain mahogany* (as are madroñe and other shrubs with reddish wood).

mariachi   In the south-west, a band of strings and brasses that plays a characteristic gay and sentimental music, often in restaurants or on the streets. Borrowed from Spanish, it's pronounced mah-ree-AH-chee.

mark   To earmark and dock the tails of lambs.

Among sheep-herders, a *marker* is a black sheep used to help in counting. Among cowboys, it is a cow with readily recognisable natural markings.

marmot   A cousin of the woodchuck that lives in the Rocky Mountains and hibernates during the winter. Also called a *rock-chuck, mountain badger, whistle pig* or by French-Canadians *siffleur*. Sometimes Westerners call prairie dogs marmots.

masa   Corn that has been treated with lye and finely ground into a flour. It is the main ingredient in tortillas and tamales and is an essential component in Hispanic diets as wheat is in Anglo diets. Adapted from Spanish (where it means 'dough'), it's pronounced mah-SAH.

matanza   In Spanish California, the killing of cattle for hides and tallow; the place where such killing was done. Borrowed from Spanish, it's pronounced muh-TAN-suh, the *a* as in *corral*.

maverick   A slick; an unbranded calf. Since it didn't follow a cow and so was of undetermined ownership, a maverick was a wonderful target for folks who wanted to increase their herds more rapidly than nature intended. This led to the verb form of the word, to maverick, to *brand mavericks*, that is, appropriate them. Throwing your brand on mavericks was called *jacking mavericks*.

In the early West, mavericking was more or less accepted as a way to get a herd started. A little later, it was controlled – at roundups mavericks were divided fairly – and free-lancing maverickers were

considered thieves. Jim Averill and Cattle Kate, for instance, were hanged (unjustly) for being mavericks, leading central Wyoming toward the Johnson County War.

Free-lance mavericks were liable to end up where they didn't want to be. The cowboy artist Charlie Russell, in *Good Medicine*, reports that one hand 'quit punchin' and went into the cow business for himself. His start was a couple o' cows and a work bull. Each cow had six to eight calves a year. People didn't say much till the bull got to havin' calves, and then they made it so disagreeable that Charlie quit the business and is now makin' hoss-hair bridles,' which was how cowboys passed the time in jail.

The term maverick is supposed to have gotten its start when a Texas lawyer named Samuel Maverick failed to brand his calves. Then the next owner started identifying every unbranded calf in the country with some phrase like, 'That's one of Maverick's,' and so claiming it as his own.

The word is also spelled *mavoric, mavorick* and *mauvric.*

By extension the word has come to signify a person of no family or faction, an independent, a loner, a misfit.

A *mavericker* was a fellow who hunted and branded mavericks. A *maverick brand* is an unrecorded brand. A rustler who killed cows to make their calves mavericks was said to be *running a maverick factory.*

mayordomo   In the south-west, the manager of a ranch or of an irrigation system. Borrowed from Spanish, it's pronounced MAY-or-DOH-moh.

The (irrigation) ditch manager supervises the cleaning of the ditch in the spring, the repair of the presas (dams) and desagüe (gates), regulates the flow and determines the amount of water each parciante (shareholder) receives. Stanley Crawford in *Mayordomo* writes of being a mayordomo: 'What good is it to be the *mayordomo* of the Acequia de la Jara? . . . A job nobody much wants. But none the less a job, one of the few that a small community can give, often reluctantly, to one of its members . . . You become even more involved and [entwined with the community]. Next to blood relationships, which rule the valley, come water relationships.'

McCarty *See* mecate.

McClellan (1) A light saddle for cavalry use. It was used for nearly a century by the US military beginning in the 1850s and was designed by Civil War General George B. McClellan after a Hungarian saddle. It had an open slot from pommel to cantle. (2) A military cap in the West of the 1870s and 1880s.

McLeod tool Among loggers, a combination hoe, rake and cutting tool with a short handle.

meat bag Trapper talk for the stomach. A *meat biscuit* was a concoction of what boils out of meat combined with flour, invented by Gail Borden of the condensed milk company. *Meat in the pot* was cowboy slang for a rifle.

mecate A rope of horsehair (or sometimes maguey) used as reins with a hackamore. It is very long (usually 22 feet) to make a long lead rope. The mecate is black and white, tied with a knot (in Spanish *la mota*) just above the heel knot and is valued by many horse breakers who prefer the hackamore style. The word is often corrupted to *McCarty*.

medicine The Indian Pidgin English term for the Indian concept of the power of the spirits. Medicine is the sway of the spiritual dimension of life, from the grand deities, from the minor spirits and from the great mysteries like sun, rain and wind. Sometimes the word seems simply to mean 'mysterious'. Almost all western Indians sought (and often still seek) medicine, the benevolent power of the spiritual in their lives.

Medicine can be made physical in medicine objects to which this power has been brought. Such an object can be natural, as in the medicine rock of the Gros Ventres or the medicine wolf (the coyote); it can be part of an animal kept for its power. It can also be man-made, such as a fetish that embodies or represents power. Or it can be made present in a ceremony or dance such as the sun dance.

A man of great medicine has strong contact with the powers, and so is likely to have strength and courage, understanding of both the apparent and the invisible worlds, harmony to live well and to survive dangerous situations, the power to heal illnesses of spiritual and physical causes, and so on.

Medicine could also mean healing among the Indians, which was often done with herbs but never entirely dissociated from matters of spirit. To *make medicine* is to appeal to Spirit via prayer, ritual or ceremony.

The word can be used in combinations with many words to mean an object or a process of power – thus *medicine arrow*, *medicine dance* and so on. It's also used for objects associated with power, as in *medicine lodge* (sweat lodge), where power is sought.

Other combinations of this kind are: *medicine bird* (the mourning dove), *medicine dream* (a dream bringing spirits and their power), *medicine drum* (a drum used for conjuring), *medicine hogan* (a Navajo hut used for conjuring), *medicine man* or *medicine woman* (a person who has contact with Spirit and who conjures), *medicine pole* (a pole hung with an object symbolising supplication), *medicine smoke* (a process of sacred smoking), *medicine society* (a Pueblo society organised for religious purpose) and *medicine song* (a conjuring song).

The word was also used in contexts where the spiritual element is less clear, which could be because of misunderstanding by white interpreters or because sacredness and mystery are being attributed to these objects. Thus a *medicine buffalo* was an ox, a *medicine dog* a horse, a *medicine iron* a gun and a *medicine talk* an important conference.

Certainly purely white meanings arose: A *medicine show* was an entertainment by whites in psuedo-Indian style. And *bad medicine* meant either bad luck or, when descriptive of a man, a dangerous hombre. To a trapper, medicine was bait to make the beaver come to the trap. It could also mean simply 'information', as in, 'I have no medicine on that.'

medicine bundle An Indian's sacred bundle, usually the skin of an animal with the owner's personal objects of medicine (spiritual power), such as sacred feathers, plants, stones, whistles and the like. Medicine bundles could also embody the medicine of an entire tribe, as the Ark of the Covenant does. In that case it was assigned to a keeper as a sacred responsibility.

medicine pipe A pipe used by Indians (and not only western Indians) to consecrate deeds or invoke spirit power. It consists of an L-shaped bowl of Catlinite (representing the earth) and a wooden stem (representing all that grows on the earth) and may be enhanced by eagle feathers (representing the winged creatures of the air). Often revered by Plains Indians as *the* sacred object. (*See* Black Elk's account of the pipe's central place in Dakota ceremonialism in Joseph Epes Brown's *The Sacred Pipe*)

The tomahawk was sometimes combined with a pipe. This device, called a *hatchet pipe* or *tomahawk pipe*, dating from colonial times and symbolising both war and peace, was an English invention.

Here is part of the blessing a modern Lakota of medicine, Lame Deer, gave to the pipe of a visiting Anglo, Kenneth Lincoln, as recounted in Lincoln's *The Good Red Road:* 'Lame Deer counselled us to sing with the spirits – and to hear the holy silence of the soul's rest, the life-stirring sounds of pulsing and breathing, gratitude and reverence, the return gifts to *Wakan Tanka* [the great spirit]. Humility, sacrifice, respect, kindliness – right listening and feeling to find others' needs – these were proper qualities and graces of a human life. He repeated his words in four different ways as a litany, tightening a circular path to a core of suffering and communion. Then he told us to consider how wide the bowl reached, to embrace all creation in a sacred hoop, offering the pipe-stem to ancient spirits in all directions.'

medicine water In Indian Pidgin English, either whiskey or a hot, sulphurous spring. The 1840s adventurer

Lt George Frederick Ruxton tells us that the mountain men also associated hot springs with spirit power: 'The American and Canadian trappers assert that the numerous springs which, under the head of Beer, Soda, Steamboat Springs, &c., abound in the Rocky Mountains, are the spots where his satanic majesty comes up from his kitchen to breathe the sweet fresh air, which must doubtless be refreshing to his worship after a few hours spent in superintending the culinary process going on below.'

Melchizedek The higher priesthood of the Church of Jesus Christ of the Latter-Day Saints. These priests are able to represent Christ on earth and perform the rituals of healing the sick, baptising, confirming and carrying out patriarchal duties. (*See* Aaronic)

menudo Tripe soup, a popular dish in Mexican restaurants. Adapted from Spanish (where it means 'cow viscera') and pronounced men-oo-doh.

merc A term for the general store still in Western use. Short for mercantile.

mericat A word of the Indians of south-eastern Utah for an American; originally any Anglo who wasn't a Mormon.

mesa A rocky, flat-topped tableland, either standing isolated or an area between valleys. More common in the south-west and a rough equivalent of plateau in the north. Borrowed from Spanish (where it means 'table'), it's pronounced MAY-suh. The diminutive form *mesilla* (little tableland) used to occur in the south-west.

mescal (1) Any plant of the genus *Agave*, such as the century plant. (2) The peyote plant, *Lophophora williamsi*. (3) A food made from the agave (maguey) by Hispanics and Indians. (4) A clear liquor made from the maguey plant (*See* tequila). Mescal is variously spelled, especially as *mezcal*.

Since the baked root of the mescal was an important food of the Apaches east of the Rio Grande, those Indians were and are called *Mescaleros*.

The practice of taking peyote (mescal)

to gain self-knowledge is called *mescalism*.

Combinations: mescal bean (a bean not of the mescal but mixed with that drink for narcotic effect), *mescal bud* (the flowering stalk of the century plant (an agave), *mescal ceremony* (a ceremony of Plains Indians involving the drinking of mescal), *mescal rattle* (a gourd rattle used in the mescal ceremony) and *mescal thread*, a fibre from the agave used by Indians.

mescal button · The top of the peyote cactus (or mescal button cactus), which when dried and then ingested causes hallucinations or (from the religious view) visions. Also called a *mescal head*.

The use of peyote has been an important religious ceremony of some south-western and Plains Indians for a long time and is now central to the ceremonies of the Native American Church.

mesquite In the south-west, a low-growing, thorny, shrub-like tree, *Prosopis juliflora*, with a hard wood. Indians made a flour from the beans, and livestock eat its seeds. Mesquite is notorious for its thickets, which are called *mesquital* or *chaparral* or *mogotes*, and make the brush country of south-west Texas nearly impenetrable. The word is variously and creatively spelled. From the Spanish *mexquite* (which in turn comes from Nahuatl and has the same meaning), it's pronounced muhs-KEET.

Combinations: mesquite bean (used by Indians as food and also as the basis of a mildly alcoholic drink), *mesquite grass* (a good forage of the genus *Boutaloua*), *mesquite meal* (a food made by grinding the bean) and *mesquite root* (a good fuel in a barren country).

mess beef A pickled or salted beef of early Texas. The *mess house* was the ranch cookhouse, the *mess room* the cowboys' dining room and the *mess wagon* the chuck wagon (which had a storage box called the *mess box*) or the freighting wagon carrying the provisions. [Adams]

mestizo A mixed blood. (*See* metis)

metate In the south-west, the bed stone on which Indians did their grinding of food with a mano.

metis A half-breed, especially one from the settlements of the Red River of the north, whose people descend from Canadian fur men (French, Scottish and British) and Indian women. Originally French-Canadian, it's pronounced MAY-tee. The French form *metif* also occurs. The people of the Turtle Mountain Reservation near the US–Canadian border in North Dakota call themselves and their language *Mitchef*. In the south-west, the Spanish version, *mestizo*, is more common.

Mexican In the south-west, a peso, or adobe dollar; a variety of sheep.

Mex is short for Mexican Spanish or, usually used with some disparagement, a Mexican person. As an adjective, it is short for anything Mexican. *Mexicano* is much like Mex, without the disparagement.

Combinations: Mexican bit (a horse's bit with a curb ring rather than curb chain), *Mexican iron* (rawhide), *Mexican oats* (nonsense [Adams]), *Mexican packsaddle* (an aparejo), *Mexican saddle* (a saddle with particularly high pommel and cantle, wooden stirrups and heavy skirts), *Mexican spur* (an ornamented spur with big rowels), *Mexican strawberry* (either a bean or a species of prickly pear said to be delicious) and *Mexico piece* (a Spanish piece of eight found in Mexico).

mezcal *See* mescal.

mico Among the Creek, Chickasaw, Choctaw and Seminole (and other Indians of the Muskogee linguistic family), a chief. Also spelled *meiko*, and pronounced MY-koh.

migra A Hispanic nickname for the US border patrol. Adapted from the Spanish word *immigración* (immigration) and pronounced mee-GRAH.

milagro (1) Miracle or wonder, as in John Nichol's *The Milagro Beanfield War*. (2) Among the Indians and Mexicans of the south-west, a black cross to which silver charms in the shape of parts of the body are nailed to promote health and healing. Borrowed from Spanish (where it means 'miracle') and pronounced mih-LAH-groh.

milk pitcher Cowboy talk for a cow that is giving milk. She may live on a milk ranch (dairy farm).

mill A circular motion that desperate cowboys hoped to get a stampeding herd into so that it would run out its fury going round and round. A mill in a river, though, called a *merry-go-round in high water*, was plenty dangerous to the beasts and the men who tried to break it up.

The word also occurs as both a transitive and intransitive verb – cowboys try to mill a herd, and cows mill.

Owen Wister described the way cowboys mill a herd: 'It seems that a mere nothing suffices to cause a herd [to] stampede. An old cow will snuff once, and the bunch starts off like lightning, as if this had been a prearranged signal. Then the two ways to stop them are, first, to have three or four men on one side continually turning them, keeping along with them and so bring them around behind the rest, thus making an ever contracting ring till the whole is a mass of animals pivoting on its centre; or a man takes the lead (which is very dangerous, because one trip means death under the hooves of the following cattle), and he rides ahead, turning on a wide circle and contracting till the rotary motion is produced.'

When hands forced a horse herd to mill, it was called *rounding up*. [Adams]

mill rider A cowboy name for a ranch hand who tends windmills. [Adams] Also called a *miller*.

milpa In the south-west, a cultivated field, especially a cornfield. Borrowed from Spanish, it's pronounced MIL-puh.

Minataree *See* Hidatsa.

mind your hair A trapper's farewell meaning 'take care', or 'watch your ass'. Literally, 'look out for your scalp lest an Indian get it'.

miner Western names for miners and men who work in mines (according to Ramon Adams) are *abajador* (supplier of tools), *banksman* (the man at the head of a shaft who handles the bucket), *butty* (a fellow miner), *cager* (a worker who attends the elevator), *company buster* (a surface worker), *double-jacker* (the fellow who swings the big hammer to separate rocks for blasting), *dyno* (an explosives handler), *gold digger* or *gold washer* (a placer miner), *hard-rock miner* or *rocker* (a miner who works underground in rock, as distinguished from a placer miner), *muckman* (any miner), *nipper* (tool flunky), *pithead man* (worker who unloads cages), *pitman* (lift and pump examiner), *powder hand* or *powder man* or *powder monkey* (explosives handler), *quartz miner* or *quartz reefer* (same as a hard-rock miner), *river sniper* (placer miner), *rust-eater* (iron-worker), *shack* (mine guard), *short faker* or *short-stage man* or *staker* or *ten-day miner* (itinerant miner), *shovel stiff* (worker with a shovel), *sluicer* (sluice operator), *tar baby* (cable lubricator), *tool nipper* (tool distributor), *tributer* (man who takes the proceeds less royalty for wages) and *wife* (fellow worker). *See* Cousin Jack and prospector.

miner's friend The safety lamp known as a Davy lamp. [Adams]

miner's lettuce A low plant (*Montia perfoliata*) that was a favourite of the forty-niners. It is now cultivated in Europe as winter purslane.

mineral entry Filing a mining claim on public land for the mineral rights. *Mineral entry withdrawal* is the removal of public lands (usually those lands that are required for administrative sites or are highly valued by the public) available for mineral entry.

mining district A Western mining area (a region of diggings defined by natural boundaries) of one or more mining camps organised for self-government before law and government arrived officially. These districts operated through what were called *miners' meetings*, and through *miners' courts* enforced *miners' law*, which could be *ad hoc*, inflexible and abrupt. In an attempt to minimise disputes, the mining recorder kept an official record of claims. *See also* claim, placer, hydraulicking and discovery.

minuteman One of a group organised by stockmen of the south-west to fight lawlessness along the US–Mexican border.

mission Indian In the south-west, an Indian living near a Franciscan mission, under its influence and presumably in the process of conversion to Christianity. The Franciscan policy was to make the Indians 'civilised', largely by teaching them agriculture, before it attempted to make them Christian.

mission stiff A parson, or a man who went to a mission and acted as though he was getting religion in order to get a hot meal and a bed.

missionary In a traditional rite of passage in the Mormon Church, college-aged young people spend up to two years in missionary work. They are supported by their families, and not only is it a time of prayer and teaching but also of abstinence from worldly concerns such as current events, dating and possessions.

Missouri A word of the Algonquian dialect meaning either 'big muddy' or 'people of the big canoes'. The Missouri Indians, who were living near the mouth of the river at the time of white contact in the 17th century, were Siouan. Never numerous, they were later removed to Oklahoma.

mix a walk A logger's expression for quitting the job.

mixed herd A cattle herd of both sexes and various ages, the easiest kind to manage.

mochila A leather covering draped over a cinched-up saddle, sometimes containing (as for Pony Express riders) pockets for mail or other goods. Variously spelled, for instance, *machilla*, *mochiler*, *mochile*. Borrowed from Spanish (where it means 'knapsack'), it's pronounced moh-CHI-luh. Also called *corus* or *macheer*.

mocho An animal with a droopy horn, gotched ear or cut-off tail. Borrowed from Spanish (where it means 'mutilated'), it's pronounced MOH-choh.

mockey A wild mare.

Mojave A yuman Indian tribe of the lower Colorado River, living around modern Needles, California, once known for its aggressiveness against whites. Their name has been given to various plants and animals of that region and to the desert itself.

The Mojave Desert lies primarily in southern California and Nevada and includes Death Valley. A basin and range topography, it receives two to five inches of rain a year (Bagdad, California in the eastern Mojave holds the record for the longest period without rainfall – 767 days). The indicator species for the Mojave is the Joshua tree, a yucca that has become tree-sized. Other dominant plants are creosote, cholla and yucca. Oases and stream beds support mesquite, willows and California fan palms.

monkey wrencher A person who defends the environment by throwing a monkey-wrench into (sabotaging) the efforts of developers, loggers, miners, drillers and the like. Destroying bulldozers and spiking trees, for instance, are acts of monkey wrenching. The late Edward Abbey coined this term in his fine comic novel *The Monkey Wrench Gang*, and it has become ubiquitous. It takes a verb form, to monkey wrench.

Another new term for sabotage on behalf of the environment is *ecotage*.

monte A gambling card game played with 40 or 44 cards, imported from Spain. The players bet on whether the suit of the card turned up will match the suits of the two cards taken from the bottom and put face up. It is not the same as three-card monte or pass monte.

Principle monte terms are *bottom layout*, *broad pitcher*, *gate*, *monte bank* (table), *monte banker* (dealer or thrower or tosser), *monte layout*, *monte sharp* and *top layout*. Borrowed from Spanish, it's pronounced mon-tee.

moon-eyed Descriptive of a horse with glassy, white eyes and allegedly with poor night vision. (*See* horse for other descriptive terms for horses)

moonlight them In cowboy talk, to night-herd cattle. To *moonshine* was to ride at night without chuck wagons for the sake of an early drive or to drive cows at night.

Moqui An older name (used particularly by Mormons) for the Hopi Indians. In some usages, it appears to mean any Pueblo people.

morada In the south-west, a chapter house where the members of the Penitente sect keep the implements for their passion ceremonies, conduct rites, and eat meals brought from the outside by the women. Adapted from the Spanish (where it means dwelling), it's pronounced moh-RAH-duh.

Mormon A member of the Church of Jesus Christ of Latter-Day Saints, a nickname based on belief in the *Book of Mormon*; as an adjective, pertaining to that Church, its members or their culture.

Mormon, in Church doctrine, was an early prophet and compiler of the *Book of Mormon*. The name means 'more good' or 'great good'.

The religion and culture are sometimes spoken of collectively as *Mormonism* or *Mormonry*. Mormon country is called *Mormondom*. *Mormonism* is the polity and doctrine of Mormons. *Mormoness* is an obsolete word for a Mormon woman, and a *Mormonite* was a Mormon. To *Mormonise* is to make someone or something Mormon-like.

Religious combinations: Mormon Bible (the *Book of Mormon* [but at one time, for a gentile to 'take a Davy on the Mormon Bible' meant 'to swear on a ludicrous object']), *Mormon Church* (a common name for the Church of Jesus Christ of Latter-Day Saints; another is LDS Church), *Mormon City* (Salt Lake City, Utah, in a usage now obsolete), and *Mormon missionary* (one of the faithful of the LDS Church who accepts an assignment to proselytise).

Historical combinations: Mormon battalion (the company of soldiers sent by Brigham Young to the Mexican War), *Mormon brake* (a log tied behind a wagon on a downhill slope to slow it down), *Mormon buggy* (a light spring wagon with a fringed top), *Mormon coin* (a gold coin of Mormon mintage in circulation about 1860), *Mormon currency* (carrots), *Mormon Expedition* (the military expedition of the federal government against the Mormons in 1857-8), *Mormon iron* (rawhide), *Mormon road* (the old trail from Salt Lake to Los Angeles via Las Vegas, or other old Mormon routes [*see* Mormon Trail below]), *Mormon Station* (the original name

for Genoa, Nevada), *Mormon tangle* (the packer's knot called a 'squaw hitch'), *Mormon Trail* (the route, much of it roughly paralleling the Oregon Trail, used by the Mormons to migrate to the Salt Lake area in 1847), *Mormon wagon* (a light, strong version of the prairie schooner used by plains-crossing Mormons), *Mormon War* (either the conflict at Nauvoo, Illinois, that precipitated the Mormon migration to Deseret or the difficulties of 1857-8 [*see* Mormon Expedition above]).

Other combinations: Mormon blanket (a quilt made from scraps of clothing [Adams]), *Mormon buckskin* (cowboy talk for baling wire [Adams]), *Mormon cricket* (a locust that plagued Mormons in the late 1840s and again in the 1930s and 1990s; according to the *Los Angeles Times* in 1990, the creatures are as 'big as a church mouse' and able to 'snap a wooden matchstick in two with their jaws'), *Mormon derrick* a crane-necked mast used to lift hay from wagon to stack in a sling), *Mormon dip* (cowboy talk for milk gravy [Adams]), *Mormon dog* (a can with pebbles, used to make a racket to control cows in place of dogs), *Mormon hobbles* (made of a metal like a puzzle, so Indians couldn't cut the hobbles and rustle livestock), *Mormon shirt-tail* (a short-tailed shirt [Adams]), *Mormon tea* (a tea made by Mormons from plants of the genus *Ephedra*) and *Mormon tree* (the lombardy poplar). (*See also* Jack Mormon).

moro A horse of bluish cast. (For horse colours, *see* buckskin)

Moroni In Mormon belief, the son of Mormon, who hid the golden plates in the earth to be revealed later to Joseph Smith. A statue of Moroni is a common symbol of Mormonism and is found on some Mormon temples.

morral In the south-west, especially Texas, a nosebag or feedbag carried on the saddle-horn. By extension, to *put on the morral* (or *put on the nose bag*) became an expression for a human being to eat. Borrowed from Spanish, it's pronounced mohr-RAL.

mosey To go, to move along. There's debate about whether it means to leave at an amble, to sneak away or to go lickety-split, and debate about whether the word comes from the Spanish verb *vamos;* therefore, there is debate about whether the word is Western.

mossy horn (1) A longhorn whose horns have wrinkled with age. (2) Sometimes an old, wrinkled cowman. Also occurs as *moss horn* and *moss back. (See* Texas longhorn)

Mother Hubbard loop In a catch rope, an extra-big loop, also called a washer woman. A Mother Hubbard saddle was an old-style Texas saddle with leather housing that detached from the tree.

mother lode The principal part of an ore vein. By extension, the real thing, the big hit, the grand stuff of fantasy.

mother up For a calf to find its mother, its milk, its haven, its comfort. In the pain immediately after branding, calves bawl until they get mothered up.

According to the Pinedale *Wyoming Roundup,* it is also cowboy talk for getting married.

motte In the south-west, a grove of trees. Adapted from the Spanish *mata* (which has the same meaning), rhymes with *not.*

mount (1) A hand's string, the horses assigned to him from the cavvy. Reportedly used on the southern rather than the northern plains. (2) A single saddle horse.

mount money In rodeo, pay for a rider in an exhibition but not in competition. [Adams]

mountain man The beaver trapper of the Rocky Mountains during the 1810–40 time period; also the other men who ventured forth with the trapping brigades, if they had wilderness skills; later any guide who knew the country. This fellow was first known as a *mountaineer* or *mountain trapper* (so called by Washington Irving and Francis Parkman), but in the 1840s Lt George Frederick Ruxton nominated him a mountain man. He's now such an American legend he's parodied in a series of Busch beer commercials.

The mountain man was one of a succession of different sorts of men who roamed, worked and settled on the plains and in the mountains and deserts in the 19th century – in the approximate order of the explorer, the trapper, the emigrant, the miner and the cowboy (plus the sorts not quite so large in myth, the freighter, the Indian fighter, lawman, badman, gambler and so on). They reflect nicely the succession of Anglo economies that dominated the West in a whirlwind of change, the beaver, the emigrant trade, gold and silver, and cattle.

Though they had something of a reputation for crudeness and bestiality, mountain men were in fact extraordinarily varied in class, race, education and social background. Around one or two camp fires at rendezvous, a visitor might have found a religious, educated Yankee (Jedediah Smith), an illiterate blacksmith (Jim Bridger), a smart black who'd lived with Indians (Edward Rose), an Irishman of some gentility (Tom Fitzpatrick), a Mexican trader (Manuel Alvarez), the son of a Missouri justice of the peace (Bill Sublette), a French-Canadian (Antoine Clement), the Iroquois John Grey and, say, a couple of Delaware Indians. And mountain men were mostly on the way to becoming Indians, with the outlook, habits, cuisine, languages and customs of red men, with red wives and children.

His talk shows aptly the mountain man's wild mix of cultures. Here's Laforey, an old trapper, begging Lt George Frederick Ruxton for some coffee: ' "*Sacré enfant de Grâce,*" he would exclaim, mixing English, French, and Spanish into a puchero-like jumble, "*voyez-vous* dat I vas nevare tan pauvre as dis time; mais before I vas siempre avec plenty café, plenty sucre; mais now, God dam, I not go à Santa Fé, God dam, and mountain men dey come aquí from autre côté, drink all my café. Sacré enfant de Grâce, nevare I vas tan pauvre as dis time, God dam. I not care comer meat, ni frijole, ni corn, mais widout café I no live. I hunt may be two, three day, may be one week, mais I eat nothin;

mais sin café, enfant de Grâce, I no live, parceque me not sacré Espagnol, mais one Frenchman." '

What mountain men had in common was daring, hardiness, a fierce yen for wilderness and adventure and extraordinary wilderness survival skills.

No white lifestyle went the way of all flesh so quickly and completely as the mountain man's. The small reason was the decline of the price of beaver. The big one was that the mountain man's life was based on wildness, on remoteness from white civilisation. The trapper was gone back to nature, gone Indian.

But that couldn't last. In 1836 the first white woman reached Wyoming in the company of mountain men. In 1847 the Oregon Trail saw about 5,000 emigrants, guided by mountain men. In 1858 the gold rush to Denver began, followed immediately by a newspaper. In 1869 the golden spike was driven, and a pregnant woman could ride in comparative comfort all the way to San Francisco. She probably thought the few mountain men left were queer old ducks, colourful but repellent with their Indian wives, children and ways. Worse than the Indians, really, because they had no excuse. From a cock of the walk to a smelly old relic in half a lifetime.

(*See* engagé, free trapper, mangeur de lard, partisan and voyageur.)

Animal combinations: mountain badger (the hoary marmot), *mountain beaver* (a sewellel), *mountain boomer* (a steep-country cow, a red squirrel, a mountain lizard or a sewellel [mountain beaver]), *mountain buffalo* (what early plainsmen called the buffalo of the Rocky Mountains, generally smaller than the buffalo of the plains, even though it is the same species), *mountain canary* (a burro), *mountain goat* (the *Oreamnos montanus* of the high northern Rockies; not a true goat but a relative of the chamois, and a denizen of the high crags), *mountain jay* (the Canada jay), *mountain lion* (the predatory cat also called a catamount, cougar, panther and puma – elusive, cunning, and fierce) and *mountain plover* (a bird that nests in a depression on the ground on the plains).

Plant combinations: mountain holly (the Oregon grape) and *mountain mahogany* (any shrub of the genus *Cercocarpus*, or in the south-west a manzanita).

Miscellaneous combinations: mountain Crow (the Absaroka [Crow Indians] of the Big Horn Basin), *mountain dew* (aguardiente Taos [booze]), *mountain fever* (an illness of uncertain origin that afflicted Mormons and others on the Oregon Trail with headache, fever, joint pain, delirium and occasionally death) and *mountain wagon* (any wagon adapted for mountain travel, usually through heavier rigging and stouter brakes). (*See* mountain oyster and mountain price)

mountain oyster One of the small dollops clipped off the calf at branding and cooked up for dinner – yes, the testicle. Sometimes animals other than cows are so victimised, especially pigs and sheep. The oyster fry or calf fry (they're usually breaded and fried, like chicken) was traditional in the high days of the roundup a hundred years ago and is traditional today. Though they're a source of levity, mountain oysters are tasty. They're also called *prairie oysters* and *Rocky Mountain oysters*.

mountain price In the Rocky Mountain fur trade period, the price for an item of manufactured goods in the West, usually at rendezvous or at a trading post. This was the price to a trapper, who would then either use it himself or trade or give it to an Indian. A mountain price might be many times what the trader paid for it back in the settlements, in compensation for the difficulty of shipment, hardship, danger and greed, and the system did its part to keep the trappers from getting rich.

At the first rendezvous in 1825, General William H. Ashley charged $1.50 a pound for coffee and sugar, $3 for tobacco, $2 for powder (which was truly essential), $2 each for knives, $5–$6 for cloth and $9 for three-point Northwest blankets. These prices should probably be multiplied by well over 10 to get modern equivalents. At the same time, Ashley was paying $3 a pound for beaver pelts.

mouth To examine a sheep's teeth to determine how old it is. A *solid-mouth* is a mature sheep with all its teeth. A *spreader-mouth* is a sheep just past its prime, its teeth are beginning to spread and will soon fall out.

move sheep A euphemism for running sheep off (sometimes off a cliff) in a range war. [Adams]

mover In the first half of the 19th century, an emigrant; later a person who kept wandering from farm to farm, failing at each place and sometimes using up the resources there.

mozo In the south-west, an assistant, especially on a pack train; a youth; a servant. The feminine form, *moza*, also occurred. Borrowed from Spanish, it's pronounced MOH-soh.

Mr John Like Lo or siwash, a general name for Indians, probably humorous or lightly derisive, as in, 'I saw by the tracks that Mr John had passed this way.'

muchacho In the south-west, boy, kid, a term of familiarity and endearment, usually applied to a youngster or a servant. *Muchacha* is the feminine form. Borrowed from Spanish, it's pronounced moo-CHAH-choh.

muck (1) In mining, dirt, gravel and other earth to be moved away. (2) As a verb, to move the dirt and gravel. A *mucker* does the work. A *muckman* is either a miner or a long-handled shovel, which is also called a *muck stick*.

muckamuck (1) In Chinook jargon, food. (2) In verb form, to eat. *High muck-a-muck* (also from the Chinook term) is a derisive expression for a person of importance.

mud wagon A poor man's concord coach, open-sided, light and low, more simply constructed.

muffoon The soft under-fur of the beaver that was used for felt hats.

mugger The header of a wild-cow milking team.

mujer Border cowboy talk for a woman. Borrowed from Spanish (where it means 'woman' or 'wife'), it's pronounced moo-HAYR.

mule Mules were called *hard-tails*, *knob-heads* and *mulas*. When white, they were *gambler's ghosts* and, when packing food, *long-eared chuck wagons*. Herds of mules were *muladas* or *mulattos*.

Combinations: mule deer (the common game deer of the West, which has a black-tipped tail and long, mule-like ears), *mule ear* (a floppy strap at the top of a boot to help with pulling it on), and *mule train* (either a train of wagons pulled by mules or a pack train of mules).

mule-skinner The driver of a mule team, or his whip. Known for short as a *skinner*, this fellow was celebrated for his stubbornness and creative profanity. When his draft animals were oxen, he was called a *bull-whacker*. Mules were faster than oxen but had to be fed corn; oxen thrived on available grass. (*See* grass freight) A mule-skinner was also called jocularly a *mule puncher* as well as a *mulero*, which meant either the driver of a mule team or an attendant on a pack train of mules. The form *mule-whacker* also occurred.

muley A hornless cow, which is defenceless and keeps to itself. Muley cows have a bad reputation with cowboys as troublemakers. Sometimes a mule deer is called a muley, and one kind of small-brimmed, low-crowned dude hat was a muley.

multiple use The management of the renewable resources of public lands (usually the national forests) in the way to 'best meet the needs of the American people' and not necessarily realise the greatest dollar return. Often multiple use is called 'multiple abuse' by environmentalists.

Murphy Murphy, Espenshied and Studebaker were the principal freight wagons of the plains after the Conestogas, which they eventually replaced. Says David Dary in *Entrepreneurs of the Old West*, they were 'made of the best timber, wide-tracked, strong and tight, high double box and heavy tyred, and covered with heavy canvas over the bows'. The Murphy, crafted by Joseph Murphy in St Louis, was the most popular.

music roots Cowboy talk for sweet potatoes.

mustang A wild horse. From the Spanish *mesteño* (which has the same meaning). By extension, anything wild, free, unrefined.

Mustang lore is rich in the West. The horse is the descendant of the Spanish horse, the continent's first modern equine. It is small, of no breeding, often a mongrel, and it was the horse of the Indians. To some early Westerners, all this meant that it was to be despised. Others rooted for it as an underdog from the wrong side of tracks. And before long the mustang developed a considerable reputation for toughness and general cowpony skills. (For much about the beast and attitudes toward it, *see* J. Frank Dobie's *The Mustangs*)

For many people, the survival of the mustang symbolises the survival of what's wild and precious in the West. The mustangs are still out there – in the Red Desert in Wyoming, for instance. The federal government now has a programme allowing people to adopt a wild horse.

A *mustanger* (or *mustang runner* or *hunter*) was a fellow who caught wild horses to sell them, as Clark Gable and Montgomery Clift did in the fine movie *The Misfits. Mustanging*, as it was called, was usually done by running them into pens or traps.

Mustang cattle, in Texas, were wild cattle. *Mustang court* was cowboy talk for a kangaroo court.

Mutual A nickname for Young Men's or Young Ladies' Mutual Improvement Association, MIA. It is an organisation in the Mormon Church for youths 12 to 18 whose purpose is to teach the faith and to provide social activities. The name has been changed in recent years to 'Young Men' and 'Young Women'.

muzzle On the northern cow ranges, a device that goes over a calf's muzzle and forces it to eat grass rather than suck. On other ranges, it's called a *blab*. [Adams]

muzzle-loader Logger talk for a bunk you have to get into from the foot. [Adams] The meaning that refers to firearms is not Western.

N

naked possessor In early American Texas, a person who held land by a long occupancy, though without title.

Nakota *See* Lakota.

naja A pendant on the bottom of a squash blossom in Navajo jewellery. From Navajo, and pronounced NAH-hah.

National Park Service (NPS) Although this Department of Interior agency administers parks throughout the country, it had its genesis in the West. The first national park was Yellowstone, which was protected by Congress in 1872, but the National Park Service did not come into existence until 1916. The Park Service has two missions – 'to conserve the scenery and the natural and historic objects and wildlife' and to provide for the public use and enjoyment of these special areas.

Native American A contemporary term meaning American Indian, often deemed appropriate (or politically correct) because it avoids the historic error of Columbus in giving the name of the Asian Indians to native peoples of this continent. (*See* Indian) In the last century, this term meant a Hispanic born in America rather than Spain.

Concerning the term Native American, Tim Giago, editor of the *Lakota Times*, writes: 'As the publisher of an Indian advocacy newspaper, the largest of its kind in America, we use American Indian, Indian or Native American, but we prefer to use the individual tribal affiliation when possible. For instance, if the subject of an article is Navajo we use that or Lakota, Ojibway, Onondaga, etc.

'We are, more and more, pulling away from using Native American, because as so many phone calls and letters have pointed out to us, and correctly so, anyone born in America can refer to themselves as Native American.

'We realise the word "Indian" is a misnomer, but for generic purposes, we are often forced to use it when speaking of many different tribes. American Indian is also acceptable in Indian country. Native Americanism, historically, was prejudice against all Native Americans except native-born Protestants. The Native American party of about 1840 promoted this intolerant view.'

Native American Church The Indian Christian Church centred on the peyote ritual. Thought by some to have been brought to the United States from the Yaqui in Mexico by Quanah Parker, it is still growing rapidly and is believed by its adherents to help contemporary Indians transcend the problems of living on reservations.

The central ceremony of the Church, always held at night, preferably in a tipi, is the eating of the peyote medicine as a sacrament. In the half-moon branch of the Church, this ceremony is supervised by a priest known as the road man, because he advocates the good, red road.

According to an April 1990 Supreme Court decision, the religious use of the drug peyote is not protected by the Constitution. Twenty-three states and the federal government give the practice legal protection.

(*See also* cross-fire)

natural bridge A span of stone formed by erosion across a stream or a wash; it's similar to an arch. The Four Corners country has many, including the celebrated Rainbow Natural Bridge.

Navajo The most numerous contemporary tribe of US Indians. They call themselves the Dine, meaning 'the people'. The word Navajo is originally a Spanish form of a Pueblo name for Navajo country; though it is sometimes spelled Navaho, the Navajos themselves usually use the Spanish spelling, with a *j*.

The Navajo have lived in Arizona, New Mexico and south-eastern Utah for over four centuries and speak an Athapascan language. Their economy was and is based substantially on raising sheep and crops, and their social organisation is strongly based on the family, extended family and clan.

Inclined to raiding and territorial expansion, the Navajo were historically often in conflict with their Pueblo neighbours. They resisted white encroachment militarily after the US acquisition of the south-west from Mexico and endured defeat during the Navajo War and subsequent internment at Bosque Redondo (once called the nation's first concentration camp). In 1868 they accepted the large reservation in the Four Corners country where they live today. Their population has increased in the last century, and they are arguably one of the tribes to have prospered through the treaties they made with the United States.

Their religion (and the art that stems from it) is expressed in a series of chants that tell their mythic stories and bring living people into harmony with the natural and supernatural worlds. Some chants, such as the Blessing Way, Mountain Chant and Night Chant, take days to perform. The Navajo sense of the world is vividly portrayed in the current mystery novels of Tony Hillerman.

The Navajo are known for the art they developed (sometimes adapting techniques from Pueblo peoples) to give voice to this understanding of the world. Navajo rugs, which comes in regional styles such as Two Grey Hills, Ganado and Teec Nos Pos, are especially prized by collectors. Silversmithing (often featuring turquoise) and sand paintings are also important Navajo arts.

Combinations: Navajo agency, Navajo blanket, Navajo country, Navajo ruby, Navajo sandstone, Navajo silver and so on.

(*See also* code talker, hogan, hosteen, pathway, sand painting and sing)

Navajo rug A wool rug woven by a Navajo woman and known for tightness and beauty of design.

The Navajos are the principal rug weavers among US Indians today. They borrowed the loom technique, but not the designs, from the Pueblo Indians. Using wool from their own sheep, Navajo women (for Navajo weavers are almost always women) wash, card and spin it, and gather natural materials for dyes (or now use commercial dyes). Then, working from the bottom of the rug up, they weave the warp and the woof in a design of their own imagination. Even a small rug takes weeks to weave.

Regional styles have developed in Navajoland, among them Two Grey Hills (the most valuable), Ganado and Teec Nos Pos.

navvy A Navajo pony. Among early Anglos, this was a term of disparagement.

navy (1) A nickname for a revolver made to US Navy specifications, smaller than the army model and of lighter calibre. Colt made a popular one. Also called a *navy six* (for six-shooter). (2) Short for Navy plug, a brand of strong, dark chewing tobacco. (*See* chaw tobacco for other brands)

Nebraska brick A facetious term for a sod square used to make a house; the soddy itself. Also called *Kansas Brick*.

neck (1) to tie a critter you want to teach to lead to a trained critter by the neck so the two move together. (2) To wean a calf by tying it away from its mother.

To *neck rope* is to catch a calf or horse by the neck with your rope, as opposed, for instance, to fore-footing it.

To *neck rein*, when applied to a horse, means for it to turn by slight pressure of the reins against its neck, the usual way Western horses are broke. They turn in the direction away from the pressure.

Nephite In Mormon belief, a member of a vanished race of Israelites who flourished from about 600 BC to AD 400 in the Western Hemisphere. The prophet Lehi led his six sons and their followers to the New World from Jerusalem. Four of the sons (Nephi, Jacob, Joseph and Samuel) were virtuous and light-skinned, and created an American light-skinned race; the remaining two (Laman and Lemuel) were dark-skinned and rebellious, and created a dark-skinned Indian race. (*See* Lamanite)

The Three Nephites are legendary disciples, immortals who travel the earth today dispensing blessings to those who need them.

In occasional Mormon usage, simply a white person.

nester A derogatory cowboy term for a homesteader, farmer, squatter or small rancher. Big cattlemen in the West regarded these small-timers as a plague, often because they fenced the land. Range wars like Wyoming's Johnson County War were conflicts between big cattlemen and nesters.

The word also has a verb form, to *nest*.

Some sources suggest that the term came into being because the homesteads were bordered by brush used to keep critters away from first crops and so looked like bird nests. Other uncomplimentary names for the small farmer are *churn-twister*, *colonist*, *granger*, *hoe-man*, *home sucker*, *honyocker*, *pumpkin-piler*, *plough-chaser*, *soddy*, *sodbuster* and *sand-lapper*.

Nez Percé   A Shahaptian tribe, the Nez Percé were originally a salmon-fishing people on the Snake River, dwelling in pit houses. After they got the horse in the early 18th century, their culture changed. They bred and traded horses, producing the appaloosa breed. They began to cross the mountains to the plains to hunt buffalo annually with their neighbours, the Flatheads, and came into conflict with the Blackfeet. As they became more nomadic, they adopted features of the buffalo-hunting cultures, including the tipi.

From first contact, with the Lewis & Clark expedition, the Nez Percé were friendly to whites, and they accepted missionaries in the 1830s. After the Nez Percé reservation was established in Idaho in 1855, the US government bought some of their land to accommodate a gold rush. Some Nez Percés never accepted this change, and it eventually led to the Nez Percé War of 1877. Under Chief Joseph, the Nez Percé fought the US military so admirably that many whites called for better treatment for them. Now many Nez Percé live on the Nez Percé and Colville reservations, both in their historic country.

Their French name has been the source of much confusion. Given them by traders (they called themselves the Nimipu), it means 'Pierced Nose'; but the Nez Percés did not wear nose ornaments. And the Indians pronounce their name not in the French way but to rhyme with *fez purse*. This custom has in turn led to confusion when Anglo sophisticates see the name

and pronounce it NAY payr-SAY, mountains and buildings get that name and so on. Courtesy suggests that Anglos pronounce the name as the people themselves do, both for the tribe and all things named after the tribe. Despite the pronunciation, the tribe retains an acute accent over the final *e* in the name.

nice kitty   Cowboy talk for a skunk.

nigger   Among the mountain men, simply another word for fellow, whether white, black or Indian. The white trappers often applied it to themselves – 'This nigger means to make meat,' and the like. Linguist J. L. Dillard says the term 'nigger' was used without offence in American English until 1928.

Also, *nigger* (like *Indian*) was often applied on the frontier to anything inferior or bad. Thus a *nigger brand* was a saddle sore. *Nigger gin* was probably rough, home-brewed stuff.

Other combinations: nigger catcher (a tab on a saddle for holding the latigo), *nigger day* (logger talk for Saturday [Adams]), *nigger driver* (what loggers sometimes called the foreman) and *nigger-in-a-blanket* (a cowboy dessert, raisins in dough [Adams]).

night herd   To ride around the cattle on the bed ground all night long to keep them settled and tranquil. The night herders on trail drives divided the night into two-hour watches. When working, each rider used an important horse in his string, the night horse, chosen for its night vision, sure-footedness and dependability. (Though never female, it was sometimes jokingly known as the nightmare.) In case of a stampede, the night horse would have the rider's life in its hooves.

Andy Adams described the normal routine of night herding in *Log of a Cowboy*: 'The guards ride in a circle about four rods outside the sleeping cattle, and by riding in opposite directions, make it impossible for any animal to make its escape without being noticed by the riders. The guards usually sing or whistle continuously, so that the sleeping herd may know that a friend and not an enemy is keeping vigil over their dreams . . . The night horses soon learn their duty, and a rider may fall asleep or doze along in the saddle, but the horses will maintain their distance in their leisurely sentinel rounds.'

And in the night herder's singing was the cradle of the one art of the West, the cowboy song.

nighthawk In the days of the open range, the night wrangler, the hand who watched the horses while others night-herded the cows; or the night wrangler for a freight train. This word was also sometimes used to mean night herder.

Nisei An American-born Japanese. The Nisei of the 442nd Combat Team fought valiantly for the United States in Italy during World War II while many of their relatives were imprisoned in camps in the West. The term comes from the Japanese, meaning second generation, and is pronounced NEE-say. *Isei* is the Japanese name for immigrant, the first generation.

no beans in the wheel Descriptive of a revolver that's unloaded and so makes you defenceless.

no man's land A name for the panhandle of Oklahoma, a narrow strip of land between Colorado and Kansas on the north and Texas on the south. At one time, it belonged to no governmental administrative unit, thus the name. It is immediately west of the Cherokee Outlet (*See* under Cherokee).

no-breakfast-forever list A figurative list of the dead, especially those burned in prairie fires. (For more expressions pertaining to death, *see* cash in your chips)

nogal In the south-west, a walnut tree. It can also be a hickory tree or, in Texas, a pecan. Borrowed from Spanish (where it means 'walnut'), it's pronounced noh-GAHL.

nooning Taking a midday stop on the trail. For Santa Fe trail caravans, the break was often long enough for two meals to be served, both breakfast and dinner. Also called *nooning it*.

nootka cypress An evergreen (*Chamaecyparis nootkatensis*) of the north-west Pacific Coast, valued for its hard wood. The *Nootka fir* is the Douglas fir.

nopal The prickly pear cactus, and its flat pads which are used in south-western cooking. From the Spanish (where it means prickly pear), it's pronounced noh-PAHL.

Norteños Northerners, as in northern New Mexicans. Isolated from the rest of Spanish colonial America, they developed in original ways. The Spanish that is spoken in northern New Mexico is distinguished by archaisms that date back to the 17th century, and is rich in contractions and colloquialisms. William deBuys writes in *River of Traps*: 'Something happened in the soil of New Mexico. Isolated by broad deserts from their countrymen to the south, the *norteños* of New Mexico drew nourishment from the land in which they lived. People from other regions rarely appreciate that New Mexico was a frontier unlike any other in our national experience. While Virginia, Kentucky, or Missouri may have represented civilisation's advancing edge for two or three generations, New Mexico remained a lonely and embattled frontier for three hundred years. It became *una patria*, a fatherland, in its own right.'

norther A freezing gale blowing from the north across Texas or other parts of the south-west. Northers had and have a reputation for nastiness and could drive cows many a mile. Also called a *Texas norther*. A particularly bad one is a *blue norther*, one with rain is a *wet norther* and one without is a *dry norther*; a windy one is a *blue whistler*.

Northwester Among the mountain men, a man of the Northwest Company, the one-time competitor of the Hudson's Bay Company for the furs of Canada and the American north-west. The *Northwest blanket* and *Northwest gun* (or fusee or fusil), a smoothbore musket, were trade items of this fur company.

Also a person of the Pacific north-west or a tall tale of that country.

nose-bag Cowboy talk for a restaurant (from the feeding of horses by nose-bags). Also a logger's term for a lunch bucket; a logging outfit that offered such lunches might have been derisively called a *nose-bag show*.

NOTCHER

notcher A killer, a gunman (from their reported practice of notching their guns to keep count of their murders). A killer horse was said to have a *notch in his tail*.

nubbing Cowboy talk for the saddle-horn.

nut pine Any of several nut-bearing pine trees of the Rocky Mountains or south-west, such as *Pinus monophyllus*.

O

obsidian A black volcanic glass used by Indians for arrow and spear points. Found mainly from the Rockies west, it was a trade item to eastern Indians.

ocelot The small, spotted wildcat (*Felis pardalis*). Its range may occasionally enter the south-west from Mexico. The name comes from the Nahuatl word. Another borderlands cat is the *jaguarundi*.

ocotillo A cactus-like shrub of the south-west, *Fouquieria splendends*, consisting of long, slender sticks that bear striking red flowers in the spring. Borrowed from Spanish, it's pronounced oh-koh-TEE-yoh. Also called *coach-whip cactus*.

off his feed Cowboy talk for someone who's looking poorly or feeling bad.

off the reservation When said of 19th-century Indians, literally off their assigned ground, with the implication that they were hunting, raiding or otherwise acting up. By extension, descriptive of a person who's out of turn or out of bounds.

A weak-minded person might have been called *off his mental reservation*. [Adams]

Oglala One of the seven principal divisions of the Teton Dakota. The Oglala lived primarily in modern South Dakota and Wyoming during the time of the Plains Indian Wars and were leading protagonists in those fights. Spelled variously, especially Ogaldala. (*See* Dakota)

oiler A slang name for a Mexican. Like greaser, it was surely derogatory.

ojala! In the south-east, an interjection of approval. Borrowed from Spanish (where it means 'I hope so'), it's pronounced oh-hah-LAH.

Ojibway A large Algonquian tribe of the Western Great Lakes region. Also known as the Chippewa. Both names refer to the puckered seam on their moccasins. They call themselves Anishinabe, 'the first men'. The tribal name is pronounced both oh-JIB-way and oh-jib-WAY.

Historically, they had a woodlands culture that was in many ways the ancestor of the Plains Indian culture: They lived in tipi-like shelters, hunted and gathered (especially wild rice) and farmed. Central to their religion was the Midewiwin or Grand Medicine Society.

Contacted early by French fur traders, the Ojibway became important in the beaver trade and major allies of the French against the British and the Americans. With the guns they traded for, this numerous and powerful tribe also drove the Dakota on to the Great Plains.

Now the Ojibway have reservations in five north-central states and two provinces of Canada.

ojo In the south-west, a spring, especially a hot spring (*ojo caliente*). Borrowed from Spanish (where it means 'eye'), it's pronounced oh-hoh.

Okie (1) A migratory worker from Oklahoma. John Steinbeck immortalised the plight of some of these people during the Great Depression with his novel *Grapes of Wrath*. Also any Oklahoman. (2) Among loggers, Okie was a derogatory term, implying an incompetent.

Oklahoma *Combinations: Oklahoma rain* (a sandstorm), *Oklahoma Run* (the Oklahoma land rush of 1889), an *Oklahoma* (a temporary shack during the Oklahoma Run) and *Oklahoma fever* (the land hunger that brought people there).

old In the West as elsewhere, a term of camaraderie or rank with no reference to age. Thus young mountain men called each other 'old coon' and 'old hoss' in comradeship. The boss of a cow outfit was called old man while still in his twenties and so on.

Combinations: Old Ephraim or *Old Caleb* (the grizzly bear), *old fruit* (in Texas slang, the genuine article, the real McCoy), *Old Hickory* (a shirt of a dark blue checked material, common on the frontier prior to the Civil War), *Old Pills* (what loggers called the doctor), *Old Reliable* (cowboy talk for the Sharps rifle), *old settler* (any early settler, especially a Cherokee who settled in the West before 1819), *old sledge* (all-fours or seven-up), *old socks* (a logger's name for a buddy [Adams]) and *old woman* or *old lady* (the cookie).

old pawn In the Indian trade of the south-west there is a tradition that jewellery pawned by Navajos or other Indians at the trading posts is superior to jewellery made for the tourist trade. At the very least such pawn has been previously owned by an Indian. Good older pieces of traditional jewellery have mostly passed from Navajo hands into private collections and museums.

olla In the south-west, a water jar of earthenware or fibre. Women sometimes carried these jars with head straps. Borrowed from Spanish, it's pronounced oy-yuh.

Omahog A jocular name for residents of Omaha, Nebraska.

on the dodge On the run from the law. Similar expressions are to *belly through the bush*, *pull freight* (or *take*) *to the tules*, *gone to Texas*, *head for the sundown* (to *be a sundowner*), *look over your shoulder*, *on the high lope*, *on the scout* or *cuidado*, *stampede to the wild bunch*, *ride the coulees* or *the high-lines* and to *whip a tired pony out of Texas*.

on the prod Full of piss and vinegar and looking for trouble. Said of both people and critters. *Combinations: on the drift* (descriptive of a wandering cowboy), *on the prairie* (a mountain man expression for 'free'), *on the skids* (doing badly, going downhill, as a log went along the skid road), *on tick* (on credit) and *on the warpath* (fighting mad).

one-armed bandit A slot machine for gambling that has one lever.

one-horse outfit A little ranch, a shirt-tail ranch. By extension, one-horse describes anything small or inconsequential.

open range Unfenced cattle country, uncontrolled and theoretically available to anyone. In practice, big ranchers often got title to the land that had water and let their cows wander freely over the public grassland, gaining a kind of *de facto* ownership. Thus fences brought the first big revolution in the Western cattle business, and the days of the open range became one of the great symbols of freedom lost.

Open-range branding, in the days of the

open range, meant branding calves when and where you found them rather than at roundup. Since rustlers branded that way, it came to be regarded with disfavour.

open-faced cows Cowboy talk for Herefords which have white faces.

opera Cowboy talk for a session of bronc-busting with spectators on the fences. The top rail was sometimes called the *opera house*.

Oregon *Combinations: Oregon grape* (*Mahonia aquifolia*, not a grape but an evergreen plant of the north-west with a fruit that resembles grapes), *Oregon jargon* (another name for Chinook jargon), *Oregon pudding-foot* (a horse bred from a draft animal and a riding horse, a type developed in Oregon, also called an *Oregon horse*), *Oregon question* (the issue of the border between US and British territory in the Pacific north-west, settled in 1846 by mutual acceptance of the 49th parallel) and *Oregon short line* (a ' 'fraid' strap, a strap on the fork of a saddle to help the rider stay on a bucking horse).

Oregon Trail A major overland trail, used not by cattle, like the big north–south trails, but by westwarding emigrants and by freighters. In 1841 trails established by Indians and beaver men were consolidated into this trail, running more than 2,000 miles from the western edge of Missouri to the new settlements in Oregon's Willamette Valley. It followed the Platte River into Wyoming, then the Sweetwater River into South Pass, then crossed to the Snake River and followed that to the Columbia River. The few way stations of 1848 included Fort Laramie, Fort Bridger and Fort Hall.

The largest migrations took place in the 1840s (including the Mormon migrations), and people and livestock kept using the trail for 40 years. (*See also* California trail, which branched off the Oregon Trail toward California)

The Oregon country was originally not the modern state of Oregon but the entire Pacific north-west from California to Alaska between the mountains and the sea. This changed in 1846 with the acceptance of the 49th parallel as the US border on the north and again in 1853 with the establishment of Washington Territory.

orejano A term of buckaroo country for a slick, a maverick, a critter neither branded nor earmarked. In early Texas, it meant a wild (thus unmarked) cow. Borrowed from Spanish, it's pronounced oh-ray-HAH-noh. *Oreja* is the Spanish word for 'ear'.

oro The Spanish word for gold, common in the names of places and businesses throughout the south-west. Pronounced OH-roh.

Osage The largest tribe of the southern Siouan Indians. The word is a version of their name for themselves, which means 'war people'.

Originally of the Atlantic seaboard, the southern Siouan Indians (also including the Kansa, Omaha, Ponca and Quapaw) lived at the time of white contact in the 17th century in Missouri, Kansas and Illinois. They dwelt in permanent lodges (mostly of earth) but hunted buffalo. They warred with other Indians, particularly the Dakota tribes, but were generally friendly to whites and in the 1870s accepted removal to Indian Territory.

Combinations: Osage hunting trail (a trail between the Arkansas and Missouri rivers made by the Osage), *Osage orange* (a tree [*Maclura pomifera*] of the country of the Osage, used by Indians to make bows [*see* bois d'arc] and by Anglos as hedges) and *Osage plum* (a wild, yellow plum known for its delicious taste).

otero Cowboy talk for a big steer. From the Spanish (where it means 'hill'), it's pronounced oh-TAY-roh.

otie A cowboy nickname for a coyote.

outfit (1) A ranch; a ranch crew. (2) An organisation or crew rigged to do any job, like freighting or drilling. (3) Someone's personal gear. (4) A pick-up truck, usually not just any pick-up but one rigged to do a job, like haul horses or hay. (5) Almost any collection of machinery or equipment – haying outfit, shearing outfit, etc. (6) Almost anything. In *Arizona Nights*, Stewart Edward White even calls a breed of chicken an outfit.

outlaw An uncontrollable horse, a man-killer; sometimes a cow that's half-wild. Horses spoiled in training or allowed to become unmanageable are often described as *outlawed*. (*See* horse for other descriptive terms for horses).

outrider A range rider; a cowboy who rode his employer's range far and yon to spot trouble. He was like a line rider, except that the area the line rider patrolled was the boundaries of the ranch only; the outrider went everywhere on the place. *Outridings* were inspection trips.

over the willows A cowboy description of a river in flood stage, because willows border most plains and mountain streams. A river over the willows threw difficulty and danger in the face of a trail herd because the animals would resist going into the water and maybe not all would come out.

over-grazed Descriptive of a range damaged by too many cattle or sheep feeding for too long. Whether the federal government properly protects public land from over-grazing is a hot subject for debate in the West.

overland stage The system of mail transportation from St Louis to San Francisco. Established in 1858 by John Butterfield, it was made obsolete by the completion of the transcontinental railroad in 1869. Its vehicle was the overland coach or stage. The stage lines carried passengers as well, at the rate of about 15 cents a mile. The trip was a trial. (Those who want to know how great a trial are referred to Mark Twain's extravagant depiction in *Roughing It*.)

Overland stage is what contemporary Indians jokingly call the cross-country bus system. The term *overland trade* meant mainly the trade on the Santa Fe Trail. Peter Watts says *overland trout* may have been a fanciful Great Plains term for bacon.

Overthrust Belt A region of the inter-mountain West (Wyoming, Utah, Colorado and Idaho) discovered in the 1970s to be rich in deep deposits of petroleum and as a result much explored in the late 1970s and early 1980s.

owl hoot An outlaw. Thus the *owl-hoot trail*, the outlaw's way of life. But to *hear the owl hoot* was to get a snootful or have lots of experiences or both at the same time. To hear the owl hoot is an expression of Indian Pidgin English meaning to have a warning of bad things coming, such as a premonition of death.

owl-head An untrainable, unridable horse. (*See* canner for other names for unfit horses)

ox train A train of wagons pulled by oxen as opposed to one hauled by mules. Ox trains pulled what was called *grass freight* because oxen could work on grass alone while mules required corn. Paradoxically, since oxen are castrated, ox trains were more often called *bull trains*.

oxbow stirrup A big wooden stirrup bent like an ox yoke, which gave a similar name to an *oxbow bend* in a river. Sometimes called an *ox yoke*. [Adams]

Ozark One name of the Quapaw, a southern Siouan tribe of Missouri and Arkansas (*see* Osage). The French called these people 'Aux Arcs', which the ungallic frontiersmen rendered as Ozarks.

P

pack (1) To ride into remote country carrying your supplies on horseback. Now it is mostly a dude's entertainment and is called a *pack trip*. Hunters also often pack in. Originally, people packed everywhere the roads weren't good enough for wagons: Mountain men, miners, surveyors, the army and others ventured into the wilderness by packing. (2) To carry loads on the backs of pack animals. (3) To carry anything regularly: A sheriff packs a star, and a badman packs a gun; cows pack irons (brands) and loggers pack balloons (bedrolls). (4) A mountain man's word for a bundle of beaver hides, grained and ready for shipment to the States. The bundles are variously reported to have weighed either about 52 or about 100 pounds each. (*See also* beaver and plew) (5) A packer's word for the load on one side of an animal's back.

Combinations: pack animal (a horse, mule or burro trained or accustomed to carrying loads), *pack cover* (a piece of heavy canvas used to keep the weather off loads), *pack dog* (a load-carrying dog, once commonly used by Indians), *pack hitch* (a diamond hitch, the most common lashing technique to keep loads where they belong), *pack-mule express* (a pack outfit serving as an express company), *pack outfit* (a firm that runs pack trips), *packsaddle* (a device that sits on the animal's back to lash loads on to [*see* aparejo and sawbuck]), *pack trail* (one suitable for pack animals; also called a *pack way*), *pack train* (a string of such animals; if made of mules, it may be called a *mule train*), modern *pack trip* (a mounted sojourn into the back country for relaxation, fishing, hunting and the like) and *Pack up!* (the instruction to get your pack animals loaded and ready to move).

A fine and funny book on packing is Joe Back's *Horses, Hitches, and Rocky Trails.*

pack rat The Rocky Mountain rodent also known as a *trade rat*. It ferrets small objects away from camps and hides them and is said to leave worthless substitutes.

pack the mail In cowboy talk, to ride fast. [Adams]

packer A man who loads the animals and delivers the loads where they're headed. Now he is almost entirely a man who guides dudes or hunters on pack trips. He's also called an *arriero, mozo* (when an assistant) and a *pack master* (when the boss).

Some of the old-time packers were legendary. David Lavender wrote of the ones who packed equipment and supplies to a mine near Ouray, Colorado in the 1930s: 'Nothing stumped them. If some piece of freight came along which they couldn't get on one mule's back – and it had to be singularly heavy and ill-shaped to occasion this – they would sling it on poles hung between two mules. Unusually recalcitrant pieces of machinery were lashed to a flat sledge and pulled up the narrow, twisting trail by a whole string of mules in tandem. In ingenuity, brawn, daring, and plain brute courage, in all the tricks of dealing with evil nature and rebellious livestock, the mountain packers have no peers.'

paddle When said of a horse, to wing out with the forefeet.

paddle wheel In the early West, a gambling game similar to roulette. [Adams]

padre A south-western expression for a Catholic priest or monk. The term is borrowed from Spanish and pronounced PAHD-ray.

paho The prayer stick of the Hopi Indians, used in a supplicating way in ceremonies. A feather or some sacred meal may be attached, and the stick was often carved and painted. Also called *baho*.

pail A range verb meaning 'to milk a cow', an onerous task to a cowboy. Sometimes it means to water a cow from a pail.

Paincourt An 18th-century name for St Louis. From the French, meaning literally 'short of bread', it came from frequent scarcity of provisions in the town. It was pronounced PAN-koor.

paint A spotted horse, white with large areas of either black, brown or red. Now paint horses are registered and must be bred from quarter horses, thoroughbreds or other paints. Historically, paint meant the same as pinto, though some observers say paint was used more in the East and pinto in the West. These horses are often called *painted horses* or *painted ponies*. appaloosas, which have small spots on the rump and back, are neither paints nor pintos. (*See* buckskin for horse colours)

Oldtime cowhands liked paints for show but not for work, thinking that they lacked bottom (endurance). Since spotted horses in those days were Indian ponies, this may have reflected a prejudice against anything Indian.

paint dauber The man who paints the brand on sheep. [Adams]

paint for war In cowboy talk, to get ready to fight. Based jocularly on the Indians' preparing for war by applying paints.

paint pot A mud pot, a boiling spring of mud. At Fountain Paint Pots in Yellowstone National Park, bubbling hot springs attack the rock, mix with the softened material and create these wonderful oddities, which range from sorrel-coloured to ochre. A mud volcano is a big paint pot.

paint your tonsils In cowboy talk, to drink whiskey. If you get drunk, you've *painted your nose*. [Adams]

paintbrush The Indian paintbrush (*Casileja linariaefolia*), a flower of the Rocky Mountain region that has the appearance of a paintbrush dipped in brilliant red, orange or yellow paint. It is the state flower of Wyoming.

pair of headlights Two eggs. Ordered with a string of flats for the engineer, says historian Francis Fugate, it means eggs with bacon.

pair of overalls Cowboy talk for two drinks. He wants them right quick for a good start. [Adams]

pair up For a cow and calf to get back together after branding; also known as *mothering up*.

paisano (1) A south-western expression for a compatriot; a fellow countryman; a

country man or peasant. When used by Anglos, it sometimes is derogatory. Borrowed from Spanish, it's pronounced py-ZAHN-noh. (2) Another name for the road runner.

Paiute A Shoshonean people of the Great Basin and California, also called Pah-Utes, Pah-Yutas, Pah-Utches and the like. Whites often simply (and contemptuously) called them Diggers. Not using the horse, they subsisted by lots of desert gathering and some hunting. They lived in brush shelters and wore little; they were skilled basket-makers. Divided into two groups, northern and southern, they now live on many small reservations in Oregon and Nevada.

palaver A parley; a long talk, such as a council between whites and Indians. Linguist J. L. Dillard says the term came into English from Indian Pidgin English, which got it from the maritime lingua franca.

paleface White man. Perhaps a word of Indian Pidgin English, dating to the early 19th century. Many occurrences, though, are of whites attributing this word to Indians, often teasingly. (For many Indian words for white man, *see* Anglo)

palo alto A slouch hat popular among California gold-rushers, resembling the later stetson called Boss of the Plains. The Spanish translates 'high pole' or 'tall tree' – palo alto was what the Spaniards named the California redwoods. It's pronounced PAH-loh AHL-toh.

Palo forms these *combinations*: *palo amarillo* (holly-grape and chamiso), *palo blanco* (the soap-berry that bears berries that can be used for soap) and *palo verde* (a green, leafless tree – also called *retama* or *lluvia de oro* – with spectacular yellow blossoms that grows in washes in the lower California and Arizona deserts).

palomino A golden horse with a cream-coloured mane and tail (for many colours and markings of horses, *see* buckskin); a colour of horse, not a breed. Borrowed from Spanish, it's pronounced pah-loh-MEE-noh.

Palouse A grassland along the Snake River in northern Idaho and eastern Washington, so named by the voyageurs from their Canadian French word for grassland, *pelouse*. Anglos called the Nez Percé Indians of that region the *Palouse* (or Pelouse) *Indians*, and the horses they bred *Palouse horses* (later appaloosas). In that country a *palouser* is a homemade lantern (a candle in a can), a greenhorn or a sunset.

pan The gold-mining gear of the common man without money, a shallow vessel the shape of a big skillet but without a handle. He uses it to wash gravel, looking for yellow.

As a verb, pan means 'to wash gravel with a pan, to be engaged in the process of panning'. Soil is said to pan well or poorly. It's also *panned out*. Something that panned out succeeded. By figurative extension, even a person may be panned (checked out closely). (*See* placer mining)

Combinations: pan amalgamation (a process of separating gold and silver from ore in a pan-like utensil [a *pan amalgamator* or *pan mill*]), *pan charge* (what's in a pan amalgamator), *pan miner*, *pain tailings* (the residue from panning gold-bearing soil), *pan test* (a test made with a pan for gold in soil), *pan washing* (or *working*) (panning gold-bearing soil).

pan-Indianism A movement among contemporary Indians to recognise common causes, beliefs, problems and so on. Now Indians of many heritages are uniting to face the dominant Anglo culture and are presenting a common front to the US government about Indian issues. Previously, historical animosities between tribes persisted (even having students from certain tribes at the same schools could cause serious difficulties), and the Indians worked together less in the political and cultural arenas.

panhandle A strip of land sticking out from a state or territory as a handle sticks out from a pan. Though this term is not necessarily Western, it is associated with several Western states – the Idaho panhandle, Oklahoma panhandle and Texas panhandle. Residents of panhandles are called *panhandlers*.

pannier In packing, a container lashed on to a pack saddle for carrying heavy loads. Bag panniers may be made of leather, cloth or canvas. Box panniers are made of wood. The gear used on pack trips is largely carried in panniers. *Pannier* comes from the French *panier* (basket). It's pronounced PAN-yer, the *a* as in *corral*.

panoche A south-western term for raw sugar or for candy made of brown sugar. Borrowed from Spanish (*panocha*), it's pronounced puh-NOH-chee and also spelled *panocha* and *penuche*.

pansaje A Texas term for a barbecue. Around the turn of the last century, pansajes were for men only. Borrowed from Spanish, it's pronounced pahn-SAH-hay.

pants rats Cowboy talk for body lice, a nice bit of cowboy drollery. A favourite Western painter, Charlie Russell, tells a funny story about them: 'It's one spring roundup, back in the early '80s. We're out on circle, an' me an' Pete's ridin' together. Mine's a centre-fire saddle, and I drop back to straighten the blanket an' set it. I ain't but a few minutes behind him, but the next I see of Pete is on the bank of this creek, which didn't have no name then. He's off his hoss an' has stripped his shirt off. With one boulder on the ground an' another about the same size in his hand, he's poundin' the seams of his shirt. He's so busy he don't hear me when I ride up, and he's cussin' and swearin' to himself. I hear him mutter, "I'm damned if this don't get some of the big ones!"

'Well, from this day on, this stream is known as Louse Creek.'

Papago A Piman Indian people of southern Arizona. Their name in their own language means 'Bean People', and their country is called *Papagueria*. Historically, they avoided conflict with the United States and allied themselves with non-Indians to fight the Apache. They are known as expert desert-dwellers and fine basket-makers and have an agricultural economy. They now live in Arizona on the San Xavier Reservation, the Gila Bend Reservation and the Papago

Reservation proper, the second largest in the US.

The Papago village Schuchuli, Arizona, has been the first village to operate on electricity provided by a stand-alone system of photovoltaic power, in an experiment of the National Aeronautics and Space Administration.

paper Marked cards used by dishonest gamblers. To *play the papers* meant to gamble.

paper bread Piki, a thin bread made from corn by the Hopi.

paper cartridge Ammunition for a muzzle-loading gun before the Civil War, black powder behind a lead ball encased in heavy paper or linen for ramming down the barrel.

paper son A ruse used by Chinese immigrants. A man with citizenship would claim that a younger man was his son so he could be admitted to the United States.

paper wagon An Indian Pidgin word for a stagecoach because stagecoaches carried the mail. [Adams]

papoose A term of Indian Pidgin English (like *squaw*, originally Algonquian) for an infant or other small child. Not a Westernism but carried West by frontiersmen. Also spelled *pappouse, papouse* and otherwise.

Papoose basket was a south-western term for a basket or bassinet for infants. A *papoose board* was a cradle-board. *Papoose root* is squaw root, or blue cohosh, used by the Indians as a diuretic.

parada A term of California and buckaroo country for a herd of cattle or sometimes a cavvy (string of saddle horses). Borrowed from Spanish (*parada* means 'stopping place'), it's pronounced puh-RAH-duh. *Parada grounds* refers to a spot you pick for working cattle. [Adams]

parade chaps A pair of chaps strictly for show, maybe for the grand entry parade at a rodeo.

pard Short for partner. Often a cowboy's pard was the fellow he was paired with daily on the range, but the word was used in other Western contexts as well.

parfleche (1) Among the mountain men and the Indians of the plains and mountains, rawhide; a hide (usually buffalo) with the hair off. (2) The boxes made by the Indians from this rawhide – big boxes or envelopes for storage, usually decorated with geometrical designs. (Other objects, such as soles for moccasins, were also made of this rawhide) (3) Among cowboys, it meant something similar, war bag or portmanteau.

The term came to English from Canadian French and is pronounced PAR-flesh. From the French, meaning to turn away (*parry*) an arrow (*flèche*), because of its ability to deflect arrows when used for a shield. It is not used in the south-west.

park In the Rocky Mountains, a natural clearing, an area of open meadows surrounded by timber or mountains. Also called a hole. New Park was the trappers' name for what is now called North Park on the headwaters of the North Platte. Old Park is Middle Park, and South Park is the celebrated Bayou Salado of the mountain men, the region in Colorado around the head of the south Platte River, which the trappers loved for its abundant game and generally shining times. Brown's Park (or Brown's Hole) was first a trapper's meeting area, then a notorious hideout for outlaws. Yellowstone National Park is full of parks, open mountain meadows. Like the great canyons, the vistas of slick-rock and the high peaks, parks are among the most beautiful places in the West.

parlour cattle car A car on a train for cattle with a passage on one side for watering and feeding without unloading, apparently a great luxury. Parlour was applied to anything luxurious, fancy or citified. Thus *parlour gun* (a derringer) and *parlour house* (not originally Western) (a fancy whorehouse, in contrast with crib).

parole A certificate given to Indian leaders by Lewis and Clark or other early US government representatives, intended to establish the recipient as the legal head of his tribe. This effort of the government ignored Indian social organisation and tradition.

partida A group, a band, especially a bunch of cattle; though the number is indefinite, the suggestion is a lot. Borrowed from Spanish (where it means political party or faction), it's pronounced par-TEE-duh.

partidario A New Mexican sheep-herder who sharecrops sheep. At the end of the season, he owes the owner a payment of wool and lambs and often does not make enough money to do much more than cover his expenses.

partisan (1) Among the mountain men, the leader of a brigade of trappers. (*See also* coureur de bois) (2) The leader of an Indian war party. Borrowed from French, the word may have come to English from the French-Canadian fur men.

pasear A walk; a trip. In the south-west, this Spanish verb became an indiscriminate verb and noun. It could be as casual as 'Let's pasear a little', but a California publication spoke in 1847 of a pasear back to the States. It was pronounced pah-say-AR. The similar *paseo* meant a stroll or ride for pleasure.

pass In gambling, to decline to bet. To *pass the buck*, in poker, is to decline to deal. In the West, a player who did not care to deal passed on an object, frequently a buckhorn-handled knife, to the next player, as a sign that he was declining.

pass In the south-west, a kind of wine or brandy made in El Paso, known to Americans as Pass wine and Pass whiskey. *Paso* means 'pass' or 'ford'.

passhico Another name for camas; the bread made by Indians from the camas root. Pronounced pa-SHI-koh.

pastor A south-western term for a sheep-herder, usually an Indian, Mexican or Basque. Borrowed from Spanish, it's pronounced PAH-stohr. Sometimes spelled *pastore*.

pat him on the lip Among loggers, to beat someone up, give him a thrashing.

patch logging An approach to logging thought to improve on clear-cutting. Instead of cutting large areas, the loggers cut in patches of 40 to 200 acres. These regenerate more quickly and pose less danger for fire and insect pests.

patent (1) Title to a mining claim gotten by patent from the federal government in exchange for work done on the claim. (2) The patented claim itself. (3) In verb form, to obtain a patent right.

pathfinder An explorer, a finder of the way. The New York novelist James Fenimore Cooper coined this word in his 1840 novel *The Pathfinder*, whose hero is Natty Bumppo, the Leather-stocking, a frontiersman who participates in both the red and white worlds. Later John Charles Frémont was known as the Pathfinder.

pathway On Navajo baskets and rugs, a slender band of light colour running from the centre to the edge. It is a break in the pattern that allows the spirit to escape. In full, the term is *weaver's pathway*.

patio (1) A courtyard within a building or connected to a building. Originally south-western (borrowed from Spanish, where it has the same meaning), the term is now used throughout the United States. (2) In mining, a yard where ores were cleaned and sorted or where silver was amalgamated. This treatment of silver, chiefly Mexican, was called the *patio process*, or *cold amalgamation process*.

patriarch In Mormonism, a man (now usually elderly) of eminence, endowed with prestige and ordained to give blessings.

patron (1) Among voyageurs and other fur men, the master or steersman of a boat. In this usage, it is borrowed from Canadian French and is pronounced pah-TROHN. (2) In the south-west, first a *hacendado* (master of a hacienda) or other man of authority or wealth; now simply a boss. As applied to large landowners, the word originally was supposed to imply a benefactor to Indians and others living on his land. In this usage, the word is borrowed from Spanish; it is also pronounced pah-TROHN.

Paul Pry A cowboy's name for a meddler. [Adams]

paulin Short for tarpaulin; used in the last century rather than *tarp*.

paunched In cowboy talk, shot in the stomach. [Adams]

paw around for turmoil In cowboy talk, to look for trouble. [Adams]

Pawnee A confederacy of Caddoan Indian people who lived in the valley of the Platte River and had a lifestyle seasonally sedentary and nomadic. Most of the year they lived in earth lodges and farmed, but in the summer they lived in tipis and hunted buffalo. The name Pawnee (derived from the word *pariki*, meaning 'horn') is said to come from the hair-dressing style of the men – many twisted the forelock into the shape of a horn. The principal bands of this confederation were the Grand Pawnee, Loup (or Mohas or Skidi or Wolf) Pawnee and Republican Pawnee.

The Pawnees of the historic period were very religious and practiced human sacrifice until 1817. They carried on generations of enmity with most other tribes, especially the Dakota, Cheyenne and Arapaho, but mostly kept the peace with white people. In the 1850s, they settled on a reservation in eastern Nebraska and subsequently formed the Pawnee Battalion under Major Frank North (who had grown up among them) to protect the labourers of the Union Pacific Railroad from the Pawnees' historic enemies. In 1877 they were moved to Indian Territory (later the state of Oklahoma), where they remain.

Combinations: Pawnee macaroni (a favourite dish of the tribe, made from antelope entrails and fish worms), *Pawnee Rock* (a landmark of the Santa Fe Trail near the Arkansas River, where the Pawnees had battles with the Comanche and later with some Santa Fe traders) and *Pawnee whistle* (a whistling sound Pawnees made to announce their arrival).

pay dirt Earth or gravel bearing minerals, especially gold, in economic quantities. The term *pay gravel* was also used among placer miners, and the terms *pay ore*, *pay rock*, *pay shoot*, *pay streak* and *pay vein* were heard among hard-rock miners. To *hit* (or *strike*) *pay dirt* was to discover such earth or gravel and by extension to strike it rich or to succeed in a large way at anything.

pay foot Twelve inches of lode. Also called a *mining foot*.

peace pipe *See* medicine pipe.

peacemaker The most famous revolver of the West. Produced by Colt from 1873 on, it was known as the *Single Action Army* and the *Frontier*. Part of its usefulness was that (after a brief time as a .45-calibre weapon), it used the same .44-calibre ammunition as the Winchester 1873 model. (*See* six-shooter)

pearl diver What loggers and cowboys called a dishwasher in a logging camp or in a restaurant.

peavey A strong pole, about as long as a man is tall, used by loggers, especially in log driving (moving logs down-river). On one end, it has a metal socket, a curved steel hook and a pike (distinguishing it from a cant hook, which has a toe ring and lip instead of a pike). Sometimes called a *peavey hook* or a *peavey log wrench*. The *peavy log* is the top log on a load.

pechita In the south-west, the mesquite bean, valued by the Papago Indians as food and used as feed for livestock. In the Papago region of southern Arizona, pechita (or *béchete*) holes are common near sources of water; these depressions are used for grinding grains and nuts. Borrowed from the Spanish (from Zapotecan), it's pronounced pay-CHEE-tuh.

peck On the peck means aggressive, on the prod, as a bull may often be.

pecker neck Cowboy talk for a horse trained for riding but not for working cows. [Adams]

pecker pole What a logger called a small tree or sapling.

pecos Literally, to shoot someone and throw the body into the Pecos River, which in the 19th century drained a lawless empire in west Texas and New Mexico. By extension, simply to kill a man. A *pecos swap* was a theft. [Adams]

Pecos Bill Cowboy talk for a teller of windies. This fellow is also known as a *peddler of loads*. The legendary Pecos Bill was a Texan who was raised by coyotes, rode a mountain lion and dug the Rio Grande by harnessing a twister. (*See also* yarn)

pedregal A rocky piece of country, especially a region of lava flow. Borrowed from Spanish, it's pronounced pay-dray-GAHL.

peeler (1) A bronc buster, a horse-breaker. To *peel horses* was to break or train them or sometimes simply to stick with a critter that was bucking. On the frontier of the eastern woodlands, a peeler had been a humdinger, an exceptional example of anything. Perhaps a man who could stick on green horses was thought a humdinger. (2) Among cowboys, especially in Texas, a man who skins cows, stripper. (3) A logger who takes the bark off redwood logs. He uses a *peeling bar* for the work.

peepstones A derogatory term of gentiles for the transparent stones of power Joseph Smith (in Mormon belief) used when translating the golden plates inscribed with the *Book of Mormon*. They are more properly called Urim and Thummin. Later, by extension, simply a magical stone.

peewee A style of cowboy boot with short tops popular in the early part of the 20th century.

peg (1) To mark a mining claim with stakes. (2) For a bulldogger to stick a steer's horn into the ground, which rodeos don't permit.

peg out Butt out; die away, become extinct. According to Joseph Porter's *Paper Medicine Man*, whites of the latter half of the 19th century expected the Indians 'to give up their old ways and become civilised, or, as one newspaper bluntly put it, "forever peg out".'

pelado A Mexican who's ignorant and broke. The word (now uncommon) is an equivalent of greaser and as contemptuous. Borrowed from Spanish (where it has the same denotation), it's pronounced pay-LAH-doh.

pelon Cowboy talk for a muley, a cow without horns. Borrowed from Spanish (where it means 'bald'), it's pronounced pay-LOHN. [Adams]

pembina The highbush cranberry (a species of *Viburnum Americanum*) of North Dakota, whose fruit both Indians and whites use for food. French-Canadian fur traders built a succession of posts named Pembina on the Red River of the north, in the area of the present Pembina, North Dakota, and many metis lived there; later the American Fur Company and the federal government built posts there; still later Pembina became a farming centre. At one time, people campaigned for a separate territory, to be called Pembina, to be formed from this part of north-eastern Dakota Territory. The *Pembina cart* (or *buggy*) was a crudely constructed cart similar to the Red River cart. Borrowed from French-Canadian speech, which was in turn based on Cree words, it's pronounced pem-BEE-nuh.

pemmican The universal preserved food of the Indians who lived on the buffalo, and later of the mountain men and other frontiersmen who learned Indian ways. Pemmican was made from buffalo meat (though occasionally deer or moose were used) that was jerked, pounded fine, mixed equally by weight with marrow fat and stored in parfleches or sewn into other skin sacks. Often dried berries were added, especially choke-cherries and service-berries. Preserved in this way, pemmican lasted for several years.

Pemmican was the staple of Indian raiding parties and of all buffalo Indians during the winter. Summer pemmican was not pemmican made in the summer but made in the later winter or spring for the summer. It was reportedly a superb food and a good diet. The voyageurs made a soup called rubbaboo by boiling pemmican in water and adding a little flour and sugar.

The Pemmican War was the struggle for dominance in the fur trade from 1812–21 between the Hudson's Bay Company and the Northwest Fur Company. Modern usages like fruit pemmican are an odd twisting of the original meaning – pemmican was mostly meat. (*See* jerky)

Penitente A member of a New Mexican Catholic sect that believes in the saving power of punishment and practices self-flagellation and even a form of crucifixion. Members (called *penitents*) scourge themselves with whips made from yucca fibre (*disciplinas*). Some become *Cristos* and carry their crosses and then are strapped to them in Good Friday ceremonies – some Cristos are said not to have survived this high, holy act. Though persecuted in the past, the sect persists today among some Hispanics, and is back in the good graces of the Catholic Church on the condition of modifying its excesses. Also known as *Los Hermanos de Luz*. From Spanish, the name is pronounced both pen-uh-TEN-tay and pen-uh-TEN-tee.

penny ante Descriptive of a poker game in which the ante is limited to a penny. By extension, anything small, inconsequential.

peon In the south-west, a member of the Mexican labouring class. In the early and middle 19th century, a peon was literally a slave or a person held by debt to a landowner in a near-equivalent of slavery.

The word had verb forms, as in, 'Juan is peoned to the patron.' Even Anglo cowboys spoke of hiring out as *peoning out*.

The system whereby peasants were held in effective servitude by debt was called *peonage*.

people of the north Same as Red River metis.

pepper-and-salt rope A rope of alternating black and white hair.

pepper-belly Cowboy talk for a Mexican who eats lots of chiles, which the cowboy calls peppers. (*See also* greaser and pelado, which also are not friendly appellations)

pepperbox A cap-and-ball or metallic cartridge pistol of the mid-19th century with five or six barrels that revolved to provide more than the one shot of the older pistol. This technology was later replaced by the revolver, in which the cylinder, not the barrels, turned. The pepperbox was also called a coffee mill.

(For many Western words for a pistol, *see* six-shooter)

peraira A common variant of prairie. Other variants are *parara* and *perara*.

percussion A term for a firearm whose charge is set off by a percussion cap rather than a flint. Percussion (or percussion-cap) weapons succeeded the flintlock from the 1820s onward, and they preceded the breech-loader. Metal cartridges incorporating percussion caps or priming compound put percussion caps out of business.

A percussion cap (sometimes called a *primer*) was and is a small piece of copper containing a fulminate charge. The cap fits snugly upon the nipple. There the hammer strikes it, causing an explosion that sends a spark through the touchhole to the powder.

A *percussion lock* is a firing mechanism that uses percussion caps; also called a *cap-lock*.

permit (1) A grazing permit on public land. (2) A timecard used as a substitute for a union card by a logger. [Adams]

Perpetual Emigration Fund Organised September 1849 in Salt Lake City to aid Mormons in need of secure transportation to the Salt Lake Valley. Donations of money, oxen, wagons, food stuffs and other goods were solicited from church members already in the valley and elsewhere. The means advanced for transportation was considered a loan, to be repaid as soon as possible after the travellers' arrival. The company was legally incorporated by the State of Deseret in 1851. When it was disbanded in 1887, it had assisted approximately 50,000 persons.

persuader (1) A revolver. (For other names for revolvers, *see* six-shooter) (2) A spur. (For other names for spurs, *see* spur) (3) A bull whip.

peso The Mexican unit of currency, as the dollar is the basic US monetary unit. The number of pesos needed to make a dollar has fluctuated widely. Now the word is often used in the south-west as a jocular reference to money. (*See* real)

Borrowed from Spanish, it's pronounced, PAY-soh.

peter out To give out, to get exhausted, as a vein of mineral might do and as people and animals do. Linguist J. L. Dillard says that this verb is a mining Westernism.

petrified forest An area where the logs, stumps and the like have become fossilised. Early Westerners were mystified and delighted by such places, such as the one in Yellowstone National Park, and they made up stories about them. Horses were said to tremble when they tried to nibble grass of rock. A hunter plunked off a bird's head, but it went on singing because it was stone. Jim Bridger jumped his horse over a huge chasm because even the law of gravity was petrified. And tale-tellers called the stone trees *putrefactions*, perhaps at first out of ignorance, later to have a little fun.

petroglyph A prehistoric carving in a rock, usually of gods, men, animals or religious symbols. In the West, petroglyphs are often the signs we have of ancient cliff-dwelling Indians (*see* Anasazi), and their meaning is much in dispute. A classic example of petroglyphs and pictographs, ancient painting on rock, is Newspaper Rock near Canyonlands National Park.

peyote A spineless cactus of the south-west, especially *Lophophora williamsi*, that yields a hallucinogenic button. These peyote buttons (discs) were used as a door to religious visions by south-western Indians for centuries (or millennia) and now are the medicine of the Native American Church, eaten ceremonially to help meditation, prayers and visions.

Adapted from the Aztec word *peyotl*, it is also spelled *payote* and *pellote*.

picacho In the south-west, summit, peak; sometimes the name of a peak. Borrowed from Spanish, it's pronounced pee-KA-choh, the *a* as in *corral*.

picaro In the south-west, a vagabound, a rogue. Borrowed from Spanish, it's pronounced PEE-kuh-roh.

picaroon Among loggers, a pole with a curved hook and a pike, used in log driving to pull logs out of eddies and the like. Also called a *pick handspike* and a *pick pole*. A similar log-driving tool is the pike pole. Of obscure origin, it's pronounced pee-kuh-ROON.

picked brand A cowboy practice of both legitimate and illegitimate purpose. The hair was picked off a calf with either pliers or a knife in the shape of a brand, which looked, at a distance, like the calf had been properly branded. When the calf was old enough to separate from its mother, it was then re-branded by the rustler. Picking a brand also describes what was done to clarify a blotched or unclear brand; the hair was removed around the brand to see the brand more clearly.

picker During shearing, the man who gathers and rolls the sheep fleeces in the shearing pen.

picket (1) On the early Western frontier, a picket was a tree trunk set straight up in the ground to form a stockade or similar obstacle to Indian attack. The word was also used to mean the resulting stockade. *Combinations: picket corral, picket fort, picket house* and *picket hut* and *picket shack*, which were used in the second half of the 19th century. Traders built a picket house on the Red River as late as 1875, setting the tree trunks into a ditch and filling in with dirt. (2) To stake a horse so the critter can feed but not stray – to stake the horse out. This was and is done with a *picket pin*, which may be anything from a crude stick to a metal stake with a ring. From the pin to the halter runs a *picket rope*, preferably of thick, soft cotton.

A *picket pin* may also be a gopher, so called because they stand straight and still. The phrase *cut your picket pin* meant 'to leave'.

Picketwire A river of south-eastern Colorado that drains the region of the Spanish Peaks. It was first called the Rio de las Animas Perdidas en Purgatorio by the Spaniards, then the Purgatoire River by the French. The Anglos, getting the name by ear, transformed Purgatoire into

Picketwire. Now it is also known as the Purgatoire or Purgatory.

pick-up A rodeo rider who helps a contestant off the critter he's been riding. The pick-up (or *pick-up man*) rides alongside and lets the cowboy get behind him. This is a considerable service since the cowboys are usually eager to get gone as soon as they've stayed on the number of seconds required. Pick-ups also help get the bucking critter away from riders on the ground and out of the arena.

pictograph An ancient native painting on a rock wall (or on hide, wood, shell and other surfaces). Like petroglyphs, pictographs usually show gods, men, animals or religious symbols in a simple and stylised way. It is not a Westernism, and pictographs are not exclusive to the West.

pie buggy A wagon sent to town for supplies. A *pie box* was a chuck wagon, and a *pie wagon* was a trailer attached to this movable kitchen.

To *have enough pie* was a California phrase for being done for.

Piegan A principal division of the Blackfeet Indians, historically living in Montana and Alberta. The name comes from *Pikuni* (poor robes), their name for themselves, and is pronounced, variously, perhaps most often PAY-guhn or pee-GAN. Confusingly, a clan of their long-time enemies the Crows is named Piegan because they acted as Piegans supposedly do – they abandoned their comrades.

pig's vest with buttons Salt pork or sow-belly.

pigging string A six-foot thong of rawhide or horsehair (nowadays made of twisted nylon) used to hog-tie calves. Now it's mostly used in the rodeo event of calf-roping, where a cowboy ropes the runaway calf, throws it and ties three feet together in as short a time as possible. Old-time cowboys seemed always to pack a bunch of pigging strings around in their pockets.

Pike Among Californians of the second half of the 19th century, a mocking name for a certain kind of Missourian who emigrated to California, originally one who was from Pike County. A Pike was supposed to be lazy, disloyal and otherwise worthless, if not a ruffian and a thief. This derogation later got applied to almost any newcomer to California. Also called a *Piker*. The term gives rise to *Pikedom*, *Pikish*, *Pike language* and *Pike Countian*.

Pike's Peaker An 1859 gold-rusher to the Pike's Peak, Colorado, area. Such folk had what was called *Peak fever* and adopted the motto 'Peak or bust!' Also known as a *peaker*.

piket A cowboy name for a skunk. Pronounced pee-KAY.

piki A wafer-like, multi-coloured cornbread of the Hopi Indians. It is baked on a piki stone, hewn by Hopi men and polished smooth by women. The stone is warmed by a fire built beneath it. Also called *paper bread*. Pronounced PEE-kee.

pile driver A name for a bronc that bucks by going straight up and pounding down on all four legs at once, stiffly.

pile the rope into a critter To rope an animal and throw it.

pilgrim (1) A greener, a fellow new to the West. It may carry the implication of a person trying to catch on to the ways of the country more seriously than a dude or greenhorn. (2) A cow that hasn't wintered on the plains, is new to the country and by implication lacks toughness. Such cows were also called *barnyard stock* and *States cattle*, that is, cattle from the United States proper. (3) Sometimes a horse that once was valuable but now has gotten too old.

Though some sources say that pilgrim was applied to cows first and men later, the actual citations indicate it was the other way around.

pillion A light woman's saddle; a pad behind a Hispanic man's saddle that a Hispanic woman rode on.

pilon Something extra given by a merchant to a customer. A term of the Rio Grande valley. Also spelled *pelon*. Borrowed from Spanish, it's pronounced pee-LOHN.

piloncillo In the south-west, a cone of unrefined brown sugar. This treat was popular with Hispanics and pioneer Anglos. Borrowed from Spanish (where *pilón* means 'sugar-loaf'), it's pronounced pee-lohn-SEE-yoh.

Pima Indians of the Sonoran deserts of southern Arizona and Sonora, a country called by the Spaniards Pimeria Alta (Upper Pimeria). The term Pima includes the tribes known as Pima, Sand Papago and Papago. Some were mainly hunter-gatherers, other farmers, all of them expert desert-dwellers. Historically, they avoided conflict with the United States and usually allied themselves with Anglos and Hispanics to fight the Apache. The Pima settled in Arizona on the Gila River Reservation, Ak Chin Reservation and Salt River Reservation.

pin grass *Erodium cicutarium*, a fine and common graze of the plains. Also called *pin clover* and *aliflaria*.

pinacate A wingless beetle of the arid West. Derived from Nahuatl but borrowed directly from Spanish, it's pronounced pin-uh-KAH-tee.

pinch (1) All the gold dust the seller can pick up with a thumb and forefinger. A pinch was the coin of the realm in the California gold regions during the gold rush and was about the smallest unit of exchange – a drink cost a pinch. (2) In mining, the narrowing of a vein. At that spot, which is also called a cap, the vein is said to be pinched. When it plays out entirely, it is said to be *pinched out* or *pinched down*.

pinch chute Cowboy talk for a branding chute.

pine beetle Beetles of the genus *Dendroctonus* that burrow into the bark of pines such as ponderosa and lodgepole, ultimately killing the trees. The stand of dead trees then became a potential fire hazard.

pine grouse The blue grouse of the Rocky Mountains (*Dengragapus obscurus*). Also called a pine hen.

pineapple cactus The Mojave fish-hook cactus (*Echinocactus polyancistrus*), which bears beautiful pink and magenta blossoms.

ping-pong In logger talk, to curry mules.

Pinkerton A detective of the Pinkerton agency, organised in Chicago in 1850 by Allan Pinkerton. Collectively, they were known (especially by strikers who disliked them) as *Pinkertonians*. The company's policy of hiring private police was called *Pinkertonism* or *Pinkertonianism*.

pinole A spicy flour of south-western Indians, usually flour from the mesquite bean mixed with parched corn meal and the whole spiced with cinnamon and sugar. Ground seeds or other ground beans are also used. Also spelled *pinol* and *pinola*. Tortillas are made from it, and it is also put into water to make a cooling drink. Borrowed from Spanish (which got it from Nahuatl), it's pronounced pee-NOH-lay or pih-NOH-lee.

piñon A pine tree of the south-west (*Pinus parryana* or *P. edulis* or *P. cembroides*). Along with the juniper it is the character-istic tree of the mesas of canyon country. Its nutlike seed was and is an important food for Indians, and its wood makes a fire with so pungently delicious a smell that it is one of the defining memories of the region. Borrowed from Spanish (where it means 'pine nut'), it's usually Ameri-canised to PIN-yuhn. Also spelled *pinyon* and occasionally pinion. *Combinations:* *piñon jay*, *piñon mouse*, *piñon pine* and *piñoneros* (Clark's nutcrackers, a bird).

Pins Members of a secret society of Cherokee full-bloods formed ostensibly to perpetuate tribal traditions but actually to oppose slavery. Named the Keetoowah Society by its members, it became known as the Pin Society because its insignia of crossed pins was worn by members on their hunting shirts and coats.

pintail The sharp-tailed grouse. (*See* prairie chicken)

pinto (1) A spotted horse; a piebald horse; a paint. Though the paint and pinto are now registered by different associations, old-time Westerners used the terms interchangeably. (2) The pinto bean, a variety of kidney bean. (*See* frijol)

The word *pinto* is borrowed from Spanish, where it means 'spotted' or 'speckled'.

pinto chaps Chaps with the hair on and spotted because hair of another colour is sewn on top [Adams]

pinwheel (1) An unusual movement in a bucking horse: it flips forward and lands on its back. [Adams] (2) A roll of a gun – the butt goes down, the muzzle up and the gun flips and lands in the hand in firing position. [Adams]

pioneer To open new country as a pioneer. (The noun *pioneer* appears to be an Americanism, and the verb *pioneer* a Westernism)

Many Western communities have Pioneer Days, festivals commemorating the achievements of the pioneers. Utah, for instance, celebrates the 1847 arrival of the Mormons at the Salt Lake each July 24, and Idaho celebrates England's withdrawal of its claim to the Oregon country each June 15. (*See also* frontiersmen)

A *pioneer bucker* is a horse that constantly hunts new territory by bucking in figure eights or in circles. [Adams]

pipe (1) In the meaning of the pipes smoked ceremonially by Indians, see medicine pipe. (2) Among the voyageurs, the distance paddled between rests for a smoke of the pipe, very approximately six miles. (3) In hydraulic mining, to wash away dirt with a stream of water.

pipestone The soft, red claystone found at Pipestone, Minnesota and used by the Plains Indians (and other Indians) to carve pipe bowls. (*See* medicine pipe) The quarries of this stone, in the country of the Dakota Indians, were and are a kind of holy land – even enemy tribes could go there in safety to renew their supplies of pipestone. According to Indian legend, the stone is made from the blood of their ancestors or from the blood of the buffalo, and so is itself sacred. Now the area is Pipestone National Monument, and stone is still quarried by Indians for their pipes.

Pipestone is also known as *catlinite*, after the traveller, painter and student of Indian ways George Catlin.

pirooting In the south-west, meandering, fooling around.

piskun A Plains Indian trap for buffalo, shaped like a V and ending in a cliff. Many tribes ran buffalo off cliffs to make large kills. Also spelled *pishkun*. From the Blackfeet language, it's pronounced PEES-kuhn.

pistol (1) A green hand, an inexperienced cowboy. (2) A pocket flask of booze. Cowboys didn't call their handguns pistols.

pita (1) In the south-west, a fibre the Indians used to make thread, cord, rope and the like. It came mainly from the agave. (2) The bag, box, net or rope made from that fibre. South-western cowboys like lassos made of fibre. Borrowed from Spanish, it's pronounced PIT-uh.

pitahaya In the south-west, a name for the organ-pipe cactus, or other large, columnar cacti (*Lemaireocereus thurberi* and *Carnegiea gigantea*), including the saguaro. Borrowed from Spanish, it's pronounced pee-tuh-HAH-yuh.

pitch (1) When said of a horse in Texas, to buck. Thus Texas cowboys speak of breaking a horse as taking the pitch out of it. A horse that insists on bucking is called a pitcher. (For more words for bucking, *see* buck) (2) The gambling game known as all-fours or seven-up. (3) Among miners, a dip in a lode. [Adams]

Pitching hay, before lots of modern machinery came along, was one of the arduous, never-ending jobs on any ranch – on to wagons, on to haystacks and then back off for winter feeding. The hay hand was teasingly known as the pitchfork, gladiator [Adams] and other teasing names. (*See* rancher)

pitch post A fence post cut with sap still in it, to make it stand the weather better.

Pitt schooner *See* Conestoga wagon or prairie schooner.

pitted Descriptive of cows caught in holes or forced into corners or draws or against fences in a blizzard. The beasts are absurdly good at getting into such spots and must be roped out or otherwise freed.

placer (1) A spot where gold is gotten by washing; a sand or gravel deposit bearing particles of gold. In such places, gold is gotten by methods using dredges, pans, hydraulicking and sluices, which utilise water and gravity. The word came from California gold-mining in 1842. (2) The word is also used as a verb – to participate in placer mining.

Placer mining is based on a convenient fact of nature: Gold, originally locked into veins in hard rock and inaccessible without lots of money and equipment, gets washed away and ground into fine particles by rains and streams. In the sand and gravel, a common man can separate the gold out in water because it's heavy and sinks. The great gold rushes of California, Idaho and Montana and (to some extent) the Black Hills were placers, and ordinary people could afford to mine. Nevada's Comstock Lode was based on mining veins.

Combinations: placer camp (a camp of placer miners), *placer claim* (a mining claim on a placer), *placer digging* (a location of placer mining), *placer district* or *field* or *ground* (a region of placers), *placer dredge* (a dredge for placering), *placer gold* (gold in flakes and grains) and *placer prospect* (a sign that placering would be productive). Many more are of obvious meaning: *placer bed, deposit, discovery, mine, miner, mining, operations, period, rush washer, working* and so on.

Plains Indians Those Indians that lived in historical times on the Great Plains and had a buffalo-hunting culture. Before the reservation period they were nomadic, got food by hunting and gathering rather than agriculture, lived mostly in tipis and followed the buffalo. (*See* Arapaho, Blackfeet, Cheyenne, Crow, Comanche, Dakota)

plains rifle A muzzle-loading rifle that was shorter than the long rifle, with a half stock and usually a tapered barrel so the weight wasn't so far forward. Noted makers of plains rifles were Jacob and Samuel Hawken, who worked in St Louis from 1822 to 1861. Also called a *mountain rifle.*

plains saddle A saddle that was on the scene by the middle of the 1870s. It was double-rigged, had skirts lined with sheepskin, had a Cheyenne roll and had a low, sturdy, leather-covered horn. It was developed in part by two saddle-making brothers, John S. and Gilbert M. Collins, in Cheyenne, Omaha, Billings and Great Falls. (*See* stock saddle)

planter In boating, a tree trunk, with one end stuck in the riverbed, acting as a snag. (*See also* sawyer)

play a lone hand To act alone, either as a policy or on a particular occasion.

play both ends against the middle In faro, to fix the game by trimming the cards at either end of the deck.

playa (1) Historically in the south-west, a depression in the desert that holds water after rains. (2) Also in the south-west, a beach, a sandy strip on the ocean's shore. From the Spanish (where it means 'beach'), it's pronounced PLY-yuh.

plaza In the south-west, a public square or an open space of a mine or fort. Borrowed from Spanish (where it has the same meanings), it's pronounced PLAH-zuh.

plew The mountain man's term for the entire pelt of a beaver. The usual derivation is that the French-Canadians called a choice pelt a *plus*, French for 'more'. Among the American trappers, who pronounced the word 'ploo', it became the word for any beaver skin.

During the height of the Rocky Mountain trade, ordinary beaver skins brought about four dollars per pound on the open market and a prime plew brought six dollars or more. At one time, fur companies were competing hotly enough that they were paying six dollars a plew for all hides, even those of kits. Prices always varied greatly, more for Great Lakes beaver, less for southern hides, more for winter hides, less for summer, and so on. When prices fell in the mid-1830s, many trappers left the trade and settled on the Pacific Coast. A few merely grumbled, 'Give this child some 'bacca, if it's a plew a plug, and DuPont and Galena [powder and lead], and it's back to the mountains.'

ploughboy   What a rider is said to do when he holds a rein in each hand and pulls the horse's head around with one while laying the other on its neck. [Adams]

plug   (1) A rectangular bar of chewing tobacco. The tobacco was sometimes seasoned with such flavourings as licorice, molasses, sugar, fruit juices and so on. (2) As a verb, to shoot something or someone.

plumb   (1) In Texas, as a verb, to *plumb a track* is to follow a faint trail. (2) As a modifier, completely or absolutely, as in, 'to hit the target plumb centre' or 'be plumb loco'.

plunder   A man's personal belongings, what he might keep in his possible sack or war bag.

plural marriage   What the Mormons called their practice of polygamy, which gentiles euphemistically called their 'peculiar institution' and which was technically polygyny. 'Not an indulgence but a divine command,' says Wallace Stegner in *The Gathering of Zion*, 'it had been revealed privately by Joseph [Smith] to his most confidential counsellors, had been put into writing in 1843 . . . and had finally been publicly admitted in 1852,' and printed in *Doctrine and Covenants*. Reports of this custom caused great animosity among gentiles toward Mormons during their days in Missouri and Illinois and during their pioneering days in Utah. John C. Frémont, campaigning for president in 1856, even called for the abolition of the great barbarisms of slavery and polygamy.

The Mormon reasoning was various: Polygamy was a practice of early Christians. It would prevent immorality. Since men often died under frontier hardships, it was a practical necessity. It would also create a larger population in anticipation of the second coming of Christ and provide bodies for righteous spirits wanting to come back to earth. Mainly, though, it was God's revelation.

Plural marriage was not for everyone but only for men of demonstrated spiritual and economic worthiness, with permission of the existing wife (or wives) and the permission of the Church. (Now some polygamous excommunicated Mormon groups require that the husband be beyond the suspicion of mere lust.) Usually the men permitted plural wives were older and influential. Perhaps less than 10% of early Mormon men were in plural marriages.

In 1890, under federal pressure, church president Wilford Woodruff issued a manifesto forbidding further plural marriage. It did not deny divine sanction of the institution but merely changed Church doctrine.

Plural marriage did survive the Woodruff manifesto in remnants. Colonies in Mexico and Canada continued the practice. It is practiced today by splinter 'fundamentalist' Mormon groups, such as the band at Colorado City on the Arizona-Utah border, and the Apostolic United Brethren. Mormons engaged in plural marriage are summarily excommunicated, and the Church treats its polygamous past as an embarrassment.

plus   *See* plew.

plute   What a logger called a rich man. Short for *plutocrat*.

poblano   Short for poblano hat, a low-crowned, broad-brimmed vaquero hat worn from the 18th century forward.

pocket   Among miners, when said of a vein, for a vein to expand into a pocket (cavity); the opposite of what it does when it pinches. Such a vein is said to be *pockety*.

   Combinations: pocket claim (a mining claim where gold pockets), *pocket diggings* (a pocket gold-mining area), *pocket hunter* or *miner*, *pocket knife assayer* (a person who tests gold with a pocket knife).

poco   The Spanish word for 'little' in the south-west. It is used in several combinations: *poco a poco* (little by little), *poco frio* (a little bit cold), *poco malo* (a little sick), *poco pronto* (right now) and *poco tiempo* (after a while).

pogamoggan   A Plains Indian war club with a stone head. From an Ojibway word, it is pronounced pah-guh-MAH-guhn.

pogonip A heavy fog that appears filled with flying bits of snow, especially in the mountains of Nevada. It is dreaded and said to cause illnesses. The word is reported variously to be Paiute or Shoshone and among the Shoshones to mean 'white death'.

point (1) The lead position for riders with a trail herd. The point riders, experienced hands, keep the herd headed the right way. The other riding positions are swing (part way back along the sides), flank (most of the way back) and drag (at the rear, where the least experienced men ride). Point riders were also called *pointers*, *point men* and *lead men*. Usually working in pairs, point riders for old-time trail drives had the most responsible and dangerous jobs on the team. (2) In the Indian trade, a black mark woven into a blanket to indicate size. A three-point blanket is five by six feet, four point, six by seven-and-a-half feet. Every Indian knew that the points told the cost, typically one plew (beaver pelt) per point. (*See also* trade blanket) (3) A wooded projection of land, especially a bend in a river. This word is a contribution of the voyageurs, who called it in French a *pointe*.

poke A small sack or bag, especially one used to hold gold dust. Often the meaning is 'the sack with the dust in it', as in, 'They stole my poke.'

poker One of several card games in which a crucial skill is placing successive bets within a hand – starting the bet, calling and raising. Poker (the term comes from the French *poque*, which sounds similar and has the same meaning) came into this country through New Orleans, moved up the Mississippi and spread all over the West. The two common forms are five-card draw, the most popular in the 19th century, and five-card stud, which uses four cards face up and the last face down.

Combinations: poker chip, poker face (an expressionless face that reveals nothing), *poker clergy* and *poker sharp* (both meaning skilled players), *poker flat, poker joint* and *poker room* (these three meaning where the game is played).

Principal poker terms are *ace high, ace in the hole, aces up your sleeve, ante, bluff, busted flush, Calamity Jane* (queen of spades), *California prayer book, cash in your chips, chips, chip in, close to the belly* (or *vest*), *dead man's hand, devil's bedposts* (four of clubs), *four flush* (and *four-flusher*), *full house, gaper, ginny up the pasteboards, jackpot, lay down your character, looloo, pack the deal* (to stack the cards dishonestly), *pass the buck, pat hand* (a hand good enough to bet on without drawing additional cards), *shiner, showdown, square deal, strippers, Sunday school, sweeten the pot, there's a one-eyed man in the game* (a warning that someone is cheating) and *you bet.*

polla In the south-west, an attractive young woman. From the Spanish word for 'pullet', it is pronounced POH-yuh and is used like the American slang *chick*.

polyg Gentile (non-Mormon) slang for a Mormon in a plural marriage. Also called a cohab.

poncho Originally a blanket with a slit so it could be pulled over the head as a cloak. Later a similar cloak made of oiled cloth, rubber or nylon. Borrowed from Spanish, it is pronounced PAHN-choh.

ponderosa The bull pine or yellow pine (*Pinus ponderosa*). This very large pine with a broad open crown is a particularly valuable timber pine in the West and is widespread. It usually grows in the mountains in pure stands; the trees are far apart with little undergrowth. The thick reddish bark smells like vanilla.

pony A mustang; any horse. A *cowpony* is a saddle horse accustomed to ranch work. A *pony beef* was a two-year-old bovine, ready to fatten for market. [Adams]

pony express A fast mail service by horseback, especially the one that operated from Missouri to California from 1860 to 1862 and was made obsolete by the telegraph. It was also called the *pony post* and was manned by *pony riders*, who sometimes used a *pony-express mount* (a jumping mount from behind). Letters were required to have *pony stamps*.

pooch Tomatoes stewed with bread and sugar.

poor bull Among mountain men, a descriptive expression for a greenhorn's ignorance, from the idea that a greenhorn could not differentiate *poor bull from fat cow*. According to Lt George Frederick Ruxton, who travelled the mountain West in the 1840s, 'the meat of the cow is infinitely preferable to that of the male buffalo . . . From the end of June to September bull meat is rank and tough, and almost uneatable; while the cows are in perfection, and as fat as stall-fed oxen.' The mountain men also said greenhorns don't 'know which way the stick floats'.

The phrase *poor bull from fat cow* was shortened to simply *poor bull* and also meant 'poor doings', anything that was bad or unfortunate.

poor doe A word applied to tough deer meat, regardless of whether from a buck or doe.

poor man's diggings A gold field that could be easily worked, such as a placer field, not requiring significant capital. Also called a *poor man's mine* and *poor man's camp*.

poor-will The Western version of the whippoorwill, with only two notes to its distinctive call instead of three.

popper The business end of the whip of a drover, freighter or stage driver. It made the whip sound like a gun when it cracked.

por favor Please. Borrowed from Spanish and common among both Hispanics and Anglos in the south-west, it's pronounced pohr fah-VOHR.

porch percher What a cowboy called a loafer. [Adams]

porcupine grass A tall Western grass (*Stipa spartea*) known for sticking to socks and pant legs. A major plant of the mixed-grass prairie, it grows two to four feet high.

porcupine quillwork *See* quillwork.

pork-eater A mountain-man term for a greenhorn. (*See* mangeur de lard)

port The raised part of a curb bit.

Port Orford cedar An evergreen (*Chamaecyparis lawsoniana*) of the north-west Pacific Coast, named for Port Orford, Oregon and commercially valuable. It's also called the *Port Orford cypress*.

portal In the south-west, an arched gallery or passageway. Borrowed from Spanish, it's pronounced pohr-TAHL.

posada In the south-west, a roadhouse, an inn. Borrowed from Spanish, it's pronounced poh-SAH-duh.

pose A term of the voyageurs for the distance they would carry goods on a portage before depositing them temporarily, resting and going back for more. It was about a third of a mile and was also called a *pause*.

posole A mush of boiled corn and meat. Borrowed from Spanish (which got it from Nahuatl), it's pronounced poh-SOH-lay or poh-SOH-lee. Also spelled *pozole and pozzoli*.

posse In the narrow Western sense, a group of riders brought together by a law officer to track down an outlaw. In the larger sense, any group assembled for a common purpose, such as a search for a lost person. It comes from *posse comitatus*, meaning 'authority of the county'.

possibles Belongings, accoutrements, especially camping gear. Borrowed from Spanish (where *posibles* has a similar meaning), it is primarily a term of the mountain men, who carried their possibles in a *possible sack*, described by Lt George Frederick Ruxton as a 'wallet of dressed buffalo skin' for carrying 'ammunition, a few pounds of tobacco, dressed deerskins for moccasins, &c.' It was a container in which you take anything you can possibly use and stuff into it as much as you possibly can. Some cowboys later used the term *possible sack* but more often said war bag.

possum (1) A crafty, dissembling or cowardly person. (2) As a verb, to dissemble or pretend, as to counterfeit sickness. (3) A hide slung under the chuck wagon to carry fuel for fires, which on the plains sometimes meant wood but usually meant cow chips or buffalo chips; in full, *possum belly*. In this usage, it was also called a *bitch*, *caboose*, *cooney*, *cradle* and *cuna*.

post (1) A frontier establishment, especially for trading. At the end of the 18th century, it began to supplant the earlier term *station*. (2) As a verb, to put up notice not to trespass and especially not to hunt on ranch property. The 'first thing these new ranchers do when they buy a ranch is "Post it",' complains one Pinedale, Wyoming resident. Posting sometimes causes resentment between ranchers and sportsmen because it prevents access, or convenient access, to public land.

postage stamp The cowboy's derisive name for what Easterners call a saddle. Cowboys don't see much use in a saddle that doesn't help you work cows. The Eastern saddle is also called a *chicken saddle, hogskin, kidney pad* or *plaster, pumpkin-seed saddle* or a *pimple*.

pot (1) In poker, the money that has been bet. (2) What a logger called a donkey engine.

pot shot An easy shot, perhaps from the notion of shooting for the pot, taking the sure shot with an eye to conserving ammunition, not as the sportsman shoots. *Pot* has a verb form: a man or critter that gets potted has been shot.

pothole A shallow depression in the land that holds rain water. Potholes can be life-savers, particularly in slick-rock country. In Texas, they're likely to become bog holes, a trap for cattle.

potlatch A word of the Chinook jargon for the giveaway ceremony of the tribes (principally the Tlingit, Haida, Kwakiutl, Tsimshian and Nootka) of the Alaska Panhandle, British Columbia and the coastal region of Washington and Oregon. This was a central religious ceremony of these Indians; an individual who wanted to give a potlatch sometimes spent years in preparation, and it was accompanied by big feasts and other hospitable gestures. A marriage, the death of an important person or even a minor life passage like the cutting of hair could occasion a potlatch; the main reason was often to affirm the status in the tribe of the giver.

potrero (1) In the south-west, a pasture or meadow. (2) Less often, a wrangler of *potros* (colts). In both cases, borrowed from Spanish and pronounced poh-TRAYR-oh. (3) A narrow ridge between canyons.

potro In the south-west, a colt or filly, often with the implication that it is unbroke. Also called *potrillo* and borrowed from Spanish (where it means 'colt' or 'wild horse'), it's pronounced POH-troh.

pouderie A voyageur (French-Canadian boatman) term for a fine, powdery snow. Pronounced poo-duh-ree.

pound leather In cowboy talk, to ride fast.

pour A contemporary Indian expression meaning 'to lead a sweat lodge ceremony'. The leader, who is given in a sacred manner the way to lead, pours water on the hot rocks a certain number of times during each round to make steam.

poverty grass *Aristida dichotoma* or one of several other grasses that grow in sandy soil where nothing else can.

powder What loggers and miners call dynamite. The man who handles it is a *powder man* or *powder monkey*. Other Westernisms for dynamite are *bang juice, dine, dinah, grease, giant powder, noise, nifty powder, puff, shot, sawdust* and *vaseline*.

powder horn A container for black powder for a muzzle-loader, in the West often made from a buffalo horn, scraped thin and occasionally scrimshawed. In the days of the flintlock, two horns were generally carried, a small one for the fine powder used in priming and a big one for the coarser powder used for the charge in the barrel. The shooter carried a charger, often made from the tip of an antler, that held the right amount of powder. Metal powder containers were called *powder flasks*. The advent of the percussion cap made the small container obsolete, and the coming of the cartridge put both out of business.

Barrels of powder at forts and the like were kept in buildings or cellars called *powder magazines*. (*See also* DuPont)

Powder River, let her buck A cowboy's battle cry, often derisive. The Powder River country is fabled as the home country of the Cheyenne Indians, and the locus of Struthers Burt's book *Powder River: Let 'Er Buck*, and looms larger in people's minds than it often does between its banks – after all, it's a plains river. Ramon Adams gives this account of the origin of the expression, and says that it originally came from cowman E. J. Farlow of Lander, Wyoming: 'Some hands trailing cows to the railroad at Casper in the autumn of 1893 bedded down near the headwaters of Powder River, near the present Hiland, Wyoming, one night. They talked about crossing Powder River repeatedly the next morning, and spoke of getting their swimming horses. The next morning one cowboy, Missouri Bill Shultz, changed horses to get a good swimmer. Making their various crossings, they discovered that in the fall at that place, Powder River was just deep enough to wet a horse's hoof, and had barely enough energy to trickle from one hole to another.

'When they got to Casper, Missouri Bill toasted the hands like this: "Boys, come and have a drink on me. I've crossed Powder River." They had the drinks, then a few more and were getting pretty sociable. When Missouri Bill again ordered he said to the boys, "Have another drink on me, I've swum Powder River," this time with a distinct emphasis on the words Powder River. "Yes, sir, by God, Powder River," with a little stronger emphasis. When the drinks were all set up he said, "Well, here's to Powder River, let 'er buck!"

'Soon he grew louder and was heard to say, "Powder River is coming up-eeyeeeep! – Yes sir, Powder River is rising," and soon after with a yip and a yell, he pulls out his old six-gun and throwed a few shots through the ceiling and yelled, "Powder River is up, come an' have 'nother drink." Bang! Bang! "Yeow, I'm a wolf and it's my night to howl. Powder River is out of 'er banks. I'm wild and woolly and full o' fleas and never been curried below the knees!"

'Bill was loaded for bear, and that is the first time I ever heard the slogan, and from there it went around the world.'

powder-burning contest A gunfight. The cowboy characteristically makes light of mortal matters.

powwow (1) A conference of war with Indians. In verb form, to hold such a conference. (2) An act of conjuring, of making magic. In verb form, to conjure or make magic. (3) A social and religious event of contemporary Indians, coming together to dance, trade or socialise. In verb form, to go to such an event. (4) Jokingly, any conference at all.

The term is originally Indian Pidgin English but not Western – it dates to the earliest colonial times. Now the third meaning is most prevalent – there is a powwow circuit, as it is called, where Indians get together (along with interested Anglos) to dance, talk, trade, camp and just hang out. Musicians and dancers travel to these get-togethers, many people wear their ceremonial best, and dance competitions are sometimes held.

pozo A well or spring or any hole in the ground. Borrowed from Spanish (where it means 'well'), it's pronounced POH-soh.

prairie Open country, level or rolling, covered with grasses and without trees. Adapted from the French word meaning 'meadow' and first used to describe the Mississippi Valley grasslands, it has different meanings in different situations with different speakers. In the early West, little prairies were sometimes known by the French diminutive of prairie, *prairillon*. It was variously and creatively spelled – *peraira*, *papara*, *perara* and so on.

Combinations: prairie belt (a cartridge belt issued by the army in 1870 [Adams]), *prairie loo* (a game of counting sightings of game as you travel across the prairies, with the less common animals weighted to count more), *prairie telegraph* (the written messages that the pioneers left beside the wagon trails) and *passed over the prairie* (a 19th-century euphemism for being raped by Indians).

Plants: prairie wool (a cowboy term for buffalo grass) and *prairie tomato* (a ground cherry).

Animals: prairie beef or *cattle* (another name for buffalo), *prairie buffalo* (a French-

Canadian name for a horned lizard of the prairies), *prairie eel* (a joking name for a rattlesnake), *prairie fox* (the kit fox), *prairie gopher* (a ground squirrel [genus *Citellus*]), *prairie lawyer*, *tenor* or *wolf* (a coyote), *prairie rattlesnake* (one of several species of rattler that inhabit the prairies), *prairie rooter* or *shark* (a hog) and *prairie runner* (what the Blackfeet called an antelope in Indian Pidgin English).

Food: prairie butter (a batter made from grease, flour and water and used as a substitute for butter), *prairie dew* (a term for booze [*see* firewater]), *prairie cocktail* (a salted and peppered raw egg drunk in booze or vinegar [also called a *prairie oyster*]), *prairie oyster* (usually a mountain oyster – fried calf testicle; occasionally a prairie cocktail [*see* above]) and *prairie strawberries* (a joking name for beans).

prairie bitters *See* gall bitters.

prairie chicken One of several species of grouse of the plains and mountains, the sage grouse (*Centrocercus urophasianus*), the greater prairie chicken (*Tympanuchus cupido*), the lesser prairie chicken (*Tympanuchus pallidicinctus*, a desert creature) and the sharp-tailed grouse (*Pedioecetes phasianellus*). Some of the creatures (perhaps all) were named *fool hens* by the mountain men because they stood still and let themselves be killed by a stone, stick or whip.

prairie dog A squirrel-like rodent (genus *Cynomys*) of the plains and mountains that yips like a dog. Ranchers don't like them. Here's the South Dakota rancher and writer Linda Hasselstrom on the subject: 'They tend to live in ever-growing communities, digging a new hole for each new generation of pups, and may bear pups several times a year. Because they multiply quickly, and dig grass out by the roots, a prairie dog colony can kill hundreds of acres of grass in a summer. Ranchers deplore the amount of grass they eat almost as much as the large holes they leave, which are traps for horses and cattle to break legs in. Natural predators like coyotes can get a few, but when they retreat to their deep holes in rock-hard dry earth, very few animals bother them.

Some ranchers used to kill prairie dogs with poison grain, but most such poisons act in a chain; that is, they kill not only the prairie dog but anything that feeds on it later: eagles, coyotes, owls.'

Prairie dogs have thus provided sport for most Western boys whose fathers will lend them a .22. Now that there are fewer prairie dogs, one animal that hunted them, the black-footed ferret, is nearly extinct.

Prairie dogs are sometimes called *barking squirrels*. A *prairie-dog town* is a network of burrows dug by prairie dogs for their homes. It's also called a *prairie-dog village*. A *prairie-dog court* is a kangaroo court.

prairie fire A fire of the grasslands. Such fires were much feared by the inhabitants of the plains and prairies because they swept all before them and destroyed everything, including the grass the cows fed on. Native Americans frequently used fire for hunting and to improve the range. The native plants evolved to live with the cycle of fire (both natural and man-made) and are dying out in areas where fires are controlled.

prairie rattler *See* sidewinder.

prairie schooner A Conestoga wagon or a smaller wagon developed from the large and cumbersome Conestoga for plains travel but still too clumsy for mountain and canyon country. Painted red and blue like the Conestoga, it got its name from the wagon's ship-like profile, and Libby Custer says they 'were well named, as the two ends of the wagon inclined upward, like the bow and stern of a fore-and-after'. It was also called a *prairie clipper*, a *prairie ship* and a *Pitt schooner*.

The typical schooner was 16 to 18 feet long and four feet wide, wheels with iron tyres and smaller in front than in back, wooden running gear that was vulnerable to drying and cracking, a hand brake, a front seat (often without springs) and a canvas top supported by bent hickory. The wagon usually carried less than a ton.

prairie turnip The prairie potato (*Psoralea esculenta*) that the Dakotas call *tipsinah*. The root of this wild vegetable was eaten either fresh or dried; it was a common item in the diet of the northern

Plains Indians. Also called *breadroot* (or *Indian breadroot*), *Indian turnip*, *ground apple* and *Cree potato*; called *pomme blanche* by the voyageurs.

prayer book A cowboys book of cigarette papers.

prayer stick The *paho* of the Pueblo Indians.

praying cow A cow that's getting up. The critter rises hind end up and the cow momentarily looks like it's on its knees.

prescribed burn A controlled use of fire. The purposes may be to reduce fire hazard by preventing a buildup of unburned fuels, to increase forest productivity, to manage wildlife, to improve habitat and so on. It's an attempt in a controlled way to recreate the natural cycle of fire in modern forests. Prescribed burning is controversial but increasingly recommended, especially after the big fires of 1988 in Yellowstone National Park.

presidency In the Mormon Church, a council made up of a president and two counsellors. The First Presidency is the highest body of this kind, consisting of the executive head of the Church and two counsellors.

presidente In the south-west, the leader of a town or the owner of a ranch. Borrowed from Spanish (where it is an approximate equivalent of the English *president*), it is pronounced pre-zuh-DEN-tee or pre-zee-DEN-tay.

presidential medal A large, bronze medal issued by the US mint at Philadelphia (in the 19th century) showing the face of a president of the country on one side and a tomahawk, peace pipe and clasped hands of white and red men on the back. These medals were frequently given to Indians at treaty councils. Indians often prized them and kept them through generations. They also wore Indian peace medals of special issue. The Jefferson medal was still being made at the Denver mint in the 1980s. As with many governmental symbols, the friendship suggested was more an ideal than a reality.

presidio A fort, originally a Spanish garrison to protect a mission, and the area it administered. The best known, in San Francisco, will soon pass from military to civilian use. From the Spanish, it's pronounced pre-SEE-dee-oh or pruh-SI-dee-oh.

prickly pear A cactus of the genus *Opuntia*, and its pear-shaped fruit, common on the plains from Montana to Texas. Longhorns are said to have been able to eat it (thorns on) as a substitute for water. The fruit and cactus pads are a valued food in the south-west. Often called the *pear cactus* and shortened to *pear*, especially when used as an adjective – 'the pear region'. Hispanics call the plant *nopal* and *tuna* – both from the Spanish (where they have the same meaning).

Pancake cactus, beaver-tail, blind prickly pear (a spineless variety) and Indian fig are all kinds of prickly pears.

prod Anything mad and looking for trouble – a man, a cow, a bear – was said to be *on the prod* (or, occasionally, *proddy*).

prod pole A stick to handle cows and keep them on their feet in cattle cars; these days a prod pole is often electric. Also called a *cattle prod*.

pronghorn *Antilocapra americana*, the critter commonly known as an antelope. Technically, it is not a member of that species but one unto itself.

pronto Right now; fast; quickly. Originally south-western, it is now used all over the United States. Borrowed from Spanish, it's usually pronounced PRON-toh, with the *o* in the first syllable a little shorter than one heard from a native speaker of Spanish.

Prophet The title of Joseph Smith, founder of the Mormon Church, and all his successors as head of the Church. Prophets are believed to receive revelations from God – they are called in full Prophet, Seer and Revelator. These revelations direct Church policy even today. Revelations include the move to Utah in the 1840s, the requirement to store a year's supply of food, the prohibition of tobacco, alcohol, and drugs, and the 10 per cent tithing.

prospect In noun form: (1) A likely spot for discovery of minerals, as in the term placer prospect. (2) The result of the first efforts to find minerals. Says Mark Twain in *Roughing It*, 'A "prospect" is what one finds in the first panful of dirt – and its value determines whether it is a good or bad prospect, and whether it is worthwhile to tarry there or seek further.'

In verb form: (1) To search for valuable minerals. (2) To examine dirt or rock in detail for minerals. A location is said to prospect well or badly.

Combinations: prospect(ing) camp, prospect holder, prospect hole, prospect operation, prospect shaft, prospect tunnel, prospect work, prospecting diggings, prospecting pan, prospecting party and *prospecting trip.*

prospector A person who searches a particular region for gold or silver deposits (or sometimes for oil) with the intention of staking a claim. In the myth of the West, he is usually a hard-bitten alkali or sourdough, often a little crazy, and operating with his grubstake lashed on to his faithful burro.

prostitute *See* calico queen.

prove (1) In mining, to take a sample of a vein of ore to evaluate it. (2) In mining and homesteading, to *prove up on a claim* is to comply with the requirements of the mining or homesteading laws to make your claim legal. The last formalities in this process are called the *final proof.*

prowl To hunt cattle. Cows have a way of getting into draws, thickets and other places where they're hard to find. When gathering them, the cowhand has to do some prowling.

proxy Among Mormons, a stand-in for ordinances performed in LDS temples on behalf of deceased persons. Ordinances can be for marriage sealing (marriage for eternity), sealings of children to parents for eternity, endowment and baptism. The object is to link all members of the family together in paradise.

public land Land owned by a government, usually the federal government, plus the school sections owned by state governments. Various government agencies administer land owned in name by the public in the West, usually amid some controversy. In the days of the open range, the big cattle ranchers tried to use public land for grazing privately owned cows and to make sure no one else's cow ate the grass they regarded as theirs. Now the battles pit those who use public land for commercial purposes (grazing, logging, mining) and those who use it for recreational purposes. Though national parks are mostly free from commercial exploitation (and that's theoretical), lands administered by the US Forest Service and the Bureau of Land Management are much quarrelled over. (*See* primitive area, wilderness, range war and grazing permit)

pudding foot Cowboy talk for an awkward horse with big feet. [Adams]

pueblo (1) A village of stone or adobe buildings, often multi-storied, where Pueblo Indians lived or live. (2) When capitalised, an Indian or tribe of Indians of the Pueblo culture of the south-west. (3) By extension, any small south-western town.

Pueblo culture had its origin around the time of Christ among the people now called the *basketmakers.* In the Classic Pueblo period a millennium later, they had large population centres at Chaco Canyon (New Mexico), Kayenta (Arizona) and Mesa Verde (Colorado) with substantial agriculture and a complex ceremonial religion. Perhaps because of drought and pressure from enemies, they vanished from the area in the late 13th century. Contemporary Pueblo Indian culture contains many of the same components: an agriculture based on maize, living in multi-family communities and the use of kivas in religious ceremonies.

The word comes from Spanish (where it means 'village') and is pronounced pyoo-EB-loh. It gives rise to the forms *puebloan* and *puebloism.*

The Pueblo Rebellion occurred in 1680. Led by a San Juan Pueblo Indian named Pope, the Indians successfully repelled the Spanish colonisers, killing 400 Spanish. Pope, however, became a despotic ruler of the Pueblos, the alliance dissolved, and after his death the Spaniards reconquered

New Mexico by 1692. (*See also* Acoma, Hopi, Laguna, Taos, Zuni, kachina, Shalako, snake dance)

puke A nickname of uncertain origin for a Missourian, usually unflattering. The Mormons especially regarded the pukes as enemies because of the conflicts the two groups had when the Saints were in Missouri.

pulaski A tool used by fire fighters for both chopping and trenching and designed by E. C. Pulaski.

pull bog In cowboy talk, to haul cows out of bog holes with a rope. [Adams]

pulque Among Hispanics, a wine fermented from the agave or maguey. It was sold in a *pulqueria*, a tavern. Borrowed from Spanish, it is pronounced POOL-kay. Mescal and tequila are distilled from the same plant.

pumpkin roller (1) What a cowboy calls a complainer in a cow camp. Also called a *freak*. (2) What a cowboy calls a green hand. [Adams] (*See* greener for similar names)

punch cows To take care of cows; to drive them; to be a cowpuncher. *Puncher* is the shortened form of *cowpuncher*.

punche A light, mild tobacco grown, used and traded by the Indians of the south-west. Of uncertain origin, it's pronounced PUNCH-ee.

puncture lady What a cowboy called a gossip. What got punctured was someone's reputation.

punk In the post-Civil War West, a sliver of wood tipped with sulphur used to help build a fire. You touched the punk to glowing tinder, and it burst into flame. On the earlier frontier, punk was dry, powdery fuel (from rotten wood to dry buffalo chips) used to help get a fire started.

pureblood An Indian whose bloodline is purely Indian, not mixed. Animals of unmixed descent are called *purebred*. The adjective form is *pure-blooded*.

push-up A repetition of part of an Indian song, like a verse or chorus. At contemporary powwows, when the master of ceremonies wants more choruses of the same song (which usually comes in sets of two or four), he asks for another push-up. These segments usually start with a sharp and dramatic rise to a high pitch – thus the descriptive name. The term is also used as a verb – 'Push it up again.'

pussy-backing A gentle kind of bucking with an arched back. Also called *cat-backing*. (*See* buck)

pussyfoot To move like a cat – softly, carefully, slyly. The word was evidently inspired by William E. Johnson, who got the nickname from the sly way he pursued fugitives in Indian territory in the late 19th century.

put a spoke in the wheel To foul things up; to stop someone. [Adams]

put him to bed with a pick and shovel To bury someone. (For other expressions of death and dying, *see* cash in your chips)

put the calk to him Among loggers, to beat someone up. The calks were studs on the bottom of boots.

put up a herd To gather up a herd of cows for the trail. In some cases, herds were put together from various owners for the long drive from Texas to the railroad.

put up or shut up Back up your words (with action, money or whatever). The expression derives from poker, where it is a demand to make your bet or fold.

Puyallup The name of a tribe of Salishan Indians, who still live on a reservation in Washington of the same name. It's pronounced poo-YAL-luhp.

Q

quarantine line A north–south line drawn at various points in Kansas during the days of the great cattle drives from Texas. East of this, Texas cattle were not to go for fear of Texas fever. Also called the *fever line*.

quarter horse *The* Western horse for working cattle. Characteristically stocky, short-coupled and big-rumped, this breed has speed in the short distance (a quarter-mile) and the ability to make the sharp cuts needed in roping. Developed on Western ranges, it was known in its early days as a *short horse*.

quartz man A gold miner. Quartz is a matrix that often contains gold, and in the 1930s, a quarter of an ounce of gold in a ton of quartz was enough to make milling profitable.

Combinations: quartz battery (a stamp for pulverising quartz ore), *quartz camp* (a camp of quartz men), *quartz claim* (a hard-rock gold claim), *quartz diggings* (a quartz mine), *quartz lead* (a vein of gold-bearing quartz), *quartz mill* or *crusher* (a machine or business establishment that pulverises quartz ore), *quartz mine, miner* and *mining, quartz on the brain* (gold fever [Adams]) and *quartz reefer* (a miner working a quartz vein [reef]).

quebrada In the south-west, a ravine, a barranca. Borrowed from Spanish, it's pronounced kay-BRAH-duh.

quelites In the south-west, wild herbs cooked and served like collard greens. Borrowed from Spanish, it's pronounced kay-LEE-tays.

querencia In the south-west, your home place, the place you were born. Borrowed from Spanish (where it means 'haunt' or 'favourite spot'), it's pronounced kay-REN-see-uh.

querida In the south-west, darling, sweetheart or a similar endearment. Borrowed from Spanish, it's pronounced kay-REE-duh. The masculine form *querido* also occurs.

quick freighting Freighting done by trains of horses or mules, not oxen, which were slower.

quick-draw artist A person skilled at getting his sixgun out quickly. He might also be *quick on the trigger* or *quick to shoot it*. Recently, the term *quick-draw competition* means a competition of illustrators and artists rendering images of Western subjects quickly.

quien sabe? (1) In the Spanish of the south-west, literally 'who knows?' A kind of philosophic shrug that sometimes suggests the unknowable. (2) What an impatient Texas cowboy calls an elaborate Mexican brand he can't read or something else incomprehensible. Sometimes pronounced kyen-SAH-bay or keen SAH-bay and sometimes kin savvy.

quillwork A technique of decoration of clothing and other leather items among Indians. It preceded beadwork historically, and many beadwork customs and patterns are taken from older quillwork.

Quillwork was done almost entirely by women and took geometrical rather than representational forms. The method is to soften porcupine quills with hot water, flatten them with the teeth, rocks or metal quill flatteners, dye them with vegetable dyes and lace them with a method like embroidery on to moccasins, shirts, pipe bags and any number of other articles. As coloured beads became more commonly available, beads often replaced quills, but quillwork is done even today. In full, *porcupine quillwork*.

quirly Cowboy talk for a hand-rolled cigarette.

quirt A rider's whip with a weighted handle about a foot long and several rawhide thongs. Most Plains Indians used quirts, often with antler handles. Cowboys sometimes made a fine craft of plaiting quirts. The weight in the handle makes the quirt effective for use as a blackjack or to whack a rearing horse in the head. Adapted from the Spanish *cuarta*, which has the same meaning. It also occurs as a verb.

quit the flats In cowboy talk, to leave the area. [Adams]

R

RM A Mormonism meaning 'Returned Missionary'. (*See* missionary)

rabbit roundup The driving and killing of jack-rabbits in areas where they create difficulties for farmers. A continuing but controversial practice.

rack (1) An ambling gait of a horse. (*See* single-foot) (2) In cowboy talk, to ride.

rafter To lie under your blankets with your knees sticking up.

rag house Among loggers and soldiers, a tent. Also called a *rag bungalow*.

rag out To dress up fancily.

rail To break sagebrush off at ground level by dragging an iron rail over it. [Adams] Ranchers try to keep sagebrush down so more grass will grow. (*See* chain)

railroad without steam A logger's expression meaning 'to go like hell'.

rain follows the plough The slogan of the 1870s promoters of lands of the Great Plains, which were previously thought of as the Great American Desert. For commercial reasons, these folks (the railroads included) wanted Americans to homestead the plains and farm them, so they propagated the idea that where man ploughed, the good Lord would send rain. The notion was even given credence by the head of the US Geographical and Geological Survey of the Territories. Even in a nation known for con artists, it was a considerable deception or self-deception.

rainbow A term for what a bucking horse does when he arches his back and shakes his head. [Adams]

rainbow trout One of two species of trout native to the coastal streams of California. Since it is a good fish for sport-fishing, the rainbow has been stocked in many Western creeks and rivers.

raise (1) To spot something far away, as in, 'He raised buffalo near five miles off.' (2) In poker, to increase the stakes.

raise hair To take a scalp; to kill someone. *Lift hair* is a similar expression;

both come from the mountain men. Sometimes the idea of the phrase was extended. 'Raise horses' sometimes meant to steal horses. An old-time Anglo view of Indians was that they never knew how to raise nothing but hell and hair.

raiz diabolica Peyote; mescal buttons. Literally 'devil root'. Borrowed from Spanish, it's pronounced rah-EES dee-uh-BOH-lee-kuh.

rake In rodeo, for a bronc rider to scratch a horse with spurs to make him buck. Also called *bicycling*.

rake up the persimmon To win, to get the prize, particularly to get the pot in poker. Also heard as *rake the persimmon* and *walk off with the persimmon*. The gambling phrase comes from Southern expressions that give high value to persimmons, such as 'I wouldn't bet a huckleberry to a persimmon,' which is like doughnuts to dollars.

ramada In the south-west, an arbor; a brush shelter. Borrowed from Spanish, it's pronounced ruh-MAH-duh.

ranahan A top hand; a good cowboy. Often shortened to *ranny*.

ranch (1) An establishment where livestock are raised. In this most traditional sense, the word normally includes the land, building, critters – the whole outfit. If this sort of ranch grows crops, they are for feed for the livestock, not a cash crop. (2) The main building of a ranch, the main house and the surrounding buildings. (3) As a verb, to raise livestock.

The word comes from the Spanish *rancho* and has taken on lots of meanings beyond these basics. In the old West, a way station for travellers could be called a *road ranch*; the word was eventually applied to every sort of establishment, even farms, leading to strange phrases like *dairy ranch* and *fruit ranch*.

Other terms for a ranch were *cap-and-ball layout*, *cocklebur outfit*, *cow outfit*, *good lay*, *layout*, *one-horse outfit*, *shirt-tail outfit*, *siwash outfit*, *spread*, *three-up outfit* and *tough lay*. A rancho (in American English) is a Hispanic ranch, sometimes a large land grant operated as a ranch. A small outfit was sometimes called a *ranchito*.

Combinations: ranch butter and *ranch egg* (foods produced on the ranch and thus fresh – in contrast to a States egg).

rancher A ranch owner-operator, whether small outfit or large. To be a cattleman has always been a source of pride in the West. The rancher was also known as *big sugar*, *raw-hider*, *suitcase rancher* or a *white-collar rancher*.

A *ranch man* or *ranch hand* is a fellow who works on a ranch, not a rancher. When he's not called a cowboy or one of the various half-synonyms for that word, he may be known, depending on circumstance, as an *alfalfa desperado* (hay hand), *Arbuckle*, *fodder forker* (hay hand), *hay slayer* or *hay waddy* (again a hay hand), *miller* or *mill rider* (hand who maintains windmills), *pitchfork gladiator* (hay hand), *stacker* (hand who works up top when stacking hay), *stiff man*, *two-buckle boy*, *windmiller* or *windmill monkey* (hand who maintains windmills) or *wood monkey* (supplier of firewood).

rancheria In the south-west, an Indian village or camp; occasionally, a ranch house. Borrowed from Spanish (where it has a similar meaning), it is pronounced ranch-uh-REE-uh. A *ranchero* is usually a Hispanic ranch owner, sometimes a Hispanic ranch hand and occasionally a ranch. *Ranchera* is an infrequently used word meaning 'ranch woman'.

range An area of uncultivated grassland, suitable for grazing livestock or serving to graze livestock.

The open range was such grassland before the days of fences and private property; the grass was free to all, or at least to the first comer. Cowmen spoke of their range – the country their cattle foraged – whether or not they owned it. Their proprietary attitudes about public land eventually led to a lot of trouble – what were called *range wars*. Among the most infamous of these were the Pleasant Valley War in Arizona, the Lincoln County War in New Mexico and Wyoming's Johnson County War.

Combinations: home range (where a man or a critter belongs), *range boss* (a ranch manager, generally for an absentee ownership), *range bum* (an out-of-work hand riding from ranch to ranch looking for a job or a free meal; also known as a chuckline rider), *range cradle* (what a sheep-herder calls his wagon [Adams]), *range horse* (a horse raised entirely on grass and usually branded but not broke), *range rider* (a cowboy assigned to ride the outlying areas of a ranch, not just the lines or fences, and do whatever needs doing), *range rights* (in the days of the open range, entitlement to graze cattle on a range by virtue of past use, not ownership), *range saddle* (a stock saddle, one equipped with a horn for rope work) and *range word* (a cowman's word of honour [Adams]).

To *be at range* is to be turned out on the grassland. To *cross over* (or *go over*) *the range* is to die. (*See also* cash in your chips) To *range brand* was to brand calves where you found them, not at roundup. To *ride the range* is to look after cows out on the range. To *run on the same range* is to grow up together, hang out together or the like.

Early Westerners sometimes spoke of the customary country of an Indian tribe as its range.

range war A conflict over grazing rights on the open range. Most often these conflicts took place between cattlemen and sheepmen, or between large and small cattlemen. Either way, they could be violent. Wyoming in particular was known for its sheepman-cattleman disputes.

ranger (1) An occasional term for a range-fed cow. (2) A cowman who range-feeds cattle.

rank How a cowboy describes a vicious, hard-to-handle horse.

rattlesnake weed A low-growing spurge (*Euphorbia albormaginta*) with tiny white flowers and a milky sap. Once thought to cure rattlesnake bites, it is poisonous when ingested. Several roots used as a palliative for rattlesnake bites are called rattlesnake root. Rattleweed is another name for locoweed.

raw A cowboy's descriptive term for a green bronc; an unbroke horse.

rawhide As a noun: (1) Untanned, dehaired hide, usually of a cow or buffalo. (2) A whip made of rawhide. (3) A name given by cowboys of the northern plains to Texas cowboys.

As a verb: (1) To whip an animal (or a person). (2) To tease. (3) Among loggers, to roll logs down a skidway. [Adams]

A *rawhider* was a small (shirt-tail) cattleman or a Westerner who was always on the move. [Adams] A *rawhiding* was a good whipping with a rawhide. A *rawhide artist* is a hand who's good with a branding iron.

Rawhide was used for everything on the frontier. Indians made drum heads, shield covers and parfleches (carrying bags) from it. Anglos used it to repair gun stocks, wheel spokes, wagon tongues – anything. Trappers made bull boats from it; cowboys made reatas and hobbles; settlers made springs, door hinges and even nails from it. It was so tough it became known as *Mexican iron* or *Mormon iron.*

Combinations using rawhide in the sense of tough: *rawhide outfit* (a hard outfit to work for), *rawhide job* (a tough job), *rawhide lumber* (slabs with the bark left on) and *rawhide Texan* (a tough hombre).

readers Among gamblers, marked cards. Cards marked with indentations were called *reflectors.*

real A Spanish coin, generally regarded as worth eight to a dollar. Adapted from the Spanish *real* (royal), it was properly pronounced ray-AHL and probably often Americanised to ree-AHL.

The Spanish peso was a silver coin worth eight reales and was often cut into halves and quarters, giving rise to the expressions two bits and four bits for a quarter and half dollar. A *quatrillo* (or *quartee*) was a quarter of the Mexican coin called a real, thus worth three cents. A *tlaco* (or *claco*) was one-eighth of a real.

reata A cowboy's rope of braided rawhide. (*See also* lariat.)

Though the word is too often used to refer to any rope, the genuine reata was and is a special item. It was usually 40 to 80 feet long, and sometimes, according to old hand Jo Mora, *reatas largas* ran

upwards of 100 feet; some vaqueros could make catches up to 60 feet away with them. Says Mora: 'The rawhide reata was the original article, and through the Spanish and Mexican cow country, reateros grew up that were masters at the craft of braiding reatas and all other vaquero rawhide tools, many of which were truly works of art. In our own country, California was where the making of reatas reached its highest peak . . .

'The finest reatas are made from the primest parts only of several young heifer hides, well chosen, properly cured, and the strands cut by an expert. The braiding must also be done with that uniformity and even tension that only your true reatero knows . . .

'Reatas are braided in 4, 6 or 8 strands. The latter two, especially the 8, if made by a top reatero, is a beautiful article and superb for light roping. For the average hard work on large stock, the 4-strand is the best. Diameters vary according to individual preference, but the three-eights inch reata is the one most used. Naturally, a hand-made reata costs considerably more than a grass rope, yet, though it is vulnerable to certain accidents, with proper care and luck it should outlast a half dozen grass ones.'

Borrowed from Spanish (where it has a similar meaning), it is usually pronounced ree-AH-tuh and sometimes spelled *riata.*

rebozo In the south-west, a shawl or long scarf Hispanic women wear over their heads and shoulders. A *ruana* is another Hispanic shawl. Borrowed from the Spanish, it's pronounced ruh-BOH-soh.

recommend Among Mormons, a certificate issued by a bishop to identify persons as members of the Church, and certify their worthiness to receive certain ordinances or blessings and eligibility to enter the temple. Job recommends are given to people in need, so that in exchange for work in one of the Church's businesses they may receive necessities for subsistence.

recorder A person chosen in each Western mining camp to record claims.

He usually inspected the claim to verify its legitimacy.

Red Power The Indian equivalent of black power; a primary object of the American Indian Movement (AIM). In the past quarter century, Indians have organised extensively and put aside old tribal rivalries in order to gain more of what they see as their birthright in this country. Battles have been fought and are being fought over water rights, mineral rights, hunting and fishing rights, rights to territory and the like – and Indians have won many battles in courts and in public opinion. At the same time renewed interest in the old religions and cultures may be leading to a renaissance. These developments have led Indians and Anglos to hope for a resurrection, a rejuvenation of spirit, among these disenfranchised people.

Red River cart A freight cart used on the trade route along the Red River of the north in the mid-19th century. It was cheap to make and was distinguished by huge, one-piece wheels cut from tree trunks. Since these wheels went ungreased, a cart train could be heard from a long distance. The wheels were removed and the carts were paddled across lakes and rivers. The carts were pulled by oxen, and each carried up to 1,000 pounds of goods. The trade route went from the country of the Red River metis (Canadian half-breeds) – its primary operators – to the area of St Paul. (*See also* carreta)

Red River metis An English, Scotch or French-Cree half-breed of the settlements of the Red River of the north or the Saskatchewan River in Canada. The French-Cree metis (often disliked and distrusted by early Americans) were very dark-skinned and noted for dressing entirely in black except for a multicoloured sash around the waists of the men.

These three kinds of metis, products of liaisons between Canada's fur men and Indian women, ran the Red River cart trade along the Red River between Canada and the United States. In 1869, when they were about to come under the jurisdiction of Canada, they formed a separatist movement under Louis Riel. In 1884–5 they again attempted independence under Riel, who was tried for treason and hanged but remains a hero to his people. They are also known as the *Bois Brûlé* (the burnt-wood people), anglicised as the *Bob Ruly*.

red road In the tradition of the Lakotas and some other Plains Indians, a way of living that is good and fruitful; it runs north and south. (The Lakota word *sha* means both 'red' and 'good'.) The black road, by contrast, runs east–west and means 'bristling with conflict and difficulty'. Thus the Lakota seer Lame Deer says his grandfather used to say, 'The earth is red, blood is red, the sun is red as it sets and rises, and our bodies are red. And we should be walking the Red Road, the good north–south road, which is the path of life.'

A *road man* is a priest of the Native American Church and gets his name because he shows worshippers how to stay on the good, red road. Red Road is now the name of an alcohol treatment programme among the Lakota.

red-eyed Cowboy talk for angry. *Red-rumped* can mean the same.

red-light district An area of brothels (the name is sometimes thought to have come from a sporting house called the Red Light in Dodge City, Kansas).

redwood The *Sequoia sempervirens*, a huge tree of California and Oregon, regarded as a wonder of nature.

Ree A nickname for the Arikara Indians; common in 19th-century literature. Another nickname was *Rickaree*.

reloading outfit Cowboy talk for eating utensils, says Peter Watts.

relocation centre A euphemistic term for the camps in which Japanese-Americans (primarily of California) were interned during World War II. The federal government established 10 such camps, much like concentration camps, in the western United States. Decades later some of these Japanese-Americans and their descendants were awarded settlements for the government's actions.

Remington Usually a rifle made by the Remington Arms Company. The Remington family of Ilion, New York made guns – rifles, pistols and shotguns – from 1816 forward. Remington was a major supplier of arms to the north during the Civil War. The armies of other nations adopted the Remington rifle as well. With Colt and Winchester, Remington was a leading manufacturer of the firearms carried in the West.

remittance man An Englishman, Irishman or European, often a younger son of a titled family, who depended on remittances from home for his living. Many Westerners felt contempt for these fellows. Says a rancher in Steward Edward White's *Arizona Nights*, 'Now you're nothin' but a remittance man. Your money's nothin' to me, but the principle of the thing is. The country is plumb pestered with remittance men, doin' nothin', and I don't aim to run no home for incompetents. I had a son of a duke drivin' wagon for me; and he couldn't drive nails in a snow-bank. So don't you herd up with the idea that you can come on this ranch and loaf.'

remuda A herd of saddle horses; a cavvy. In the old West, every big outfit had a remuda, usually with scores of horses (geldings only), and each cowboy was assigned a string of a half dozen or more for his use. When not being ridden, the horses were herded by a *remudero* (wrangler) or kept in a *remudadero* (horse corral). In the south-west, also called a *remonta*. Adapted from the Spanish word meaning 'remount', it's pronounced ruh-MOO-duh; some south-western cowmen say ruh-MOO-thuh.

rendering ring A packer's word for the cinch ring on an aparejo.

rendezvous The annual trade fair of the mountain men during the heyday of the mountain fur trade, held mid-summer each year from 1825 through 1840. As many as several hundred trappers and several thousand Indians would gather at a pre-appointed spot (most often along the Green River) to meet the pack caravan from the settlements. The official business was exchanging beaver pelts (plews) for powder, lead, tobacco, beads, maybe some clothing, maybe some traps or a new gun and almost certainly some whiskey. The unofficial agenda was getting drunk, getting a woman, trading news, getting letters, gambling, indulging in competitions of horse, foot, knife and gun and joining up with someone to trap with during the autumn. The main idea was to have a blowout.

Today's rendezvous is a hobby of people who recreate the ways of those old times, often under the sponsorship of the National Muzzle Loading Rifle Association (NMLRA). Several thousand attend the larger rendezvous, wearing primitive dress and living in lean-tos and tipis, shooting muzzle-loading guns and the like.

renegade An outlaw cow or horse. A *renegade rider* was a cowboy who rode to outlying ranches to gather stock belonging to his outfit. (*See also* rep)

rep A cowboy, usually a top hand, representing his outfit at a roundup. His job was to gather his outfit's strays and a fair share of the mavericks and trail them home. The cows and calves he claimed were known as the *rep's cut*. He was sometimes known as the *outside hand*.

represa A small earthen dam used in arid country to hold water from run-off. Also called a *presa*. Often the resulting water holes are very small. Borrowed from Spanish, it's pronounced ruh-PRAY-suh.

re-ride In rodeo, a second chance for a contestant to try an event when the horse fails to perform. When a calf or steer is used a second time for roping in the same go-round, it's called a *re-run*.

reservation A tract of land held in trust for the use of one or more Indian tribes as a nation within the United States, under tribal (and to some extent federal) jurisdiction but not always subject to the laws of the surrounding state. The legal history of reservations is long, complex and bloody.

These reservations at first were principally ways of controlling Indians and opening their former lands to passage or settlement by whites. Often the lands set aside for Indians were considered useless, making subsequent attempts to teach the Indians to farm them hypocritical. In some cases, the lands set aside turned out to have great mineral value; then the whites often found ways of taking them back; sometimes the Indians got the mineral royalties and the last laugh.

The reservation system had dubious success from the start. Congress, Indian agents and even freighters constantly found ways to reduce (often by theft) the annuities the Indians had accepted as payment for settling on a reservation. Abraham Lincoln is said to have defined a reservation as where Indians live surrounded by thieves. Though the Indians were often hungry, they were not always permitted to leave the reservation to hunt. The old way of life had been taken away, and no new one provided. Starting in the late 1880s, federal policy was to end the Indians' communal ownership of their reservations, allot lands to individual Indians and give the Indians what were considered the advantages of private property (and not incidentally to open unalloted lands to white settlement). Through this policy, some two-thirds of Indian lands passed into white hands over the next 50 years.

The recent social history of reservations is little better. Many of them are centres of deep poverty, unemployment, alcoholism, high infant mortality, broken families and other symptoms of troubled spirits. Perhaps the Red Power movement, which is primarily political, and the resurgence of traditional religion and ways among Indians will heal some of these troubles.

The slang of contemporary Indians and some Anglos for a reservation, sometimes lightly derisive, is the *rez*. The Canadian equivalent of reservation is *reserve*, and that form is sometimes used in American English as well.

To *be off the* (or *your*) *reservation* originally meant for Indians to be away from their assigned lands and (from the Anglo's point of view) likely causing trouble. It has come to mean 'to be crazy, to be going wild', sometimes 'to be committing infidelity'.

reservation hat A tall, unblocked (uncreased), flat-brimmed, black hat originally issued by the federal government, now worn almost exclusively by Navajos and Crows.

retablo A painted or carved panel made by a *santero* (a person who carves religious images).

revolver Usually a handgun (old-time Westerners did not say *pistol*) capable of shooting repeatedly because it had either several barrels or a multi-chambered cylinder with separate charges or cartridges. The first popular one was made by Samuel Colt.

rib up (1) In cowboy talk, to persuade. (2) To stiffen an aparejo with sticks. [Adams]

ribbon shirt A shirt decorated with glossy ribbons, worn by Indians at powwows and other dress-up occasions. A ribbon dress is the equivalent for women and girls. The Navajo have a ribbon dance.

Rickaree *See* Arikara.

rico In the south-west, a rich man. The rich are also known in the West as *bums on the plush* and are said to be *in the chips* or *wallowing in velvet*.

ride Many combinations are formed with this word. In cowboy talk: *ride fence* (ride along an outfit's fences regularly to check their repair), *ride for a blind bridle* (work for farmers, whose horses wore blinders [Adams]), *ride for a brand* (work for a cattle outfit), *ride herd* (keep watch on cows – or people – while riding in a circle around the herd or a person or a situation), *ride line* (ride the understood boundaries of a ranch), *ride the chuck-line* (*see* chuck) or *grub line*, *ride the rough string* and *ride sign* (check for sign that your cows have strayed).

Cowboys also use these expressions: *ride herd on a woman* (court her), *ride into someone's dust* (follow them), *ride out a horse* (ride a horse until it quits bucking), *ride like a deputy sheriff* (ride recklessly

[Adams]), *ride slick* (ride a bucker without benefit of cheaters such as a bucking roll), *ride straight up* (ride erect in the saddle with the reins in one hand, as you should ride), *ride on one's spurs* (hook one's spurs into the cinch [Adams]), *ride out of town with nothing but a head* (have a hangover [Adams]), *ride over that trail again* (explain something better [Adams]) and *ride the bed wagon* (be laid up hurt or sick [Adams]).

In rodeo, competitors *ride a beast with a belly full of bed springs* (ride a bucking horse) and *ride the shows* (compete on the rodeo circuit).

In reference to badmen: *ride the coulees* or *the high lines* (move along keeping one step ahead of the law [Adams]), *ride the owl-hoot trail* (follow the outlaw life), *ride with an extra cinch ring* (improvise brands with cinch rings [Adams]) and *ride under a cotton-wood limb* (get hung [Adams]).

Similar phrases among loggers: *ride Aunt Polly* (or *board with Aunt Polly*) (to be collecting pay while off work because of illness or injury), *ride her out* (what a logger had to do when a log jam gave way unexpectedly on a river drive), *ride shank's mare* (to walk [Adams]), *ride the saw* (not to do your share on the crosscut saw, or generally be lazy).

And last, the old phrase *a man to ride the river with* is a high compliment. A trail-drive expression, it means a fellow who will stick no matter how tough the going gets. Drives often had to cross rivers in the spring that were flooding and dangerous.

ride bog To ride the boggy areas of a ranch looking for cows that are stuck and probably weak and pulling them out with your rope. It's hard work.

ride circle To search out the cows in a large area and drive them to the gathering spot, one of the principal chores of a roundup. It took on a metaphoric meaning: to complete your circle meant to finish your task, your earthly responsibilities, your life.

riffle In placer mining, a slat or bar in the bottom of a sluice box. Riffles catch the particles of gold, which sink to the bottom as the water flows through.

They're also called *riffle bars* and *riffle blocks*. Sluice boxes are sometimes called *riffle* (or *ripple*) *boxes*.

rig (1) Cowboy talk for a saddle. (Saddles are also said to be rigged in certain ways, meaning to have a certain arrangement of the cinch or cinches. [*See* single-rig.]) The complete arrangement of cinch, rings and other saddle leathers is known as its *rigging*. (2) Almost any kind of vehicle, from a plains-crossing wagon to a contemporary pick-up truck, especially if the pick-up is outfitted with a stock rack (animal pen) or other extra equipment. (3) In oil drilling, the equipment for drilling a well.

rigging pecker Among loggers, an IWW (Industrial Workers of the World) organiser.

right-hand man Either a ranch foreman or his assistant; the straw boss; the most valuable man.

rildy Cowboy talk for a blanket or quilt.

rimfire Descriptive of a saddle rigged with a single cinch well forward. Such a saddle is also called a *Spanish rig* or a *rimmy*. (*See* single-rig)

To *rimfire a horse* is to put a burr under the blanket, a prank that is likely to get the next rider bucked off. [Adams]

rimrock Steep rock on the rim of a canyon, channel or basin. All over the West, rock has been left high and dry by water that may be either hundreds or thousands of feet below or have disappeared centuries ago. It makes climbing out of canyons difficult or impossible. To *get rimrocked* is to get penned in by rimrock. This has happened to most Westerners who've done much wandering on foot or horseback – even to the one-armed explorer John Wesley Powell climbing in the Grand Canyon. It can be dangerous.

To *rimrock sheep* was to kill them by stampeding them over cliffs. A *rimrocker* is a horse sure-footed enough for rimrock country.

rincon A protected spot, a valley or a nook, good as a location for a house or a settlement. Borrowed from Spanish (where it has a similar meaning), it's pronounced ring-KOHN.

ring bit A curb bit with a ring that slips over the lower jaw. In careless hands, it's hard on the horse. Also called a *chileno*.

ring herd To keep cows going in a circle in order to keep them together.

ring toter A rustler; a man who carried an extra cinch ring so he could burn any brand he wanted.

ringey (1) Cowboy talk for riled up. [Adams] (2) When referring to a woman, nervous, high strung; taken from the way a horse will wring its tail when nervous.

rio In the south-west, a river. It occurs mostly in proper names – Rio Grande, Rio Gavilan and so on. Borrowed from Spanish, it's pronounced REE-oh.

ripper A Great Basin term for a big horse with plenty of bottom (endurance). (*See* horse for other descriptive terms for horses)

ristra A string of dried red chiles used decoratively and functionally in south-western kitchens. From the Spanish, and pronounced REES-truh.

river mining Mining done in a dry riverbed when the stream has been diverted. [Adams]

river rat Among loggers, a log driver (or river driver), a man who floated logs from where they were cut down-river to the sawmill, a dangerous job because of log jams.

river sluicing When done along a river, hydraulic mining (mining with powerful streams of water).

road agent A highway man, a stagecoach holdup man. It occasionally took the form *road agentry*. Road agents were sometimes called *roadsters* (this was the era before the automobile).

From this term came the phrase *road agent's spin*, or *Curly Bill spin*, said to have originated with Curly Bill Brocius (or Graham). It was a trick spin of a revolver into shooting position. Appearing to hand the gun over butt first and upside down, the road agent spun it on the trigger guard, cocking the hammer as it came under his thumb, and shot.

road brand A brand put on Texas herds during trail drives. For a time, such a brand, high on the left side, was required by law for cows going north out of the state. Also used as a verb.

road man A priest of the Native American Church. He shows worshippers how to stay on the good, red road.

road ranch A name for an establishment providing supplies to travellers on a trail.

road runner The chaparral cock of the south-western deserts, which was legendary even before it hooked up with Wile E. Coyote. The name comes from its habit of running a trail ahead of riders or wagons. It is said to eat rats, mice, lizards and snakes – including rattlesnakes, which may be why it's regarded as cuckoo. Among its many names is *ground cuckoo*. Others are *chaparral bird, churrea, cock of the desert, lizard bird, paisano, runner bird, snake-killer* and *snake-eater*. Josiah Gregg commented in 1840 that a road runner will perform all the vermin-eating duties of a cat.

road stake Among loggers, the wages a man has saved up to take away to another job.

roadhouse A rustler's holding corral for stolen animals, usually in an out-of-way place.

roadometer A Mormon term for the mechanical means of measuring road distance that they worked out on their way to the Salt Lake in 1847, based on revolutions of a wagon wheel.

roaring camp A mining camp that was wide open, with plenty of booze, gambling and prostitutes. Both a common and proper noun, as in Bret Harte's 'The Luck of Roaring Camp'.

robber's roost Descriptive of a place frequented by outlaws, as in such-and-such a place was 'a real robber's roost'. When capitalised, the hideout of the notorious gang the Wild Bunch in Utah's San Rafael Swell area, about 40 miles from Hanksville.

roble   In the south-west, an oak (*Quercus lobata*). It occurs principally in place names. Borrowed from Spanish, it's pronounced ROH-buhl.

rock   *Western combinations: rock dog* or *rabbit* (another name for a pika) and *rock wren* (any of several wrens of rimrock country).

rockchuck   Another name for a marmot.

rocker   A primitive trough for separating gold from dirt. The miner shook gold-bearing dirt and water in the rocker (or *rocking cradle*) and retrieved gold from the riffle bars in the rocker or the cloth below. Also called a *rocker sieve* or sometimes a *tom*.

To use a rocker is to *rock*, or *rock out*, *gold*.

Rocky Mountain   *Combinations: Rocky Mountain canary* (a jocular name for a burro), *Rocky Mountain goat* (either a mountain goat or a bighorn sheep), *Rocky Mountain sheep* (a bighorn sheep), *Rocky Mountain pine* (the ponderosa or bull pine) and *Rocky Mountain* oyster, a mountain oyster.

Rocky Mountain College   The mountain man custom of reading during the winter, or learning to read; Shakespeare, Byron, Scott, Miss Jane Porter and the Bible were favourites. In Osborne Russell's camp near Fort Hall, Idaho, books could be borrowed so the literate could teach the illiterate to read. Some contemporary buckskinners mistakenly use the phrase to mean 'the learning of wilderness skills'.

rodeo   (1) First, in the south-west, a roundup, a gathering of cattle. (2) Later, a competition among cowboys of roping and riding skills that were originally developed from working cows. Still later, these competitions developed into today's rodeo circuit, a sequence of events sanctioned by the PRCA (Professional Rodeo Cowboys Association) with substantial prize money and official world championships. The five standard events are bulldogging, calf roping, bronc riding, bareback riding and bull riding; team roping is also a recognised event.

In the first sense, which is pretty well obsolete, the word is pronounced roh-DAY-oh, in the second, ROH-dee-oh. Both stem from the Spanish *rodear* (to surround or encircle). (Among buckaroos, a rodear is a group of cattle that's been cut out.)

Combinations: rodeo clown (a skilled rider dressed up as a clown; while entertaining the audience, he deliberately distracts the horses and bulls who have thrown their riders so the cowboys can high-tail it), *rodeo chaps* (heavy chaps to protect against chutes and fences; they're often painted with resin to make the legs grip tightly), *rodeo cool* (descriptive of a beer that's cool enough to drink at a rodeo but not cold), *rodeo cowboy* (an athlete who works the arenas, not ranges), *rodeo arena*, *rodeo ground* and *rodeo producer*.

Loggers sometimes called their log-rolling competitions *roleos* after the cowboy contests.

roll   (1) An exhibition shooting trick. The shooter spins the gun on the trigger guard from and to the normal shooting position, cocking it with the thumb on the way around. In the border roll, the gun was spun the reverse direction of the usual roll, the butt going down first and the barrel up. (*See also* road agent and border shift) (2) A flip of the cowboy's rope that sends a corkscrewing wave along the string. It's often used to retrieve a rope from cows' heels. (3) A cowboy's name for his bedroll. (4) In rodeo, the bucking stock waiting to get into a chute.

Combinations: rolling faro (a faro game played with a wheel, like roulette, instead of cards [Adams]), *rolling mustang* (a gambling game), *roll in* (to go to bed or, depending on context, to arrive; among loggers, to *roll them* meant to go to bed), *roll its tail* (what a cow will do with the near end of its tail just before it runs; also said of a man about to head out fast), *roll logs* (to float them downstream), *roll the cotton* (for a cowboy to roll up his bedroll and go [Adams]), *roll the guff* (among loggers, to talk), *roll up* (when said of a horse, for it to take advantage of the saddle's coming off to roll on its back), *roll your own* (to make your own cigarette from tobacco and paper [and, figuratively, to make anything yourself instead of buying it]; the trick of rolling a cigarette with just one hand was a well-known test of cowboy ability) and *roll your wheels* (to get going [Adams]).

rollway A slope where logs were rolled into a river; the pile of logs to be rolled.

romal A whip or quirt braided from the end of reins, popular among the Californios. It often was about three feet long. Adapted from the Spanish *ramal* (strand of rope), it is pronounced ruh-MAL, the *a* as in *corral*.

Roman riding A rodeo stunt in which a rider stands on two horses' backs with a foot on each moving horse. Also known as a *hippodrome stand*.

roostered Cowboy talk for drunk. A drunk is called (in the south-west) a *borracho*. He's a man who has *bottle fever*, *keeps the double doors swinging*, *cuts his wolf loose*, *freights his crop*, *hears the owl hoot*, *goes on a bender*, *goes on a high lonesome*, *goes on a jag*, *puts the rollers on* or *ties on a bear*. When he's loaded up, he's a *walking whiskey vat* and often somebody has *stolen his rudder*.

rope In the West, this word usually doesn't mean just any sort of line but the string a cowboy uses on cows and horses, that is, a catch rope, lariat or reata, usually made of rawhide, hair, hemp, sisal or cotton. He does everything with it – catches his horse in the morning, throws and holds cows, pulls critters out of bogs, hauls firewood, pickets mounts and builds rope corrals. In the old days, he even administered what he thought of as justice with it.

All this proceeded historically from one necessity: the vaquero and his successor the cowhand needed to catch horses so they could ride them and catch cows so they could brand them (or earmark them, doctor them, etc). That led to the defining equipment of the Western rider, the saddle horn and the rope. Movies notwithstanding, most hands took far more pride in their riding and roping skills than in their competence with guns.

Some hands could and can do fancy tricks with ropes, but in the heyday of the open range, many hands could boggle the minds of greenhorns with rope skills needed for everyday work, like throwing the noose in a figure eight throw so that the upper loop caught a calf's head and the lower loop its front feet. More rope throws are *backhand slip* (a rope throw over the calf behind the roper's horse), blocker loop, *California twist* (a rope throw with no twirl), *cotton-patch* or *community loops* (large nooses in the rope), *fore-footing* (a front feet catch), heel, hoolihan, *head catch* (catches the head rather than the feet or horns), *mangana* (an overhand throw), *overhand toss*, *peale* (a hind foot catch), *pitch* (an overhand with a horizontal loop rope throw), *roll* (a flip of the rope that starts a corkscrewing motion and frees it from a cow's heel), *roll-up*, *slip* (an overhand with a vertical loop rope throw), *washerwoman's loop* (a big flat loop) and *underhand pitch*. (See also dally)

Some roping tricks are *body spin* (around the roper's own body), *complex spin* (two ropes simultaneously), *butterfly* (looks like a butterfly), *juggling* (a variation of the body spin), *roll-over* (rolls the noose up and down his arm), *stargazing* (a body spin while lying down), *skipping* (jumping in and out of a vertical loop) and *setting spin* (jumping in and out of a vertical loop in a sitting position).

The most common cowboy words for throwing ropes were *catch rope, lariat, lasso* and *reata*. Others were *catgut* (when it was made of rawhide), *clothesline, coil, fling line, grass rope* (when of fibre), *gut line* (when of rawhide), *hemp* (when of manila), *lass rope, line, maguey* (when of century-plant fibre), *manila* (when of that), *seago* (when of hemp), *skin string* (when of rawhide), *string, tom horn* and *whale line*.

To rope a critter is to catch it with a rope. When applied to a man, it often means 'to entrap'.

A *roper* can mean either a man skilled with a rope or a horse trained to work with a rider in roping cattle. Such a horse has lots of smarts: it knows to catch up with a cow on the left side but not pass it, watch to see if the throw is accurate, face the catch straight on and sit back hard on its hindquarters with the forefeet braced.

Combinations: rope corral (a pen improvised with lariats, or other ropes, to hold horses at a camp that has no corral), *rope shy* (descriptive of a critter that jumps away from a thrown rope), *smooth roper* (one who does his job without fancy tricks), *rope someone in* (to trick someone), *rope tosser* (a roper who ropes calves in a herd with the rope starting on the ground behind him, without swinging it above his head [Adams]) and *roping out* (catching the mounts in a corral [Adams]).

rope and ring man Cowboy talk for a rustler, because he used a rope and an extra cinch ring to acquire cattle.

rosadero The leather fender that goes underneath the saddle leathers, between the rider's knee and the horse, not to be confused with a *sudadero* (sweat pad on the underside of a saddle). Borrowed or adapted from Spanish, it is pronounced rohs-uh-DAYR-oh.

rosebud Cowboy talk for a knot in the dallying end of his rope. Other such names are *turk's head*, *crown knot* and *Matthew Walker knot*.

rosette A flower-shaped, decorative piece of leather on a saddle or bridle.

rotten logging Cowboy talk for a couple's sitting on a log and necking. [Adams]

rough rider A hero-making name for a cowhand, perhaps first used in print by Teddy Roosevelt himself. It may have derived from rough-string rider. Later, Roosevelt's Spanish-American War cavalry outfit, recruited from the Western cow country, was called the Rough Riders.

rough string A cow outfit's bunch of half-broke or unbroke horses. On a big outfit, every hand was assigned a string, and there were usually some horses in the cavvy that had never been ridden – the rough string. The hands who paid extra to break these cayuses were known as rough-string riders and were thought to have more guts than brains. (*See* break a horse)

Combinations: rough-break a horse (to stick with it two or three times, maybe get the kinks out, and call it broke), *rough gambler* (in the gold-rush days of Montana and Idaho, a thief or road agent; the term also took the form *rough gambling*), *rough-lock*

a wagon wheel (to use a chain or other primitive device to brake it) and *rough out a horse* (the same as to rough-break it).

roughneck A worker on a drilling crew in an oil field.

roundup The gathering of cattle, usually to brand calves or to ship steers to market.

Over the years, the Western roundup has varied considerably. In the early days, the Texans called it a *cow hunt*, procedures and rules were made up as folks went along, and beef wasn't shipped to market.

During the heyday of the open range, in the couple of decades following the Civil War, it became the custom to round up the cows once in the spring for branding and again in the fall for shipping. The hands of the various cow outfits of the region would meet at an appointed place and time (sometimes several successive places and times) under a roundup boss and an understood set of rules. The men would ride circle to gather the cows; then they'd cut (separate) them by brand and make decisions about mavericks; then they would do the jobs that needed to be done. (*See* branding) Since this process wore out horses, each hand had his own string of horses, with different mounts for circling, cutting and roping.

These open-range roundups were huge enterprises. In *Cowboy Culture*, David Dary describes a big one in Texas in 1881. Eight or 10 stockmen got together and rigged one chuck wagon and headed for the roundup; altogether 10 chuck wagons representing a total of 90 stock outfits showed up. The hands made dry camps overnight and then drove the cattle into one enormous herd. At the instruction of the roundup boss, the home outfit cut its cattle out and drove them back on to the range. Other outfits then took turns cutting while others held the herd. If disputes arose over unclear brands, the roundup boss settled them. The reps were given their cuts. Mavericks were claimed by whoever had best title. Then each outfit proceeded to do its branding. And then each chuck wagon with its herd headed for the *next* roundup.

Roundup was a big social occasion. Hands got to socialise with friends they seldom saw and jaw around the chuck wagon and camp fire.

When the ranges were fenced, roundup changed. No longer were such vast areas to be ridden, and no longer were different brands mixed indiscriminately. But outfits (especially small outfits) continued to help each other. Today ranchers in a region often round up and brand on consecutive weekends at each other's places.

By metaphoric extension, last roundup came to mean the cowhand's final reward.

roundup captain The boss of a roundup. In the days of the open range, he had a huge job – coordinating the efforts of perhaps scores of outfits with chuck wagons, many cowboys to a wagon and a string of horses for every cowboy. He sent men to ride circle on various parts of the range, oversaw the gathering, cutting and branding and kept the peace between rival outfits. Though he might not be an owner, here he was a monarch.

roustabout *See* worm.

route Among loggers, the time of operation for a logging camp, or a logger's time on that job. [Adams]

rowel The wheel of a spur, the business end, the part that scratches. Rowels come in a wide variety of styles and shapes, some with many small points and others with a few big, sharp points.

rub out To kill. The expression dates at least to the mountain men. Linguist J. L. Dillard suggests that it came from the Plains Indian sign meaning 'to kill', a rubbing motion. (*See* dry-gulch)

run (1) A stampede. (2) A land rush.

Combinations: run cows (to operate a cattle ranch or to work cattle), *run cows off* (to stampede them so you could steal them), *run buffalo* (or *run meat*) (to hunt them on horseback), *run mustangs* (to rope them from horseback), *run a rapid*, or a stream as a whole (to navigate it in a boat), *run down his mainspring* (what a rider may let a runaway horse do, run unchecked until it decides to quit [Adams]), *run like a Nueces steer* (to run fast and recklessly [Adams]) and *run a brand* (to draw it on a hide with a running iron).

In rodeo, a *runaway bucker* is a kind of bucking horse; it runs like the devil for a distance before starting to buck, then gives a tremendous leap and comes down hard. Among Santa Fe Trail traders, a *runner* (sometimes called in French an *avant courier*) was a man sent ahead of a caravan to get provisions and send them back and make other necessary arrangements. *Running mate* is cowboy talk for partner or wife. A *running mount* is a jump on to the back of a horse without benefit of stirrup. A *running W* is a hobble.

running iron A branding iron without a stamp on the end. Using a plain rod or one with a little curl at the tip, the brander would draw his brand freehand. Though the running iron had legitimate uses (for instance, applying a neighbour's brand when you didn't have one of his irons), it was the mark of the rustler. If a man was caught with a running iron in his boot, he was often required to answer nasty questions from men ready to consider themselves judge, jury and executioner. Running irons were outlawed in Texas in the 1870s.

rurales The Mexican equivalent of Arizona Rangers – a paramilitary police force that operated in rural areas. During the Mexican Revolution the enforcement corps consisted of killers and bandits released from prison that terrorised the campesinos of northern Mexico.

rusher A person who participates in a human stampede for gold or land. (*See also* forty-niner and sooner)

Russian drag A method of trick riding, boot in a strap and head hanging off to the side of the horse. [Adams]

rust the boiler In cowboy talk, to drink alkali water. [Adams]

rustler First, a hustler, an active enterprising fellow, then a critter good at foraging (rustling up something to eat), then a horse wrangler, then a ranch cook and, finally and most memorably, a cow thief. Some authorities suggest that a fellow who was a hustler at mavericking (putting his brand on unbranded calves) when that practice was common became a thief when mavericking was no longer accepted.

The verb form 'to rustle' occurs with all the meanings above.

In the meaning 'cow thief', a rustler was also called *brand artist*, *brand blotter*, *brand burner*, *brand botcher*, *Cattle Kate* (if a woman), *cow thief*, *cross brander*, *hoodoo*, *mavericker*, *ring toter*, *rope and ring man* and *tongue-splitter*. He was a fellow said to be *careless with his branding iron* or *handy with his running iron*. Similar expressions were *he doesn't keep his twine on the tree* (doesn't keep his rope coiled on the saddle horn), *he keeps his branding iron smooth* (not rusty), *he rides with an extra cinch ring* (for range branding), *he swings* (or *throws*) *a big loop*, *his calves don't suck the right cows*, *his cows have twins*, *he has a sticky rope*, *he packs a long rope*, *he's too handy with a rope*, *he works ahead of the roundup* and *he works (alters) brands*.

One rustling technique was to change the brand. For instance, a lazy Y can easily be altered to a dumbbell. Another method was rebranding through a wet blanket. (*See* hair brand) One of the most common methods was sleepering, earmarking a calf without branding it in the hope that the real owner wouldn't notice the missing brand; when it was weaned and left its mother, the rustler would recrop the ear and put his own brand on it.

Some authorities say that there's more rustling going on today, when trucks can move stock away quickly, then in the bad old days.

Combinations: *rustler's pneumonia* (cold feet, fear) and *rustle the pasture* (to bring in the horse herd [Adams]).

S

sab-cat   What a logger called a saboteur. [Adams] It came from the black cat in an Industrial Workers of the World (IWW) emblem.

sabe   In the south-west, savvy. As a noun, it means 'knowledge, understanding'. Thus Jack London wrote in *Valley of the Moon*: 'We ain't got the *sabe*, or the knack, or something or other.' As a verb, it means 'to understand' – 'Do you sabe?' Also used as an adjective – 'a beaver is a sabe critter'. Borrowed from the Spanish *saber* (to know), it is pronounced SAH-bay.

sabino   A red roan with a white belly. A *sabina* is a cow with red and white spots. Borrowed from the Spanish, it is pronounced suh-BEE-noh. (*See* buckskin for other horse colours)

sacatone   A popular forage grass of the south-west, *Sporobolus wrighti*. Also spelled *zacaton* and also called *sacate*, it is adapted from the Spanish *zacatón* and pronounced sah-kuh-TOHN.

sack   In logging, to trail after a drive and push grounded logs back into the water. It was laborious work. Also called *sacking the rear*. A man who did it was a *sacker*, and he was a member of the *sacking crew*.

sack a horse   When breaking a horse, peelers (bronc busters) often rub a bronc with a sack or blanket and flip it at him to get him used to being touched and handled. Also called *sacking him out*.

sacred hoop   In the world view (or religion) of the Lakota and other Plains Indians, a symbol of wholeness and completeness – the wholeness of the family, the tribe, even the species. Thus it is the sacred hoop, and when it is broken, the people are sundered, their health and spirit destroyed. The hoop is the particular gift, says Black Elk, of one the cardinal points, the south, and in its centre the tree will bloom.

saddle   *Combinations*: *saddle slickers* and *saddle stiffs* (cowboys), *saddle bums* (cow-country drifters), *saddle tramps* (cowboys who spent their time riding the chuck line), *saddleman* (a man on horseback), *saddlebag doctor* (a doctor who rode to see his patients and took his medical implements in his saddlebags [sees sawbones]), *saddle-blanket gambler* (a small-time gambler or a cowboy who gambled on a blanket [Adams]), *saddle pockets* (another name for saddlebags), *saddle strings* (the leather strings used for tying gear on), *saddle gun* (a carbine – a short, light shoulder arm handy for use on horseback; it rides in a heavy leather case called the *saddle scabbard*), *saddle stand* (the wooden contraption, approximating the shape of a horse's back, for storing your saddle), *saddle mule* (the prairie-schooner mule ridden by the driver [a nigh mule] or a mule broke for riding as opposed to a pack mule or mule to broke to harness), *saddle-broke* (a term for a horse broke enough to tolerate a saddle on its back but no more) and *saddle stock* (a ranch's saddle horses, its cavvy or remuda). In logging, a saddle is a transverse log shaped to guide other logs down a skid road. [Adams]

Saddle-backed is an expression meaning 'set across something like a saddle'. The miners used to say that the Rockies are saddle-backed across the rangeland in Colorado. (For more on Western saddles, *see* stock saddle. For names for English saddles, *see* postage stamp)

saddle blanket (1) A pad or blanket that protects the horse's back against the chafing of the saddle. In the earliest days, an apishemore (buffalo-calf hide) was used. For a long time, the Navajo blanket was the most popular. Now the cool pad is the favourite. Also called a *saddle mat*. (2) A griddle cake. (3) A dollar bill. [Adams]

saddle tree The frame of a saddle.

saddle-bronc riding One of the principal competitions of a rodeo. The rules specify that the rider must use an association saddle, use just one rein, not touch anything with his free hand and stay on the horse for eight seconds.

sage Sagebrush, the ubiquitous plant of the plains and desert; an area covered with that plant, as in, 'they walked off into the sagebrush together arm in arm'. The big sage (*Artemisia tridentata*), more than head-high, black sage (*Artemisia arbuscla*) which grows at elevations below 5,800 feet, and *Artemisia nova*, which is only one to two feet high, are all members of the wormwood family rather than true sages (*Salvia* sp.). Sage is blue-grey-green and in thousands of places so thick and far-reaching, it looks like an ocean. It is beautiful.

Westerners call sage *dogwood* (from its smell), *hickory*, *estafiata* and *artemisia* (Spanish names). Plants and animals with sage in their names are simply a version of that critter that lives in the sagebrush: *sage chipmunk*, *sage chicken*, sage grouse, *sage hare*, *sage quail*, *sage sparrow*, *sage thrush*, *sweet sage* and *sage willow*. The land is described as *sage country*, *sage desert*, *sage flat*, *sage hill*, *sage land*, *sage plain*, *sage prairie* and *sage range*. Cowboys call people who live out in the boonies *sagebrushers* [Adams], and a *sage rat* is the equivalent of a desert rat. *Sage hen* is used, fancifully, for girls and young women.

sage grouse A big grouse that hangs out in the sagebrush. Also called a *fool hen*, *sage hen*, *sage cock*, *pine hen*, *prairie cock* and *prairie turkey*. The sage grouse has a wonderful mating ritual, done in early spring. The males group together and strut, posture, show off their tail feathers and boom (make plopping noises with their air sacs). The females and immature males watch, the females pretending not to be interested. Birds slip off into the sage (not always excluding immature males) and before long there are chicks.

sagebrush process A method of attempting to amalgamate gold or silver from ore – with a tea brewed from sagebrush.

Sagebrush Rebellion A political movement of the latter 1970s and early 1980s. Some people in the Western states rebelled against the influence of the federal government in their states through control of public land. Usually the sagebrush rebel was a fellow who favoured exploitation over preservation of public resources.

sagebrusher A sagebrusher is any inhabitant of the West, especially one in a remote area. He can be a person who camps out on his own (by implication in the sagebrush) instead of staying at hotels. This meaning seems to have originated in Yellowstone National Park, where sagebrushers offended the proprietors of the great hotels and their tip-hungry staffs. The park developed its own lingo: camp employees were *savages*, waitresses were *beavers*, bellmen were *pack rats*, maids were *pillow punchers*, bus drivers were *gear jammers*, and couples dating were said to be rotten logging.

saguaro A huge cactus (*Carnegiea gigantea*) of the south-west that grows in columns to the size and shape of a well-ordered tree, up to 60 feet high. The Indians and Anglos made (and make) syrup and wine from its fruit. Borrowed from Spanish, it's pronounced suh-WAR-oh or suh-WAR-oh and spelled variously, especially *sahuaro*. Also known as the *pillar cactus* or *pitahaya*.

Sahara Club The mocking name some Westerners, especially Utahns, give the Sierra Club, which they see as opposing economic progress with its environmental activities.

sail away To take off quickly, to vamoose.

saint (1) A common name for one of the faithful of the Church of Jesus Christ of Latter-Day Saints, used both by Mormons and gentiles and often capitalised. (2) *Winter saint* was a term of early Utah Mormons for a gentile emigrant who spent the winter in Salt Lake instead of risking the crossing of the Great Basin and the Sierra Nevada with cold weather approaching. (3) Without capitalisation, a rustler's name for a cowboy who's honest. [Adams]

sakey In the south-west, an irrigation ditch; short for acequia; also called a *sequia*. Also spelled saykee.

sala In the south-west, a big room; sometimes a big hall used for dancing. Borrowed from Spanish, it is pronounced SAH-luh.

salado Said of a wind-broke horse (a horse with breathing trouble). [Adams]

Borrowed from Spanish (where it means unlucky, salty), it is pronounced suh-LAH-doh.

salal A chinook word for a small shrub also called *shallon* (*Gaultheria shallon*) or its berry, valued as food. First mentioned in the journals of the Lewis and Clark expedition.

sale brand A brand burned over the original to show that the cow has changed hands. (*See* brand)

sale ring Where the rancher goes to sell his cows at auction, mostly to buyers representing big meat-packing companies. Many times the sale ring tells the cattleman whether he's survived to ranch another year.

salea A sheepskin used as a pad between a saddle and saddle blanket or beneath a pack saddle. Borrowed from the Spanish *zalea* (which means 'sheepskin'), it's pronounced suh-LAY-uh.

saleratus Baking soda. William A. Baillie-Grohman in *Camps in the Rockies* called saleratus 'the grandest word in the trapper's very abridged dictionary'. He meant the trapper of the later 19th century, for the early fur men had no baking soda, indeed no bread. A *saleratus lake* is an alkaline body of water, and *saleratus water* is alkaline.

salina A salt lick, salt pond or the like. Borrowed from Spanish (where it means 'salt mine'), it's pronounced suh-LEE-nuh. Likewise *salinera* is a salt pit.

sallie A cowboy's name for the cook. (*See* cookie for other names)

salmon chuck In the Pacific north-west, a stream full of salmon. (The Chinook word *chuck* means 'stream'.)

saloonist A Westernism for a saloon keeper. The word 'saloon' appears to have been born in the south, even if it earned most of its bad reputation in cow towns.

salsa A spicy sauce used in Mexican cuisine. A recent Westernism, it is borrowed from Spanish (where its means 'sauce') and pronounced SAHL-suh. Usually tomato-based, it can also have other ingredients; *salsa verde* is made from chiles and tomatillos.

salt (1) Often a synonym for alkali in the West – thus terms like *salt flat* and *salt plain*. Gleaming white on the arid earth, alkali looks like salt, and salts can mean, instead of table salt, 'saline minerals' such as alkali. A *salt desert* is a desert of alkaline soil, and a *salt flat* is an alkali pan, a flat stretch of alkaline soil. (2) To give livestock salt. (3) To put mineral into a mine to make it appear valuable. (The gold dust, precious stone or other stashed mineral is itself called salt.) (4) In forestry, to spread salt and other minerals over a piece of country to get the animals redistributed. The country is then called *salt ground*.

Plants using salt in their names are *salt grasses* (like *Distichlis spicata* and *Spartina* that grow on salt or alkali flats or marshes), *salt sage* (greasewood), *salt weed* (a variety of *Atriplex*), *salt bush* (shad scale) and *salt wood* (*Purshia tridentata*, useful as forage in the winter).

Salt chuck is a Chinook expression for the sea. *Salt horse* is a word for corned beef.

saltillo blanket A blanket that often served as a poncho in Texas before hands had slickers, according to Peter Watts. It was made in Saltillo, Coahuila, Mexico.

salty dog Anyone who's really good at his work. [Adams] Also, according to other sources, a tough fellow (*salty bacon* or *ham*). Salty means 'full of spirit and fight'. When said of a hand, it's a compliment. But a horse that's salty may be mean.

salvage cutting The harvesting of trees that are damaged, diseased, dying or dead before they become worthless as timber.

sancho A lead goat.

sand (1) Courage; grit; what a man has in his craw when he's brave. A fellow with sand is the sort you want to ride the river with. (2) Among loggers, a word for sugar.

Plants using sand in their names are *sand bur* (the prickly pea of any of several Western plants, especially bur grass), *sand cherry* (*Prunus besseyi*) and *sand mat* (a euphorbia).

Combinations: sand flat (an arid, sandy stretch of flat country, usually alkaline), *sand hills* (hills or dunes made of sand, as in the Sand Hills of Nebraska; the Blackfeet speak of the dead as having gone to the sand hills), *sand storm* (a wind that blows sand up from the ground and into everything, particularly the eyes, nostrils, mouths and ears of people, horses and other critters, a nasty bit of work), *sand auger* (a little whirlwind of sand; a dust devil) and *sand wagon* (a stagecoach especially built to cross rivers with quicksand; it had high clearance and wide tyres [Adams] and was also called a *sand liner* [as in ocean liner]).

sand painting A ritual of Navajo, Pueblo and sometimes Apache and California Indians. Sand painting, though valued as art by Anglos, is to Indians not aesthetic but religious. As part of a religious act, each one is destroyed at completion of the ceremony. Designs are not created by the makers but prescribed by tradition.

The paintings are made on the floor of a hogan or kiva or sometimes on a piece of buckskin or outdoors. The materials, sands of different colours, powdered minerals, charcoal, pollen, cornmeal, leaves and flowers, are gathered in a ritualistic way. These are spread on a base layer of sand by assistants working under the direction of a singer, a man of medicine. The ceremonies often last for many days and are centred on the recitation of the chants that restore harmony to the natural and spiritual worlds.

Principally through the efforts of singer Tl'ah Hastiin (Hosteen Klah), many reproductions of sand paintings and other elements of Navajo life are preserved in Santa Fe's Museum of Navajo Ceremonial Art. The process of making sand paintings is also called *dry painting*.

sand-cast Jewellery such as bracelets, rings and bow-guards made from molten silver (often from Mexican coins in the old days) and poured into a two-part mould carved from soft tufa or pumice blocks wired together. These soft moulds were usually only good for a few pours.

sandhill crane A gangly grey bird (*Grus canadensis*) that inhabits marshes in the West. It sometimes congregates in large flocks and shares a similar habitat to the whooping crane.

sandia A south-westernism for watermelon. Borrowed from Spanish, it's pronounced san-DEE-uh. When capitalised, it refers to the mountains on the east side of Albuquerque, New Mexico or the pueblo just north of that city.

sandlapper What old-timers in the Oregon desert called the homesteaders of the first two decades of this century. These newcomers ploughed up the desert in hopes of raising crops, but the desert wasn't vanquished. (For other names of homesteaders, *see* nester)

Santa Ana In the Los Angeles area, a name for a hot wind that blows from the Mojave Desert toward the west. Old-timers say it's properly pronounced san-TA-nuh, the *a* as in *corral*.

Santa Fe Trail A route of commerce between Missouri and the present capital of New Mexico, pioneered by William Becknell in 1821. It ran from Franklin or Independence, Missouri to Council Grove and on to the Arkansas River. From the Arkansas in south-central Kansas, travellers followed one of two branches: The Cimarron Cutoff, starting with a dry jornada of 60 miles to the Cimarron River, or the Mountain Branch, past Bent's Fort and over Raton Pass. The 800-mile journey took two or three months for the freight-laden Conestoga wagons. Josiah Gregg drew a detailed picture of the traders, caravans and life on the trail in *Commerce of the Prairies*, published in 1844. Since Santa Fe was the northern end of the Camino Real, the trail thus connected the major trade routes to points south. Since the Santa Fe Trail continued to function until superseded by the railroad in 1878, it endured longer than any of the cattle trails.

Combinations formed with Santa Fe: *Santa Fe tea* (tea made from the leaves of *Alstonia theaeformis*), *Santa Fe expedition* (an effort by Texas in 1841 to lay claim to eastern New Mexico), *Santa Fe town* (any town in the part of New Mexico claimed by the Santa Fe expedition), *Santa Fe trader* and *Santa Fe wagon* (one used on the Santa Fe Trail).

Santee A group of the Dakota Indians, made of the Mdewakanton, Wahpekute, Wahpeton and Sisseton tribes. In the 19th century, the Santee lived in southern Minnesota as farmers. In the rebellion of 1862, they killed over 700 Anglos and suffered harsh reprisals. Now they live on the Santee Reservation in Nebraska, the Sisseton Reservation in South Dakota and the Devil's Lake Reservation in North Dakota.

santero A south-western expression for a person who carves religious images, especially santos (statues or images of saints).

sateen A satin-like fabric made of cotton; popular among the Navajos (along with velveteen and silk plush) for clothing.

Sauk The Sac or Ousaukie Indians, an Algonquian woodlands tribe. They lived in what is now Michigan but were pushed west by the French and settled in Illinois and Iowa, allying with the Fox (properly Mesquakie) Indians there. Under Black Hawk, they fought unsuccessfully against white encroachment in 1832; over the next two decades, they made a series of cessions of land to the United States. They now have Sauk-Fox communities in Iowa and Stroud, Oklahoma.

savanero A Sante Fe Trail expression for the fellow who guarded the mules at night to keep them from straying. From the Spanish *sabanero* and related to an English word for plains (savanna), it's pronounced sa-vuh-NAYR-oh.

save To kill. Hunters sometimes spoke of saving deer, frontiersman of saving Indians. After the Utah War in 1856, says Wallace Stegner in *The Gathering of Zion*, among Mormons 'the phrase "to save" a man came to have the precise meaning of our modern euphemism "to liquidate".' (*See* dry-gulch)

savvy What a sensible man has – an understanding. It's used in several forms. A wise man has savvy (a noun form).

Cowboys are savvy about cows (an adjective form). A trapper savvies beaver (a verb form). A common Western query was, 'Do you savvy?' (Do you get it?) Here the Spanish *sabe* was used interchangeably with savvy. The linguist J. L. Dillard, though, says *savvy* came to the West from the maritime lingua franca through Indian Pidgin English, not directly from Spanish, as most authorities have believed.

sawbones A doctor, especially a surgeon. The expression likely arose because, in the days before sepsis was understood, wounds often required amputating limbs, which necessitated sawing through bones. Westerners also called a physician (according to [Adams]) *Epsom salts*, *Genuine Jimmy*, *old pills*, *pill roller*, *Quinine Jimmy* and *saddlebag doctor*.

sawbuck A name for a packsaddle. The usual packsaddle has ends that look like a sawhorse, or sawbuck.

sawdust What a miner called dynamite. [Adams] (For other Westernisms for dynamite, *see* powder)

sawyer (1) A log or tree caught in the river bed, bobbing up and down in the stream and so a menace to boats. (2) A bucker; a logger who cuts trees into logs; sometimes a fellow who both fells and saws them (*see* faller). A log the right size for sawing is called a *saw log*.

scad In placer mining, the gold left in a pan after a washing.

scaffold Among many Plains Indian tribes, a platform for the dead, either on four crossed poles or in the fork of the tree. Often weapons, food and clothing were placed to accompany the dead on their journeys. The bodies were placed in a high place to be protected from scavengers, and once the flesh had decayed, some Indians made a ceremony of taking the scaffold down and placing the bones in a safe place, such as a crevice in a rock or in the ground.

scalawag A worthless cow, a likely cull. The meaning with regard to people (a rascal) is an Americanism but not a Westernism. *Scalawag bunch* are the horses useless for working cows (the rough string).

scale (1) In logging, for logs to produce lumber, as in the phrase 'the number of feet a tree will scale'. (The lumber is measured in board feet.) (2) To calculate or estimate the amount of lumber in logs; this fellow is called a *scaler*.

scalping The custom of cutting off part or all of the scalp of an enemy, not necessarily a dead one, was practised in North America by most Indian tribes and some whites and Hispanics. Scalping was a venerable practice, performed not only in North America, but in Europe, Asia and Africa. Often, as here, it stood for the taking of an enemy as a ritual of war and as an insult to the fallen man and his tribe. It was widely performed by native peoples (but not by all tribes) both before and after white contact. Among some peoples, up to recent times, the taking of the entire head remained a more powerful act.

After white contact, the practice spread, partly because Anglo and Hispanic governments offered bounties for the scalps of native peoples who were causing difficulty. Some whites became scalp hunters, and other whites (for instance, mountain men) took scalps. The popular recent notion that white men corrupted the red man by teaching him to take scalps is a notable exaggeration.

Techniques of scalping varied. Sometimes the skin of the entire upper half of the head was taken, including the ears. Other times only a patch of skin (a topknot) with scalp lock was cut off. Among Indians, the deed was an act of medicine, and the resulting trophy was an object of power. So scalps were kept, displayed, treasured and sometimes traded. Among Anglos and Hispanics, a scalp was more often a symbol of vengeance and a hide that could be turned in for a bounty.

Combinations: scalp dance (a solemn Indian dance performed after fighting with the enemy), *scalp feast*, *scalp hunter*, *scalping knife* (or *scalper*), *scalping party*, *scalp shirt* (a shirt decorated with scalps), *scalper* (a person who scalps or the knife he uses) and so on.

In logging, to scalp is to strip away turf.

scatter-gun A shotgun with a short barrel.

school section From 1802, one section of land (a section is one square mile) out of every township was given by the federal government to the state governments for the support of public schools. It was often called the 16th section because it was the 16th in the 36 in each township surveyed. In the West, if not used for actual schools, these sections often have been leased to ranchers for grazing; thus left undeveloped, they sometimes are both producers of revenues and sanctuaries for wildlife.

scissorbill A term of contempt generally; among cowboys it's a word for a shirker or incompetent. Among loggers, it is a fellow of bourgeois values, one not of the true working class.

scoop A derogatory word for a Mormon, said to have been coined by canyon-country river runners. Also *double scoop*. It's nasty – it comes from the notion of brains having been scooped out.

scoot A single sledge for dragging logs. Also known as a *go-devil* and a *lizard*.

scorcher An off-hand word for a branding iron.

score In rodeo, the length of the head start given a calf or steer in a roping or wrestling event. [Adams]

Scotch cap A woollen cap with a short brim and a pillbox top, usually navy blue but sometimes a colourful plaid, worn by men who work outdoors, from carpenters to cowboys, on the northern Plains.

Scotch hobble A hobble (fetter) that runs a rope from a horse's neck and lifts the hind leg off the ground several inches.

scours A foul-smelling diarrhoea that debilitates calves. These days it's treated with *scours pills* (antibiotics) the rancher gets from the vet.

scout On the scout meant 'on the lam from the law'.

Scout itself, in the sense of a guide, a lookout, is not an Americanism. Historically, the army found itself half-helpless in the face of Western country, customs and Indians, so it employed what it called a scout to find the way, find the water and find the natives; then to explain the Indians, interpret their languages, make promises to them and, when convenient, to kill them. This fellow was usually a former mountain man, who didn't wear the blinders of civilisation, or an Indian of a tribe other than the one being sought. Scouts like Tom Fitzpatrick and Jim Bridger, wise beavers around the mountains, were the most valuable hands the army had and they tried to keep Indian–army encounters from being mere slaughters.

Later another sort of fellow altogether called himself a scout, a show-off fellow in buckskin, fringes, beads and long hair and full of lies. Says Bernard DeVoto in *Across the Wide Missouri*, 'The West has been fecund in the production of phonies: the Scout was one of the earliest and just about the most noisome.'

scrape A difficulty, a predicament, a fight. So a *shooting scrape* is a gun fight (with droll Western understatement), and a *water scrape* is a long ride or drive across a dry stretch of country.

scraper (1) Among the Plains Indians, a tool for scraping flesh and fat off hides, usually made of elk antler; also called a dubber. (2) Among miners, a big blade like a hoe, dragged by a cable.

scratch In rodeo, to keep your spurs moving on the bucking animal you're trying to ride, to urge it to buck. The rules mandate scratching, and screwing down is not permitted.

screw Another word for a cowboy.

screw bean In the south-west, the screw-pod mesquite.

screw down In rodeo, when riding a bucking animal, to put your spurs into the cinch instead of scratching. It's forbidden, because it helps the rider, and scratching is required.

scrub Among cowboys, any critter of poor breeding; a runt. Among loggers, brush or stunted trees that aren't sellable.

seago A rope woven from grass or hemp. Arizona cowboys called it a *yacht line*.

sealing An ordinance performed in Mormon temples in which a marriage union is sealed for time and eternity. The sealing ordinance and temple marriage are performed for newlyweds, and children born to that union are considered sealed to their parents, or 'born under the covenant'. Couples previously married in a civil ceremony can participate in the sealing ordinance, and have any children already born sealed to them. Sealings can be performed for widows, widowers or deceased children; a proxy stands in for the deceased.

seam squirrel A body louse.

Sears Roebuck guy What loggers called a novice. [Adams] The equivalent among cowboys was an *Arbuckle*.

seco In the old south-west, the brass and aluminium tokens made by individual traders for use in place of silver coins. The silver coins were used in jewellery-making.

second growth forest In logging, trees that have grown up since the cutting of the virgin forest.

see a man about a horse To urinate. A fellow drinking with his buddies will often excuse himself for a moment with the excuse (intended to fool nobody), 'I've got to see a man about a horse.'

see daylight What the spectators do when a rider bounces high in the saddle of a bucking horse – they see it between bottom and saddle. It's considered poor form.

see the elephant What you had to do at the climax of your journey – see whatever was there to be seen and do whatever there was to do. Often it had the implication of to see enough and more than enough and to head home in disappointment. Gold-rushers said optimistically on the way West that they were going to see the elephant and said in disgust on the way back that they'd seen it. Trail hands spoke the same way about Kansas cattle towns.

seed forest In logging, a forest primarily of trees grown from seed.

sego Also called *sego lily* (*Calochortus nuttalli*), it is the state flower of Utah, growing thickly in beds on dry hillsides. The Indians and Mormon pioneers used the bulb for food.

segundo The second in command; the assistant to the boss; the straw boss. Used particularly on trail drives. Borrowed from the Spanish segundo (meaning 'second'), it is pronounced suh-GOON-doh.

seismic crew A gang of workers hired by oil exploration companies to find oil and gas, especially in the overthrust belt. These workers (called *juggies*) set explosives on the surface of the earth, detonate them, record the resulting sound waves and use computers to determine the rock structure. They were common in the Overthrust area during the late 1970s and early 1980s but with falling oil prices have mostly disappeared.

seldom hombre An unusual man. John Russell, the hero of Elmore Leonard's fine novel *Hombre*, is both a real hombre and a seldom hombre.

selective cutting In logging, a kind of cutting that harvests only trees of a certain size, value or both, or trees that are diseased. (A forest that has been cut selectively is called a *culled forest*.) Controversy burns in the West today over clear-cutting versus selective cutting. Many loggers argue that clear-cutting is more economical and efficient. Many environmentalists argue that selective cutting is more visually appealing and healthier for the forest.

señor A Hispanic man, especially a gentleman. Also an equivalent of Mister. Borrowed from Spanish, it is pronounced sayn-YOHR or seen-YOHR. A *senora* is a lady, and a *señorita*, a young girl.

sent for supplies Among sheep-herders, an expression for crazy, driven around the bend by loneliness. [Adams] Such a fellow was sent to town for supplies to get him back among folks.

As grizzlies are fierce, coyotes skulky and antelopes swift, sheep-herders (Westerners do not say shepherd) are legendary among cowboys for being crazy. Cowboys said they went crazy trying to determine which side of square sugan was the long side and spoke of sheep-herding as *trying to find the long end of a square quilt*. No doubt the sheep-herders spend too much time by themselves; and probably most cowboys never get to know them.

Some Western expressions for crazy are *loco*, *crazy as a sheep-herder*, *hunting for water* and *short of hat size*.

sequoia A genus of trees that includes two huge California conifers, the redwood (*Sequoia sempervirens*) and the Big Tree of the Sierra Nevada. Also called a *Washington cedar*, it was named after Sequoyah, the Cherokee who devised a syllabary for his native language.

serape A shawl or blanket worn as an outer garment, especially by Hispanics. Borrowed from the Spanish *sarape* (which has the same meaning) and pronounced suh-RAH-pay. Sometimes spelled *sarape*.

service-berry The dark blue fruit of the service-berry shrub, genus *Amelanchier*. The fruit is used as food by the Indians and Anglos. Sometimes spelled as two words or as *sarvisberry*, and pronounced *sarvisberry*; also called a *saskatoon* or a *june-berry*.

set (1) A placement for a trap. (2) The ready position of the crewmen of a keelboat, poles firm in the river bottom. The men then walked down the running board on each side of the craft from bow to stern, pushing the boat up-river. (3) Among cowboys, a short version of *settler*. [Adams] (4) Among miners, also according to Adams, a piece of ground worked by a tributer, a fellow who works a claim for wages.

Other expressions starting with set: *set down* (to be fired, to be kicked off and set afoot), *set the buck* (to ride a bucking bronco successfully [Adams]), *set the hair* (to ride a horse until he gentles a little [Adams]), *set up* (to treat people, as in, 'Johnny set up the drinks' [free]) and *set-down* (what a friendly householder might give a bum – a chance to come in, wash and 'set' [sit] down to eat).

set close to the plaster For a rider to keep a tight seat in the saddle, not to show daylight. [Adams] (*See* see daylight)

settlement company A group of people who agreed to go to a certain place (often to cross the continent to the West Coast), to perform actions such as clearing the land together and to take up their lives together there. It might have a bond, such as a religion or a utopian dream, or might simply be a practical assemblage. This term gave rise to similar ones like *settlement duty*, *settlement road*, *settlement store* and so on.

Seven Cities Ancient cities of New Mexico, probably the Zuni pueblos, whose legendary wealth drew the Spanish into that country. (*See* pueblo)

Seven Council Fires The alliance of the Dakota Indians, commonly known as the Sioux. The seven groups were the Mdewakanton, Wahpekute, Wahpeton, Sisseton, Yankton, Yanktonia and Teton.

Seven Persons A term of Indian Pidgin English among some Plains Indians for the Big Dipper.

seven-up The popular gambling card game also known as all-fours.

seventy In the Mormon Church, one of offices in the Melchizedek Priesthood. Seventies are elders with a special call and ordination to do missionary work. Members of the First and Second Quorums of the Seventy are General Authorities of the Church, aid in the administration of Church affairs and act under the direction of the Council of the Twelve Apostles.

severe Wild, headstrong. A horse was sometimes said to be severe. So was a fellow who 'never killed a man who did not deserve killing'.

sewellel The so-called mountain beaver, a squirrel-like creature of the Pacific north-west. The word was originally the chinook name for a robe made from the skin of these animals. Also called a *boomer* and a *showt'l*.

shabrack A large piece of cloth, often ornamented, worn over the saddle pad to protect the rider from contact with a dirty and sweating horse. Also called a *chevrac*.

shack (1) A hut, a shanty. Mathews makes the case for it as a Westernism, indicating that the term came to English from the Aztec *xacalli* through the Spanish *xacal* (later *jacal*). *Combinations: claim shack, cook shack* and, more recently in the West, *ski shack*. (2) A cowboy word for the bunkhouse. [Adams] (3) To hole up for the winter. (4) To amble along.

shad scale A salty forage bush (*Atriplex canescens*) of the south-western deserts.

shading Resting. What a cowboy does when he finds a shady spot on the range, which is mostly treeless. Old hands in the inter-mountain West advise that when you find shade, even the sliver made by a metal fence-post, you should stand in it.

shadow jumper Said of a horse that is skittish, apt to use any excuse to shy or scotch.

shadow rider A rider who's so vain he goes along admiring his own shadow.

shag out A Texas expression meaning 'to run out on someone, to back out', as in, 'His partner shagged out.'

shaganappi Thongs of buffalo rawhide used to bind or hold anything and everything; ubiquitous in the north-west and sometimes called *north-western iron*. Originally a cree word, it is pronounced sha-guh-NAP-pee.

shake hands with Saint Peter Among cowboys, to die. [Adams]

Shalako The winter solstice ceremony of the Zuni Indians.

Shanghai To spirit someone away, using force, drugs or other means; especially to recruit sailors for long voyages (such as Shanghai) by force. Mathews says that the expression is believed to have originated in San Francisco about 1850.

shanty A frontier term for a rude cabin or shack in a lumber camp. *Shanties*, in the plural, often means 'a lumber camp'.

Combinations: shanty boy or *man* (a logger), *shanty cake* (an unleavened bread), *shanty gang* (a timber crew), *shanty queen* (a logger's wife), *shanty team* (the same as a shanty gang) and *shanty town* (a poor district full of shanties). Also *claim shanty, cook shanty, lumber shanty* and *timber shanty*.

shapeleel A chinook word for grain or an Indian of the north-west. Pronounced SHAP-uh-leel.

Sharps Any of several models of firearms devised by Christian Sharps and produced by the Sharps Rifle Company until 1881. The firm was primarily known for its breech-loading rifles, though it also made a derringer. The most popular Sharps were Old Reliable, the cavalry carbine and the heavy-calibred, single-shot buffalo-hunting rifle. This monster was said to 'fire today, kill tomorrow'.

shave-tail (1) A broke horse, in contrast to the *broomtails*, wild range horses (usually mares). In the days of the open range on the northern plains, it was customary to pluck the tails of horses as you broke them to make them easy to distinguish from the unbroke critters. (2) Among soldiers, a new, uneducated army mule. When new mules came on the scene, they weren't bell-sharp, that is, they didn't respond to bell commands. The soldiers shaved the tails of the new ones to identify them. Thus a shave-tail was a mule that didn't know what it was doing. (3) A brand-new officer, a second lieutenant, so called precisely because he didn't know what he was doing.

she stuff Female critters, whether women, girls, fillies, cows or heifers. Fully grown cattle were called *grown stuff*, and cows and heifers, *she cattle*.

shearing factory Sheepmen had elongated frame sheds where sheep came from up to 50 miles to get sheared. David Lavender described the process as it took place in the 1930s in *One Man's West*: 'Generally the shearing is contracted to professionals who move from ranch to ranch. Piece payment, averaging twenty-five cents for a ewe, half a dollar for a big, husky ram. Their job folds on them with the season, and so they have developed astonishing skill. A good man can make twenty dollars a day.

'Inside the shed a gasoline motor drives an overhead shaft, powering a line of a dozen or so clippers, one man to a clipper. Behind each worker is a small pen, kept filled with sheep. He reaches into it, seizes an animal by the hind leg, drags it out, wrestles it into a sitting position, and kneels by its left side, using his left hand to hold its under-jaw.

'The sheep lies helpless on the round of its rump, dumb terror in its yellow eyes. *Snip-snip-snip.* Along the neck and side from back to belly travel the shears. Sweat pours from the operator. This is work, holding a ninety-pound mutton with one hand while the other races against time. *Snip-snip-snip.* The fleece comes off in one unbroken greasy mass. The shearer – his hands are always debutante-soft from the lanolin in the wool – folds it with the clean hair inside and tosses it on to a conveyor belt running overhead. He pushes the shorn animal through a door in the outside wall, reaches back for another.'

Sheepmen used to have shearing contests, men racing to get the most wool off in a set time. Ivan Doig describes one contest vividly in his fine novel *Dancing at the Rascal Fair*.

sheep Sometimes a verb: A sheepman will sheep a cattleman, that is, claim he's obliged by circumstance to drive sheep across the cattleman's range. To get sheeped, in the days of the open range, was somewhere between annoying and infuriating.

A *sheep camp* is the moving home of the sheep-herder, consisting mostly of a *sheep wagon*, a canvas-covered wagon where the sheep-herder sleeps and stores his cookstove, bedding and other gear. Range sheep require constant attendance, so the camps were and are supplied by camp tenders who drive out periodically from town. Sheep wagons were called *maniac dens* or *mansions* by cowboys [Adams] and *cradles* by sheep-herders.

A *sheep dipper* is a man who treats sheep with dip (a liquid disinfectant); *sheep feeder* is a man who puts sheep into feed lots to fatten them for market; and a *sheep grower* or *sheepman* is the equivalent of a cattleman, the owner.

Sheep fever is the fervent desire to go into the wool-growing business, regarded by many cattlemen as a sickness. *Sheep-herding, sheep meat* (for mutton), *sheep herd, sheep spread* and *sheep range* are also Western coinages.

sheep deadline A line marking sheep range from cow range. Such lines were strictly creations of cattlemen, who used to form associations and committees to declare such lines and order sheepmen to stay the hell out. In Jackson Hole, Wyoming, the cattlemen formed a 'committee of safety' in 1897 and declared the area unblemished cow country. The object of cattlemen in Wyoming generally was to restrict sheep to the desert lands where cattle couldn't thrive anyway. The country over-grazed by sheep (or in a cattleman's view, grazed at all by sheep) was said to be *sheeped off*. The sheepmen wanted the grass – thus Wyoming's sheep wars.

The supposed destruction that sheep do to grazing lands was much exaggerated by cattlemen, and now many Wyoming stockmen raise both – cattle for respectability, as they like to say, and sheep for profit.

Sheep-Eaters A branch of the Shoshone Indians who lived in high, remote country and hunted bighorn sheep instead of moving on to the plains, employing the horse and adopting the buffalo-hunting culture. Their name in their own language, *Tukuarika*, means 'sheep-eaters'. They survived as a separate group, living on the Lemhi Reservation, until 1912, when they relocated to Fort Hall Reservation.

sheep-herder The Westerner's word for the fellow who nursemaids sheep on the range, as cowboys might put it disparagingly. Shepherd is a much older word – sheep-herder dates only from 1871 – and probably sounded too pious to cowboys.

Western sheep-herders are often Basques. Regardless of their ethnic origin, they have generally been regarded as about half crazy. When one gets strange from having spent too much time alone, he's sent for supplies. Cowboys derogatorily call the sheep-herder a *drop-band herder, jockey, lamb licker, mutton puncher, scab herder, snoozer, sheep puncher, social herder* or *wagon herder*. He's also known more respectfully as a *campero, pastor,* or partidario.

shelterwood In logging, a form of selective cutting. It employs two or three cuttings so that the larger remaining trees provide shelter for young trees. The shelterwood approach preceded clear-cutting as the usual technique; now it is making a comeback because it leaves a more attractive-looking forest than clear-cutting and one that's better for wildlife and recreational forest users.

shenanigan A trick, a bit of nonsense or tomfoolery. The word appears to have been born in California in the 1850s but is of obscure origin; Webster speculates that it comes from an Irish verb that sounds similar and means, 'I play tricks'.

shepherd's bible What a cowboy called a mail-order catalogue. [Adams] Adams tells a funny story about a hand who ordered a dress under the illusion that the girl who modelled it was part of the bargain. He then bragged that, since everything came postpaid, he didn't even have to pay a freight charge on her.

sheriff's deadline The equivalent of a sheep deadline for sheriffs – outlaws in Texas, for example, called the Nueces River a line those law officers could not pass.

shift boss In mining, the foreman of one shift. Also known as a *shifter*.

shindig A dance, a party.

shine To do well, to stand out. This was a favourite verb of the mountain man, as in, 'You can't shine in this crowd.' *Shining times* were stand-out times, to be savoured and remembered.

shiner A reflective surface that a card sharp uses to see the faces of the cards as they're dealt. [Adams] It might be anything – a ring, coin, etc. Also called a *glimmer*.

Shining Mountains The name some early explorers used for the Rocky Mountains, perhaps because some of them are always snow-covered.

shinnery The scrub oak (*Quercus gambelii*, *Q. undulata*) common in Texas, also called *shinnery oak* and *shin oak*; a thicket of scrub oak.

ship close A cattleman's term for sending every halfway ready head of cattle to market. Such cattle were held in a little pasture called a *shipping trap*.

shirt-tail ranch A small ranch, probably with too few cows, too few hands, too little land and too little money. Also called a *rawhide outfit*, *greasy sack outfit*, *one-horse outfit*, *three-up outfit*, *two-by-four outfit*, *ranchito*, *cockle-bar outfit*, *starve-out ranch* and *stump farm* (when it's on newly cleared land).

shit-kicker A redneck in high heels; a Western redneck.

shivaree A noisy serenade, especially for a newly married couple. The verb form means 'to serenade' them and perhaps annoy them. A chivaree was sometimes thrown to indicate community opinion that a couple *ought* to get married. Unpopular people didn't get a shivaree. Also spelled *charivari* or *chaveree*.

shongsasha The bark of a red willow, mixed by Plains Indians with tobacco for smoking. (*See* kinnikinnick)

shoofly A mine's passageway.

shoot Among loggers, to shoot a jam is to dynamite a log jam to get it loose. Among miners, shooting is getting oil or gas to start flowing with a blast of dynamite. A *shooting affair* is a gunfight, usually a duel between two men with pistols (also called a *shooting affray*), and to shoot centre is to shoot accurately.

shooting iron A firearm, usually a handgun. The first use of this expression is evidently in 1787.

shootist A marksman with a gun. Glendon Swarthout wrote a fine novel called *The Shootist*.

shop-mades Custom-made boots. [Adams] Adams speaks of the cowman's scorn for ready-made boots. I think that's mostly a thing of the past, perhaps because profit in the cattle business is a thing of the past.

short A man who's past due to head somewhere else is short, as in, 'You're short in this town.'

Combinations: short bit (a dime; since two bits make a quarter, one bit would be twelve and one-half cents), *short staker* (among loggers, an itinerant worker; also known as a *boomer*), *short horse* (once a name for a quarter horse), *short yearling* (a calf just short of a year old), *short age* (a word for cattle under three [Adams]), *short of hat size* (what a cowboy called a sheep-herder who was a little crazy [Adams]), *short-trigger man* (a fellow who was quick on the trigger or with his temper, a gunman) and *shorten his stake rope* (to get someone under control, cramp his style).

shorthorn (1) According to some Westerners, any cow of a breed other than Texas longhorn, the original Texas cattle; thus any of various breeds that are imported and therefore foreigners, including the most common of contemporary range cattle, Herefords. But other Westerners observe that the Shorthorn is a distinct breed, imported later than the Hereford. (2) A tenderfoot. Perhaps this application to people is an extension of the notion that shorthorns are imported cows, not natives.

shortwood logging The traditional method of logging, felling and cross-cutting on the spot.

shosh The Navajo word meaning 'bear'; part of various place names around the Navajo Reservation in New Mexico and Arizona, like Shos-B'toh near Fort Wingate. The bear is a taboo animal for the Navajo.

Shoshone An Indian tribe of the Uto-Aztecan family. At the beginning of the 18th century, they lived along the Rocky Mountain front from what is now Alberta to Wyoming and in southern Idaho and northern Utah. Acquiring the horse at that time from the Spanish settlements through the Utes, the Idaho-Utah Shoshone began to adopt a buffalo-hunting culture and to supply their relatives on the east side of the Rockies with horses, which allowed them to hunt the buffalo more easily, also. (Other desert Shoshone of the Great Basin continued in the old ways.) After smallpox and the Blackfeet drove the Shoshone out of Montana and Alberta, they congregated into seven principal groups: the largest band, which hunted around what are now Idaho Falls and Pocatello; another buffalo-hunting band that lived along the Wind River in Wyoming; the Lemhi band, which lived along the Salmon River in Idaho and subsisted principally on salmon; a band along the Bear River in Idaho and Utah; and another salmon-eating band in south-western Idaho. (In addition to these four, the Indians of the Great Basin that whites called diggers were often a detached variety of Shoshones.)

The Shoshone were mostly friendly to Anglos. The woman interpreter for the Lewis and Clark expedition, Sacajawea, was a Shoshone. During the 1820s and 1830s, the mountain men held most of their rendezvous in Shoshone country. Washakie, the great Shoshone chief, was an advocate of peace. The opening of the Oregon Trail through their country caused resentment, though, as did the establishment of Mormon colonies, and the Shoshone sometimes took reprisals. In 1863 Colonel Patrick Conner led California volunteers in a sneak attack on a village of Shoshone on Idaho's Bear River and killed several hundred Indians, mostly women and children. Treaties from 1868 created reservations in traditional Shoshone hunting grounds near Pocatello and along the Wind River. The reservations remain today, but disagreement about rights continue – even now the Shoshones of the Wind River Reservation, along with the Arapaho and the Shoshone-Bannocks at Fort Hall, Idaho are engaged in major disputes with the federal and state governments over water rights.

Though most academics spell the tribal name *Shoshoni*, the press and the Indians themselves generally prefer Shoshone. An idiosyncracy is that when the word is used as an adjective in areas near the two Shoshone reservations, the final *e* is often silent.

shot In mining, a packet of dynamite used for blasting. (*See* powder)

shot gold The pellet gold found in placer mining. Also known as *shotty gold*.

shotgun (1) A smoothbore long arm that fires a load of shot instead of a single ball or bullet. Surprisingly, this term appears to be a frontierism, first recorded in the early days in Kentucky and acknowledged by James Fenimore Cooper as 'the language of the West'. It was also called a *two-shoot gun*, *two-scatter shotgun*, *scatter-gun*, *shot-scatter gun* and so on.

Shotguns were relied on in the West by men who had to defend against groups, for instance, lawmen and stage guards. Thus an express messenger was also called (though the references are of later date) a *shotgun messenger*. He had a difficult and demanding job, keeping him awake for days on end to guard the valuables on the stagecoach against road agents. The way shotguns scattered their pellets made it difficult to miss at short range, and if the barrel or barrels were sawed off, the shot scattered over a greater area.

(2) Shotgun also became a description of a long, narrow, unelaborate shape: *Shotgun leg* was a term for chaps that followed the straight and narrow; *shotgun shack* meant a little house that went straight as a barrel from front room to bedroom to kitchen.

Combinations: shotgun cavvy (the bunch of saddle horses made by putting the mounts of several outfits at one roundup together [Adams]; *see* cavvy), *shotgun freighter* (a fellow who wasn't a regular trader but took trade goods to a gold field or other trading spot [Adams]; farmers, for instance, might take eggs, butter and other farm products), *shotgun pasture* (a homesteader's little pasture with a fence around it, protected against big trail herds with a shotgun [Adams] and *shotgun wagon* (a wagon that didn't join the main roundup but worked independently [Adams]).

shoulder draw Pulling your pistol from the shoulder scabbard or shoulder holster.

shoulder scabbard A holster for a hidden pistol, out of sight under the clothing in the armpit. The cowboy turned Pinkerton detective Charlie Siringo tells us he owned such a holster for 40 years. Also called a *shoulder holster*.

shove-down crew A group of riders used to bring down cattle from the high country to lower ranges. [Adams]

show bucker In rodeo, a bucking horse that looks good but is easy to ride. [Adams] This horse bucks straight away with his head between his front legs.

showdown In poker, what happens when the bet is called – the players have to show their cards, to put up or shut up. By extension, any decisive confrontation, the mythical classic being a gunfight.

shuck (1) A name for a cigarette or cigar made by rolling tobacco in a corn shuck, a particular custom of Hispanics. More fully called a *shuck cigar* or a *shuck cigarillo*. (2) An Anglo cowboy's word for a Mexican because Mexicans liked shuck cigars. Like greaser, it's a disparaging term. (3) As a verb, to take something off or get rid of it, as in shucking wet socks. (4) To get shucked out, though, is to get thrashed, as in a usage in Mark Twain's *The Celebrated Jumping Frog of Calaveras County, and Other Sketches*.

si One way of saying yes in the southwest, often by playful Anglos. Borrowed from Spanish, it is pronounced *see*.

Sibley A tent often used by the US Army in the West after the Civil War, said to have been designed by General Henry Hastings Sibley on the pattern of the Dakota tipi. The *Sibley stove* was a small heating stove (also designed by Sibley) commonly used in the US Army during the period of the Indian Wars.

side Among loggers, the crew and equipment needed to perform one task – the high lead side, skidder side, etc. The foreman of a side was called a *side push*, and the boss of the yarding crew a *side rod*. A *side axe* is an axe with both a bevelled face and a flat face, for better hewing. A *side boom* is a barrier of logs (a boom) along the side of a stream to keep floating logs from escaping.

side rider A mounted man who accompanied a stagecoach through country suspected of harbouring road agents (highway men). [Adams]

side-line To hobble a horse by fixing a front leg and the hind leg on the same side together rather than two front legs. The horse is then said to be *side-hobbled*, *side-lined* or *lined*. To side-line a steer is for a buster to tie a rope from its neck to its hind leg.

sidewinder (1) A desert rattlesnake - that moves by looping itself along sideways, leaving a succession of discontinuous tracks. Also called a *side-liner*, *side-wiper* and *horned snake*, it is regarded by many Westerners as especially dangerous. The principal Western rattlesnakes are the *prairie rattler*, which is widely distributed, and the *diamondback* and *sidewinder*, which are mainly south-western. (2) A sneaky man, one who comes at things sideways or 'left-handed'. (3) A tree knocked down by a falling tree; a tree that, while falling, hits another tree and is knocked from its path, thus not completing its fall and becoming dangerous. [Adams]

sierra In the south-west, a range of hills or mountains. Borrowed from Spanish, it's pronounced see-AYR-ruh. Sometimes a common noun, it is more often a proper name, as in Sierra Nevada and Sierra Madre. In California it is usually short for Sierra Nevada and is used in various combinations with that sense: *Sierra bighorn*, *Sierra Big Tree*, *Sierra creeper* and so on.

siesta In the south-west (and now anywhere in the United States), a nap. Borrowed from Spanish, it's pronounced see-ES-tuh.

siffleur A name given the marmot by the voyageurs, meaning 'whistler' in French. The French-Canadians used marmots as food.

sign camp Another name for a line camp, where line riders (or sign riders) lived while working. This term traces its lineage at least back to Charlie Siringo's *A Texas Cow-Boy*, but has apparently fallen into disuse.

sign language The method of hand signalling that Plains Indians, and later Anglos conversant with it, used to communicate in the absence of a common language. Each tribe had its own identifying signals, and trades could be arranged with sign language alone. Normally the term 'sign language' does not include gestures of communication intended to carry over substantial distances, such as waving a blanket, riding a horse in a circle, sending signals with smoke and so on.

Siksika The name of the Blackfeet proper, also called the North Blackfeet, not including the other tribes of the confederation.

silk (1) The whip used by a driver of a stagecoach. Thus the driver is known as a *silk-popper* or *knight of the silk*. (2) Among cowboys, a word for barbwire. [Adams] *Silk grass* is bear grass, *Yucca filamentosa*.

silver claim A mineral claim where the pay dirt is supposed to be silver.

silver exchange A jocular name for a gambling hall.

silvertip Another name for the grizzly bear. The beast is called a silvertip because the ends of its hairs are sometimes silvery, as though frosted.

simpatico Literally, sympathetic, but more than that – congenial, even endearing. Borrowed from Spanish and used mostly in the south-west, it's pronounced seem-PAH-tee-koh.

sing (1) An Indian ceremony for healing, casting out evil spirits, divining and the like, in which song has an important part. Used principally to refer to ceremonies of the Navajo, it may also mean rituals of other Indians, even Plains Indians, especially in these days of pantribalism.

Among the Navajo, a sing is given by a singer (shaman) elaborately trained for it – he will have memorised songs, chants, dances, sand paintings and other religious gestures, or all of these, that go on sometimes for more than a week. Examples are the Blessing Way, the *hatal* (a curing ceremony), the Mountain Change and the Beauty Way. The purpose is to restore harmony in the natural and spiritual worlds.

(2) The Navajo word *entah*, according to Cornelius Smith, is also translated 'sing'

but refers to an elaborate social get-together, with dancing, story-telling, games and contests and general good times.

singing to them A cowboy term for riding night guard on cows. The practice of singing while you rode was not a matter of lullabying the critters to sleep but of entertaining yourself and also letting them know you were nearby, so your approach wouldn't spook them and cause a stampede. One hand commented that the cowboy usually 'has a voice like a burro with a bad cold, and the noise he calls singin'd drive all the coyotes out of the country'.

single jack In mining, a heavy hammer with a short handle used for hand drilling.

single rig A saddle with just one cinch, which may be placed as far forward as the forks (the front end of the saddle) or as far back as the middle of the tree (saddle frame). Also known as *single-fire* or *single-barrelled*.

The Mexican saddle, father of all Western saddles, was Spanish rigged, that is, the single cinch hung directly down from the forks. The Texas cowboys, wanting to rope big, wild cows in difficult terrain and tie hard and fast and never have the saddle slide, added another cinch farther back, creating what was called the double rig. That saddle would stay put, regardless. (*See* tie-hard-and-fast man)

On the other hand, the early Californians thought the cinch hanging from the forks tended to slip forward and chafe the horse. They moved the cinch back to the middle, creating the centre-fire or California saddle (also known as the California rig). Later they experimented with moving it forward part way, giving us the five-eighths, three-quarters and seven-eighths styles. But they stuck to a single cinch.

Other rigging styles are: the Montana rig, with the cinch just forward of the centre-fire position; the seven-eighths rig, with the cinch placed well forward, but not as far as the rim-fire; and the rim-fire, with a single cinch well forward.

Today all these rigs are used. The double rig is preferred by the Texas cowboys who tie hard and fast, the single by the cowboys who dally. The double-rig crowd says the single rig lets the saddle whump you in the ass when the horse bucks. The single-rig crowd says a horse with a single rig doesn't buck as much.

single steer tying A rodeo competition that is not offered at most rodeos. As in calf roping, the animal is roped and thrown and its feet tied with a pigging string. But in single steer tying, the horse, not the cowboy, throws the roped animal – by running away from it. Also called *steer-roping*.

single-foot A horse's fast comfortable walk, also known as a single-foot rack. A horse with such a gait is called *single-footed* or a *single-footer*. To move or ride at this pace is called 'to single-foot'.

sink (1) A depression in the land surface where water has no outlet and simply stands. The word is usually applied to dry lake beds, where the evaporating water has left alkali and other mineral salts. The deserts of the Great Basin are full of such lake beds. (2) By extension, from the notion of water disappearing, where a stream goes underground is a *sinks*. Thus the spot above Lander, Wyoming, where the Popo Agie River goes beneath the surface (to reappear a half mile or so downstream), is known as the sinks.

sinker (1) A jocular word for a biscuit, which is also called a *hot rock* and a *sourdough bullet*. (In this century in many parts of the country, sinker has also come to mean dumplings, muffins and especially doughnuts.) (2) Among loggers, a log too heavy to float.

Sioux The Indians who call themselves Dakota. Although this word is a shortened form of the Ojibway word for enemy, the Dakota now use it officially. The adjective form is Siouan.

sisal A Mexican rope made from the fibre of the leaves of the agave. Like the maguey and rawhide lariat, the sisal gave way to the more popular rope of manila hemp.

Siskadee Name of the mountain men for the Green River; it means 'sage hen' and was borrowed from the Crow. The literature spells it with wonderful creativity – not only Siskadee but *Siskeedee, Seeds-ka-day, Seedskeeder* and so on.

This river was heaven on earth for the mountain men, who found in its country beaver a-plenty, more sage hens than you could beat off with a stick and friendly Indians, the Shoshones. Most of their rendezvous were held near or on the Siskadee.

Early travellers called it Spanish River. With the Colorado, it forms canyon country, culminating in the Grand Canyon.

sisters A word among the early Mormons for plural wives. Present-day saints often refer to each other as sister and brother.

siwash (1) A Chinook word for an Indian tribe of the Pacific north-west and the trade jargon they used. As used by Anglos, it was often derogatory. Other Anglo words for Indians were *feather-duster, gut-eater, hair-lifter, heap big chief, Lo, Mr John, redskin* and *scalp lifter*. (2) To bivouac, to camp in the open, without shelter. (3) To cook over an open fire with a stick. [Adams] (4) As an adjective, Indian; often meant in an uncomplimentary way. For instance, the *siwash side* of a horse is the wrong side, a *siwash outfit* a poor ranch.

Combinations: siwash tree (among loggers, used to change the direction of a cable), *siwash coat* (a long, loose gown worn by Siwash women), *siwash dollar* (a cylindrical shell used for money among the Siwashes) and *siwash onion* (an edible root of siwash country, known principally as camas).

Among cowboys, to be *siwashed* is to be blackballed. [Adams]

six-shooter The most common generic term for a revolver in the West, though five-shooters and four-shooters were also around. The name got fixed when the Texas rangers adopted the Colt version in 1847 and called it a six-shooter. Remington, Starr and Smith & Wesson also were well-known manufacturers, and .44 was perhaps the most common calibre. (The so-called navy revolvers were .36 calibre, since that was the official navy

bore.) In the years immediately after the Civil War, these weapons shot black powder and were set off by percussion caps; later they used self-contained cartridges, as modern weapons do. In *The Look of the Old West*, William Foster-Harris reminds us that hand weapons in those days were not called guns – that term was reserved for cannons. Other names for the kinds of revolvers cowboys carried were *belly gun, black-eyed Susan, blue lightning, coffee mill, Colt, cutter, dewey, dragoon, equaliser, flame-thrower, forty-five, forty-four, hog leg, life preserver, lightning conductor, lead chucker, navy, old cedar, one-eyed scribe, parrot-bill, peacemaker, pepperbox, persuader, plough handle, slip gun, six gun, smoke pole, smoke wagon, talking iron, thumb-buster* and *Walker*.

Six-shooter coffee is proper cowboy coffee, strong enough to float a six-shooter, and *six-shooter law* is the law of the gun.

sixteen-shooter A rifle with a magazine holding sixteen shots. This term came to suggest some special kind of mean. Thus W. S. James in *Cow-Boy Life in Texas* in 1898 speaks of 'some fiend incarnate tank[ed] up with "sixteen shooting liquor".'

six-weeks grass Any of various quick-growing grasses, especially in the south-west. An example is *Poa annua*.

size up To take the measure of a man or situation; to estimate his or its nature and especially strength. Early uses are in the *Santa Fe Weekly New Mexican* (1885) and Libby Custer's *Following the Guidon* (1890).

skate A lousy horse; a nag, a plug.

skid In logging, peeled poles laid so that logs can slide (be skidded) along them. In verb form, to do that skidding.

Combinations: skid greaser (the man who oils the poles to facilitate the sliding), *skid road* (the prepared skidding route) and *skidway* (poles on which logs are stacked).

Skidder may mean a man who skids logs, a steam engine that does the same thing (with the help of what was called a *skidder crew*) or the boss of a crew that builds skid roads.

skid road A district of derelicts and cheap bars, first called a *skidroad area*. According to linguist J. L. Dillard, 'The big skidroad in Seattle first attracted men and money and then honky-tonks and their usual accompaniments, thus becoming a bad area.' *Skid road* gave rise to the misnomer *skid row*.

skillet of snakes An Anglo cowboy's mocking description of the elaborate cattle brands used by Hispanics. Another name for them was *map of Mexico*.

skim diggings Shallow deposits of placer gold. Ramon Adams says these are also called *skin diggings*.

skimmy A calf raised on skim milk.

skin (1) To skin mules is to drive them; thus the driver is a *mule-skinner*. (2) To skin your gun is to draw it from a holster. [Adams]

Combinations: skin canoe (an occasional name for a bull boat), *skin lodge* (another word for a tipi), *skin trade* (the fur trade) and *skin string* (an occasional term for any rope made of rawhide).

skinner (1) A skinning knife. (2) A workman with a buffalo-hunting crew whose job was to skin the beasts. Usually the skinners made some key cuts and the robe was pulled off using mules or horses. (3) In Texas, a hand employed to skin cattle after a die-up. Winter was the skinning season. (4) Short for mule-skinner. (5) Nowadays short for buckskinner (mountain-man hobbyist). (6) In logging, a *cat skinner* is the man who drives a Caterpillar.

skinny skis Contemporary slang for cross-country skis; so called because they are narrower than downhill skis.

skipper Among loggers, a foreman. [Adams] (For more logging boss names, *see* supréme being)

skipping A show roper's trick of jumping into and out of a noose that's spinning vertically. [Adams]

skookum (1) A noun from the chinook trade jargon meaning a demon, evil spirit or disease. (2) As an adjective, strong or powerful.

A *skookum house* is a jail on an Indian reservation.

skull cracker What cowboys called a tomahawk. [Adams]

skunk egg An onion. [Adams]

skunk wagon A comical Wyoming and Montana name for an automobile. [Adams] Adams says an old Indian named Black Coal in Lander, Wyoming got a whiff of his first car and said, 'Heap skunk wagon', and that amused cattlemen picked it up. No one then could have known how prophetic Black Coal would turn out to be, for Yellowstone National Park is now skunk-wagon land.

sky farmer A farmer in arid country who ploughs and plants a piece of land that has no irrigation, hoping for manna from heaven. [Adams] Such a field, a huge one, lies on the south of the road between Shoshoni and Casper, Wyoming, on the high plains. Sometimes there's a crop, and sometimes there isn't. (*See* dry farming)

sky pilot One name cowboys used for a preacher. (*See* black robe for other such names)

skyline logging A technique of logging in which a heavy cable called a skyline (often two inches thick and over 2,000 feet long) is stretched between two spar trees. A powered carriage, called a sky hook, travels along the cable, hauling logs. The donkey engine that provides the power is a *swing donkey*, and the cable that guides the loading boom is the *swing line*. Also called *cable logging*, *highline logging*, *aerial logging* and *aerial skidding*.

slab (1) A person's rib. Cowboys called people with their ribs showing *slab-sided*. (2) A paved road. Mathews identifies it as a Westernism.

slack In today's over-booked rodeos, a means of letting contestants compete outside the normal hours, usually early in the day or after the paying crowd has gone home.

slash (1) In logging, the residue left on the ground after cutting – tops of trees, branches, stumps, twigs, bark and leaves. The debris left by a wind storm is called *wind slash*. (2) An earmark – a diagonal slit.

slave   Among loggers, a man who works for wages. The *slave driver* is the foreman, especially a tough one. He's also called a *slave pusher* or *slave puncher*. A *slave market* is an employment office.

sleep   A day, as 'The big bend of the Wind River is seven sleeps away.' Used by Anglos in imitation of the manner of some Indians in measuring time. This frontier expression dates to early colonial times, so is not a Westernism. Likewise *moon* and *winter* mean month and year.

sleeper   A calf in the midst of being cleverly rustled. Here's how it worked: New calves were branded and earmarked to establish ownership. In the days of the open range, if a cowboy saw a slick (a calf that wasn't branded and earmarked) sucking at one of his outfit's cows, he would stop and do the job. The rustler's first task was to make it look like these matters had been taken care of when they hadn't. So he'd make a sleeper: he'd earmark the calf properly but brand it lightly or not at all, or pluck the hairs instead of burning them. Until weaning time, the calf would stick with its mother, and the cowboys would mostly just look at the ears, which stuck up conveniently, instead of making a hard examination of the brand. When the calf left its mother, the rustler would slap his own brand on, re-cut the earmark into a different shape and declare himself the proud owner of the little critter. In those days, he didn't even have to take it away. He'd wait for roundup, and when the calves were sorted (cut) by brand, the sleepered calves would be herded in with his. This process was known as *sleepering*.

A brand unknown on a particular range is a *sleeper brand*.

sleeve gun   A hideout gun (a small, concealed pistol) in a gambler's sleeve. [Adams]

slick   (1) A maverick; an orejano; an unbranded calf, which is called a slick or slick-ear because it isn't earmarked. Unbranded horses are also known as slicks. A slick is sometimes called a full ear. In the days of the open range, calves were sometimes missed in the spring roundup and turned up as slicks at the next roundup. Men who made a practice of branding slicks were considered enterprising in the early West and called rustlers later on. (2) Sometimes a fat cow, especially one with no calf. Since she's not giving suck, her hair is shiny and glossy-slick.

slick fork   Narrow shoulders on a saddle; the opposite of *swell fork*, or fork with projections on each side of the horn.

slickens   The residue from hydraulic mining. This powdery soil washed downstream from the gold fields. It so degraded the water and the land downstream that legislatures enacted strict environmental standards.

slickensides   Among miners, the smooth, polished surface of the vein or its walls.

slicker   An oilskin coat to ward off the rain, carried by many cowboys tied behind the cantle (the raised back of the saddle seat). Also called a *fish*. A cowboy's bedroll wrapped in his slicker is a *slicker roll*.

Horses are sometimes *slicker-broke* – the slicker is dropped off the left side of the horse. When the horse learns not to kick at it, he'll also be less spooky in general, less of a shadow jumper.

slick-heeled   Among cowboys, descriptive of a man who's not wearing spurs.

slick-rock   The red sandstone of the canyon country of the Four Corners (the area where Utah, Colorado, New Mexico and Arizona meet), hundreds upon hundreds of miles of bare rock to walk upon, rise and fall with, wander through. It is the skeleton of the earth exposed beneath the soft flesh of its soil, hard, sculpted over centuries by the ever-whispering wind, flowing, undulating, swelling, soaring, grand beyond human comprehension, speaking to us of time and eternity.

slide   (1) In logging, a chute for moving logs, usually a rough path down a mountainside. (2) In mining, a 'vertical dislocation of a lode'. [Adams] (3) An occasional word for a branding chute.

sliding leather blind A leather strap that covers a horse's eyes, used on a horse by a bronc buster to immobilise the critter long enough to get the saddle on and get mounted. Then the rider slid the band up the headstall, and all hell broke loose.

According to Jim Bramlett in *Ride for the High Points*, the peelers (bronc busters) in the old days were mostly breaking full-grown horses unaccustomed to human beings and soon learned that a shirt or bandanna tied over the beast's eyes gave the rider a little edge. Then they refined that into a three-inch-wide sliding leather band, which moved up to become a browband when not in use.

sling In packing, a manila rope about 30 feet long used to tie the packs together on the mule's back. [Adams] As a verb, it means to do such tying, as in *slinging the load*, *cross-slinging*, *double-slinging* and *double-cross-slinging*.

sling his head What a horse may do to object to pressure from the bit, which means he isn't neck-reining properly. Says Max Evans, in his fine comic novel *The Rounders*, 'If you have to turn a horse by force and pressure from the bit only, you are going to ruin his mouth. He will get high-headed and start slinging his head. That kind of horse is a disgrace to any cowboy.'

sling joint Among loggers, to work with your hands.

sling lead To shoot your gun, at least in movies and books.

slip gun A pistol fixed to fire when the thumb is slipped off the hammer. [Adams] Usually the trigger was rendered non-functional, the spur on the hammer lowered and the barrel sawn off so the pistol would fit in a pants pocket. *Slip shooting* is firing a gun by thumbing the hammer, which is more accurate than fanning. [Adams] (*See* fan)

slipped his hobbles Said of a horse that has gotten out of its hobbles or a human being who 'has fallen from grace'. [Adams]

slope In states on or near the continental divide, the terms 'eastern slope' and 'western slope' designate one side or the other of that high country. In Colorado, for instance, the folks on the western slope often complain that they don't get the consideration due them in state political matters because most of the population is on the eastern slope in cities such as Denver. Thus *eastern sloper*, *western sloper*, *Pacific sloper* and so on. Adams says that people who lived on the Pacific Coast were called *slopers*.

Slota The Dakota name for Red River metis.

slouch hat A wide-brimmed hat of soft felt, very common in the West in the decade after the Civil War, perhaps the most common hat of all. Also worn in the 1870s were the bowler, the homburg, the plug hat and even the high silk hat. Social distinctions were naturally made according to the hat you wore, fur indicating high status and wool low, because wool was cheaper and held its shape poorly. (*See also* stetson)

slow elk Beef from another man's cow, taken without his consent. It was said of many an old-time cattleman that he never tasted his own beef, unless it was at another man's table. Also known as *big antelope*.

slug (1) A nugget of gold or other precious metal. (2) A big gold coin issued privately in California around 1850.

sluice (1) In placer mining, a long, inclined trough or series of riffle boxes for washing gold-bearing dirt. Gravel and sand were shovelled in at the top and washed down, cleats on the bottom catching the gold. (*See also* flume and long tom)

Combinations: sluice box (a riffle box), *sluicing claim* (a claim where sluice mining is done), *sluice fork* (a sluicing tool), *sluice head* (enough water to flush out a sluice), *sluice mine*, *sluice mining*, *sluice process*, *sluice robbing*, *sluice tailing* (a tailing of sluice dirt), *sluice trough* (a sluice) and *sluiceway* (a sluice).

(2) In logging, a trough that floats logs downhill; also called a *flume*, *water slide* and *wet slide*. The *sluicer* is the logger who helps push the logs through. As a verb, it

means to do such washing down of dirt or logs. But to *get sluiced* is to be caught in a rush of logs out of control.

slum-gullion (1) Stew of meat and vegetables, especially potatoes and onions, also called *slum* and known for its mongrel vigour. Thus the fine Western essayist Edward Abbey called one of his collections *Slum-gullion Stew*. Its quality is suggested by its origin, which is the next meaning. (2) The mud that comes out of the downhill end of sluices.

small-loop man Among cowboys, a roper who used a small loop, as brush poppers (brush-country cowboys) did.

smart aleck A know-it-all. Also spelled *smart Aleck* or even *smarty*. The adjective form is *smart-alecky*.

smart as a whip Very clever; first used in Salt Lake City in 1860.

Smith & Wesson A pistol invented by gunsmiths Horace Smith and Daniel B. Wesson and made in Springfield, Massachusetts by the firm Smith & Wesson. Though the firm was innovative – it was the first (in 1857) in its field to use a metal cartridge – and the pistols were popular, they were never as much in demand with Westerners, or with the army, as the colt.

(For the many words the cowboy used for his pistol, *see* six shooter)

smoke (1) Among the Indians generally, to have a council. (2) A smoke among Indians or mountain men or other Anglos could be a social occasion, time spent smoking pipes and talking. *Smoke the peace pipe* is an Anglo expression for making a treaty with Indians or just making up with a friend. (3) To subject something to smoke. Meat smoked would dry and take on a smoky flavour. Hide would harden, perhaps for a shield made of hide. (4) Among the Sauk and Fox Indians, to *smoke a horse* was a custom by which one acquired a horse via a ceremony. (5) Among the Cherokees and perhaps the other Five Civilised Tribes, to *smoke someone* means to use medicine (usually smoking tobacco) against someone. (6) Among cowboys, a smoke came to mean not only a cigarette but a short

break, a period of relaxation spent smoking.

To *smoke out cattle* is to chase them out of brush or other hiding places by shooting. A horse that *smokes its pipe* has a torn lip where the bit sits. [Adams]

smoke pole Originally a pistol; now, among buckskinners, a muzzle-loading rifle. (*See* six-shooter) To *smoke up* is to shoot.

smoke signal A genuine long-distance communication, Indian-style, or informally any sort of signal.

smoky Shady, devious, snaky.

smooth out the humps To take the rough edges off a horse [Adams], something a mount often needs in the spring after a winter of not being ridden. (*See* break a horse) A *smooth horse* is an unshod one, and a *smooth-mouthed horse* is 10 years old or older and has teeth worn down with age.

smudge Among contemporary Indians, to use smoke or steam in a ceremonial manner, especially for purification. In the sweat lodge, for instance, participants waft steam rising from the hot rocks on to their bodies. People also pass sacred objects through smoke from burning cedar.

snaffle bit A bridle bit; like a bar (one piece) bit but made of two pieces joined flexibly in the middle.

snag (1) A tree or branch obstructing a river and dangerous to navigation; a sawyer or planter. (2) In logging, a standing dead tree consisting mostly of a trunk; if less than 20 feet high, it's called a stub. (3) A plug, a skate, a skin – a worthless horse. (4) As a verb, to cut away snags, whether in the water or on land. (5) To get snagged means 'to get caught on a snag in the river'. (6) *Snaggy* described a river full of snags.

snail Among cowboys, to drag with a rope. [Adams]

snake Another name for the Shoshone Indians, generally thought to have come from the sinuous sign language gesture for that tribe. The gesture, which meant weaver, was misinterpreted to mean snake.

snake A longhorn left in the brush after most have been gathered.

Combinations: snake's alarm clock (his rattles), *snake blood* (meanness), *snake eater* and *snake killer* (a road-runner), *snake-headed* (a mean, ornery man), *snake hole* (in mining, a bore hole), *snake fence* (a zig-zag fence of rails, built without posts) and *snake a critter out* (to haul him out of the bog with a rope).

snake dance A ceremony of the Hopi Indians performed in alternate years for eight days to bring rain. The handling of live rattlesnakes by dancers during the final day of the dance, followed by the release of the reptiles, has made it much remarked on by outsiders; but much of the ceremony takes place in the kiva.

snake-head whiskey Rotgut whiskey, reputedly made with ingredients that included the heads of snakes; other reptilian words for whiskey are *snake juice*, *snake poison* and *snake water*. (*See* firewater)

snaky Descriptive of a man who's devious, shady, treacherous.

snare To catch something with a rope, especially a cow you've come on unexpectedly.

snipe In logging, to trim the end of a log. The rounded end is referred to as *snipe-nosed*.

snipe-gutted Among cowboys, said of a horse or other critter that's slender in the barrel. [Adams]

snirt A word for the mixture of mud and dirt you get on the northern plains in the spring; a nicely inventive coinage.

snooper A cowboy who spotted another man's hideout bottle (hidden liquor bottle) at a dance and sneaked a snort or two. [Adams]

snoose Among loggers and sheep-herders, a strong, moist variety of snuff introduced to the West by Scandinavian loggers, sometimes called *Scandihoovian dynamite*, *Swedish condition powder*, *rest powder* or *heifer dust*.

snorty Said of a contrary or belligerent cow, of an irascible man and of a high-spirited horse.

snow (1) An Indian Pidgin English term for year; another translation is *winter* – an Indian would speak of something that happened four snows or winters ago. (*See also* sleep) (2) What a miner calls a dusting from the roof that augurs a cave-in. (3) The West has various terms for forms and qualities of snow, which are of particular interest to skiers: *corn snow* (a heavy, granular spring snow), *hominy snow* (a term born in Kansas for a granular snow, like hominy grits), *powder snow* (a dry, fluffy snow adored by *powder hounds*) and *sugar snow* (loose unconsolidated snow). In Jackson Hole fresh powder brings people outside the way sunshine does in Seattle.

snow surveyor A government worker who measures the amount of snow in the mountains as a means of predicting how much water will be available for irrigation the following summer. Thus the combinations *snow survey* and *snow surveying*.

snowbird (1) A soldier of the period of the Indian Wars who enlisted for the winter for the sake of food, clothing and shelter and deserted in the spring. (2) An Arizona term for folks who desert cold climates for Arizona in the winter. *Sunbirds* make the reverse trip, leaving Arizona in the summer.

snowmobile A machine for travel over snow, with runners in front and a bogie wheel in the rear. It travels well on unploughed roads and through trackless country. Though used mostly for recreation, snowmobiles are also used in the West for transportation to remote ranches and for work such as running trap lines. This word is not a native Westernism. A related word is *biler*, short for snowmobiler.

snowshoe An early Western term for a ski. The verb *snowshoe* and noun *snowshoer* thus require caution – they sometimes meant 'to ski' and 'skier'. (The use of this word to mean a racket-like device lashed to the foot for travelling over snow in winter is as much Eastern as Western.)

Combinations: snowshoe dance (a ceremony of some Indians performed after the first snow of each winter), *snowshoe disease* or *snowshoe evil* (inflammation and swelling of tendons stressed by snowshoes) and *snowshoe rabbit* (a Rocky Mountain hare, *Lepus bairdi*).

snub; snub up (1) To tie an animal with a short rope to either a post or a saddle horn. You do this to a calf or cow you want to control and especially to a horse that's going to buck when you get on him. (2) To dehorn cattle. (3) In logging, to use a brake drum (a *snubber*) and a cable (a *snubbing line*) to keep a log being skidded downhill from getting out of control.

Combinations: snubbing post (a stout timber set in the ground in a corral to snub wild critters to) and *snub horse* (in rodeo, the horse used for snubbing; the cowboy is the *snubber*).

snuffy Descriptive of cattle or horses that are wild and spirited and likely to cause trouble.

sny A word of the Missouri and Mississippi Rivers signifying a narrow passage between the shore and an island. Pronounced SNY, it derives from the French *chenal* (channel) through the French-Canadian *chenail* (which is pronounced shuh-NY).

soak Among cowboys, to rest, to loaf.

soapweed Any one of several plants in the west and south-west used by Indians and Anglo pioneers to make soap, especially yucca. *Soap apple* (also called *soap bulb*) was a California plant used for soap. Others, especially the *palmilla* of the south-west, were called *soap plant*. *Soap wort* is another name for soapweed, and *soap ball* refers to the flowery head of yuccas.

sobre paso A slow trot of a horse. [Adams] A south-western expression borrowed from Spanish, it is pronounced SOH-bray PAH-soh.

sobrecincha A south-western term for a surcingle, cinch or girth, according to Cornelius Smith. The band or strap that passes under a horse's or mule's belly to hold a saddle or pack on. Borrowed from the Spanish (where it has the same

meaning), it is pronounced soh-bray-SEEN-chah.

sod corn Indian corn, which needed little water; the whiskey made from that corn.

sod house A soddy. A *sod house claim* was claim of public land with a sod house on it. A *sod fence* was a wall on the plains made of sod and dirt.

soda (1) As an adjective, soda is often an equivalent of alkaline, or mineral-salt. Thus a *soda spring* is an alkaline spring, a *soda butte* a hill in alkali country, a *soda lake* a dry lake with a salt bed and a *soda prairie* a prairie of mineral-salt soil. (2) In faro, the first card, the one turned face up. The last card is called the *hock*, giving rise to the expression from *soda to hock*, meaning all of it, from soup to nuts, from *a to z*.

soda sinker A doughnut made with soda.

soddy (1) A sod house, a primitive plains dwelling built from the turf itself. About half an acre was stripped of sod, which was cut in three-foot lengths and stacked like brick. Some soddies were combined with dugouts, that is, part of the house was dug into a hill. The inside was always a problem – the ceiling leaked water during rains and dropped dust when the sun was shining. Such were the first homes of many homesteaders. (2) A homesteader, because many of them lived in soddies. Also called a sodbuster. (*See* granger for other names)

sod-pawing mood A cowboy's expression for anger, because that's the way snorty bulls acted. [Adams]

sod-soaker A good rain.

sofky Among the Creek Indians, hominy, often flavoured with wild meat. They prepared this dish during their time in the South and after the forced migration to Oklahoma.

soft Said of a horse that wears out easily, that has little endurance. *Soft-mouthed* is a term for a horse that's sensitive to the bit, just as sweet-mouthed is.

soft grub What a cowboy called fancy food; hotel food. Also called *fluff duffs*.

sold his saddle Said of a cowman or cowboy who's hit bottom, who's lost his status. The bottom might be financial – he went belly-up; or personal – he went crazy; or moral – he sold us out. Philip A. Rollins told an apt story in *The Cowboy*: 'A school kid in Montana, asked by his teacher who Benedict Arnold was, answered, "He was one of our generals and he sold his saddle." '

sold to halter An expression for a horse being sold with absolutely no guarantee.

solo A card game. Owen Wister described it as new when he played it with some army officers in Arizona in 1895.

sombrero A hat, especially a cowboy hat and more especially a Mexican style of hat that used to be common in the south-west. It had a high-curved wide brim, a sugar-loaf crown dented at the top and a long, loose chin strap. Like cowboy hats generally, it kept off the sun and rain, fended off the branches and served as a handy bucket or cup. Borrowed from Spanish, it is pronounced sohm-BRAYR-oh.

some An adjective of admiration, especially among the mountain men, as in, 'He was some hoss.' Sometimes it was used as an emphatic positive, as in, 'That hoss could shoot some.'

son-of-a-bitch stew A spicy stew of marrow-gut from a freshly killed calf, said to have gotten started because calves couldn't keep up on trail drives and so were expendable. Adams says that the liver, tongue, kidneys, heart, sweetbreads and brains were used, plus any vegetables that were handy. Jean Burroughs writes in *New Mexico* magazine that it 'contained the vital parts and everything edible but the "hair, horns and holler".' Of course, there were as many versions as there were cookies to cook it.

The name varied. When female ears were present, it was *son-of-a-gun stew*. And after the jurisprudence system arrived and proved to be even more political than it is today, the dish naturally came to be called *district attorney*.

Maybe some purveyor of the *nouvelle cuisine* will revive this fine, traditional Western offering and call it a veal dish, which will be worth a chuckle.

son-of-a-bitch-in-a-sack Dough and dried fruit sewed into a sack and steamed. One authority suggests the name came from the difficulty of making it. Also called, of course, *son-of-a-gun-in-a-sack*.

sonora A California expression for a winter rain that comes from the south, the direction of the Mexican state of Sonora.

Sonoran Desert The hottest of the American deserts and the desert with the widest variety of plant life. Located in southern Arizona and California and northern Mexico, it is home of the saguaro, the ocotillo, the mesquite, the organ-pipe cactus and the palo verde.

Sonoratown In the south-west, a town's Mexican quarter. One writer tells us, 'In most cases, the Chinatowns had developed around the adobe huts of Sonoratowns.'

Sons of Dan A vigilante organisation of Mormon men and a scourge of the Church's opponents and of apostates. The name alludes to Genesis 49:17 – 'Dan shall be a serpent by the way, an adder in the path . . . ' Members were also known as the *Danites*, *Big Fan*, *Shanpips*, the *Destroying Angels* and *Daughters of Gideon*. Their job was sometimes to save people, in that deft usage where 'to save' means 'to liquidate'. They were organised in the late 1830s in Missouri, in response to persecutions by non-Mormons there.

sooner (1) In general, a person who jumped the gun, who got some place too soon. The term applied particularly to people who claimed land in the Cherokee Strip before it was legally open or to premature claimants of any Oklahoma Indian land or any land reserved to Indians. That tendency came to be known as *soonerism*. Oklahomans still call themselves sooners. (2) Men who branded ahead of the roundup. [Adams] In the days of the open range, the cattlemen's associations would set dates for the roundup in each area, but some hustlers would work the cows ahead of the roundup to get any mavericks and slicks (unbranded calves) for themselves.

soopollalie   A north-westernism for the buffalo berry (a shrub – *Shepherdia canadensis* – with an edible, but bitter, red berry). It is from the Chinook jargon word *olallie* and is pronounced soo-puh-LA-lee.

sop   What old-time Westerners called gravy. In a boarding house, says Libby Custer in *Following the Guidon*, 'an Eastern man, a "tenderfoot", on one occasion asked someone to pass the gravy, whereupon the bouncer placed his pistol on the table and quietly remarked, "Any man as calls sop gravy has got to eat dust or 'pologise." '

Cowboys called the cookie *sop and taters*. Loggers call sop *goozlam*. [Adams]

sopaipilla   A Hispanic fritter, deep-fried in fat, like a buñuelo. Borrowed from Spanish, it's pronounced soh-puh-PEE-yuh.

sorrel   A reddish brown horse with mane and tail of the same colour, unlike a bay, which has a black mane and tail. (*See* buckskin for other horse colours)

sotana   A south-western term for a robe, a cassock; Bret Harte speaks of a priest's sotana. Borrowed from the Spanish, it's pronounced soh-TAH-nah.

sotol   A south-western plant similar in appearance to the yuccas. The plant (*Dasylirion*) is long-leaved and was used (according to J. Frank Dobie) for torches and for fibres and food. Also a fermented drink of the poor, similar to pulque. Borrowed from Mexican Spanish (which in turn borrowed it from Aztec), it is pronounced soh-TOHL. Sometimes called the desert spoon.

sound the horn   To grab the saddle horn when your horse bucks. Also known as *choke the horn and claw the leather*.

sourdough   From the original meaning, bread dough with active fermentation, come Western meanings and combinations: (1) An old hand, a fellow who's alkalied (adapted to the country), likely an old-timer (speaking in strictly relative terms) and likely a prospector. In this sense, the word had its greatest currency in Alaska and the Northwest Territories.

He got this name because he ate (perhaps essentially lived on) bread made from sourdough. (2) A bachelor. (3) Among cowboys, a cook [Adams], or simply a bachelor.

Combinations: sourdough biscuit, sourdough bread, sourdough bullet (a biscuit), *sourdough keg* (the container for sourdough), *sourdough pants* (blanket-lined pants for northern plains winters), *sourdough rolls* and *sourdough starter* (a piece of fermenting dough used to set a new batch of dough to fermenting).

sour-mouth   What a cowboy calls a horse who worries at the bit. He ends up hard-mouthed.

souvenir   A States egg too old to be eaten; that is, an egg shipped out from the United States proper (when the West was mostly territories) that's gotten hoary.

sovereign squatter   A settler in Kansas in the 1850s who thumbed his nose at Stephen A. Douglas's notion of 'popular sovereignty', the doctrine that each new state should choose to be a free or slave state by popular vote. The *sovereign squats* (or *squatters*) held out for free-state status.

spade bit   A long, wide bit that fills a horse's mouth. One of the great debates of Western horsemen is the curb bit versus the spade bit. Early-day cowboys of Texas and the plains used the curb bit in breaking and riding their horses, rode them tight-reined and regarded the spade bit as too hard on a horse. They also didn't spend much time breaking their horses. The Californios and the descendants of the buckaroos took more time to break their horses, using hackamores, riding them loose-reined, and graduating to a spade bit. Old Hand Jo Mora, conceding that each way has its points, nevertheless wrote in *Trail Dust and Saddle Leather*, 'On a horse that's been properly broken and reined with a hackamore, bitted by a good hand, and ridden by a loose-rein stockman who knows what it's all about, I consider the spade bit tops.' Mora adds that the bit is cruel only in the hands of the unskilled. One cowboy name (surely derisive) for a spade bit was *stomach pump*.

Spanish dollar A silver Spanish American coin worth eight reales (*see* real), valued as hard currency.

Spanish grant A land grant (often very large) from the government of Spain.

Spanish horse The Barb brought to the New World by the Spaniards. A kind of big pony, it weighed on average 600 pounds and stood under 14 hands high. It was the horse of the Plains Indians, and they showed spectacularly what it could do. Though sometimes dismissed by Anglos as a runt and a mongrel (and associated with 'those dirty Injuns'), it made a terrific reputation as a cowpony because it was tough and sturdy. It also was the ancestor of the mustang. Says Jo Mora in *Trail Dust and Saddle Leather*, 'The Spanish horse should have been called the American horse. He certainly rated that honour. He was the very first equine to set foot on American soil, and his get populated practically the entire hemisphere.' (*See also* cayuse)

Spanish figures in other horse terms: *Spanish bit* (a bit similar to a spade bit, with a high port), *Spanish rig* (a saddle with the cinch hung straight down from the forks, the style of the old Mexican saddle [*see* single-rig]), *Spanish saddle* (a saddle from Mexico, usually heavy, elaborate and decked out with silver), *Spanish spurs* (a spur favoured by many Mexican riders, with a long shank and sharply pointed rowels), *Spanish trot* (an easy swinging trot), *Spanish cattle* (properly, the black cattle running wild in Texas at the beginning of American settlement; loosely, any cattle of Mexican origin), *Spanish fever* (another name for Texas fever, a cow disease caused by the cattle tick) and *Spanish Trail* (a cattle trail that went from Texas to New Orleans, a cattle trail from Texas to California and a mission trail through Utah and Nevada to California).

Plants using the word Spanish are: *Spanish bayonet* (one of several species of yucca, particularly *Yucca aloifolia*), *Spanish dagger* (a yucca) and *Spanish needle* (porcupine grass, an irritant to the mouths of horses and cattle).

Spanish brick is an Anglo word for adobe

and *Spanish monte* is another name for the gambling game monte.

Spanish River The Green River.

speck A prospector's short version of the verb 'to prospect'. [Adams]

Spencer A lever-action, repeating rifle (often a carbine) invented by C. M. Spencer, popular in the West in .52 and .56 calibres in the post-Civil War period.

spick A derogatory word for a Mexican or Mexican-American. Also spelled *spic* and *spik*. (For similar words, *see* greaser)

spider (1) Among loggers, a little tool that checks the set of sawteeth. [Adams] (2) A socket attached to the cinch ring on the offside to serve as a rifle scabbard.

spike Usually a young bull elk with spike-like, unbranched antlers. He's also called a *spike* (or *spiked*) *bull*. A young buck (also called a *spike buck*) with spike-like antlers. Historically, a young buffalo bull with short horns.

spike a tree To commit a contemporary form of monkey-wrenching (sabotaging), driving spikes into trees that may be sold or have been sold for cutting. According to the head monkey-wrencher himself, the late Edward Abbey, 'One spike in a log can strip the teeth from a ten-thousand-dollar circular saw, put a crimp in profits, deter further logging, and thus preserve those living breathing respirating trees whose right to continued existence is at least as legitimate as that of any other creature including, but not limited to, the human.' No doubt others have other opinions, but the author is not obliged to quote them, and Abbey will rest more peacefully if I don't.

spike team (1) A team of three draft animals hitched with one in front of the others. (2) Five draft animals pulling a stagecoach, hitched with the heaviest two at the rear and the lightest one alone in front. [Adams]

spike your horse's tail What a cowboy does when he brings his horse to such a sudden stop that it sits right down on its tail. [Adams]

spinner Among rodeo cowboys, a horse with an inclination to buck in tight circles, which makes the rider dizzy and soon puts him in the dirt.

spirit trail   In Navajo weaving, a line of contrasting yarn that runs from the central motif to the edge of the piece. Navajos in particular have a taboo against designs that form an unbroken border, whether in weaving, basket making or other crafts. The simple explanation was that the maker's soul might be trapped in the piece, so the spirit trail provided an escape. Spider woman gave the Navajo weaving and its associated lore – hence the alternate term spider trail. In early times a small hole was often left in the centre of a weaving or basket for similar reasons.

spiritual   A synonym for sealed one, a woman sealed to a Mormon man in celestial marriage. In full, *spiritual wife*. In practice, in the days of plural marriage, it was used to mean a wife beyond the first. Mormon wives referred to each other as sister. In the 19th century some Mormon women were spiritual wives of past leaders such as Joseph Smith and Brigham Young. The custom of having spiritual wives is known as spiritual wifery.

spiritual widower   A California expression meaning 'a married man who is away from home chasing gold'. The woman he left behind was called a *California widow*.

spit   Among miners, a lighted fuse. To light the fuses for the blast is to *spit a round*.

splash   A head of water released suddenly to wash logs downstream. Previously it would have been held back by a *splash dam*.

splatter dabs   A cowboy word for pancakes, which he also called *hen-fruit stir*.

split   (1) An earmark consisting of a split in an animal's ear, reaching neither the tip nor the head. [Adams] (2) In rodeo, for a pair of contestants to agree to pool their winnings and share equally. [Adams]

split the tail   To cut a cow's tail lengthwise, a practice once believed to prevent blackleg, usually a fatal disease.

spoiled herd   Among cattlemen, a herd inclined to take any excuse to stampede.

spoiled horse   A horse mistreated while getting broke and so ruined.

Spokane   A tribe of Salishan Indians that historically lived below the falls on the Spokane River in Washington. They subsisted primarily on salmon. After the Northwest Company established Spokane House at the mouth of the Little Spokane River, the chief's son, Spokane Garry, went to the Red River Settlements to learn Anglo culture. He later taught some of his people how to read, build log cabins and grow some crops. During the gold rushes of the area in the 1850s, troubles arose between the Spokanes and the whites but passed without major incident. The Spokanes were put on a reservation in their historical country, where they live today.

spook   To frighten horses, cattle or other critters. They're then spooky – jumpy, nervous.

spool your bed   Among cowboys, to get your bed rolled and ready to go.

spoon   (1) To turn over in your sleep. In the West, two men sometimes slept spoon-fashion in a small space. When one man wanted to turn over, he would tell the other to spoon. (2) Among miners, a rod for cleaning drill holes. [Adams]

spotted pup   Rice pudding; rice or tapioca cooked with raisins.

spotter   Among loggers, a man who spies for the company.

spraddle horns   Among cowboys, longhorn cattle. For a cowboy to get *spraddled out* was for him to be dressed up in his Sunday-go-to-meeting clothes. [Adams]

spread   A ranch – land, buildings, hands and critters together. Used to identify a kind of ranch, as in *sheep spread*, or its owner, as in the *Chisum spread*.

spread the mustard   Among cowboys, to put on airs. [Adams]

spreader dam   A dam of earth used to make surface run-off spread out rather than form a gully.

spree   This word sometimes occurs in the West as a verb. Thus Owen Wister writes, 'Hank bein' all trembly from spreein' it in town, he says . . . '; A similar expression is *on a high lonesome*.

spring Among cowmen, to be about to calve. A cow *springing heavy* is near her time, and a *springing heifer* is carrying her first calf. A *springer* is any cow carrying a calf.

Spring range is the grazing ground for cows that's used before they're driven to their summer ranges. Cattle that are skinny from the winter are called *spring poor*. The *spring roundup*, also called the calf roundup, is primarily for branding new calves. The fall roundup is primarily for gathering cows for market or moving them to winter range.

A *spring creek* is fed by a spring rather than run-off or snowmelt; often sought in the West as excellent for trout-fishing because it is clear all year round.

A *spring wagon* is a light wagon whose wheels were set individually on springs. Watts says such a wagon 'was something of a luxury in a land of rough trails and rutted roads'.

Springfield A rifle made at Springfield, Massachusetts by the United States Armory and used by the US Army from the Civil War to World War I. The most common Springfield in the West was the Trap Door, a single-shot model adopted by the army in 1873.

spud (1) Among loggers, a hand tool for stripping bark from felled trees. (2) In oil drilling, to drill the first 50 or 60 feet of a hole with a drill attached to a rope and a drum. Such a rig is called a *spudder*. Nowadays, spud simply means starting the hole.

spur Though all spurs consist of a heelband, a shank and a rowel, the Western versions of these devices for giving the get-go to a horse are various. Historically, the main differences were between two styles – the Plains style, east of the Rockies, and the Californio style, in California, the south-west generally and buckaroo country. In general, the California spur was bigger and fancier, the Plains spur smaller and simpler. Sometimes the old Californios wore spurs

so curved they couldn't walk in them.

The *spur leather*, also called a *spur strap*, is the piece that goes over a rider's instep to hold it in place, and sometimes it's decoratively tooled, carved or ornamented with conchas. The *spur chains*, usually two or three of them, go under the arch. People who don't ride sometimes assume that spurs are cruel, especially big ones. In fact, they're only as severe as the man using them, and the ones with more points prick less. They're used as reminders and emergency starters. Other words for spurs are *buzz saw, California drag rowels, can opener, cartwheel, Chihuahuas, diggers, gad, galves, gooseneck, grappling irons, gut hooks, gut lancers, gut wrenches, hell-rousers, hooks, Kelleys, pet-maker, persuader, rib wrenches, steel, star rowel, sunburst, sunset rowel, tin belly* and *wagon-spoke rowel*.

square deal In card-playing, a fair game. The term arose from the dealer's using a pack of square-edged cards, which are harder to cheat with. By extension, any kind of fair arrangement. A square deal was Teddy Roosevelt's slogan in the 1904 campaign. When the term square is applied to a man, it is a compliment meaning that he's straightforward and trustworthy.

squatter (1) A person who claimed land without legal rights was called a squatter, often a term meant and taken unkindly in the West because squatters accelerated the breaking up of the open range. (2) In Texas, a longhorn that hid out in the brush during the roundup.

Combinations: squatters' association (an organisation of squatters, created to give credibility to the claims of squatters), *squatter's deed* (a claim to first right when an area was opened to settlement), *squatter law* (a structure of law made by squatters for their mutual protection), *squatter* or *squatter's right* (the legitimacy of a squatter's claim) and *squatter sovereignty* (the right of squatters to govern themselves and their right to their claims).

The land you squatted on was your squat. A *squatteree* was a squatter's cabin. *Squatterism* meant the ways of squatters. *Squatterphobia* was antagonism to squatter sovereignty.

squaw (1) An Indian woman. Used teasingly, it can also mean an Anglo woman. This word started life as an Algonquian term meaning 'wife', then became part of the lingua franca developed by eastern Indians for purposes of trading and was carried west by frontiersmen, according to linguist J. L. Dillard in *All-American English*. The Plains Indians saw it as a white man's word and found it objectionable and almost all contemporary Indians find it objectionable. (2) To get squawed was to marry an Indian woman; hence the expression *squaw man*.

Combinations: squaw axe (a small axe of the Indian trade, used mostly for splitting wood), *squaw blanket* (a trade blanket), *squaw camp* (a camp of Indian women and children while the men were out fighting or hunting), *squaw dance* (an Indian dance where the squaws chose their partners), *squaw fire* (a small fire), *squaw horse* (an Anglo word for a horse not worth having), *squaw medicine* (an Anglo word meaning 'Indian quackery'), *squaw pony* (among US soldiers, a horse fit only for carrying loads, not men), *squaw saddle* (a blanket or quilt rigged out as saddle, after the fashion of Indian women's saddles), *squaw side* (the off side, the wrong side for getting on a horse; also called *Indian side*), *squaw talk* (women's talk), *squaw wind* (a chinook), *squaw winter* (a little winter preceding an Indian summer) and *squaw wood* (light, easily gathered wood used for cooking).

Plants: squaw carpet (*ceanothus*, a shrub of the buckthorn family, common in the Sierra Nevada), *squaw corn* (soft-grained, multi-coloured Indian corn), *squaw currant* (*Ribes cereum*), *squaw grass* (bear grass, also known as *squaw lily, Xerophyllum tenax*), *squaw root* (one of various plants believed to have worth as a medicine or a food, especially *Canopholis Americana*), *squawweed* (one of several plants – a ragwort, *Senecio obovatus*, used medicinally; horseweed, *Erigeron canadensis* or any of the *squawberry*), *squaw cabbage* (miner's cabbage, *Montia parviflora*, also called *Indian lettuce*; also the desert trumpet, *Eriogonum inflatum*), *squawberry* (a bewildering number of plants in the West:

osoberry, *Osmaronia cerasiformis*; deerberry, *Vaccinium stamineum*; sumac, *Rhus aromatica* or *Rhus trifoliata; Mitchella repens* [which has bright red fruit], a plant of the genus *Lyceum*, or its fruit) and *squawbush* (one of several shrubs – Indian tobacco [*Cornus stolonifera, Cornus serica* or *Cornus canadenisis*] or a Western sumac, *Rhus trilobata*).

squaw tits Two leather pads that are tied on to the front forks of a saddle. Also called bucking rolls. When the horse starts to crow hop, the rider is thrown back in the saddle. (*See* buck)

squeeze chute A narrow chute to hold cattle for branding. Also called a *squeezer, snapping turtle* or a *branding chute*.

squeeze spindle A device used for cheating by the operators of gambling wheels, such as roulette wheels. The squeeze spindle, also called a *squeeze wheel*, stops the wheel secretly where the operator wants.

squeeze them down In driving a trail herd, for the cowboys to reduce the width of the line of cows, perhaps to herd them across a river. This was also called *narrowing the string*.

squip Among miners, a fuse.

squirrel can A big can used by the camp cook for scraps.

stackwad A lazy cowboy who looks for the easy jobs. [Adams]

stag (1) When said of cattle, an animal not castrated until it reached maturity. (2) In the sense of a social event for men, as in a stag dance or stag party, it appears also to be an expression of the frontier, when men were often without women. (3) Among loggers, to cut off your pants at calf level.

stage station Where the stagecoach stopped *en route* to give the passengers a break as well as to change horses. The passengers might have found some soap, something to eat and drink, perhaps a bunk and surely a handy deck of cards. The larger stations (also called *home stations*) were usually homes to the station masters, their families and other stage line employees. Small communities often grew up around them. They were usually about 50 miles apart on the line. The smaller stations, placed closer together and often called *swing stations*, provided only a change of livestock. Stage stations were also called *stage stands*.

stagecoach A wheeled, horse-drawn vehicle of public transportation; a principal object of desire for road agents (highwaymen); a principal locale of Western adventure stories.

Though the West made stagecoaches famous among modern Americans, they were not native sons – they'd been used to move the public, its mail and its valuables around for two centuries before they became common on the Western frontier. The best-known stagecoaches in the 19th century were the concord coaches, made in Concord, New Hampshire from the 1820s. These were luxury vehicles, built for comfort, with three seats holding three passengers each comfortably, elaborately sprung and cushioned; the middle seat could be shifted into a bed. Two boots for luggage were provided, one under the driver's box and the other in back. The coaches were pulled by two or three pairs of horses.

The stagecoaches scratched their ways to almost all the population centres of the West, from the edge of the prairies at St Louis to the edge of the continent at San Francisco. This journey took about $200 and 25 days. You travelled night and day at the rate of four or five miles an hour, on the average, changing horses at relay stations, eating, cleaning up and sometimes sleeping at stage stations or road ranches. It was a rugged trip – modern readers wanting to enjoy the experience vicariously need only to turn to Mark Twain's *Roughing It*. They'll have a lot more laughs than Sam Clemens did or any other traveller of the time.

But if you were John Ford, a little later, you could put just the right mix of the brave, the helpless and the villainous in one and make a fine movie, like *Stagecoach*.

It was also called simply a *stage* and in this form makes various combinations pertaining to stagecoaching: *stage barn*, *stage connection*, *stage holdup*, *stage line* (a stagecoach system) and *stage station*, *stage house*, *stage post* or *stage ranch* (all terms for a stopping point on a stage line). A stage was a section of road between stage stations.

stake *Verb combinations: stake a claim* (literally to mark it with stakes or in any way to make a mineral claim; figuratively, one could stake a claim to anything, including a pretty girl) and *stake a person* (to supply someone with the means for a project such as prospecting; to grubstake someone).

In the Mormon Church, a stake is a district, according to Wallace Stegner in *Mormon Country*, 'roughly equivalent to the dioceses of the Catholic Church'. Stakes are subdivided into small units called *wards*. Combinations are *stake house*, an assembly building, and *Stake of* (or *in*) *Zion*, referring to a stake in the 'tent of Zion'.

In mining, a *staker* is an itinerant worker, and a *stake notice* is a declaration of a mining claim posted on a stake.

Among loggers, *stakey* describes someone with enough money to be itchy to get to town, and *stake-bound* is being well-off enough to quit your job. [Adams]

A *stake horse* is a horse tethered by a stake; *stake-broke* describes a horse accustomed to being staked; *stake pin* is a picket pin for a horse; *stake rope* is what a Texan calls a picket rope; and *staking ground* is what teamsters called the space near a wagon where horses were staked. [Adams]

To *make* or *raise a stake* is to earn some money, perhaps enough to start a business or otherwise get started in life; to *move stakes* is to change where you live; and *staked to a fill* is to have your stomach full. [Adams]

staked plain A wide treeless plain, perhaps so barren that you had to mark the trail across it with stakes; sometimes called a *staked prairie*. The Staked Plain was the Llano Estacado of Texas and New Mexico, 40,000 miles of barrenness and even larger in the tales told about crossing it.

stamp axe Among loggers, an axe for log-branding. Also called a *branding axe*.

stamp iron Any branding iron with a brand forged at the business end, as opposed to a running iron, which is adaptable for writing any brand whatever.

stampede (1) What every open-range cowman used to fear, especially on a trail drive – a blind, lurching, crashing take-off of cattle (or for that matter horses or buffalo). It was always serious trouble and sometimes disaster. The animals would run until they were worn out, which damaged their condition for the trail drive and seriously reduced their weight and thus their value for market. They also got broken bones, got trampled, got lost and got drowned.

Anything could and did start a stampede, 1,000-pound critters being not only afraid of jack-rabbits but nearly anything that moved. The most frequent causes were storms. It happened suddenly: 'The remarkable thing about it,' said the veteran cattleman Charles Goodnight, 'was that the whole herd started instantly, jarring the earth like an earthquake.' The hands tried to keep them from getting clear to hell and gone by getting alongside the leaders and turning them into a circle, using up their furious energy running round and round on safe ground, instead of having them end up in the river or off the top of a mesa. Some cowboys, though, believed that the best strategy was to get in front of them, make yourself the leader and gradually slow down. Riding hell for leather to catch the leaders or in front of them, often at night, was risky business and killed many a hand.

The stampedes of buffalo were formidable – 5,000 and 10,000 beasts half again the size of cows on the rampage, utterly unstoppable, a force of nature.

Now that cattle are tended by people from birth and not allowed to get wild and snorty off by themselves and are mostly kept within fences, the stampede is primarily a danger of the past.

(2) In verb form, it means to set off on a flight, whether you're a critter or a person; to cause a stampede, a common technique of horse thieves both Indian and Anglo;

to rush into anything, as to stampede into marriage. (3) A charge of gold miners to new diggings was called a stampede. Such stampedes were a subject of much hilarity, even among the miners themselves.

This story comes down to us: A miner came to the pearly gates and asked for permission to enter. But St Peter said heaven couldn't stand another miner. Why, just the week before the critters were breaking up the pavement of the gold streets with picks and assaying their harps. So the miner proposed a bargain: If he would get rid of these trouble-makers, would St Peter let him stay in heaven? Agreed.

By the end of the day came a stampede of miners, lickety-split, for the lower place. At its end came the miner who had made the bargain with St Peter, his gear packed and headed out. St Peter asked in amazement how the fellow had managed to get all the miners to leave voluntarily. The fellow said he'd just started a rumour that someone had struck colour in hell. St Peter chuckled, but went on to ask why the miner himself was packed up and headed south. 'Well,' drawled the fellow, 'you never know.'

(4) Stampede is one of the early words for rodeo, as in Calgary Stampede. (5) A *stampeder* may be an animal prone to start stampedes, a horse inclined to run off blindly, a man who causes a stampede or who simply takes part in one, or a miner who rushes into a new mineral area. (6) To *stampede to the wild bunch* meant 'to go on the dodge, to cast your lot with outlaws'. [Adams]

Often pronounced *stompede* by old-timers, the word comes from the Spanish *estampida*, which also means a sudden flight of beasts. Early forms of the word in American English were *stampedo*, *stampido* and *stampado*.

stand (1) What buffalo runners called an episode of shooting into a herd. Interested only in quantity of kill, the runners would approach and shoot undetected from downwind. Some authorities say the leaders were killed first. Often the beasts would not pay attention to the disturbance and would stand until the hunter had felled as many as 20 or 30 animals. Some stands are said to have run into the hundreds. And thus were the great herds decimated. (2) A stallion's breeding efforts; the place where he is available for breeding. In verb form, such a stallion is said to be *standing at stud*. Not a Westernism but now most common in the West.

stand hitched This is what a well-trained horse will do when the reins are dropped – stand as if hitched to the ground. Also, how you should act when a gun is pointed at you and how you hope your partner will act when you're in trouble.

stand pat In poker, to accept your hand the way it was dealt the first time. What you keep is called a *pat hand*. Figuratively, to stick where you are or with what you've got. 'Stand Pat with McKinley', was a campaign slogan, says linguist J. L. Dillard.

stand up An occasional synonym for 'to hold up', what a robber does to a bank or a stagecoach.

standard event The Professional Rodeo Cowboy's Association recognises five standard events: bareback riding, bulldogging, bull riding, calf roping and saddle bronc riding.

standing feed What a cowman calls grass and hay still growing. [Adams]

standoff A situation where neither side has the upper hand. The term comes from card gambling.

staple A device used to nail barbwire to a fence post, U-shaped and sturdy. In Texas, it's called a *steeple*.

star A patch of white on a horse's forehead. Stars, blazes and stockings are among the markings most commonly used to identify horses. Also a term for a four-directions wheel of the Indians.

star candle A candle of stearine, an army-issue candle when George Armstrong Custer was on the Plains.

star chief *See* hasher.

Star Navy A brand of chewing tobacco. (*See* chaw tobacco for other brands)

star rowel A rowel made of just five or six points and thus likely to be rough on the horse.

stargazer Said of a horse that goes around with his head high in the air, and not said kindly. Often the result of the trainer being rough with the bit.

star-pitch To bivouac, to sleep outside without a tent or other covering. [Adams]

start a bronc To break a horse; to give an unbroke horse its first ride, often a hair-raising experience for mount and rider.

start the swim *See* swim the herd.

starter (1) A batch of sourdough used to set new dough fermenting. (2) A logger who gets logs started downstream on the first spring rise. (3) *For a starter* or *as a starter* means 'as a beginning', as in, 'He gave me twenty bucks for a starter.' The first uses of these expressions are Western.

star-toter An officer of the law, so called from his badge.

starve-out A horse pasture without water and grass. Hands used to pen horses there overnight to make them easy to catch in the morning. Probably this word gave birth to the term *starve-out ranch* in Elmer Kelton's fine novel *The Man Who Rode Midnight*, meaning 'a ranch short on water and grass'.

States Short for the United States. In the early West, it meant the settled half of the country as opposed to the unsettled West. The settled areas were divided into states, but most of the West hadn't even been made into territories. Until 1846, the south-west was Mexico, and the north-west was disputed with Britain. Thus a trapper in the Rockies or a fur trader on the Pacific shore would speak of heading back to the States.

Combinations: States blood (genes from the eastern United States introduced into the mustang line), *States cattle* (also called *pilgrims* and *barnyard stock*; cows from the eastern United States as opposed to the native longhorns), *States eggs* (eggs from the eastern United States; in early frontier days, chickens were few, and eggs had to be shipped out from the settled areas) and

States fruit (also called *hen fruit;* the same as States eggs).

station (1) A stage station. (2) In the latter 18th century on the frontier of Kentucky, Tennessee, and the Old north-west, a residence (usually of several families) fortified against Indians. (3) In mining, a landing place at different levels of a mine.

Combinations: station agent (the fellow in charge of a stage station), *station drink* (the drink, evidently free, a stage driver was entitled to at each station), *station house* (a stage station) and *station keeper* (on the Oregon Trail, a station agent).

steal (1) For a ewe to give birth to a lamb out of season. Her offspring is called a *stolen lamb.* (2) In poker, to *steal a pot* is to bluff a player with a better hand into folding. (3) To *steal a start*, in the old days, meant for a cowboy to get enough mavericks (or otherwise pilfer enough calves) to start his own herd and become a cowman.

steamer day In San Francisco, from the 1850s, people called the day before the next steamship sailed for the States steamer day, a big day for merchants, bankers and other businessmen to settle bills. Later, in Virginia City, Nevada, it was extended to mean any Monday, when businessmen were supposed to make good on their contracts.

steer A male cow that's been castrated. Not a Westernism but a term whose significance seems mostly lost outside of cattle country. Steers are what you raise for beef. Cutting (castrating) them re-channels their energy from fighting and fornicating, making them easier to handle and their meat more flavourable. A *feeder steer*, in cow business lingo, is one raised for beef and sold to a feedlot man for fattening for slaughter; a *blackjack steer* is a skinny critter from timber country [Adams]; a *bulling steer* is a castrated animal that nevertheless has some sexual odour and draws other steers; a *lead steer* was the one who got at the head of a trail drive and led 'em out; a *rough steer* is a runt with a poor bloodline.

Steer busting is roping and throwing steers single-handedly. You ride up on the left side of the beast, rope its horns, loop your rope around its right hip and around its hind end and then ride off sharply to the left, jerking the critter off its feet.

There are many rodeo events featuring steers: *steer roping* or *single steer tying* (the horse throws the steer and the cowboy ties its feet with a pigging string), *steer wrestling* (bulldogging), *steer decorating* (a gentler form of bulldogging, usually a ladies event, where a ribbon is grabbed off the steer's back).

Stetson The most popular brand of broad-brimmed hat in the West – so popular that, like Colt and Winchester for handguns and rifles, it became a generic name for hat. What someone called a Stetson might be another brand. Now the principal alternatives to the Stetson brand are American Hat, Bailey and Resistol.

Official Stetsons, familiarly called John B.s or J. B.s, were made by John B. Stetson of Philadelphia from 1865 onward. The model most popular with cowboys in the early days was the Carlsbad; the first Western style was the Boss, another the high and wide Buckeye. A Stetson cowboy model cost almost as much as boots, 10 to 20 bucks or more. (When you consider that in those days a hand probably made 30 dollars a month, the price of head cover was substantial.) But you needed a hat: it kept the sun out of your eyes and off your neck. It was an umbrella. It gave you a bucket (the crown) to water your horse and a cup (the brim) to water yourself. It made a hell of a fan, which you need sometimes for a fire but more often to shunt cows this direction or that. Stetsons (and Western hats generally) were and are made of felt, which is in turn made from wool or animal fur, especially beaver fur. Stetsons are made from beaver, rabbit and hare fur. The more beaver in it, the more durable and resistant to weather the hat will be. Stetson indicates the amount of beaver with Xs – 100 per cent beaver being 20X. Stetsons now range from $70 to 10 times that much. They're supposed to stand up to a terrific beating –

they're not even broken in until they've been trampled in the mud and manure by horses – and should last halfway to forever.

Of course, Western hats were and are sometimes for show (for example, Dallas stockbrokers wear them to work). In that case they're likely to be decorated with a band of some sort, woven horsehair, snakeskin, concha-studded leather, beadwork, quillwork or whatever, even (heaven help us) fancy concoctions from pheasant feathers.

An important consideration for show is the shape. Old-timers used to be able to tell where a hand was from by the shape of his hat. These days the most popular is the rancher or cattleman crease, dented straight down the middle and on both sides, the crease flat from front to back. Newly popular is the Gus crease, or the Montana slope, named after the one worn by the character Gus in the television mini-series *Lonesome Dove*. It's a modification of the Montana peak, in which the crown stands high and is creased sharply from the top toward the brim. Many hands like the rodeo crease, the bull-rider's crease (which used to be called the RCA crease, for Rodeo Cowboys of America), the quarter horse crease and the tycoon, with a pinched front.

But you can be a cowboy without a cowboy hat. I heard a recent story about a cowboy and a tourist in Jackson Hole. The tourist saw some hands moving cows along a highway and noticed one was wearing a baseball cap. Curious, this greenhorn pulled up alongside the rider and asked why he wasn't wearing a cowboy hat. The cowboy tugged at his cap brim and, perhaps thinking of pheasant feathers, replied, 'Don' wanna look like a goddam truck driver.'

Not all broad-brimmed, Western hats were or are cowboy hats. *See* beaver, Kossuth hat, reservation hat and slouch hat.

stew A miner's name for nitroglycerin.

stick ears Cowboy talk for cows that have been earmarked.

stick horse A horse that doesn't want to work and has to be forced. [Adams]

stick like a postage stamp What a good bronc rider does on a bucking horse.

sticky rope What a cowboy calls a rustler, because his rope has a way of sticking to other men's cows. [Adams]

stiff (1) A corpse. (2) A stiff man – a fellow who burned carcasses on the range. [Adams] (3) An important person, especially a self-important person, a mucky-muck. Perhaps this usage stems from the stiffness of the fronts of their boiled shirts. (4) Among loggers, a word for a white-collar worker. [Adams] (5) A labouring man. Thus *hard rock stiff* (a miner), a *shovel stiff* (a labourer with a shovel), *saddle stiff* (a cowboy) and *lumber stiff* and *bindle stiff* (both a logger).

This word sometimes appears to mean simply 'person', as in *working stiff* (any worker). It is also a hobo's word for hobo, and a *mission stiff* is, wonderfully, a bum who goes to a mission and pretends to get religion in order to get food and a bed.

stinger (1) A Johnson bar, the back, hand-held bar of a fresno (a wheelbarrow-like device for building earth dams). When it kicks, it stings like hell. (2) What loggers call the part of a logging truck that sticks out behind the trailer's wheels. [Adams]

stinkweed Another name for *Datura meteloides*, commonly called *jimson weed*.

stirrup The support for the rider's foot that hangs from the saddle tree. Though stirrup is a very old word in English, elements of the Western stirrup were distinctive: the stirrups of the early range were big affairs carved from a single piece of wood; they were called *oxbows* or sometimes *doghouse stirrups*. Later the wooden bar that went beneath the instep was wrapped in rawhide and still later was made of steel. Westerners often wore and wear their stirrups with *tapaderos*, covers for the front part of the boot, open at the back.

Combinations: drop stirrup (a leather loop dropped below the stirrup for short riders to use to get a leg up), *hobbled stirrups* (stirrups linked beneath the horse's belly with a strap; though they make it easier to stay on a bucking horse, they're dangerous, and good riders are scornful of them), *stirrup hood* (a tapadero – a covering for the rider's boot), *stirrup iron* (the part of the stirrup that goes beneath the foot and supports it; in the early West it wasn't made of metal [*see* above]) and *stirrup leather* (also called by the Spanish word *ación*, the leather straps that hang from the saddle framework and support the stirrup iron).

stock Short for *livestock*, which in the West usually means cows, sheep or horses rather than other critters raised for market.

Combinations: stock buyer (at one time a man who bought draft animals for stage lines; now a cattle buyer for the big packing houses), *stock car* (a railway car for shipping cows and other livestock to market, which became a huge business on the Great Plains in the decades after the Civil War), *stock corral* (a pen for horses, cows or sheep), *stock country* (any land more fit for grazing than tilling, especially the grasslands of the Great Plains), *stock horse* (a brood mare), *stock inspector* (a person who checks brands to make sure stock is being transported or sold legally; also called a brand inspector), *stock law* (the body of law governing the stock-raising industry), *stocker* (a calf being raised for slaughter, not yet a feeder), *stockman*, *stock-raiser*, *stock grower* or *stock rancher* (the raisers and breeders of cattle, horses or sheep, not farmers or dairymen). A *stock tank* is a big container on the range for water for the stock to drink, usually supplied by a well, *stock train* (a railroad train of stock cars), *stock water* (water for the stock to drink, in the West often in stock tanks or reservoirs, in contrast with irrigation water) and *stockyard* (a pen where cows are held for shipping or more often for slaughter).

stock contractor A person who provides the stock for a rodeo – bucking horses, calves for roping, bulls to ride and steers to bulldog. He may also be the rodeo producer.

stock growers' association An organisation of cattlemen formed to protect what they saw and see as their rights. Such associations began to spring up after the first great trail drives after the Civil War. They sought to keep 'their' range for themselves, to fight against rustlers, to co-ordinate roundups, to get recognition of their brands, in some areas to keep Texas fever out and to face other common problems. Eventually they hired brand inspectors and stock detectives. Tom Horn was a stock detective for the Wyoming Stock Growers' Association when he was convicted and hanged in 1903 for the bush-wacking of Willie Nickell, the teenage son of a sheepman.

In the days of the open range, the associations often fought against what homesteaders and small ranchers saw as *their* rights. One result of such conflict was the Johnson County War, in which the powerful Wyoming Stock Growers' Association in 1892 went against the small ranchers of Johnson County, thought to be mavericks.

Because stockmen continue to have common interests and problems, their associations still exist. Sometimes they're called *cattlemen's associations*, *stockmen's associations* or *stock grazers' associations*.

stock saddle (1) The Western stock saddle is different from the English riding saddle, which Western riders used to refer to derisively as a postage stamp. The principal difference is the high horn, which the cowboy uses for dallying or tying hard and fast when he ropes. Bruce Grant, in *How to Make Cowboy Horse Gear*, lists the parts of the Western saddle as a tree (frame), the seat, the cantle, the horn, the swell and gullet, the front jockey and back jockey, skirt, fender (or rosadero), stirrups, stirrup-leathers, cinch rings, latigo, conchas and tie-strings.

Stock saddles were and are usually named for the maker or the shape of the tree. Common Western saddles are the association, California, charro, Conestoga, eight-string (ordinary work saddle, whose leathers are secured with eight sets of strings), Great Plains (or Texas Trail), McClellan, Mother Hubbard, Pony Express, Santa Fe (a mountain-man saddle) and Spanish. For rigging, *see* single-rig. In the old days you could tell where a rider hailed from by the way his saddle was rigged.

stogie (1) A cheap cigar. The people from Lancaster County, Pennsylvania rolled the local tobacco into cigars, and many of them drove Conestoga wagons. Thus the cigar got called a *Conestogie*, which was shortened to stogie. (2) What cowboys used to call cheap boots. Both are also spelled *stogy* and *stoga*.

stomp What a cowboy is likely to call a dance.

stone on the chest A miner's name for tuberculosis, the disease he fears.

stool pigeon Among gamblers, a capper for a faro bank; any shill or gambler's decoy.

stool-and-bucket cow What a cowboy may call a co-operative milk cow. [Adams]

store tobacco In the middle period of the Far West, many items available from merchants were referred to as store this and store that, as opposed to homemade – *store boots, store candy, store cheese, store dress, store goods, store medicine, store pants, store sugar, store teeth* and so on. Tobacco in the earlier days was kinnikinnick or came from traders, either in twists (long pieces as thick as your thumb twisted around themselves) or plugs (brick-like hunks).

storm cellar The south-central plains, northern Texas, Oklahoma, parts of Kansas and Arkansas, are twister (tornado) country, and many houses are outfitted with outside cellars with doors low to the ground for protection against such storms.

storm the puncheons One of the old-time cowboy's figures of speech for dancing. [Adams] In pioneer days, many floors were made of puncheons (rough timber split from a log and hewn on one side), which was often the first step up from dirt. And the cowboy's style of dancing was often vigorous to a fault.

stove up Beaten up, worn out, banged up, damaged. Often said of an old cowboy who has peeled (broke) too many broncs in the rough, old way, which makes old men out of young ones in a hurry.

straddle bug Three boards put up in tripod form to mark a land or mining claim.

straight buck A horse's buck that's straight ahead, without twists, turns or curlicues. A horse that does this is said to be bucking straight away, and however vigorous he may be, he's comparatively easy to ride.

straight goods The truth. The usage seems to appear in print first in a story by Western novelist Owen Wister – 'I'm givin' yu' straight goods, yu' see.'

straight-coloured horse A solid-coloured horse like a buckskin or sorrel, traditionally the preference of the cowboy. This preference is quite possibly ethnocentric: such horses were what Westerners called American horses, brought out from the East. Multi-coloured horses, such as paints, pintos and appaloosas, are descendants of mustangs (ultimately of the Spanish Barb) and are associated with Indians.

strainer The part of the saddle tree (framework) that supports the middle, where the rider sits. It is galvanised iron and is covered with leather.

Strangite A follower of J. J. Strang, who laid claim to leadership of the Latter-Day Saints Church after Joseph Smith died in Illinois. Strang led his group to Beaver Island in Lake Michigan. Their beliefs were called *Strangism*.

strangler A vigilante, so named because he enforced his opinions with ropes around the neck. That made the victim do what was called the *strangulation jig*. Some vigilance committees were even named the Stranglers. (*See* string party)

strapped on his horse toes down Sent home dead. [Adams] Adams points out that since a loose horse would usually find its way home, it could be used to send a message in a range war, the body of its rider. (*See* dry-gulch)

straw boss A ranch foreman who works under the superintendent; any boss who's second dog to the top boss.

stray A cow that has wandered from its range. (Wandering horses were called *stray horses*, not just strays.) Such critters were sought out by what were called reps, *stray hands* or *stray men*, riders assigned to visit ranges or especially roundups outside their outfit's usual territory and bring back strays.

stretch out (1) An expression used by traders and freighters meaning 'to get the caravan going'. (2) To stretch a critter out is for two cowhands to rope it by the horns and hind feet and stretch its legs out. It's now standard practice in team roping in rodeo. (3) To *stretch the blanket* is to tell a windy, spin a tall tale.

stretching frame A square of wooden poles devised by trappers to hold buffalo skins while hair was scraped from them.

strike (1) A sudden discovery of valuable ore or oil. In verb form, to come upon a vein, to hit oil or pay dirt. This use appears to have originated during the California gold rush, as did the expression *strike it rich*, meaning to get great wealth suddenly. (2) The expression to *strike camp*, meaning to take down and pack the camping gear, also appears to be originally Western.

string (1) The group of horses assigned to a cowboy by his outfit. (2) A cowboy's rope (called a *skin string* when made of rawhide). (3) A leather tie on a saddle. (4) Among loggers, a group of logs floated downstream together. (5) Among miners, a fuse. (6) Among trappers, 12 traps, the usual number one man would tend.

A cowboy's string of horses was essential. Typically it comprised four to six mounts or more – a circle horse, a cutting horse, a roping horse and a night horse plus one or two broncos who were learners. The string belonged completely to the cowboy it was assigned to – he was responsible for it, and it was hands off to everyone else. Outfits kept strings together from each rider to his successor. The new cowboy was never told anything about the horses in the string – the assumption was that he rode well enough to need no advice. If a cowboy broke his string by losing a horse or getting one hurt, that was a bad omen. For the boss to break the string by assigning one of the horses to someone else was the same as telling the cowboy to find another job.

To *string a greener* is to play a joke on a dude; to *string a whizzer* is to tell a windy, a stringer, spin a tall tale [Adams]; to *string them out* on a trail drive is to get the cattle off the bed ground and on to the trail. [Adams]

string party A hanging. Expressions for this fate are: *to be guest of honour at a string* (or *necktie*) *party*, be a *cotton-wood blossom*, *decorate a cotton-wood*, *die in a horse's nightcap*, *die with throat trouble*, *gurgle on a rope*, *do a mid-air dance*, *do a strangulation jig*, *get exalted*, *get dressed in a hemp four-in-hand*, *get hemp fever*, *get used to trim a tree*, *gone up*, *gurgle on a rope*, *look through cotton-wood leaves*, *look up a limb*, *ride under a cotton-wood limb*, *telegraph him home*, do a *Texas cake-walk*, *stretch hemp* and *string up*.

stringhalt A disorder of horses' nerves that makes their hocks swell and leaves them with an awkward pigeon-like walk.

stripper (1) A person who skins the hides from buffalo or cattle. [Adams] (2) A dry cow or a heifer. (3) People trying to get land in the Cherokee Strip were called strippers. (4) In faro or poker, strippers are cards trimmed for cheating.

stronger than the nuts An expression for a gambling game tilted excessively in favour of the dealer or house. [Adams] The nuts meant the shell of the old shell game, so the implication is, less honest even than the shell game.

Stroud A wool cloth common as a trade item in the fur trade and known for its bright colours. It was named for Stroud, Gloucestershire where it was made. Also called *strouding*.

stub In logging, the trunk of a tree broken off to 20 feet or less, standing bare of leaves and branches.

stub-horn An old bull of many fights whose horns are now chipped down. [Adams] Also said of battle-scarred men.

stud A stud horse, a stallion, a male horse kept for breeding, so not cut (castrated). Now his owner gets a stud fee for his covering (copulating with) a mare. Western Indians are said to have preferred studs as war horses because they had lots of aggressiveness. Because studs are a nuisance to mares and to their riders, Anglos traditionally prefer to ride geldings. The term is applied by extension to young, virile men. An occasional south-western term for a stud is *garañon*.

Studebaker A well-known freight wagon first built by the Studebaker Brothers in 1852. (*See* Murphy and Conestoga)

stuffed shirt A man of pompous, over-formal manner, which in the West included most Easterners. *Stuffed-shirtism* meant the tendency to such qualities.

stuffing dudes This is the time-honoured practice of having a little fun with dudes by telling them tall tales. It comes naturally in the West, where half of what's real is so crazy or spectacular that greeners can hardly believe what they're seeing. So the old-timers string them along with stories like this one from David Lavender's fine memoir, *One Man's West*. When a greenhorn ventured that it was cold, often a safe conversational opening, an old hand replied, ' "I wouldn't say so. Now when it gets so that a man rides along whistlin' to himself and the whistle don't make any noise on account of freezing solid and fallin' to the ground as fast as it comes out, then it *is* cold. You'll notice it in the spring," he said. "The woods sound like a steam calliope loose and the stops tied down – all them frozen whistles thawin' out and poppin' off. It spooks the mules considerable and the first few days. For a fact," he said, solemn as an owl.'

stump sucker A cribber, a horse that sets its teeth into wood and sucks wind.

stumpage In logging, standing timber; the value of standing timber; the right to cut it. Such wood is said to be worth so much at or in the stump, meaning 'as it stands, unfelled'. A *stump detective* is a person who calculates the amount of waste in standing timber.

Sublette's Cutoff A shortcut on the Oregon Trail from the west side of Wyoming's south pass to Bear River and the Fort Bridger–Fort Hall trail. Though it meant travelling fewer miles, some emigrants avoided it because 30 of them were waterless. Also called the *Sublette Road* and *Greenwood's Cutoff*. *Sublette's Lake* was the trappers' name for Yellowstone

Lake, discovered by William Sublette in 1826.

suck lick A salt lick that's liquid enough to drink, which some Western licks were in wet weather. Also called simply a *suck*.

sudadero The leather lining of a saddle's skirt. It's not the same as a rosadero, which is attached to the stirrup leathers, though the sudadero is sometimes used that way. Borrowed from the Spanish word for sweat cloth, it's pronounced soo-duh-DAYR-oh.

sugan A heavy blanket or comforter homemade from patchwork materials and the mainstay of the cowboy's bedroll. Also spelled *soogan*, *soogin*, *suggan*, *sugin* and *sougan* and pronounced soo-guhn. Evidently adapted from an Irish term.

sugar eater What a cowboy calls a pampered horse.

sugar pine A pine of the Pacific Coast (*Pinus Lambertiana*) whose gum is said to taste like sugar mixed with turpentine.

suicide gun A pistol hardly big enough to irritate a man, such as a .32-calibre. A rancher considering carrying such a gun once is said to have asked his foreman what would happen if the rancher shot the foreman with the little thing. The hand answered that, if he noticed it, he'd up and whup his boss.

suicide horse What a cowboy calls a horse that goes crazy when anyone tries to ride it, that bucks in any direction and into anything. So called because it's likely to kill itself.

suitcase rancher A man who owns a ranch but lives elsewhere and only visits. Suitcase ranchers have been in the West as long as ranching has. Many owners of ranches on the Great Plains in the 1870s and 1880s were Britons and Scots looking for big profits. The winter of '87, with its huge die-ups, inhibited their adventuring. In the 1960s and 1970s, some suitcase ranchers were stars of the entertainment industry who bought cattle ranches as tax hedges. The latest source of resentment is ranchers from Japan.

Local people see suitcase ranchers as involved in ranching mainly for reasons of finance, not reasons of emotion, lifestyle and sense of connection with the land, so lacking in motive to be conservators and stewards.

sull To act sullen. It is said especially of a cow that, regardless of a cowboy's cajoling, pleading or provocation, absolutely refuses to move. This, and not cattleman-sheepman conflicts, is what should be called a range war.

summer range Grazing land for cattle or sheep that is appropriate for use in the summer. It's likely to be in country that's deep in snow during the winter and a long trail drive or truck ride from the main ranch.

summer tent A summer shelter of tipi-dwelling Indians. When these Indians found their tipis cumbersome in the summer, they would use temporary shelters of branches and poles set in a semicircle and covered with hides or blankets.

sun dance A central religious ceremony of about two dozen tribes of Plains Indians, especially the Dakota, Cheyenne and Arapaho. The name 'sun dance' is Anglo, though most Indians now keeping the practice use it. The Dakota originally called it the *sun-gazing dance*, the Cheyenne, the *medicine lodge ceremony*, and other tribes, the *thirsting dance* because participants did not drink during the actual four days of dancing.

The entire ceremony lasts about a week. It is held during the summer months, usually in July. The goal is to put the tribe in harmony with itself and with the spiritual powers; the dancers are not worshipping the sun.

Generally the ceremony follows this form: A tree is chosen, cut down (symbolically attacked), trimmed and erected (with religious emblems attached) as the centre pole of an enclosure. An altar is made, featuring a buffalo skull and facing east. At the proper time, the men who have pledged themselves begin their four days of dancing, neither eating nor drinking, intermittently blowing eagle-bone whistles. Among most tribes women do not dance, though one woman and a berdache, or half-man–half-woman, may

have key roles in preparation. The ceremony was historically understood as an act of the whole tribe, an expression of their oneness as a people. The dancers are expressing their awareness of the paramount importance of the common good.

Different tribes perform the ceremony in different ways. It is famous for the one gesture of self-scourging: Some dancers permit skewers to be passed under the skin of the chest or the back, then are tied by leather thongs to a pole, and rip out the skewers by leaning back against the thongs. Not all tribes accepted this piercing historically – it principally belonged to the Oglala Dakota – and some forbade it. Early missionaries and Indian agents were horrified by it and had the ceremony itself officially banned for a long time. Today the sun dance is practiced among many Western tribes, and piercing continues among the Lakotas and some others.

sun dog A pale, rainbow-like spot in the winter sky, caused by sunlight illuminating ice crystals. Sun dogs are often a sign of impending weather change. James Willard Schultz indicates in *My Life as an Indian* that the Blackfeet understood sun dogs to be warnings of approaching danger.

Sunday horse The horse a cowboy rides for dress-up or festive occasions. It likely has some style and some looks but may not be worth a damn for work. A counterpart of Sunday-go-to-meeting clothes (which is not a Westernism).

Sunday school Among loggers, a poker game. They worked six days and played cards on Sunday.

sundown Descriptive of the Pacific Coast country, as in reference to Oregon as a *sundown land*. It sometimes simply meant 'further west'. To emigrate to the West was sometimes expressed as to *seek a home beyond sundown*. A *sundowner* was a man headed west to stay ahead of the law. [Adams]

sunfish A way of bucking. The horse throws its middle violently to one side, then the other, so that it seems its shoulder may touch the ground and the critter sun its belly. Such a horse is called a *sunfisher*.

sunset trail A figure of speech for the death of an individual or a group. The Indians of the West, being pushed aside by Anglos, were sometimes said to be on the sunset trail, headed for extinction. (For other Western words and phrases for death, *see* cash in your chips)

supreme being What loggers called their superintendent, no doubt behind his back. Also known as *brass nuts*, *big bull*, *big savage*, *bigwig*, *enemy*, *gaffer*, *governor*, *grandpa*, *skipper*, *uncle* and *walking boss*.

surcingle A strap that goes around a horse's belly. Used as an added precaution to hold a saddle on or for riding with stirrups but no saddle. The term did not originate in the West.

sure as shooting Damn sure; as in, 'That bear is sure as shooting going to make dinner out of us.'

sure cure A remedy that won't fail. Often used in a jocular way, as a cowboy might say that getting your teeth punched out is a sure cure for cavities. Mathews shows the first appearance of the phrase in print in the *Oregon State Journal* of Eugene, Oregon.

surface coal What a cowboy calls buffalo chips or cow chips for the fire. Also called *surface fuel*, *prairie coal* and *Babcock coal*.

surface diggings In mining, diggings at or near the surface of the earth.

Combinations: *surface dirt* (ore-bearing dirt near the surface), *surface lead* (a vein of ore near the surface, with the implication that it doesn't go far into the earth) and *surface placer*.

surface fire Among fire fighters, a fire that moves along the forest floor, burning the spruce duff, other surface litter and small vegetation. Same as a ground fire. Its opposite is a crown fire.

surround A way of hunting herds of game used primarily by Indians. The hunters encircled the animals, often antelope or buffalo, and herded them over a cliff or drove them into a hidden pen or other trap and shot them. Lots of Indian hunting was a way of getting a large quantity

of meat for a large number of people as surely and efficiently as possible.

sustainable A government term that describes an activity that can be continued indefinitely without destroying the resource. Sustainable timber harvests are thought to be of the size that will permit them to continue indefinitely.

sutler A civilian who traded goods to soldiers on or near a military post. This was the fellow who sold necessities of life like cloth, buttons, knives and tobacco, plus whiskey, of course, and was licensed or otherwise approved by the commander, as opposed to the fellow who sold whiskey and women at the hog ranch. The world 'fell into disuse' in the mid-1870s, says memoirist Martha Summerhayes in *Vanished Arizona*, apparently in favour of *post trader*. And sometime later the sutler's store became the *post exchange*. The word *sutler* was not originally a Westernism.

swag A low place, a depression in the ground.

Swainson's hawk A hawk (*Buteo swainsoni*) seen especially on the Great Plains, with a dark breast-band and white colouring underneath. William Swainson's name (he was a British naturalist) was also given to the Western (or Swainson's) warbling vireo (*Vireoslyva gilva swainsoni*)

swallow its head For a bucking horse to put its head and tail way down and arch the devil out of its back. (*See* buck)

swamp In logging, to clear underbrush away, make a place for a skid road and get trees out of the woods.

A *swamper* is a worker who's low on the totem pole. In logging, he clears underbrush for skid roads or trims trees for the sawyers. On a freighting team, he's the assistant to the skinner. In a cow camp, he helps the cook. On a river-rafting trip, he takes care of the camp. In a saloon, he does a little of everything.

swap ends What a bucking horse is said to do when he makes a quick half-circle, putting his hind end where his front was an instant ago.

swear-off A promise to abstain, as in, 'This new year's resolution is going to be the big swear-off (of booze).'

sweat lodge Among western Indians, a low hut for sweating as a ritual of purification and to cure illness. Now the huts are framed of willow branches and covered with tarpaulins, rugs and the like, with a fire pit and a low entrance facing east. In the last century they were generally covered with hides. The ritual varies from tribe to tribe and leader to leader. Usually herbs and water are thrown on to fire-heated rocks to create very hot steam; and prayers are offered. The ritual sometimes takes place in several sessions, called rounds, with a short break between each. To lead such a ritual is sometimes called 'to pour' because the leader pours the water on the rocks. The Dakota called this ritual the *inipi* (stone-people lodge ceremony). It was called by Apaches the *tá-a-chi*. The sweat lodge was also sometimes called a *sweat house* or *sweat tipi*.

Swede fiddle What a cowboy calls an accordion and what a logger calls a crosscut saw.

sweeney Atrophy of a horse's shoulder muscles; a horse with that condition is said to be *sweenied*.

sweet sage Among contemporary Plains Indians, a common plant of the northern plains, *Artemesia cana*, used for ceremonial purposes. For instance, the dirt floor of the sweat lodge is covered with sweet sage.

sweetgrass A grass (*Torresia ordorat*) of the northern plains often burned in rituals for purification or as a welcoming of the spirits. Wallace Black Elk writes in his book *Black Elk*, 'Sweetgrass is Mother Earth's hair. It is a perfume. When my grandma's spirit comes she carries that smell, that perfume, and you can smell it. That's why we use the sweetgrass as a prayer at the altar.'

sweet-mouthed Said of a horse that's sensitive to the bit; the same as soft-mouthed and opposite of hard-mouthed or dead-mouthed.

swell fork On a stock saddle, projections on either side of the horn that a rider can press his knees under when the horse bucks; the opposite of a slick fork.

swim the herd On a trail drive, to get the herd across a river. They could be ornery about going into rivers. Sometimes they went freely. Sometimes they'd follow the horse herd or a swimming horse (a horse chosen for its swimming ability) across. Sometimes they'd sull and balk for days.

swing Part of a trail herd, checked by the swing riders. Swing riders minded a trail herd, staying about a third of the way back from the point riders and in front of the flank riders.

swing station A place on a stage line where the draft animals were changed. These stations were about 10 or 12 miles apart and offered no services. Principal stage stations, also called *home stations*, were usually about 50 miles apart.

swingdingle Among loggers, a kind of chuck wagon on runners that brought the workers a hot lunch.

swipe To steal. The first appearances of this verb in print are Western, dating from 1889 in Seattle.

switch man Among some Plains Indians, a man chosen to keep people dancing at a ceremony; also called a whipman. He used (and uses – the custom is not dead) a horsewhip and switches people's legs. But if he drew blood, a serious offence, he had to pay one horse.

switchback A reversal in the direction of a trail as it angles up or down a hill or mountain. It also takes a verb form, as in, 'We switchbacked up the ridge.'

switch-tail A nervous horse. Also called a *switcher*. (*See* wring-tail)

Sydney bird A California gold-rusher from Australia, often a convict and regarded as a ruffian or worse. These men were also called *Sydney ducks* and *clipped ears* because such convicts' ears had been cut as a punishment.

T

tablita The name of a ceremonial headdress worn by Pueblo people.

taco From the south-west and now used throughout the United States, a Hispanic food, usually meat, cheese, lettuce, tomato and salsa stuffed into a folded hard tortilla called a *taco shell*.

tail The vaqueros made a sport of tailing cattle, or *tailing them down*. The rider came alongside the cow on the left and grabbed the tail and twisted it until the critter went down hard. Sometimes other moves are ascribed to the rider.

Anglos developed a method of tailing for branding – throwing a calf by twisting its tail so you could slap a brand on it.

Cowboys also tail cows up – get them on to their feet by twisting their tails. It is used, for instance, to get cows out of bog holes.

Tail rider was another name for drag rider. To *roll your tail* or to *tail out* is to head out in a hurry.

tailings (1) The refuse of the mining process. They're taken away suspended in water (called *tail water*) in a *tail race*. Uranium tailings now litter the canyon country, and sometimes these are called *tailings dumps* or the *tail end*. A *tail sluice* is the end sluice. (2) The stragglers of a cattle herd.

take your dust to town To go to town.

talking Westerners have lots of expressions for talking, too much talking and people who won't shut up. A *talking load* is enough whiskey to make a hand talkative. [Adams] To *talk like a Texan*, naturally, is to brag. Other expressions include: *chew the fat* or *cud*, *coyote around the rim*, *dally your tongue*, *diarrhoea of the jawbone*, *flannel mouth*, *giggle talk*, *leaky mouth*, *medicine tongue*, *more lip than a muley cow*, *powwow*, *slack in the jaw*, *talking talent*, *tongue oil* and *wag your chin*.

What stockmen do most is talk cows or maybe talk horses. For their next favourite, telling big stories, *see* yarn.

talking iron Cowboy talk for a pistol.

tall timber Wilderness, especially deep wilderness. To *head for tall timber* is to skedaddle to where people can't find you.

tallgrass country The prairies, in contrast to the plains, shortgrass country. To be *in the tall tules* is to be in trouble.

tallow factory A business establishment where cow carcasses were boiled for tallow. This practice was common in Texas until markets developed for beef and the days of the great cattle drives began.

Tallowweed is a forage (*Tetraneuris linearifolia*) of southern and western Texas known for putting fat on cows.

tally hand The fellow who kept count of the calves at branding, often a hand too old, too young or too stove up to wrestle calves. Sometimes he used knots on a string or pebbles to keep track of every 10 calves. The result was called the *tally* and was kept in the *tally book* (or on the *tally sheet*). Counting cows was called *tally branding*.

The sheep world has a different language – the fellow who weighs the wool after shearing is a *tallier*.

tamale A Mexican main dish – spicy, minced meat rolled in corn meal and (originally) steamed in a corn shuck. Sometimes prepared in the form of a pie. The *real tamale* means 'the real McCoy'. Borrowed from Nahuatl by way of the Spanish, it's pronounced tuh-MAH-lee.

tamarisk A shrub-like tree (*Tamarix chinsensis*) introduced to the West at the turn of the century. It has been too successful and now chokes irrigation ditches in the south-west. Called *tammy* for short.

tame Indian A friendly Indian, as opposed to a hostile. As Peter Watts points out, the adjective implies that Indians are animals.

tank In the south-west; a hollow in the ground (often in sandstone) that holds water during the rainy season; sometimes a reservoir made by damming runoff water. Later a stock tank (metal tank for watering stock).

Taos A Pueblo people of the northern Rio Grande. The name, derived from Tewa, means 'red willow place'. The people are now sometimes called Taoseños or Taosans.

Taos became the site of an early mission and then of a settlement well known to mountain men and traders. In 1847 the Taos pueblo was the centre of an unsuccessful revolt against the Americans who were occupying New Mexico during the Mexican–American War. In this century, the pueblo and town named for it have become large art markets. Much of the art work is based on traditional Indian design. Taos Indians share the culture of the other Pueblo Indian groups of the Rio Grande River.

Taos lightning was a fierce variety of firewater popular among the mountain men.

tapadero A leather covering for the stirrup, open at the rear; valued in brush country as protection and in general to keep the boot from slipping too far forward in the stirrup, which could cause a rider to be dragged by the stirrup. Adapted from the Spanish *tapadera* it's pronounced tap-uh-DAYR-oh.

Tapaderos with conchos on the toe are called *hog-nosed taps*. Tapaderos are also called *taps*, *bulldogs*, *eagle bills* and *monkey noses*.

tapajo A blind for a horse or mule, usually attached to the headstall. It is often used to help with mounting an unbroke horse or to keep a mule still for loading. Adapted from Spanish (where *tapa ojo* literally means 'eye cover'), it's pronounced tah-PAH-hoh. Sometimes spelled *tapaojos*.

tarrabee In the south-west, a wooden hand tool used to spin the threads for making cinches. Adapted from the Spanish *taraba* or *tarabilla*, it's pronounced TAYR-ruh-bee.

tasajo (1) In the south-west, jerky (dried meat). Borrowed from the Spanish, it's pronounced tuh-SAH-hoh. A *tasajero* was a building where meat was dried. (2) A cactus of the genus *Opuntia*, which looks like strips of jerky.

tata A title of south-western Indians for whites, showing respect. Borrowed from Spanish, it's pronounced TAH-tuh.

team roping A standard rodeo event. Two ropers, a heeler and a header (who rope the critter by the heels and head respectively), rope a steer and tie it, against time. After the steer's head and two hind feet are tied, the header faces his horse to the steer. A winning time is five to six seconds, although four seconds is sometimes seen.

tecolote A small burrowing owl of the south-west. Borrowed from Nahuatl by way of Spanish, it's pronounced te-kuh-LOH-tee.

teeth in the saddle Among cowboys, descriptive of saddle that rubs a horse's back raw. [Adams]

Tejano A Texan. From the Spanish name of that state, Tejas, which came from the name given to an Indian tribe by early explorers.

temescal In the south-west, originally a hot springs where Indians took baths, then a sweat lodge. The Plains sweat lodge was made from branches covered with hides, but the temescal was branches caulked with mud. In both, red-hot stones were put inside and water poured over the stones to make steam.

tenderfoot A newcomer, an inexperienced person, a greenhorn, a pilgrim, a pork-eater. First applied to imported cattle (which were tender-footed), then used by miners for ignorant males of the human variety.

The tenderfoot has been a object of a good deal of teasing in the West, much of it unkind. A nice trick played on the innocents was the one that the Wyoming writer Struthers Burt used on the Easterners who came to his dude ranch each summer. In those early days, visitors had to travel to Jackson Hole by stagecoach from Idaho. Burt had his dude wranglers mask themselves and rob the stagecoach on Teton Pass – pick the guests completely clean, money, luggage, the lot. When they got to the ranch, the dudes were amazed and hugely grateful to find their belongings in their rooms and even laid out in their drawers.

ten-gallon hat An over-sized stockman's hat, one with an extra-high crown and an extra-wide brim. Maybe the ten-gallon part, meaning how many gallons of water the crown would hold for a thirsty horse, was originally a Texas brag.

tenting Raising newborn lambs in tents during a cold spell in spring. [Adams]

tepary In the south-west, a bean (*Phaseolus acutifolius*) that is particularly resistant to drought.

tepee *See* tipi.

tequila An alcoholic drink made from the maguey plant. The first stage of fermentation produced pulque, the next mescal, and tequila was distilled from mescal. The name came from Tequila, Mexico, which made a particularly good distilled spirit from the maguey. Old-timers call it cactus juice.

tesquite An alkali of commercial value that oozes from the earth around south-western bodies of water.

teton (1) A mountain, when its shape suggests a breast. Used in place names such as the Teton Range and the Grand Teton. This meaning derives from the French *téton* (breast). (2) The largest and most powerful branch of the Dakota Indians. This meaning derives from an Indian word meaning 'prairie dwellers'. (*See* Dakota)

Teton Sioux *See* Lakota.

Tewa (1) Pueblo people living in villages of northern New Mexico and at the Hopi Reservation in Arizona. The name is the Keresan word for moccasin and is also spelled *Tegua*. (2) The ankle-high moccasins originally made by these people and worn by many Indians, Hispanics and Anglos of the pioneer and modern south-west.

Texan Both a person and a cow. The cows called Texans were Texas longhorns, half-wild and in need of considerable subduing, like some of the people. Texas people are also known as *beef heads*, *rawhiders*, *Tejanos*, *Texians* and *Texicans*. The lore of the state (the equivalent of Americana) is called *Texana*. The language is *Texan*, and its characteristic expressions are *Texanisms*. The Texan Republic was the sovereign state founded by Texans after independence from Mexico and before admission to the Union, lasting from 1836 to 1845.

Combinations: Texas butter (gravy made from rendered animal fat, flour and water), *Texas cake-walk* (a hanging), *Texas gate* (a gate made of three strands of barbwire and wide-spaced poles, ubiquitous in ranch country), *Texas house* (two log cabins with a covered dog trot in between; also called a *double log cabin* or a *saddlebag house*), *Texas itch* (a skin disease of cattle also known as scabies), *Texas Panhandle* (the northern piece of the state that extends between Oklahoma and New Mexico, famous for its barren plains; sometimes referred to as *down in the skillet* [Adams]), *Texas leg* (descriptive of shotgun chaps that go all the way around the leg), *Texas rig* (any double-rigged saddle), *Texas saddle* (the Texas adaptation of the old vaquero stock saddle, with small, high horn, high cantle, square skirt and two cinches [a double rig]), *Texas skirt* (a square saddle skirt such as was the rule in Texas until the late 19th century), *Texas tie* (the tying of the catch rope to the saddle-horn, the way tie-hard-and-fast men do it), *Texas tree* (the saddle tree of a Texas rig) and *Texas yell* (a ferocious holler bellowed in combat, rousing the yeller and intimidating the foe, perhaps adapted from the Comanche or Creek Indians).

Texas fever (1) A parasitic fever that made Texas cattle sick and killed other cows. From the mid-1850s, Kansans, Missourians and Indians of the five civilised tribes tried to keep Texas cattle from coming into their country. In the 1860s, laws were passed against the importation of Texas cows, and all through the era of the great cattle drives, quarantine lines kept these cows west of certain points in Kansas. The Jayhawkers also used the fever as an excuse to steal cows. Later, Texas fever was discovered to be caused by a tick the Texas cows carried. Texas fever was also called *Spanish fever*, *Southern fever*, *splenic fever* and *Texas murrain*. (2) A powerful desire to go to Texas, felt especially by people in trouble with their creditors or the law. The cure was sometimes symbolised by the initials GTT. – Gone to Texas.

Texas longhorn   The wild cow of Texas. Known for its wide span of horns, the longhorns were also called *broadhorns*, *coasters*, *sea lions*, *cactus boomers*, *horned jack rabbits*, *Indian cattle*, *mossy horns* or *backs*, *Texas cattle*, *Spanish cattle* and *twisthorns*.

Descended from the mission cattle of old Mexico, these cattle thrived on their own until the time of the settlement of Texas and during their years of independence developed considerable hardiness, not to mention wildness, cantankerousness and even nastiness.

The longhorn can forage on barren lands that more delicate cattle starve on. Its hardiness led cattlemen to drive the longhorns in the 1870s and 1880s from Texas to the great ranges of the northern plains. But there the longhorn gave way to various shorthorn breeds because these cattle produce more as well as more tender beef and don't have the nuisance of long horns, which make shipping difficult. After near extinction at the beginning of the 20th century, the longhorn has made a modest comeback. The classic book about these critters is J. Frank Dobie's *The Longhorns*.

Longhorn can also mean a person – a Texan or any old-timer.

Texas Rangers   A fabled group of Indian fighters, soldiers and mounted police in Texas. They were first organised while Texas was still part of Mexico to protect settlers against Indians. They operated in military units in the war against Mexico, and by the 1870s were an important police force, though not bound by formalities such as uniforms.

theodore   An Americanised version of fiador, a cord running from the bosal around the horse's ears.

there goes hoss and beaver   Mountain-man talk for, 'We just lost everything,' which they too often did to raiding Indians, raging waters and so on.

there's a one-eyed man in the game   In gambling, a warning that someone's cheating. Ramon Adams says it came from a superstition that one-eyed gamblers gave other players bad luck forever.

three saddles   A professional bronc buster's expression for a horse that he's broke. In the 19th century, a horse ridden three times was considered broke, which was some distance yet from trained or gentled. (*See* break a horse)

three-legged riding   Riding with a tight rein and sawing on the bit.

three–seven–seventy-seven   At Virginia City, Montana, in the 1860s, a code name for the Vigilance Committee. Says Berry, the fictional trader in James Willard Schultz's *My Life as an Indian*, who is a stand-in for the actual trader Joseph Kipp, 'You don't know who they are, but you may be sure that they are representative men who stand for law and order; they are more feared by criminals than are the courts and prisons of the East, for they always hang a murderer or robber.' The code name often appeared as numerals, and may have meant the number of days, hours and minutes offered to get out of town. (*See* vigilante)

thriftiness   A sheep that does well on the range; it does not lose weight and is unlikely to be culled.

through herd   A herd of cows being driven or shipped through to a further point. Through herds were a problem to local stockmen during the days of the great trail drives, for local people didn't want to provide free grass and bed grounds to those passing through.

throw a hitch   To tie a knot, a hitch, which in the West is not tied but thrown.

thumb the hammer   To fire a revolver by pulling the hammer back with the second joint of the thumb and letting the hammer slide forward from the thumb's web area. A man who used the hammer this way, instead of a trigger, was called a *thumber*. The older revolvers, with stiff hammers, were called *thumb busters*.

thunderbird   One version of what Indians call *thunder beings*, spirits of power associated with the West, with lightning, thunder and rain. The thunderbird is an icon particularly in the religious art (and all of their art is religious) of south-western Indians; it causes the thunderstorm by fighting with a giant serpent.

tie *Combinations: tied to the ground* (descriptive of a horse trained to stand still with the reins dropped to earth, as secure as if he were tied, ground-hitched), *tie down a steer* (to rope it and hog-tie it, as in a rodeo), *tie-down man* (a gunman with his holster tied to his leg to facilitate his draw), *tie on the bear* (to become inebriated), *tie rail* (a hitching rail), *tie rope* (either a mecate or a pigging string) and *tie strings* (leather strings on a saddle [usually through a rosette] used to tie on a bedroll or other gear).

To *tie on to something* means 'to rope it'. *Tie one to that!* is an invitation to top a good story. [Adams]

tie hack A man who cut railroad ties. These men often lived in a *tie camp* and hewed the lumber into the ties on site, sometimes as many as forty a day. Wyoming, with its stands of lodgepole timber, which were used chiefly for railroad ties, had many tie camps. Once the ties were made, they were driven down the river in the spring runoff.

tie-hard-and-fast man A roper who ties his rope to the saddle horn instead of taking dallies to stop the critter he's roped. This style has been most popular in Texas and on the Great Plains generally. This fellow is also known as a *tie man* or *tie peeler*. (*See* dally.)

tienda In the south-west, a store, a shop. Borrowed from Spanish, it's pronounced tee-EN-duh.

tiger The game faro, because of the tiger conventionally painted on the faro box. Thus to play faro was to *buck* (or *twist*) *the tiger*.

tight-legging Riding a horse with the legs pressed right against it. The rules in rodeo require the competitor to be scratching, not tight-legging.

tilikum Chinook jargon for a friend; tilikums may also mean plain folks. Also spelled *tillicum* and pronounced TIL-uh-kuhm.

timber *Combinations: timber beast, timber head, timber-jack* (lumberjack is little used in the West), *timber savage* and *timber wolf* [Adams] (all names for a logger), *timber cruiser* (a man who looks for commercially valuable tracts of timber – goes on *timber cruises* or *timber hunts*; also called a *timber looker* or *tree looker*), *timber claim* (a section of public land with a claim filed for its timber, often with the condition of planting a portion in trees), *timber marking* (blazing, painting or otherwise marking trees for timbering [Adams]), *timber cattle* (cows that range in timber), *timber fall* (an area of blowdown) and *timber-line* (in mountain country, the elevation where trees give way to shrubs and grasses; also called *treeline*).

tin dogs A string of tin cans rattled by a sheep-herder to get the sheep to move along. [Adams]

tin pants Heavy, woollen, water-resistant trousers such as loggers and other outdoorsmen of the north woods use. A *tin coat* is made of similar material.

tinaja A natural water hole, especially in rock; a water hole dug by Indians; a tank. Adapted from Spanish (where it means 'a big earthen jar'), it's pronounced ti-NAH-hah.

tin-belly Cowboy talk for a cheaply-made spur.

tinhorn A gambler of the flashy sort.

tipi The lodge of the Indians of the Great Plains, a dwelling shaped like an upside-down cone. Typically, it was made from buffalo hides (later of canvas) stretched over a frame of poles of peeled lodgepole pine. From the Dakota *tipi*, meaning 'used to live in', it is also spelled *teepee* and *tepee*.

Tipis were as small as 12 feet in diameter for a small travelling family and could be very large when intended for councils. Women made them, women owned them, and only women erected them. A centre fire kept the lodge warm in winter, and lifting the lodge skin from the bottom allowed a breeze in the summer. The entrance faced east, a gesture of acknowledgment of the spirit powers. Modern Indians and interested Anglos still use tipis, especially at powwows and rendezvous.

Much lore of the tipi and practical instructions for putting one up are found in Reginald and Gladys Laubin's *The Indian Tipi*.

Tipi rings are circles of stone used to hold down the cover of a hide tipi. They are still found, half in the ground, at popular Indian camping sites on the Plains.

tiswin A sweet Apache drink made from corn, says Cornelius Smith, but usually confused with its fermented form, *tulapai*, a kind of beer. Tulapai was used religiously but was also known for getting Apaches drunk and troublesome. This bit of doggerel by Charles Poston, called the father of Arizona, sets the story straight:

The Tizwin drink is much enjoyed,
    to make it, Indian corn's employed.
They bury the corn until it sprouts,
    destroying food for drinking bouts.
They grind it in a kind of tray,
    they boil it strong for one long day,
Strain off the juice in willow-sieve
    and in the sun to ferment, leave.
Fermented juice is then Tulpai
    on which Apache chiefs get high.

From the Spanish *tesgüino* (which has the same meaning), it's pronounced tis-WEEN and also spelled *tizwin*.

tobacco tie Among Plains Indians, a prayer symbol made of a small square of cloth around a pinch of tobacco, closed and tied on to a string. Originally these ties were made of dyed buckskin; after traders made cloth available, the custom changed. Also called a *tobacco-tie garland* or a *prayer tie*.

tobiano A pinto horse whose white colour is on top, on the back and on the hind quarters and extends downward.

toggle A piece of wood or chain fixed to the front foot of a horse or cow so that the critter can walk but will step on the toggle if it tries to run. That way it can graze but not run off. [Adams]

tom In placer mining, to wash gold-bearing gravel in a long tom. A sheet of perforated iron put over the riffle box to strain out the larger stones was called a *tom iron*.

tomatillo A vine-like plant (*Physallis ixocarpa*) that produces tart green fruits that are an important ingredient in Mexican sauces.

tombé In the south-west, an Indian drum made from a hollow log with a piece of hide stretched over one end, said to produce a far-carrying sound. The word is of obscure origin.

tong An American Chinese word for a fraternal organisation among Chinese in the United States, especially in San Francisco, often used to control gambling interests. San Francisco's tong wars over gambling began about 1899.

tongue-splitting A practice of rustlers. When they cut a calf's tongue, it couldn't suck so would stop following its mother and so would become a maverick and belong to the first claimant. Thieves who did this were called *tongue-splitters*.

too much mustard Descriptive cowboy talk for a prickly fellow or a braggart. [Adams]

too thick to drink, too thin to plough An eloquent description of Powder River or the Platte or many another Western river with everything but enough water to get a decent drink from.

tool nipper Miner's talk for the worker who distributed the tools in a mine; also called an *abajador*. The *tool-pusher* is the superintendent of an oil rig.

toothing Checking a horse's or sheep's teeth to find out how old it is.

toothpick timber Among loggers, a mocking term for little trees.

top *Combinations:* topknot (a scalp), *top out* or *top off a bronc* (to take the kinks out of it), *top-railer* (a person who sits on the top rail of the corral and gives advice) and *top screw* (to both cowboys and loggers, a foreman).

top hand A first-rate cowhand. Also called a *top waddy*.

In cowboy talk, top was and is added to a number of other nouns to indicate superiority – thus top man, top roper, top cutter, and so on. But among miners, a top hand was a recruit off the farm.

toro An occasional name for jerked buffalo meat, from the Spanish word meaning 'bull'. Also an occasional word for bull, used in the circumspect 19th century as a euphemism for the male bovine, which wasn't mentioned in front of ladies. Later a general US word for bull, often used jocularly.

torreon In the south-west, a lookout spot, such as a hill. Borrowed from Spanish (where it means 'big tower'), it's pronounced toh-ray-OHN.

tortilla Especially in the south-west, a thin, flat, unleavened bread made from flour or ground corn. Originally tortillas were baked on a slab of hot stone, later on hot iron. Borrowed from Spanish, it is pronounced tor-TEE-yuh.

tostado An open-faced tortilla covered with beans and cheese.

touch him up In cowboy talk, to spur a horse.

tornillo In the south-west, the screwpod mesquite (*Prosopis pubescens*) or its bean, which cows and horses feed on. Borrowed from Spanish, it's pronounced tawr-NEE-yoh.

touron A derogatory name for a tourist used in the vicinity of Grand Teton National Park and Yellowstone National Park. It derives from the combination of 'tourist' and 'moron'.

trace A track made by animals, wagons and so on – *buffalo trace*, *wagon trace*, *Comanche trace*.

trade blanket A heavy, wool blanket made for trade to the Indians. Blankets were from the beginning a staple of the Indian trade. Probably the best-known brand was the Hudson's Bay Company's; others were the Witney and Northwest blankets (Hudson and Witney are still made today). They became so closely associated with Indian ways that the expression for a red man's returning to his tribal traditions became *back to the blanket*. The blankets were identified by size, shown by stripes woven into the fabric; a four-point (-stripe) blanket cost four beaver skins (plews), a six-point six skins and so on. Coats, leggings and other items of clothing were also made from the blankets. (*See* capote) From the reservation period forward the most popular brand has been Pendleton.

trading post The commercial establishment of an Anglo trader for trade with the Indians and for supply of trappers roaming the country for beaver. Though goods surely were exchanged with Indians from the time of earliest white contact, the term trading post wasn't used until 1796, and then was applied mostly to the West. The great trading posts, from Fort Vancouver to Fort Leavenworth were situated beside the great rivers – the Missouri, Platte, Arkansas, Snake, Columbia and Yellowstone. The traders in charge of these posts usually became expert in Indian ways and languages; some later became Indian agents; others even became Indians.

The Indian trade was the basis of Western economies from the beginning of colonisation of the continent. The fur trade of Canada and the United States, in fact, was the motivation for exploration. At the heart of this activity was trading goods like blankets, hatchets, knives, guns, beads and whiskey for beaver plews.

The prices of these items were high enough to make the greedy gleeful – or so the Anglos thought. The Indians probably saw four beaver hides for a blanket or a gun as trading the common for the rare and wondered at the whites who would do it. So both sides profited at the time, though Indian dependence on trade goods contributed significantly to their downfall.

Some such American posts were operated by the big fur companies, Hudson's Bay Company and American Fur. Others, like Bent's Fort and Fort Laramie, were built by independent traders. As the West changed, so did these outposts. Laramie was typical. It started as a fur post, became a centre for the emigrant trade and finally turned into a military post. Later the federal government licensed trading posts on the reservations.

David Lavender's *Bent's Fort* gives a marvellous picture of life at a major trading post.

trail (1) To drive cattle from one place to another, not necessarily on a trail. (2) A more or less permanent track beaten by human use (possibly a Westernism, it first occurred in the journal of Patrick Gass on the Lewis and Clark expedition).

After rivers, trails were the first major roads of the West. The great emigrant trails chiefly ran from the Missouri settlements to the West – the Santa Fe Trail to New Mexico, the Oregon Trail to the Pacific north-west and so on. The great cattle trails ran from Texas north, at first to the Kansas railroad towns, later to the grasslands of Colorado, Wyoming and Montana.

One trail of legend was a forced emigrant trail: the Trail of Tears was the route of the US government removal of the Cherokee people to Indian Territory (present-day Oklahoma), a trip of great suffering.

Combinations: trail blazer (one who finds the way and marks it), *trail boss* (the man in charge of a cattle drive, especially responsible for finding good water, good grass and good bed grounds and for handling the trail crew), *trail-broke* (descriptive of cows accustomed to the cattle trail and therefore manageable), *trail crossing* (a place where a cattle trail fords a river, sometimes remembered for the deaths that took place there), *trail cutter* (an inspector responsible for checking passing cattle herds for cows that didn't belong in them; what he did was called trimming the herd [Adams]), *trail hand* (a trail driver, a cowboy engaged in taking cows up the trail, which was one of the ambitions of most Texas cowboys) and *trail ride* (a dude activity on most guest ranches, horseback riding on a trail to a pleasant spot – not anything to do with a cattle drive).

Verb phrases: take the trail for somewhere (to set out for that destination), *camp on someone's trail* (to follow someone), *cut someone's trail* (to come upon his track; to block his trail while you inspect his herd), *hit the trail* (to leave) and *break trail* (to make a way through obstacles, especially through deep snow).

trail drive *See* cattle trail.

travel with the grass In the days of the great trail drives, to trail cows north as the grass comes green, starting in Texas early in the spring and getting to the northern ranges as the snow clears and the grass comes.

travois A vehicle for hauling belongings; the horse Indians' equivalent of a wagon. The word is an adaptation of the French-Canadian *travail* and is also spelled *travée*.

A travois was made by taking a pair of lodge-poles (which one already had for the tipi), criss-crossing the small ends on a horse's back, letting the butt ends drag behind, slinging skins (or straps of skin) in between and tying gear on. Small children might be put on, also. Before Indians had the horse to drag big travois, they hitched small ones on to their dogs.

An Indian village on the move was carrying everything it owned, most of it on travois. It was slow, it lacked mobility, and the butts of the poles, dragging on the ground, left a big trail, called a *travois trail*. Such a village was vulnerable and needed defence, which was provided by the young men.

Since they were in roadless country and had no wheels, mountain men often adopted the travois. Later, lumbermen used travois to transport logs and developed the transitive verb 'to travois'.

treasure box A stagecoach's strongbox, the main object of the road agent's desire. A stagecoach carrying gold away from diggings and designed for defence against road agents was called a *treasure coach*.

treaty Indian An Indian whose tribe had come to a peace agreement with the federal government and was therefore 'pacified'. This notion caused a lot of misunderstanding in the West, partly because Anglos didn't understand the nature of Indian leadership. The whites were always designating one Indian as head of a band or a tribe, often because he was co-operative. But that fellow might not have had any real leadership, and his people might not have felt obliged to respect any agreements he made. Also, the Indians regarded by whites as chiefs often were only leaders in war. The US government made this mistake in coming to terms with Red Cloud but not the real leaders of the Oglala Dakota in 1868 at Fort Laramie.

Another important matter about Indian leadership: Indians acknowledged the rights of individuals to do what they thought right (often to do what their medicine indicated), regardless of what the group did. Altogether, a treaty Indian might have been warlike, in his view, without violating any promises.

From early colonial times, *treaty* referred not only to an agreement with Indians but to the conference at which the agreement was reached.

tree a town An expression of trail-drive cowboys. When they strutted and drank and shot their guns until they had a whole town scared and buffaloed, including its law officers, they said they had it treed. They also spoke of *treeing the marshal*. It's all an extension of the notion (from the Eastern frontier) of making an animal you're hunting take refuge in a tree.

tributer A miner who works a claim, taking mineral as wages, without rights as owner or leaser.

tricks Especially in Texas, belongings, personal possessions, what the mountain man called *possibles*.

trigger is delicate Cowboy talk for a man with a quick temper or maybe literally quick on the trigger. [Adams] This latter fellow is said to have *trigger itch* [Adams] and to be *easy on the trigger*.

trigueño In the south-west, descriptive of a brown horse. Borrowed from Spanish (where it means 'dark, swarthy'), it's pronounced tree-GAYN-yoh. (For horse colours, *see* buckskin)

trim his ears with a hat For a rider to fan his horse with his hat.

trinchera In the south-west of the 19th century, a fortified position. Borrowed from Spanish (where it means 'entrenchment'), it's pronounced trin-CHAYR-uh.

trip rope A rope tied to the front foot of a difficult horse when it's being trained and used to jerk it off its feet as a lesson.

tripas In the south-west of the 19th century, a socially acceptable word for guts. Borrowed from Spanish, it's pronounced TREE-puhs.

tripping In oil drilling, pulling all the pipe out of a drill hole in order to replace the drill bit.

tromper During shearing, the worker who stands in the wool sacks and compresses the fleece with his feet. Usually the job is given to a boy or an apprentice.

trouble wagon A wagon used to transport the cowboy who looked after the windmill, pipes and water troughs, and to haul salt. [Adams]

tulapai An Apache beer made from corn. (*See* tiswin)

tule In the south-west, especially California, either of two bulrushes of the genus *Scirpus*, often used by Indians to thatch huts. Borrowed from Spanish, it's pronounced TOO-lee.

To *pull freight for* (or *take to*) *the tules* meant 'to go on the dodge, to run from the law'. To *be in the deep tules* means 'to be in trouble'. *Tulares* are areas overgrown with tules; they were also a band of Indians living on San Francisco Bay.

Combinations: tule balsa (a raft of tules), *tule boat* (a boat somewhat like a keelboat made of tules), *tule elk* (the small California elk), *tule fog* (in California, a fog on the Sacramento or San Joaquin Rivers), *tule root* or *potato* (the tuber of the tule, used for food in California by Indians, Chinese and some Anglos) and *tule wren* (the California marsh wren).

tumbleweed The Russian thistle (*Salsola australis*), which breaks off its roots when finished growing, blows and rolls all over the country and ends up caught on fences. The tumbleweed has become a symbol of a footloose, roving Western fellow, liable to drift in any direction and stay nowhere long.

Tumbleweed was accidentally introduced to South Dakota in 1877, and rapidly spread over the West. It grows in disturbed and agricultural areas, causes the destruction of range land and is dangerous to motorists and livestock. Also called *saltwort*, *Russian cactus* and *wind witch*.

A *tumbleweed wagon* was a jail on wheels that took prisoners to more permanent calabooses.

tum-tum In Chinook jargon, the heart, the mind or the will. The word imitates the beating of the heart.

turkey A bedroll. Or, among loggers, a bag to carry tools in. *Turkey season* is tourist season. Surely an extension from the common derogatory slang term 'turkey'.

turn on a dime and give you back five cents change   What a first-rate cutting horse can do. A horse that makes quick cuts is also said to have *turned through itself*. [Adams]

turron   A dessert blended of almonds and honey, a favourite of Hispanics in Arizona a century ago. Borrowed from Spanish (where it means 'a confection of nuts'), it's pronounced TOO-ROHN.

turtle   A rodeo cowboy; a member of the Cowboy's Turtle Association, the ancestor of the current Professional Rodeo Cowboy's Association. One story about how the first rodeo rider's union got named is that someone called the rodeo cowboys turtles because they were practically the last working men to organise.

Turtle Island   Among Indians, this continent or the Western hemisphere, by extension this world we live in. From the Algonquin legend that the earth rests on the back of a turtle.

tus   A jug-shaped basket of the Apaches, from the Apache word for it. Other tribes have similar baskets now sometimes called by the same name, some even saturated with pitch to make them hold water. Pronounced TOOS.

tusker   A person who takes the canine teeth (tusks) of elk for sale as souvenirs, charms and decorations. Such men poached thousands of elk in Jackson Hole and the Yellowstone country, but in 1906 vigilante action in Jackson put a stop to the tusking.

Twelve Apostles   In the Mormon Church the members of the Council of Twelve, often referred to simply as the Twelve. The principal ruling body of the Church under the first Presidency. Members of the Council of Twelve are also set apart as 'prophets, seers, and revelators'. (*See* prophet)

twenty-one   *See* blackjack.

twist   A rope of tobacco; one of the two

chief forms in which chewing and smoking tobacco were traded and sold in the old West, the other being *plug*. It was seasoned with such flavourings as licorice, molasses, sugar, fruit juices and so on and was sold in substantial hunks. For mountain men and Indian hobbyists, tobacco is still available in twist form.

twist down   For a bulldog to force a steer down by twisting its neck. To *twist a horse*, or *twist it down*, is to break it. (*See* break a horse)

twister   (1) Slange for a tornado. Tornados are common on the southern and central plains. (2) A bronc buster. (3) A cord put around the lip of a difficult horse and twisted with a stick to inflict pain and teach a lesson; perhaps this is the source of the term *bronc twister*. (4) A nail on the end of the pole of a railroad cowpuncher, used to catch in the tail of a troublesome critter and twist.

two bits   A quarter of a dollar – originally of a Spanish or Spanish colonial dollar. These dollars were called pieces of eight, eight reales to a dollar, and the frontiersmen called the reales bits. Prices were high in the old West: two bits for a shot of rotgut, four bits or a dollar for a meal at a stage station, compared to a short bit (dime) for a full meal in many St Louis restaurants, coffee and pie included. (*See* real)

two whoops and a holler   Cowboy talk for a short distance. But *two jumps ahead of the sheriff*, meaning 'on the lam', was never far enough.

two-by-four outfit   A shirt-tail outfit, a rawhide outfit, a little ranch.

two-gun man   A gunman who wore two pistols and shot with both hands, a rarity in the West and a dubious advantage.

two-track   A crude road, not graded but merely two tracks made by the passage of tyres; the native road of ranch country. The automotive explorer who hasn't explored the West via two-tracks hasn't begun to explore.

tyee   In Chinook jargon, a chief or other person of special consequence.

U

Uncle Tomahawk The Indian equivalent of an Uncle Tom, an Indian who is over-accommodating or subservient to whites. The Indian equivalent of what blacks call an Oreo (black outside and white inside) is an *apple*.

uncork a horse To take the edges off a bronc, the beginning of breaking it; to ride a horse that's bucking into submission. Also said as *unrooster*.

United Order The United Order of Enoch, an economic utopian concept of Joseph Smith's. He proposed that all worldly goods be shared communally by Mormons. They experimented with it in Ohio and Missouri but failed; in the 1870s, they made an effort at Brigham City and Orderville, Utah, but failed. Though polygamist factions have experimented with this style of co-operative living even in this century, the orthodox Church no longer advocates it.

unshucked Cowboy talk for naked. And an unshucked gun is one that's out of the holster. [Adams]

untrack a horse To lead a horse forward a little before mounting. If the horse is in a mood to blow up, he's likely to show it at that point. Old hands don't get on a horse without untracking it.

up and down as a cow's tail Cowboy talk for honest, straightforward. [Adams]

up to trap Said by mountain men of an experienced trapper, a man who knew what he was doing. Another expression with the same meaning is *up to beaver*.

uranium on the cranium A Utah description of the mental state of uranium prospectors in canyon country.

Ute A Uto-Aztecan people who lived, from the time of white contact, in western Colorado and eastern Utah. The name of the tribe, meaning 'high up' or 'land of the sun', is also rendered as *Utah*, *Utaw*, and *Eutaw*. The Indians called *Ute Diggers* were Paiutes. In the 19th century, Anglos called them *Goshutes*, *Grasshopper Indians* and *Land Pitches*.

Primarily hunter-gathers, when they acquired the horse in the late 1600s they adopted a nomadic life similar to that of the Plains Indians, yet they rarely hunted buffalo. In the 19th century, they developed a formidable reputation as horse thieves, venturing as far as California on raids.

Through the leadership of Chief Ouray, the Utes received a large reservation in western Colorado by treaty in 1863, but after their killing of Indian agent Nathan Meeker in 1879, the government took away their Colorado reservation and gave them two small pieces of land in Utah. In the late 1940s the Utes won a large judgment against the federal government as reimbursement for their Colorado reservation.

V

vaca The Spanish word for cow, used commonly in the south-west, sometimes jocularly. Pronounced VAH-kuh. A *vacada* is a herd of cows.

vacheur An occasional south-western-ism for a vaquero, a cowboy. Borrowed from French and pronounced vah-shur. Ranches were sometimes called *vacheries*.

vaciero In the south-west, the fellow who brought supplies to the camps of the sheep-herders because they couldn't leave their herds. From the Spanish, and pronounced vah-SYAYR-oh.

vag Slang for a vagabond. The first uses appear to be in the West.

valgame Dios! In the south-west, an exclamation, literally 'God help me', and the approximate equivalent of 'for heaven's sakes'. Borrowed from Spanish, it's pronounced VAL-gah-may-dee-OHS.

valley tan In Mormondom, a derisive term for anything homemade. First it was applied to a second-rate leather made in Salt Lake, then generalised to anything made at home. It particularly applied to a potent brand of whiskey also called *leopard sweat*.

vamoose Let's go, let's get a move on, let's get out of here. Adapted from the Spanish verb *vamos*, which means the same, it's pronounced vah-MOOS or va-MOOS. The term started in the south-west and has spread all over the United States. American practice widened the term to looser usages, such as the infinitive (to vamoose), the gerund (vamoosing) and even the transitive verb. Thus Libby Custer writes, 'they vamoosed the ranch'.

vaquero A cowboy, especially a Hispanic cowboy, or an Anglo hand of the border country or California. Borrowed from Spanish, it's pronounced vah-KAYR-oh by most Americans and bah-KEH-roh by those with a finer tongue for Spanish. Also spelled *vacquero* and *baquero*.

The vaqueros of New Spain and Mexico discovered and refined much of the gear, technique and lore that became the standard equipment of American cowboys.

Early Texans learned it from vaqueros and sent it north to the Great Plains with the great trail herds. David Dary's excellent *Cowboy Culture* shows how cowboy learning developed and was disseminated.

vara A Spanish yard, 33 inches. Borrowed from the Spanish, it's pronounced VAHR-uh.

varruga In the south-west, a cut in the jaw or wattle that made a strip of flesh hang down (a mark of ownership like the earmark). Borrowed from Spanish (where it has the same meaning), it's pronounced vah-ROO-guh.

vega A meadow; a grassy plain or valley. Borrowed from Spanish, it's pronounced VAY-guh.

vent brand A sale brand; a brand replacing the original brand of ownership and indicating that the cow has been sold. To *vent a brand* was to put on such a brand and perhaps burn a slash through the old brand. Derived from the Spanish *venta* (a sale). That Spanish word became a south-westernism meaning 'inn'.

verdad This Spanish word for truth is sometimes used in the modern south-west to mean 'really, truly, for sure'.

viga In the south-west, a peeled log used to support a roof in an adobe structure and usually sticking out beyond the walls. These are often combined with crossing latias (slender, peeled poles) in a style called viga-and-latia construction. Borrowed from Spanish (where it means 'rafter'), viga is pronounced VEE-guh.

vigilante A member of a vigilance committee. Also called a *regulator*, or *vigilant* or a *vigy*. The form *vigilancism* was used in California in the 1850s; the first uses of vigilante date from Colorado and Montana in the 1860s, in both cases in newspapers during times of vigilance committee activity.

Citizens banded together in the West as vigilance committees, without legal sanction and usually in the absence of effective law enforcement, to take action against men viewed as threats to life and property. The usual pattern of vigilance committees (also called *hemp committees*, *committees of vigilance* or *associations of vigilance*) was to grab the 'bad' guys, stage a sort of trial and hang their enemies. Others of their enemies then were likely to see discretion as the better part of valour and vamoose.

These committees started not in the West but the South, where they arose to intimidate blacks and abolitionists. In the West, they usually claimed to set out to make life safe for ordinary citizens. In Montana of the 1860s gold rush, they were respected men and probably acted from commendable motives. But other vigilantes may have been motivated by religious or racial intolerance or a desire for power and were afflicted with blood lust after they got started. Most areas of the West saw some vigilancism.

The committees sometimes signed themselves VC, so that a traveller might see a grave with a marker bearing a name and the ominous inscription, 'Died by the hands of the VC'.

vinegarroon   In the south-west, the whip scorpion, which also has been called a *vinagrillo*. The name comes from the vinegarish stink of the critter when disturbed. Adapted from the Spanish *vinagrón*, which suggests a strong vinegar smell, it's pronounced vin-uh-guh-ROON.

Visalia   A popular saddle tree (the wooden framework of a saddle) that thus gave its name to the saddle; *Visa* for short. [Adams] Other well-known trees have been California, Ellenburg and Frazier.

vision quest   A traditional form of seeking among Indian men and sometimes women, very widespread. Typically, during adolescence the quester purifies himself in a sweat lodge, isolates himself for four days, does not eat or drink during that time and seeks medicine, which is most likely to be revealed in the form of a dream. He may repeat the quest several times during his life.

This custom, once common to many primal peoples and still vital among Indians, is now spreading in a modest way to women and to Anglos, who seek not medicine specifically but life-guiding wisdom. *See* the excellent *The Book of the Vision Quest* (1980) by Steven Foster and Meredith Little for this new form of an ancient rite.

viva!   In the south-west, an exclamation of approval. Borrowed from Spanish, it's pronounced VEE-vuh.

volante   (1) In the south-west, a light two-wheeled vehicle drawn by horses or mules. (2) A veil-like woman's head covering. Adapted from Spanish, it's pronounced voh-LAHN-tay.

volunteer   A rodeo hand who sets calves and steers free from the competitors' ropes and pigging strings.

vomito   A virulent form of yellow fever, often accompanied by black vomit. Borrowed from Spanish, it's pronounced VAH-mi-toh.

voucher   In Texas and perhaps more broadly through the south-west, a scalp taken for bounty.

voyageur   A French-Canadian boatman (*voyageur*). He was a hired labourer with a canoe paddle. For an appreciation of him, see Peter Newman's *Caesars of the Wilderness*. Borrowed from Canadian French, it is pronounced vwa-yah-JHER.

W

waddy One of the words for cowboy, especially a cowboy who drifted from ranch to ranch and helped out in busy times. Jo Mora and Ramon Adams both suggest that the word derived from *wad*, something used to fill in, but this notion isn't widely accepted. Neither is the suggestion that it comes from a wad of chewing tobacco. To add to the mystery, waddy first meant 'rustler', then 'cowboy'. Also spelled *waddie*.

wagh! An interjection of the mountain men, indicating vigorous assent, amazement or the like. Some authorities speculate that it may have derived from the grunt of an Indian or of a grizzly bear. A more likely suggestion is that it came from an exclamation of Santa Fe Trail men, Hua! meaning 'Get along!' which in turn comes from the Spanish exclamation *Gua!* meaning something like 'Gracious!' Many mountain men first came West on the Sante Fe Trail in the 1820s and 1830s, and the first recorded use among the mountain men is by Lt George Frederick Ruxton in the late 1840s.

wagon boss The wagon master, the leader of a train of freight, often reported to be an absolute monarch on the trail, in charge of finding grass and water, choosing places for nooning and camping, security against Indians and so on. Also a name for the roundup captain.

wagon train A group of wagons bearing emigrants west or sometimes bearing freight. (Trains of freight wagons were more likely to be called bull trains, grass trains and so on.)

The emigrant train has been one of the yeasty myths of the West, giving birth to tales of epic adventure, heroism, cowardice, villainy and the like. Emerson Hough's *The Covered Wagon*, a hugely popular novel and movie, and A. B. Guthrie Jr's *The Way West*, which won the Pulitzer Prize, describe the experience.

The wagon of legend and history was the prairie schooner. For the Oregon Trail, the principal emigrant trail, and the Santa Fe Trail, these wagons generally assembled at Westport, Missouri and started in the spring when the grass was good. They bunched up in trains big enough to offer protection against Indians, which the emigrants imagined to be the biggest danger, though they weren't. Thunderstorms, dust storms, high rivers, lack of water, scarcity of game, steep grades and disgruntled companions all took their toll on the emigrants. The Plains Indians, perhaps after being placated with some gifts, most years simply let the wayfarers pass. The most celebrated disaster of the emigrant period came from starvation – when the Donner party got stuck in the Sierras in 1846 and had to winter there.

Most emigrants passed without disaster to Oregon or California or to the kingdom of Deseret or to wherever they were going and set up a new life or even a hoped-for utopia.

wakan Among contemporary Plains Indians of various tribes, sacred, spiritual. Borrowed from the Dakota language (where it has the same meaning), it's pronounced wah-KAHN. One Dakota word for deity is *wakantanka*. Similar words existed in other Siouan languages.

walkaheap Indian Pidgin English for an infantryman, who walked rather than rode. Also heap-walk-man.

walk-down A technique of catching wild horses. The hunters ride slowly along behind the animals, at a distance, careful not to spook them, and finally exhaust them. This has even been accomplished on foot.

Walker A .44-calibre, six-shooting Colt produced by Samuel Colt and Eli Whitney Jr from 1847 into the 1860s. It was named after Texas Ranger Sam Walker.

wallet A saddle sack for a cowboy to carry his food and personal gear in. It was tied behind the saddle.

wallflower Among loggers, a bum, especially one who cadged drinks in a saloon.

wampus cat An imaginary critter loggers attribute night sounds to.

wannigan What a sheep-herder called his supply wagon or even his sheep wagon.

Among loggers: (1) A box for storing small items; a chest for storing clothes. (2) The logging camp office where loggers got paid. (3) A boat carrying the men and equipment of a woods logging camp. (4) A shelter loggers lived in. It is from an Abenaki word and variously spelled.

wapiti The American elk, which the British call a stag. The name (sometimes occurring as *wapiti deer* and variously spelled) comes from a Shawnee word meaning 'white rump'; the Cree have a similar word. For a study of these creatures and part of the country they inhabit, *see* Margaret and Olaus Murie's *Wapiti Wilderness* (1966), which views the animals both scientifically and from personal experience.

war *Combinations* created by Anglos relating to Indians and war, not necessarily exclusively Western: *war budget* (a sack containing an Indian's war medicine and trophies), *war chief* (a leader in war, who would suggest military missions and methods a war chief, being young and committed to making war, was not usually a leader of the people for broader purposes]), *war dance* (an Indian ceremony, including dancing, held as a preparation for war to solicit the help of the spirit powers; an Anglo imitation of the dancing, often done in jest), *war eagle* (the golden eagle, whose feathers represented prowess in fighting), *war paint* (paint applied by a warrior to his face or body [or both] in a design revealed to him to offer protection against injury, and perhaps offer fighting prowess; not all paint was war paint; also a mixture of soot and grease cowboys put on their faces as a protection against glare of the snow), *war party* (a group of Indians on a mission of war and by extension a bunch of whites out for blood), *war path* or *trail* (first a trail used to go to war; later a military expedition or the way or mode of war generally, first applied to Indians, then, sometimes jokingly, to whites and even to housewives), *war shield* (a shield made of heat-treated parfleche and made powerful by medicine), *war tent* (Indian Pidgin English for the Sibley tent used by soldiers on the Great Plains) and *war whoop* (an Indian war cry, understood by whites to be a joyous and bloodthirsty outburst, but these whites usually didn't understand the words; also occurred in verb form).

war bag A cowboy's bag for his personal possessions, often canvas but sometimes just a flour or grain sack. In the days of the open range, a snoop probably would have found some town clothing, the makings (for cigarettes), cartridges and maybe some letters from home in it. The word has survived to today, and the contents have changed with the times. It's also called a *war sack*, a *tucker bag* and a *possible sack*.

war bonnet Among the Plains Indians, and many other Indians, Indian Pidgin English for a hat of medicine, worn either in war or on ceremonial occasions or both. The medicine typically protected the warrior against injury or death and usually required certain behaviours on his part.

In popular imagination this hat has become a full-length eagle-feather headdress worn by the Plains Indians like the Sioux (Dakota) and Cheyenne. Actual war bonnets were made of many materials, especially the skin of the buffalo, and often included horns. The full eagle-feather version was also real, mentioned by John C. Frémont as early as 1845.

George Bird Grinnell was fortunate enough to get the story of a famous war bonnet, the one worn by the Cheyenne warrior Roman Nose, directly from the man who made the bonnet, White Bull. Discovering that White Bull had seen protection against lightning in a dream, Roman Bull asked him to make a war bonnet like the one dreamed. To make paints, White Bull pulverised stones and animal bones, and he gathered minerals and clay and charcoal. 'In the front of the war-bonnet, close to the brow-band, and over the warrior's forehead, stood a single buffalo-horn. Immediately behind this horn, on top of the bonnet, was the skin of a kingfisher, tied to the hair. At the right side of the head was tied a hawk-skin. This hawk represented the person who in White Bull's vision had held in its claws [a] gun and sabre. From the headpiece, on either side, two tails of eagle-feathers ran down toward the ground, the feathers on the right side being red, and those on the left side white. At the back of the head, part way down on the war-bonnet, was the skin of a barnswallow, while to the right side of the war-bonnet, where the feathers were red, was tied a bat, so that the warrior might safely fight in the night, for a bat flies at night and cannot be caught.'

White Bull goes on to explain that when an enemy shoots at the man on horseback, the real person will be the bat, above, or the barn swallow flying close to the ground. The kingfisher was to close holes made by bullets in the body, as the water closes over the kingfisher when it dives.

war bridle A painful halter used to lead unruly horses, made of a noose hitched on to a horse's mouth and around its head.

war knot A knot in the tail or mane of a horse, tied by buckaroos and Californios to keep the long hair out of the way when working.

ward A congregation in the Mormon Church, headed by an executive known as a bishop; similar to the Catholic parish. The local church building, often referred to as the *ward house*, is the centre of a Mormon family's religious and social life. (*See also* stake)

warrior society Among the Plains Indians, a kind of club or association that men belonged to and fought with. Admission to such a society was an important mark of standing for a young man. Also called an *akicita*.

These societies had varying functions within the tribes. Most typical were police-like duties, maintaining order on the march and on the buffalo hunt and protecting the rear of the people during retreat or flight. The position of chief of a warrior society was considered a heavy responsibility, and a man who accepted the position had to be prepared to die at all times.

Many tribes had the same societies – the kit fox men, for instance, was a society in various tribes. George Bird Grinnell reports seven soldier societies of the Cheyenne – the kit foxes, elk soldiers, dog soldiers, red shields, crazy dogs, bowstrings and chief soldiers, the latter band consisting of the 44 chiefs of the tribe.

wash (1) A ravine; a dry, flat-bottomed gully with steep walls created by occasional run-offs. (2) Descriptive of gold-bearing earth and gravel, as in the usages *wash dirt* or *washing stuff*; also occurs in the noun form – the wash, meaning the 'wash dirt'. (3) A bear den; a hole dug in the bank of a stream by a beaver.

Combinations: wash gold (gold found in placer diggings rather than in veins in rock) and *wash pan* or *washer* (an implement [pan] for panning gold).

washinango In the south-west, a person of mixed Indian and Negro blood. Also called a *Zambo*. (In Louisiana and east Texas, a person of red, black and white blood is a *redbone*.)

Washoe A name for the territory that became the state of Nevada, after Indians of that name who lived on the Truckee River. A Washoeite was a person who came to the great silver mines of the Comstock lode (Sam Clemens was one) and later any Nevadan. Pronounced WAH-shoh.

Washoe canary is a name for a burro. The *Washoe process* was a method of treating silver ore by grinding and adding mercury, blue vitriol and salt. The *Washoe zephyr* is a strong west wind in Nevada.

wasna Pemmican. Originally a Dakota word with the same meaning and pronounced was-NAH.

watap The roots of the spruce or pine used for weaving or sewing. Indians pounded the roots and separated the fibres to make the threads and could weave a bowl tight enough to hold water. From Canadian French and presumably based on an Indian word, it's pronounced wa-TAHP, with the first *a* as in *corral*.

water *Combinations: water hole* (a spot naturally containing water – a tank, a wallow, a water pocket – where you can water stock; it's also a place where a cowboy wets his whistle with whiskey), *water master* (a supervisor of an irrigation system), *water-shy* (descriptive, among cowboys, of a person who doesn't bathe often enough), *water wally* (a batamote, the seep-willow tree) and *water trap* (a corral at a water hole, with a gate that closes when the horses are in).

Verbal expressions: water at night (to be on the dodge) and *water a herd* (in the days of the open range, to drive the cattle into and out of the river in such a way that all cows got clean water, enough water and didn't stampede – it was a tricky job).

water scrape A waterless stretch of country to cross. (*See* jornada) Cornelius Smith says the origin was that, if water was to be found, it had to be scraped for. A good many of the great stories of the West come from crossings of water scrapes, with stock half-mad from thirst.

waterbelly An affliction of steers, the blocking of the urinary canal with stones, often leading to death.

watermelon under the saddle Among cowboys, descriptive of a horse that arches its back a lot. [Adams] (*See* horse for other descriptive expressions for horses)

wattle A mark of ownership, like a brand or an earmark, consisting of a flap of skin cut from the jaw or neck of livestock so that it hangs.

wave around Especially in the days of the open range, to wave your hat in a signal for someone to ride around and not come toward you; a not-welcome sign.

wawa In Chinook jargon, talk, speech. Also used as a verb, to speak. A council was a *hyas* (big) *wawa*, and even one newspaper had wawa in its name. Pronounced WAH-wah.

weaner A newly weaned calf; a calf ready to wean. Calves are often weaned in a *weaning corral*. By extension among cowmen, a human infant.

wear the bustle wrong To be pregnant. Good cowboy humour, based on a mental picture.

weaver A horse that bucks with a weaving motion rather than straight away, a hard horse to stay on. [Adams] Also a term of buckaroo country for a horse that continually sways in the stall.

weaver's pathway *See* pathway.

webfoot A resident of Oregon, because of the wet weather.

wedding vase A tall, double-necked pot where the two necks are joined by a handle. Made by the Hopis, it was never part of a traditional marriage ceremony.

well-heeled Well off, depending on context, for either money or firearms.

Welsh Indian One of the will 'o the wisps of the West. Reports of Welsh-speaking Indians with fair skin, beards and blue eyes led to efforts by a good many explorers to find this lost tribe and to accounts of its discovery. Legends of 12th-century colonies established in America by Welshmen inflamed the speculation. The Mormons were especially keen to find this tribe as confirmation of declarations in *The Book of Mormon*, and they sometimes thought they spotted Welsh words in the language of the Hopi.

wet stock Livestock stolen in Mexico and forced to swim the Rio Grande. Thus *wet horse* and *wet cow*.

wetback A derogatory term for a Mexican who gains illegal entry to the United States by swimming the river. Such a person is also called *mojado* (from the Spanish word 'wet'), *alambrista* (fence climber), *illegal alien* and *undocumented worker*.

whang A leather string, such as hung from deerskin hunting shirts and still hangs from saddles. Such hide strips were used to repair almost anything, as baling wire is used in the West today. On saddles, they're used to tie things to the saddle.

what I know about that you could put in one eye I don't know a damn thing about that. A nice example of self-deprecatory cowboy humour. It also occurs in an even better form: What I know about that you could put between your eye and your eyelid and it wouldn't scratch.

wheel Cowboy slang for the cylinder of a pistol. *No beans in the wheel* means an empty gun.

when cows climb trees! A cowboy expression for when he'll do what he doesn't mean to do – never.

whey-belly Cowboy talk for a pot-gutted (second-rate) horse. (*See* canner)

while the gate's open Rancher talk meaning 'while the opportunity is there'. [Adams]

whiskey trader A fellow who traded whiskey to the Indians for hides, which was illegal but profitable and gave these small traders an advantage over the government's trading posts and forts. A *whiskey Indian* was one who was fond of booze. (*See* Indian whiskey) Westerners of the last century called places that sold whiskey *whiskey holes, joints, mills* and *ranches.*

whistle Cowboy talk for a young 'un, a button. Whistle was also a 19th-century word for the call of the bull elk in mating season; it's now called *bugling.*

A *whistler* (or *whistle pig*) may be either a marmot (because of its cry) or a horse that wheezes because it's wind-broke.

whistle judge In rodeo, the official who signalled you had stayed on the horse or bull long enough to qualify. These days a Pro Rodeo official called the timer blows an air-horn up in the crow's nest; the judges in the arena have stop watches.

whistleberry A cowboy's name for a bean. He also called them *strawberries* (Arkansas, Mexican or prairie) and *ribstickers.*

white A description of a fair, decent, right sort of man. Though this usage may be pre-Western, most of the early citations are from the West, like this one: 'Although your colour is cinnamon, and you may have Spanish, Navajo, or even Apache blood in your veins, you treat me white all the same,' wrote John Cook in *The Border and the Buffalo.* A similar phrase

was, 'That's mighty white of you.' Normally the notion of who was white included only northern Europeans and Americans of that descent (sometimes even Germans were left out).

Combinations involving people: white Cherokee or *Choctaw* (a member of one of those tribes with considerable white blood), *white doctor* (a physician who practiced scientific medicine [was not a medicine man] even if an Indian), *white flesh* (white people, considered collectively), *white Indian* (either a member of a tribe noted for light skin or a white man who adopted an Indian way of life, often a mountain man married into a tribe) and *white-water man* (a logger's name for a log driver).

Other combinations: white bear (the grizzly), *whiteface* (a Hereford cow, red with a white face), *white heart* (a red bead with a white centre made popular in the Indian trade by the French, who called it a *coeur blanc*), *white horse* (a notice to a logger that he's fired and is to get his pay and leave [go to town on a white horse]), *white house* (one of the cowboy's names for the main ranch house [Adams]), *white mule* (what a logger called cheap whiskey [Adams]), *white sage* (a plant, *Salva apiana*, with whitish leaves, used ceremonially and medicinally by Indians) and *white weasel* (among old north-west traders, an ermine).

white buffalo A buffalo that is cream-coloured or even spotted dark and white. These creatures were sacred objects to nearly all the Plains tribes. When a hunter found and killed one, its hide was tanned especially well and made a gift to the sun. This act brought blessings not only to him but his entire tribe. Though it is often assumed that white buffalo were albinos, white Indian James Willard Schultz says their eyes were of normal colour.

white-collar rancher Same as suitcase rancher.

whittle whanging Cowboy talk for quarrelling.

whooping crane The tallest bird (*Grus americana*) in North America and one of the rarest. Almost brought to extinction by hunting and habitat pressures, small populations are making a comeback. The largest flock winters in the Aransas National Wildlife Refuge in Texas; there is an experimental population at Grays Lake National Wildlife Refuge in Idaho.

whoop-up An establishment that traded whiskey to Indians; an Indian who liked to drink. Ramon Adams says that the term comes from a bar called Fort Whoop-up on the Canadian–American border. The border literally ran through the building, and the proprietors sold whiskey to Indians.

wickiup A brush hut used by western Indians, principally those who were not tipi dwellers, and especially Indians of the desert south-west. Often crudely woven from willow branches, reeds or ocotillo stalks and the like, and covered with brush, hides or blankets. Probably from a Sauk, Fox and Kickapoo word for dwelling and pronounced wɪ-kee-up. Sometimes Anglos applied this word jocularly to their own houses.

widow-maker Among cowboys, an outlaw horse; among loggers, a falling tree or a branch apt to fall; among miners, an excavating drill; uncommonly, a revolver.

wild bunch (1) A bunch of horses not accustomed to being handled. (2) A gang of outlaws, such as the one usually called the Wild Bunch, which was led by Robert Leroy Parker, best known as Butch Cassidy.

wild cow milking A rodeo event in which a pair of cowboys ropes a wild cow, milks her and hooves it to the judge's stand with some milk.

wild horse race A rodeo event in which a trio of cowboys catches and saddles a wild horse and rides it across the finish line.

wild rice Not rice but an aquatic grass (*Zizania aquatica*) that grows in northern Minnesota and Wisconsin. Difficult to cultivate, it is mostly harvested from the wild by the Ojibway Indians and is a major source of revenue.

Wild West show An outdoor entertainment showing 'characteristic' scenes from the days of the 'Wild West'. Buffalo Bill Cody, though not the first entrepreneur of a Wild West show, created the best-known in *Buffalo Bill's Wild West*, which started in Omaha in 1883. Cody staged for his audiences exhibitions of shooting, riding bucking broncos, roping, an attack on a stagecoach, pony-express-style riding and so on. Annie Oakley and Sitting Bull were among the performers. The show even toured Europe and was a direct ancestor of the rodeo. Also called a *Bill show*.

wild Willie west Cowboy talk for a dude ranch.

wildcat In California from the 1860s, a mine of dubious value; later an oil well dug in a new oil area. Men who dug such wells or sold such mines were called *wildcatters*. *Wildcatting* meant 'engaging in dangerous or highly speculative activities'. Combinations like *wildcat claim, mine, oil company*, etc., also developed.

wilderness Land protected by the 1964 Wilderness Act which has managed to preserve its natural condition. Each wilderness area is usually 5,000 acres or greater and reserved for travel by foot or animal. Hiking, grazing and hunting have been deemed compatible uses; in most instances, drilling and logging are not permitted, and no permanent improvements for human habitation are made.

Primitive area was the name for areas designated by government agencies rather than by congress; these areas are now incorporated into wilderness areas or are called *wilderness study areas* if they may be included in a future wilderness area.

willow backrest The chair of the Plains Indians. The user sat on the floor and leaned against it. It was made of strips of willow peeled and laced together and was hung from a tripod to give support for the back. Many were beautifully decorated with pieces of blanket and buckskin or beads, and only a poor tipi was without at least one. Indians and hobbyists still use them, primarily at powwows and at rendezvous.

win your spurs To earn your place or standing, usually as a cowboy but in any endeavour. Thus novelist Owen Wister, talking about a favourable review, wrote, 'They say I've already "won my spurs", and if not "spoiled by undue literary petting" I shall probably etc., etc. I don't think I've won my spurs, though I propose to. But I'm glad they think so, and as many other friendly critics as possible.'

Winchester A repeating rifle. As Colt came to mean any pistol and Stetson any hat, Winchester came also to mean any repeating rifle. The company that made it, the Winchester Repeating Arms Company, was a reorganised form of the New Haven Arms Company, which made the Henry rifle, and the first Winchester in 1866 was even known as the Improved Henry. Then Winchester put out the Model 1873, a .44-calibre, centre-fire, 15-shot rifle, and it became 'the rifle that won the West'. The .30-.30 Winchester became hugely popular in the 20th-century.

Other Western names for rifles were *Big Fifty*, *buffalo gun*, *fusil*, *Hawken*, *Henry*, *lightning stock*, *long tom*, *meat in the pot*, *needle gun*, *reliable*, *saddle gun*, *smoke pole*, *trade gun*, *Worcestershire* and *Yager*.

wind-broke Descriptive of a horse with partially paralysed vocal cords. Because of its wheezing, it's called a *whistler*. (See canner)

windmiller A hand hired (on ranches big enough for one) to keep the windmills in repair. Also called a *windmill monkey*.

windy (1) A tall tale, a yarn, a fanciful story. (2) A cow hard to drive from the canyons on to the flats; Ramon Adams says this use comes from the fact that such work exhausts the cowboys.

winter In Indian Pidgin English, a year. Thus an Indian toddler was two winters old, and the Plains Indian calendar was called a *winter count*. To winter was to spend the winter in the Western wilderness, among trappers a mark of an experienced man. (See hivernant)

Combinations: winter horse (a horse not turned out for the winter but grained and kept ready for work), *winter kill* (cattle killed by cold weather; sometimes wild animals such as elk killed by cold weather), *Winter Quarters* (the temporary home of the Mormons on the west side of the Missouri River on their great 1846-7 migration from Nauvoo, Illinois to the valley of the Salt Lake in Utah) and *winter saint* (an emigrant who spent a winter among the Mormons at Salt Lake instead of attempting to cross the remaining deserts and mountains to the West Coast late in the season).

winter count An Indian history book, a pictographic record of past years painted on hide by Plains Indians. Each pictograph would indicate what happened in one year, such as the year Crazy Woman Creek flooded, the year of the big prairie fire, the year the three kit fox men got killed and so on. Winter counts are now important both as art objects and as historical records.

wipe One cowboy word for a bandanna, his jack-of-all-tools.

wire road A trail (or road) following a telegraph line. [Adams]

wirecutters A combination of pliers, cutters and small hammer carried by Westerners who ride the range these days on horseback or in pick-ups. Along with the wire stretcher, wirecutters are one of the essential tools of the modern cowboy.

A century ago a wirecutter was a person who cut a fence in a range war or started a range war.

wish book A mail-order catalogue, a chief source of news on the latest developments for remote ranches.

wohaw A term of Indian Pidgin English for cattle. It spread to cattlemen as well and also occurred in the form *wohaw John*.

The source of the word has been attributed to the cries of the bull-whackers to draft animals: whoa, gee and haw. Though a recent lexicographer doubts this, it appears to be confirmed by Lt George Frederick Ruxton, who in the 1840s called the wagon driver's talk to his oxen 'wohaws'. It has also been suggested that wohaw is an Indian adaptation of the Spanish word for cow, *vaca*.

wolfer A man who hunted wolves for money, using traps or poison. Often he was paid by ranchers and also collected a bounty from the government. Wolves were a threat to livestock in the older West, but references to them in diaries and journals are to be handled with care – often the coyote (prairie wolf) was meant, not the wolf.

Wolfing is wolf hunting.

wood hawk A man who cut wood along a river for steamboats, which he stacked at wooding stations.

wood ranch An area (particularly in treeless country) where wood was available.

wooden overcoat A coffin. See, for instance, Paul St Pierre's wonderful story 'Antoine's Wooden Overcoat'. Also, in the army, a barrel worn as a punishment.

woolly (1) A sheep. Sheep are subject to all kinds of derisive names: *Ba-ah, grass shavers, hoofed locusts, maggots, stinkers, stubble jumper, underwears* and *wool locusts.* (2) As an adjective, descriptive of a wild place or person.

Woollies are angora chaps with the hair on.

woolsey A second-rate cowboy hat, probably one made entirely of wool felt rather than beaver or a beaver-wool blend.

woosher In cowboy talk, a hog. [Adams]

work a brand over To change a brand, once a cause for lynching if unauthorised.

To *work cows* is to handle them – round them up, drive them, cut them and so on. To *work a horse* is to train it. [Adams] To *work ahead of the roundup* was to get there early and claim the mavericks.

To *work the bed ground* was for a sheepherder to help the ewes and their lambs get together. [Adams] To *work like a beaver* was to work hard, an expression perhaps made common by the mountain men.

worm The lowest worker on an *oil rig.* The name comes from the 1920s when an imported weevil (worm) started putting Western farmers out of business. The farmers headed for the oil patches of Oklahoma and Texas where they got the lowest jobs and were called the worms.

wrangler Once the hand who took care of the horses; now any cowboy, especially one who leads dudes on rides. The word is an American version of the Spanish *caballerango;* it also occurs in the form *caverango* and in the verb form *to wrangle.*

Historically, taking care of the horse herd (cavvy), at the ranch or on the trail, was a beginner's job. Ironically, the word has come to imply experience and expertise. The top awards of the National Cowboy Hall of Fame are called Wranglers.

A wrangler was also called a *cavvy man, dew wrangler* (one who has the early morning shift), *horse pestler, horse rustler* (in Texas), *jingler, wrangatang* or *wrango.* The saddle horse he kept at hand to bring in the horses was the *wrangle horse.*

wreck pan The tub for dirty dishes at the chuck wagon. Also called the *wreck tub.*

wrestling calves See flank.

wring-tail A horse that is nervous or over-tired, because it then wrings its tail as it runs.

wrinkle-horn An old steer with wrinkled, scaly horns; a wise, experienced person. Also called *mossy horn.*

Y

yack Cowboy talk for a stupid person.

yah-tay The Navajo equivalent of hello, which has come into use among some Anglos in the Four Corners country. This spelling comes by ear from the Anglo pronunciation.

Yakima A tribe of Shahaptian Indians that lived along the Columbia and Yakima rivers in Washington. After they got the horse in the 1730s, they became skilled horsemen and added to their salmon fishing the custom of crossing the mountains and hunting buffalo; they also incorporated some elements of Plains Indian culture.

The Yakima had difficult relationships with the early fur traders, but when Washington became a territory, they agreed to accept a reservation and permit whites to use trails across their lands in exchange for annuities. Disagreements about this treaty led to the Yakima War of 1855–6. In the 1860s, many Yakima became involved in the Dreamer Cult. In this century, the dams on the Columbia River have destroyed many of their traditional salmon-fishing areas, and the federal government has paid them millions of dollars in reparations.

Since the Yakima were well-known horse traders, *Yakima* also became a word meaning 'horse', in the way that *cayuse* derived from the Cayuse Indians.

yampa (1) One of two herbs (genus *Atenia*) with an edible tuber. (2) The Yampa tribe was a division of the Utes.

yamping Stealing; theft.

yannigan bag A logger's equivalent of a cowboy's war bag or a trapper's possible sack – what he carried his personal gear in.

yarb woman In the south-west, a Hispanic woman who knows how to use herbs medicinally. It derives from the Spanish word for herb, *hierba*.

yard the grub In logger talk, to eat. [Adams]

yardlight The mercury vapour lamp kept on through the night in most ranch yards today.

yarn To tell a tale, probably an adventure, and probably a tall tale. It has a noun form – the tale is a yarn.

Yarning is an old Western custom, a campfire entertainment and an occasional way of teasing dudes. (The custom is not exclusively Western – the East had its own tall tales in the Pennsylvany hurricane and the Caroliny swamper.) Some greenhorns mistook yarning for prevaricating. A Montana newspaper editor missed an international scoop by refusing to report the existence of the fabulous Yellowstone region – he didn't want to get caught printing old Jim Bridger's lies.

The yarn was first and most tellingly associated with the mountain man. Black Harris's tale of the 'putrefied' forest is a classic, and Bridger told encyclopedias of them. Here's one from David Lavender's *One Man's West* that shows the later West kept the tradition alive and well: ' "Why, these mosquitoes ain't nothin'. You ought to see 'em in Greasewood. They put scouts along the trails, an' when a man shows up you can hear 'em holler, 'Here comes meat!' They fly over in droves that shade the sun. They sound like a millrace. Oncet I thought to fool 'em by takin' along a copper wash boiler. When I saw 'em headin' my way I crawled underneath it. But do you think that stopped 'em? No sir! They lit on it an' began to bore like woodpeckers. *Rat-a-tat-tat* – it near broke my eardrums. I picked up a rock an' when they drilled through I clinched their beaks over like you would a nail. It weren't no use. They reared back, picked up the boiler with their beaks, an' flew off with it. The rest really did go for me then. If a forest fire hadn't come up an' smudged 'em off, I never would of got away." '

yedra In the south-west, poison ivy or poison oak. Adapted from the Spanish *hiedra*, which means 'ivy', it is pronounced YAYD-ruh.

Yeibechai In Navajo mythology, deities. Also a dance with masked dancers representing the Yeibechai.

yellow belly (1) A denigrating term for a Mexican. (2) A Mexican breed of cow.

yellow leg A name for the cavalryman of the post-Civil War period, from the yellow stripe down the seam of his britches. Likewise an artilleryman was a red leg. Though infantrymen had blue piping on their trousers, they weren't called blue legs (the entire uniform was blue).

yellowcake Uranium oxide, the fissionable material in carnotite ore; highly valuable. The hunt for yellowcake tore up a good deal of the Four Corners country during the uranium-rush days of the 1950s.

yellowdog In oil drilling, a water pump.

yerba buena (1) One of several kinds of mint used medicinally by the California Indians (the literal translation would be 'good herb'), especially *Satureja douglasii*. (2) An early name of what is now the city of San Francisco. (3) Another name for Goat Island in San Francisco Bay. Adapted from the Spanish *hierba buena*, it is pronounced YAYR-buh BWAY-nuh.

Other medicinal herbs are *yerba de vibora*, used by California Indians to alleviate the effects of snakebite (*vibora* being Spanish for viper); *yerba santa* (sacred herb, *Eriodictyon californinum*), used by California Indians to treat respiratory and stomach problems; *yerba del manso* (*Anemopsis californica*) used by the pimas to treat syphilis.

yeso In the south-west, gypsum. Borrowed from Spanish, it is pronounced YAY-soh.

yo Sheep-herder talk for a ewe.

yosemite A valley formed by glacial action, having a flat floor and steep walls, such as Yosemite Valley in the national park. It also forms the adjective *yosemitic*. The original native (Miwok) word, which *yosemite* is a recreation of, means 'grizzly bear'.

you bet A standard strong affirmative in the West, derived from the popularity of gambling.

younker A kid, a youngster (though in the East, a man of position).

Yucca A genus of arid-land plants of the lily family, sometimes tree-like and bearing white blossoms. The yucca of the south-west has creamy flowers, its root was used by Indians and Hispanics to make soap, and it is also called *soapweed, palmilla, Spanish bayonet* or *Our Lord's Candle*. South-western Indians used yucca fibre for weaving. Yucca palm is another name for the Joshua tree.

Yuma An Indian tribe of the lower Colorado River, more properly known as the Quechan. Their Yuman-speaking relatives (such as the Cocopa, Halchidhoma, Havasupai, Maricopa, Mojave, Walapai and Yavapai) live along the Colorado, Salt and Gila rivers in Arizona. Traditionally, the Yuma have been an agricultural people, known for their baskets, beadwork and pottery.

In historic times, they controlled the crossing of the Colorado near the mouth of the Gila. The Spanish built a settlement there, but the Yuma attacked and killed the settlers. In the 1840s, Americans began heavy use of this crossing. The Yuma charged to raft people across the river until subdued by the Army. From 1884 they have lived on the Fort Yuma Reservation.

Z

zacate In the south-west, forage. Borrowed from Spanish, and pronounced sah-KAH-tay.

zacaton *See* sacatone.

zaguan In the south-west, a gate, entrance, vestibule. Borrowed from Spanish, it is pronounced sah-WHAN.

zanja An irrigation ditch. The main ditch was called a *zanja madre* (mother ditch), and the man who dug ditches was a *zanjero*. It is borrowed from Spanish and pronounced SAHN-hah. (*See also* acequia)

zapato A boot or shoe. Borrowed from Spanish, it is pronounced suh-PAH-toh.

ZCMI Zion's Cooperative Mercantile Institution, the first department store in the United States. It was founded in·1868 by the Mormon Church to compete with the gentile merchants in Utah Territory, and its stock was sold only to faithful Saints. Now it is a large and successful chain of department stores throughout Mormon country.

zebra dun A dun horse with a dorsal stripe and sometimes zebra-like stripes on the legs. (*See* buckskin for horse colours)

Zion (1) In Latter-Day Saint thought, theologically refers to the name given by the Lord to his Saints; identifies both a geographical area and a group of people. Joseph Smith counselled the Saints to move west and 'build Zion in the tops of the mountains', a goal realised in Salt Lake City. (2) In Mormon scripture, the Lord's chosen, 'because they were of one heart and one mind, and dwelt in righteousness'. (3) Also appears in adjective form such as Zion First National Bank, Zion Book Store, etc.

zopilote In the south-west, a turkey vulture, a buzzard. From Spanish (which got it from an Aztec word), it's pronounced soh-pee-LOH-tay. Sometimes spelled *sopilote*.

zorrilla A line-backed Texas longhorn, often speckled white on the flanks and belly.

Zuni A pueblo of western New Mexico; the pueblo's people. The Zuni have a ceremonial religion like the other Pueblo tribes and a unique language. Their central religious ceremony is Shalako, near the winter solstice each year. Their economy historically was agricultural.

Coronado sought Zuni as one of the fabled seven cities of Cibola, and the Spanish established a mission there in 1629. Relations between Zunis and Americans were generally peaceful in the 19th century, and they still inhabit their original territory. Today the Zunis are primarily known for their fine silversmithing and jewellery-making.

The name Zuni is a Spanish version of a Keresan word whose meaning is lost. Though occasionally spelled with a tilde, it is pronounced zoo-nee.

FURTHER READING

Language is a communal creation, and a dictionary is a compendium of the knowledge of a huge number of people. To find out more about the variety of American English used in the West, today and in the past, we drew not only on decades of living in the West and the knowledge of other living Westerners, but upon scores of books, magazines and newspapers. Those who want to study the subject further may want to walk some of our trails.

Every day, incessantly, we used these dictionaries and reference books:

Adams, Ramon, *Western Words: A Dictionary of the American West*, Norman: University of Oklahoma Press, 1968. (Generally regarded as the standard work, and a good book, but Adams was vulnerable to error when he strayed far from the people and places he knew best, cowboys and Texas.)

Audubon Society, *Deserts*, New York: Knopf, 1985.

Castillo, Carlos and Bond, Otto F., *The University of Chicago Spanish Dictionary*, Revised and enlarged by Canfield D. Lincoln, Chicago: University of Chicago Press, 1987.

Craighead, John J., Craighead, Frank C. Jr and Davis, Raj J., *A Field Guide to Rocky Mountain Flowers*, Boston: Houghton Mifflin, 1963.

Gaamez, Tana de (ed.), *Simon & Schuster's International Dictionary, English-Spanish, Spanish-English*, New York: Simon & Schuster, 1973.

Lamar, Howard R. (ed.), *The Reader's Encyclopedia of the American West*, New York: Crowell, 1977. (An essential source.)

Mathews, Mitford M., (ed.) *A Dictionary of Americanisms on Historical Principles*, Chicago: University of Chicago Press, 1951. (Because of the quotations from early sources, a truly indispensable book.)

Murray, James A. H. (ed.), *Oxford English Dictionary and Supplement*, Oxford: Oxford University Press, 1884, 1928, 1972.

Smith, Cornelius, *A South-Western Vocabulary*, Burbank: Clark, 1985. (Like Adams, susceptible to error.)

Watts, Peter, *A Dictionary of the Old West*, New York: Knopf, 1977. (A sound book, limited to the second half of the 19th century.)

Weseen, Maurice, *A Dictionary of American Slang*, New York: Crowell, 1934.

We also recommend these references:

Adams, Ramon F., *The Cowman Says It Salty*, Tucson: University of Arizona Press, 1971.

Adams, Ramon F., *Cowboy Lingo*, Boston: Houghton Mifflin, 1936.

Beattie, Russell H., *Saddles*. Norman: University of Oklahoma, 1982.

Cassidy, Frederic G. (ed.), *Dictionary of American Regional English*, Cambridge: Harvard University Press, from 1985. (Two volumes (up to the letter H) of this excellent dictionary have been published to date.)

Chapman, Robert L., *New Dictionary of American Slang*, New York: Harper & Row, 1986.

Clapin, Sylva, *A Dictionary of Americanisms*, New York: Louis Weis and Co., 1902.

Dillard, J. L., *All-American English*, New York: Random House, 1975. (Good on Pidgin English and frontier speech.)

Dillard, J. L., *American Talk: Where Our Words Came From*, New York: Random House, 1976. (Good sections on cowboys, mountain men and gamblers.)

Foster-Harris, William, *The Look of the Old West*, New York: Viking, 1955. (Good for sketches of clothes, tools and the like, plus descriptions of how things worked, but not entirely reliable.)

Ford-Robertson, F. C. (ed.), *Terminology of Forest Science, Technology, Practice and Products*, Washington, DC: Society of American Foresters, 1971.

Hodge, Frederick W., *Handbook of Indians North of Mexico*, Washington, DC: Bureau of American Ethnology, 1912. (Two volumes. Available currently in several reprints.)

Larson, Peggy, *The Deserts of the South-West*, San Francisco: Sierra Club Books, 1977.

Ludlow, David H. (ed.), *Encyclopedia of Mormonism*, Macmillan Publishing Co., 1992.

McCullough, Walter F., *Woods Words: A Comprehensive Dictionary of Loggers Terms*, Portland: Oregon Historical Society, 1958.

McDermott, John Francis, *A Glossary of Mississippi Valley French, 1673–1850*, St Louis: Washington University Press, 1941.

Mencken, H. L., *The American Language*, New York: Knopf, 1986; first published, 1919. (Valuable for understanding the development of American English.)

Potter, Edgar, *Cowboy Slang*, Seattle: Hangman Press, Superior, 1971.

Sturtevant, William C. and Ortiz, Alfonso, *Handbook of North American Indians: South-West*, Washington, DC: Smithsonian Institution, 1983. (Volumes 9 and 10 of the series are a remarkable and authoritative [if forbidding] resource. *See also* volume 7 by Sturtevant and Wayne Suttles (1990) on Indians of the north-west coast and volume 11 by Sturtevant and Warren L. D'Azevedo, (1986), on Indians of the Great Basin.

Wentworth, Harold and Flexner, Stuart Berg, *Dictionary of American Slang*, 2nd ed., supplemented, New York: Crowell, 1975.

Yenne, Bill, *The Encyclopedia of North American Indian Tribes: A Comprehensive Study of the Tribes from the Abitibi to the Zuni*, Greenwich, Conn.: Bison Books, 1986.

In general the reader should roam through first-rate histories of the West by Westerners.

BRIEF RECOMMENDATIONS:

On cowboys, particularly the books of David Dary, J. Frank Dobie, Jo Mora and Philip Aston Rollins.

On Plains Indians, especially the books of George Bird Grinnell, George Hyde, Robert Lowie and Peter Powell.

On mountain men, Bernard DeVoto (especially *Across the Wide Missouri*), LeRoy R. Hafen, David Lavender, Peter C. Newman (on the Canadian fur men) and Paul Chrisler Phillips.

On Mormons, Wallace Stegner (especially *The Gathering of Zion* and *Mormon Country*) and Fawn Brodie.

On gamblers, Herbert Asbury's *The Sucker's Progress*.

We found the journals, memoirs and as-told-to biographies of Westerners a treasure trove. Examples:

On the life of women in the West, those of Frances Anne Mullen Boyd, Elizabeth Custer, Martha Farnsworth, Alice Kirk Grierson, Martha Summerhayes and Teresa Griffin Vielé.

On the life of Indians, the narratives of Black Elk, Plenty Coups, Pretty Shield, Son of Old Man Hat, Don Talayesva, Two Leggings, Yellow Wolf and others.

On cowboys and trail drivers, the recollections of Teddy Blue Abott, Charlie Siringo, Andy Adams and Charlie Russell, among others.

On mountain men, James Clyman, Warren Angus Ferris, Josiah Gregg, Joe Meek, James Ohio Pattie and Osborne Russell.

Various Mormons, Indian traders, travellers on the Oregon Trail, miners and so on have also left their recollections and much of their language – the possibilities for discovery are vast.

In addition, the better works of fiction are worthwhile, especially when written by Westerners. We recommend for study the language in the fictions of Edward Abbey, Vardis Fisher, A. B. Guthrie Jr, Will Henry, Oliver LaFarge, Frederick

Manfred, Jack Schaefer, James Willard Schultz, Wallace Stegner, Mark Twain, Stewart Edward White and Owen Wister.

Among novelists whose work is more recent, Don Berry, Richard Bradford, Ivan Doig, William Eastlake, Max Evans, Linda Hogan, Tony Hillerman, Elmer Kelton, M. Scott Momaday, Leslie Marmon Silko, James Welch and Norman Zollinger.

Some modern essayists are rich in Western language. To mention Edward Abbey, Gretel Ehrlich, Linda Hasselstrom, Joseph Wood Krutch and Barry Holstun Lopez is only to begin.

DISTRIBUTORS
for the Wordsworth Reference Series

AUSTRALIA

Reed Editions
22 Salmon Street
Port Melbourne
Vic 3207
Australia

Tel: (03) 646 6716
Fax: (03) 646 6925

GERMANY, AUSTRIA & SWITZERLAND

Swan Buch-Marketing GmbH
Goldscheuerstraße 16
D-7640 Kehl am Rhein
Germany

GREAT BRITAIN & IRELAND

Wordsworth Editions Ltd
Cumberland House
Crib Street
Ware
Hertfordshire SG12 9ET

ITALY

Magis Books SRL
Via Raffaello 31/C
Zona Ind Mancasale
42100 Reggio Emilia

Tel: 0522-920999
Fax: 0522-920666

SINGAPORE, MALAYSIA & BRUNEI

Paul & Elizabeth Book Services
Pte Ltd
163 Tanglin Road No 03-15/16
Tanglin Mall
Singapore 1024

Tel: (65) 735-7308
Fax: (65) 735-9747

SPAIN

Ribera Libros S.L.
Poligono Martiartu, Calle 1-no 6
48480 Arrigorriaga, Vizcaya

Tel: 34-4-6713607 (Almacen)
34-4-4418787 (Libreria)
Fax: 34-4-6713608 (Almacen)
34-4-4418029 (Libreria)

PORTUGAL

International Publishing Services Ltd
Rua da Cruz da Carreira, 4B
1100 Lisboa

Tel: 01-570051
Fax: 01-3522066

SOUTHERN AFRICA

Struik Book Distributors (Pty) Ltd
Graph Avenue
Montague Gardens
7441
P O Box 193
Maitland
7405
South Africa

Tel: (021) 551-5900
Fax: (021) 551-1124

USA, CANADA & MEXICO

Universal Sales & Marketing
230 Fifth Avenue
Suite 1212
New York, NY 10001 USA

Tel: 212-481-3500
Fax: 212-481-3534